Merger Arbitrage

Founded in 1807, John Wiley & Sons is the oldest independent publishing company in the United States. With offices in North America, Europe, Australia, and Asia, Wiley is globally committed to developing and marketing print and electronic products and services for our customers' professional and personal knowledge and understanding.

The Wiley Finance series contains books written specifically for finance and investment professionals as well as sophisticated individual investors and their financial advisers. Book topics range from portfolio management to e-commerce, risk management, financial engineering, valuation, and financial instrument analysis, as well as much more.

For a list of available titles, visit our web site at www.WileyFinance.com.

Merger Arbitrage

*How to Profit from
Event-Driven Arbitrage*

THOMAS KIRCHNER

John Wiley & Sons, Inc.

Published by John Wiley & Sons, Inc., Hoboken, New Jersey.
Published simultaneously in Canada.

For general information on our other products and services or for technical support, please
contact our Customer Care Department within the United States at (800) 762-2974, outside
the United States at (317) 572-3993 or fax (317) 572-4002.

Wiley also publishes its books in a variety of electronic formats. Some content that appears in
print may not be available in electronic books. For more information about Wiley products,
visit our web site at www.wiley.com.

Library of Congress Cataloging-in-Publication Data:

Kirchner, Thomas, 1968–
    Merger arbitrage : how to profit from event-driven arbitrage / Thomas Kirchner.
        p. cm. – (Wiley finance series)
    Includes bibliographical references and index.
    ISBN 978-0-470-37197-8 (cloth)
    1. Arbitrage.   2. Consolidation and merger of corporations.   3. Stock exchanges and
current events.   I. Title.
    HG4521.K48 2009
    332.63′2–dc22

                                                                    2009004118

Printed in the United States of America

10 9 8 7 6 5 4 3 2 1

Contents

Preface

Merger arbitrage, also known as risk arbitrage, has grown exponentially over the last two decades from small operations within Wall Street firms to stand-alone arbitrage funds directly accessible to the public. Yet surprisingly little has been written on the topic. A number of academics have written studies about various aspects of the strategy. For the general public, I can count only five books on the topic. This small number pales in comparison to the information overload that other areas of finance experience. Since Guy Wyser-Pratte's two monographs in the 1970s, only three other books about merger arbitrage have been published. One of them is Ivan Boesky's *Merger Mania*. Maybe potential writers fear that authoring a merger arbitrage book stands under a bad omen because Boesky was arrested a few weeks after the publication of his book. As the author of a merger arbitrage book, I certainly hope that writing a book and getting arrested are linked only by correlation and not by causality.

In this book I try to go beyond a mere description of the arbitrage process to incorporate some thoughts on the benefits of adding merger arbitrage to an investment portfolio and the vehicles investors can utilize to access the strategy. The expansion of the book's horizon will make it more relevant to a broader investment audience. Nevertheless, the focus of the book remains on mergers and merger arbitrage, not asset allocation or portfolio management.

The book is organized into three parts: the first four chapters introduce the basics of the arbitrage process, Chapters 5 through 11 discuss what can go wrong, and Chapters 12 and 13 deal with some practical questions of investing in merger arbitrage.

Chapter 1 explains the basic types of mergers and how to set up the arbitrage. Chapter 2 expands the basic arbitrage by incorporating risk. Probabilities of failure and potential losses are incorporated into the return calculation to find an expected return of the arbitrage. Chapter 3 discusses different sources of risk and return in more detail, in particular the timing of mergers, leverage, and short sales.

The difference between mergers and tender offers is not well understood by many investment professionals. The terms are often used interchangeably.

Chapter 4 goes into details and should be of interest to all investors, not just those seeking to read up on merger arbitrage.

Financing is often one of the most critical parts of an acquisition, and so Chapter 5 looks at different financing options.

Mergers are subject to a plethora of legal requirements, and I discuss them under different angles. Readers should keep in mind that this is a financial book, not a legal textbook. Many aspects are touched on only in a cursory manner. Boards of directors have to follow a number of procedures to ensure that a merger is fair to shareholders. This is discussed in Chapter 6.

Unfortunately, the law that is supposed to protect shareholders often is disregarded when managers buy the companies that they are managing as agents of their shareholders. Chapter 7 looks at management incentives for getting mergers done and how managers' interests are often diametrically opposed to those of shareholders.

Similar conflicts of interest among managers, acquirers, and shareholders can be found in buyouts by private equity funds, discussed in Chapter 8. Now that the buyout wave of the monetarily lax Greenspan years has come to a halt, this is likely to be less of a concern for investors.

Minority squeeze-outs present risks of their own to merger arbitrageurs and therefore are discussed in a chapter of their own, Chapter 9.

The government gets involved in the merger process on several levels, both federal and state. Despite the obvious importance of government regulations, I have decided to relegate their discussion farther to the back of the book because I believe that the motivations of the market participants—management, financiers, board members—are more relevant by far to the success of a merger than government regulations, discussed in Chapter 10. As they say: Where there is a will, there is a way.

Next, I step into a minefield by encouraging investors to seek to exercise their rights and get full value for their shares when a company is taken over. Chapter 11 describes methods that shareholders can use to that end. Too often have I seen investors resign when their company gets taken over for a lowball price. Most investors view themselves as stock pickers and throw in the towel too early. I hope that this chapter convinces investors, perhaps even some institutional investors, to fight for full value.

Chapter 12 explains the historical performance of merger arbitrage as an investment strategy and how it can be added to a diversified portfolio. This chapter in particular is relevant for investors who are looking to add merger arbitrage to their portfolio. Some background in modern portfolio theory is helpful for the understanding of this chapter, but readers without such knowledge should also be able to follow the thoughts and conclusions.

Finally, Chapter 13 gives some practical tips on investing in merger arbitrage. In particular, readers should recognize that cash holdings of event-driven investment strategies are dependent on events and not a deliberate asset allocation decision. As a result, merger arbitrageurs can have highly variable cash positions that are not an indication of their view of the market.

Chapter 13 contains some mathematical material. Stephen Hawking remarked in the introduction to his well-known *A Brief History of Time* that his publisher advised him each formula would reduce the potential readership by half. I trust that readers of financial books can handle a few formulas.

At the time of writing, the markets were in the midst of the worst financial crisis in a generation, the type of event that statisticians claim occurs only once in the lifetime of the universe. Financial markets could change dramatically once the crisis is over. It is difficult to forecast how much of the change will be mandated by the government or the financial industry's self-regulatory bodies and how much will be the result of Schumpeterian creative destruction. Writing any finance book in these times carries a severe risk of obsolescence of the text by the time it is printed. Even though I expect that the focus of the financial industry's changes will be in areas other than mergers, in particular in fixed income, without a doubt, collateral damage will affect arbitrageurs.

THOMAS KIRCHNER

Acknowledgments

I thank the editorial team at John Wiley & Sons for their support throughout the development of the volume, in particular Laura Walsh, who first contacted me with the idea for this book, Emilie Herman, Rosanne Lugtu, and Meg Freeborn.

Ron Charnock has been very supportive and encouraged me with many helpful tips. Others who have given me ideas, sometimes unwittingly, that are incorporated in the text are Geoffrey Foisie, Randy Baron, Juan Monteverde, and Marc Weinberg. Many more friends not listed here have helped with ideas and encouragement.

Adam Mersereau recognized the potential behind applying the newsvendor formula to the cash management problem and referred me to Warren Powell, who developed the algorithm in Chapter 13 with Juliana Nascimento.

Most of the analysis in this book was performed using the statistical software package R. R is an open source competitor to S-Plus, a commercial statistics package. The maker of S-Plus, Insightful Corp., has struggled with the competition from R and ironically was taken private by TIBCO Software through a merger while I was writing this book.

Ashish Tripathy worked with me on analyzing probabilities for the closing or failure of mergers. Sthaporn Witoonchatree helped me retrieve some of the data used in analysis throughout the book.

Finally, I thank all authors who have given me permission to reprint tables or figures from other studies.

T. K.

The Arbitrage Process

CHAPTER 1

Introduction to Merger Arbitrage

Arbitrage is one of the oldest forms of commercial activity. *Merriam-Webster's 11th Collegiate Dictionary* defines it as:

1. The nearly simultaneous purchase and sale of securities or foreign exchange in different markets in order to profit from price discrepancies
2. The purchase of the stock of a takeover target especially with a view to selling it profitably to the raider

Unfortunately, both definitions fail to describe arbitrage properly. In a world of instant global communications, the first type of arbitrage is rarely viable. A much better definition of arbitrage is that used by economists, who define arbitrage as a "free lunch": an investment strategy that generates a risk-free profit. Academic finance theory formalizes this definition as a self-financing trading strategy that generates a positive return without risk. Three different degrees of arbitrage can be distinguished, as shown in Table 1.1.

A simple location arbitrage in commodities would be the purchase of crude oil in Rotterdam, the rental of a tanker, and the simultaneous resale of the oil in New York. Today, most arbitrage activity occurs in financial markets. An arbitrageur might take positions in a currency spot rate, forward rate, and two interest rates. Arbitrage transactions of this type are known as cash-and-carry arbitrage. This type of arbitrage can be understood easily as the purchase of oil and the simultaneous sale of an oil futures contract for the delivery of that oil at a later time. (An arbitrageur would also have to arrange for storage.) In practice, few such simple arbitrage opportunities are available in today's markets. The key idea in arbitrage is the absence of risk. Arbitrageurs eliminate risk by taking positions that in the aggregate offset each other and compensate arbitrageurs for their efforts with a profit.

TABLE 1.1 Orders of Arbitrage

Degree	Definition	Example
First order	A strong, locked-in mechanical relationship in same instrument	Currency triangular arbitrage Location arbitrage Conversions and reversals for European options "Crush" and "crack"
Second order	Different instruments, same underlying security	Cash-future arbitrage Program trading Delivery arbitrage Distributional arbitrage (option spreading) Stripping
Second order	Different (but related) underlying securities, same instrument	"Value" trading Bond arbitrage Forward trading Volatility trading
Third order	Different securities, different instruments, deemed to behave in related manner (correlation-based hedging)	Bond against swaps (asset spread) Cross-market relationships Cross-volatility plays Cross-currency yield curve arbitrage

Source: Nassim Taleb, *Dynamic Hedging: Managing Vanilla and Exotic Options* (New York: John Wiley & Sons, Inc., 1997). Reprinted with permission of John Wiley & Sons, Inc.

Arbitrageurs are often referred to affectionately through the abbreviation "arb."

Arbitrage in general plays an important economic function because it makes markets more efficient. Whenever a price discrepancy arises between two similar instruments or products, arbitrageurs will seek to profit from the discrepancy. Such discrepancies can arise temporarily in any market—oranges, stocks, lease rates for dry bulk carrier vessels, or sophisticated financial derivatives. As soon as arbitrageurs identify a price discrepancy, they will buy in the cheaper market and sell in the more expensive one. Through their actions, they increase the price in the cheap market and reduce the price in the more expensive market. In due time, prices in the two markets will return to balance. Ultimately this benefits all other market participants, who know that prices will never diverge significantly from their fair value.

Suppose government regulations were introduced to curtail the activities of arbitrageurs. This would leave market participants with two options:

1. Accept the price in their local market and risk overpaying.
2. Research all other markets to find the "true" value of the product.

In either case, there are costs involved—either the cost of overpaying (or underselling) or the information cost of price discovery. Both outcomes are not optimal and will make markets less efficient.

It is also important to recognize that arbitrage is not a synonym for speculation. Speculators assume market risk in their trades. They will acquire an asset with the hope of reselling it at a higher price in the future. There are two differences between speculation and arbitrage:

1. In speculation, the purchase and acquisition are not made simultaneously, so speculators face prices that can change with the passage of time. They assume full market risk until they sell. Arbitrageurs, however, will execute the purchase and sale simultaneously.
2. Speculators do not know at which price they will be able to sell. There is no guarantee that they will be able to sell at a higher price. Arbitrageurs, however, know exactly at which price they can sell, because the purchase and sale transactions are executed simultaneously.

Similar observations can be made about the difference between arbitrage and price scalping.

In theory, arbitrage is a completely risk-free undertaking. However, most trades referred to as arbitrage in reality involve some risk and should really be referred to as quasi-arbitrage trades. Basis trades in bond futures are one such example. In a basis trade, an arbitrageur buys a bond, sells a bond futures contract, and then delivers the bond upon expiration of the futures contract to the clearinghouse. In reality, the opportunity for a risk-free delivery of a bond into a futures contract, known as a positive net basis in bond parlance, hardly ever exists. Instead, basis traders focus on trading the negative net basis, and they profit as long as they anticipate the cheapest-to-deliver bond correctly. Readers interested in a more detailed description of bond futures basis trades should consult the extensive literature on the topic. Merger arbitrage is another example of such a quasi-arbitrage.

In a strict sense, merger arbitrage is a misnomer because it, too, involves some risk. The type of risk in merger arbitrage is unlike the market risk that financial risk managers are familiar with and build models around: beta risk. Instead, merger arbitrage is about event risk, the event that the merger is not completed. It is not directly related to the movements in the overall market.

This does not mean that merger arbitrage is completely independent of the market, especially during large dislocations in the market. However, market movements are not the principal determinant for the successful completion of a merger. It is very difficult to capture event risk mathematically. In most statistical risk models, event risk falls into the unexplained component, the error term. As part of the error term, it is uncorrelated to market risk. It is precisely this property that makes investment strategies based on event risk appealing in the construction of portfolios that seek to reduce exposure to market risk. This topic is discussed in more depth in Chapter 12.

More specifically, the risk in merger arbitrage is primarily the nonconsummation of the announced merger. Much can go wrong between the announcement of a merger and its closing. For example:

- Financing for the transaction can dry up.
- Antitrust authorities can block a transaction.
- The economic environment can change, making the merger less appealing.
- Fraud or other misrepresentations can be discovered.
- A spoiler bidder (a.k.a. "white knight") can intervene.

It is the role of the arbitrageur to weigh these risks against the profit opportunity.

Merger arbitrage generally is used to describe a wide range of investment strategies around mergers, many of which have little to do with actual arbitrage. These investment tactics can be organized into a risk spectrum (see Figure 1.1) from the most speculative activity, which is the most removed from an actual arbitrage, to least risky, which is merger arbitrage in a proper sense.

At the most risky end of the spectrum is speculation about potential takeover targets. Some investment magazines occasionally publish lists of takeover targets based on financial characteristics, typically price relative to cash on balance sheet and earnings before interest, taxes, depreciation, and amortization (EBITDA). The idea is that these companies could potentially be bought out based on attractiveness of their accounts for leveraged buyouts. Of course, there is no guarantee that anybody actually will have an interest in acquiring any of the firms on the list. Many more factors must align before a financial buyer might be interested in acquiring a firm.

Of similar riskiness albeit occasionally more founded in reality is the Wall Street rumor mill. There is little doubt that the spreading of such rumors is facilitated by investors who hold the relevant stock. Internet message boards have been a particularly fruitful breeding ground for all sorts of takeover speculation. Sometimes rumors enter analyst reports or

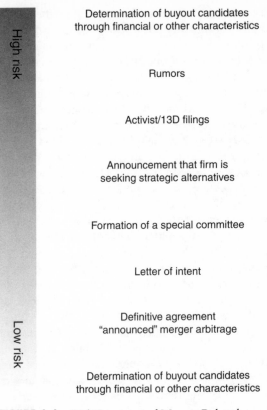

FIGURE 1.1 Risk Spectrum of Merger-Related Investments

newspapers. At that level, rumors are often somewhat more reliable—to the extent that the word "reliable" can be used in describing a rumor. One publication that made itself a name with sometimes-accurate reports of ongoing acquisition discussions in the apparel industry is *Women's Wear Daily*. In August 2005, it reported accurately that J. Jill was to be sold. A few months later, Jill rejected an acquisition proposal from Liz Claiborne and was eventually sold to Talbots.

A more reliable, although still speculative, merger investment strategy is to follow activist investors who try to get a company to sell itself. Activists file their intentions with the Securities and Exchange Commission (SEC) under Schedule 13D. These filings can be a source of potential merger targets; however, companies that are targets of activists are often in less-than-perfect condition and pose significant investment risk. This is, after all, why activist investors target these firms in the first place. Some commercial services monitor 13D filings and provide additional analysis.

Companies sometimes announce that they are for sale. These announcements are usually phrased as a "search for strategic alternatives, including a sale" or other transaction. Sometimes these announcements come in response to an attack by activist investors; sometimes a company's board decides on its own to explore the possibility of a sale. Compared to the previously discussed scenarios, investing in a firm whose management is actively pursuing a sale is much safer, but it still is no arbitrage because the company may well be sold for less than it can be purchased for at the time of the announcement. In addition, the outcome of such an investment depends highly on the market environment. In a bull market, it is relatively easy for management to sell the firm at a premium. In contrast, in a bear market, no buyers may materialize and the stock may fall along with the market.

Potential acquirers sometimes enter into a letter of intent before signing a formal merger agreement. Investing after a letter of intent can be very speculative. Most merger partners enter into a definitive agreement right away. Letters of intent are a sign of adverse selection: Either the buyer or the company is not yet quite ready to sign a definitive agreement. In the case of the acquisition of CCA Industries by Dubilier & Co., a private equity firm managed by the son of a cofounder of Clayton, Dubilier & Rice, a letter of intent led to a busted buyout because the acquiring private equity fund could not arrange the requisite financing. Had the firm found it easy to arrange the financing, it would have entered into a definitive agreement rather than a letter of intent in the first place.

Hostile bids are of a similar degree of risk as letters of intent. If the target fends off the bidder successfully, its share price may well revert to a lower, prebid level. Even worse, if an arbitrageur has set up a short position in the acquirer (discussed later in the chapter), a short squeeze could ensue, leading to losses on both the long and short side of the arbitrage.

The only real merger arbitrage occurs when the arbitrageur enters the position after a definitive agreement has been signed between the target and the acquirer. Arbitrageurs who specialize only in this type of transactions refer to it as announced merger arbitrage to differentiate it clearly from the other, more risky investment styles shown in the risk spectrum in Figure 1.1.

The remainder of the book addresses transactions in which a definitive agreement has been reached.

Merger arbitrage resembles in many respects the management of credit risk. Both are concerned with the management of a large asymmetry in payoffs between successful transactions and those that incur losses. A

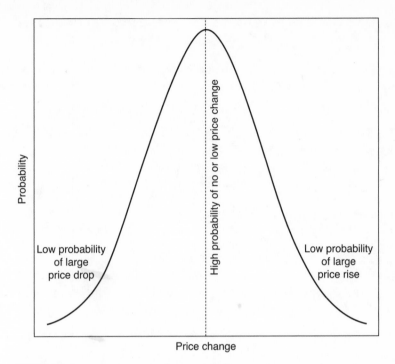

FIGURE 1.2 Payoff Distribution for Stock Investors

typical stock investor is faced with an almost symmetric payoff distribution (see Figure 1.2). The stock price is almost as likely to go up as it is to go down. The likelihood of a small gain is roughly the same as the likelihood of a loss of equal size. Larger changes in value are also almost equally likely. The downside is unlimited, or limited only by a complete loss of the investment. The upside, however, is unlimited. Every now and then, an investor gets lucky and owns the next Microsoft or Berkshire Hathaway. A small upward drift in stock prices means that in the long run, stocks trend up.

The situation is different for merger arbitrage and credit managers (see Figure 1.3). The upside in a merger is limited to the payment received when the merger closes. Likewise, the most credit managers will receive on a loan or bond is the interest (or the credit spread if they manage a hedged or leveraged portfolio). The downside is unlimited: If a merger collapses or a loan goes into default, a complete loss of capital is possible in a worst-case scenario. The only reason why investors are willing to take risks with such an asymmetric payoff distribution is that the probability of a large loss is

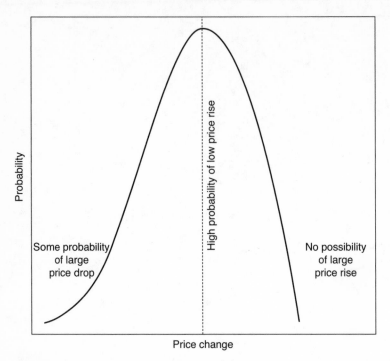

Probability

High probability of low price rise

Some probability
of large
price drop

No possibility
of large
price rise

Price change

FIGURE 1.3　Asymmetric Payoff Distribution

very small and the probability of a small gain is very large. The skill in
merger arbitrage, as in credit management, is to eliminate investments that
have a high probability of generating losses.

Another field in finance has payoff distributions very similar to those
of merger arbitrage and credit: option selling. An option seller expects to
make only a small return in the form of the option premium but can suffer a
significant loss when the option is in the money. Option strategies are often
depicted in payoff diagrams, such as that of a short (written) put option in
Figure 1.4. If at expiration the stock price rises above the strike price, the
option seller will earn only the premium. However, if the stock price falls
below the strike price, the option seller will suffer a significant loss. Merger
arbitrage and credit resemble this payoff pattern. Figure 1.5 shows the payoff
diagram for a simple merger arbitrage, where a buyer proposes to acquire
a company for cash consideration. If the transaction passes, the arbitrageur
will receive only the spread between the price at which she acquired the
target's stock and the price at which the firm is merged. However, if the
merger collapses, the stock price probably will drop, and the arbitrageur

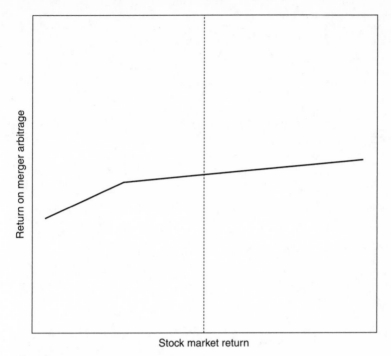

FIGURE 1.4 Put Option Characteristics of Merger Arbitrage

will incur a loss that is much larger than the potential gain if the merger is closed.

From an arbitrageur's point of view, the most important characteristic of a merger is the form of payment received. Therefore, merger typology used by arbitrageurs uses payment method as the principal classifier. Other merger professionals, such as tax advisers or lawyers, may use other criteria to categorize mergers. For example, tax advisers distinguish between taxable and tax-exempt mergers, whereas legal counsel may distinguish mergers by its antitrust effect. There are three principal categories of mergers and one rare category.

1. *Cash mergers.* The shareholders of the target firm receive a cash consideration for their shares.
2. *Stock-for-stock mergers.* The shares of the target firm are exchanged for shares in the acquirer.
3. *Mixed stock and cash mergers.* The target company's shareholders receive a mix of cash and a share exchange.

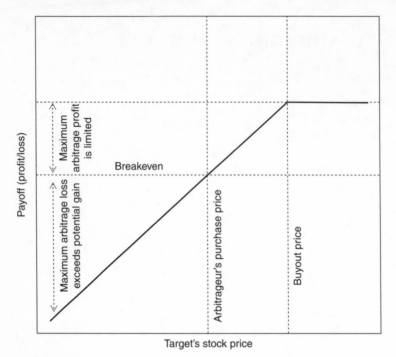

FIGURE 1.5   Payoff Diagram of Cash Mergers

4. *Other consideration.* In rare instances, shareholders of the target firm receive debt securities, spun-off divisions of the target, or contingent value rights.

The remainder of this chapter discusses the first three types of merger consideration and how arbitrageurs will set up an arbitrage trade and profit from it.

CASH MERGERS

The simplest form of merger is a cash merger. It is a transaction in which a buyer proposes to acquire the shares of a target firm for a cash payment.

We will look at a practical example to illustrate the analysis. An announcement for this type of merger is shown in Exhibit 1.1. This is the press release announcing the purchase of Trustreet Properties, a real estate investment trust, by a subsidiary of GE. It is typical of announcement of cash mergers.

EXHIBIT 1.1 PRESS RELEASE ANNOUNCING ACQUISITION OF TRUSTREET PROPERTIES BY GE CAPITAL

Orlando, Fla. (October 30, 2006)—Trustreet Properties, Inc. (NYSE: TSY), a leading restaurant real estate investment trust (REIT), announced today that it has entered into a definitive agreement to be acquired by GE Capital Solutions, Franchise Finance ("GE Capital Solutions"), a leading lender for the franchise finance market in the United States and Canada. The transaction is valued at approximately $3 billion, including the payment of $17.05 per outstanding share of Trustreet's common stock, in the form of cash, and the assumption or refinancing of Trustreet's outstanding debt. GE Capital Solutions will add Trustreet's preeminent restaurant 1031 trading platform to its own Franchise Finance business, and will also establish an East Coast office at Trustreet's headquarters in Orlando, Fla., where all sale-leaseback financing and related asset management will be handled for GE Capital Solutions' Franchise Finance business.

The transaction is expected to close during the first quarter of 2007 and is subject to the approval of Trustreet's common shareholders and other customary closing conditions....

GE Capital Solutions will acquire all of the outstanding common stock of Trustreet for $17.05 in cash. Trustreet is permitted to pay its quarterly dividend for the quarter ending December 31, 2006, but is not permitted to pay any additional dividends on its common stock thereafter unless necessary for Trustreet to maintain its status as a REIT. Dividends paid after December 31, 2006, may have the effect of reducing the merger consideration payable to the holders of Trustreet common stock.

The terminology used in mergers is quite straightforward: A Buyer, GE Capital Solutions in this case, proposes to acquire a Target, Trustreet here, for a consideration of $17.05 per share. The difference between the consideration and the current stock price is called the spread. When the stock price is less than the merger consideration, the spread will be positive. Sometimes the stock price will rise above the merger consideration, and the spread can become negative. This happens occasionally when there is speculation that another buyer may enter the scene and pay a higher price.

In a cash merger, the buyer of the company will cash out the existing shareholders through a cash payment, in this case $17.05 per share. An

arbitrageur will profit by acquiring the shares below the merger consideration and holding it until the closing, or alternatively selling earlier.

Arbitrageurs come across press releases as part of their daily routine
search for newly announced mergers. This one was released on October 30,
2006, at 9:00 AM. For regulatory reasons, companies announce significant
events like mergers after the end of regular market hours or in the morning
prior to the opening. This is meant to prevent abuse by investors with
slightly better access to news. With the growing importance of after-hours
trading and the availability of 24-hour trading of U.S. stocks through foreign
exchanges, this restraint has already become somewhat pointless but is still
considered best practice.

The first observation an arbitrageur will make is that the stock of
Trustreet jumped almost immediately upon the announcement of the merger.
As can be seen in Figure 1.6, Trustreet closed at $12.51 on October 27, the
last day before the announcement of the merger. It opened at the same level
on October 30, quickly moved above $17.00, and closed at $16.97. Some

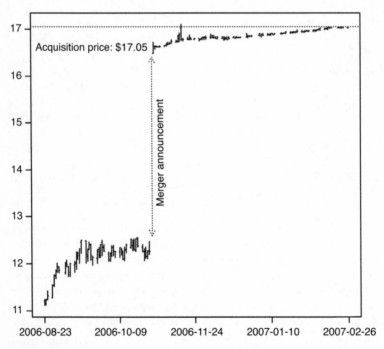

FIGURE 1.6 Stock Price of Trustreet Properties before and after the Merger
Announcement

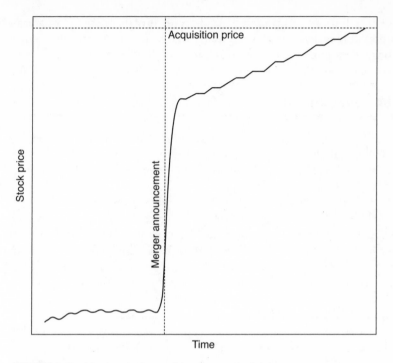

FIGURE 1.7 Idealized Chart of Stock in a Cash Merger

lucky investors bought shares at the opening price, and because there must be a seller for every buyer, some unfortunate sellers parted with their investment at a low price. However, it was not practical for any investor to acquire any significant number of shares at the open. It is most likely that these shares were acquired by specialists on the New York Stock Exchange, where the stock was listed. An investor had a realistic chance to acquire shares around $17.00.

A chart like that shown in Figure 1.6 is typical of stocks undergoing mergers. The buyout proposal is generally made at a premium to the stocks' most recent trading price. This leads to a jump in the target's stock price immediately following the proposal. As time passes and the date of the closing approaches, the spread becomes narrower. This means that the stock price moves closer to the merger price. An idealized chart is shown in Figure 1.7, whereas Trustreet's actual chart is more typical of the behavior of most such stocks.

In some instances, the buyout proposal is made at a discount to the most recent trading price. This rarely happens and is limited to small companies where the buyer is in a position to force the sale. It often leads to litigation and a subsequent increase in the consideration. A transaction at a discount to the last trading price is called a "takeunder."

INSIDER TRADING

Investors looking at the large jump in Trustreet's stock on October 30 will be tempted to calculate the profits they could have made with a little advance knowledge of the upcoming merger. Insider trading is a crime, not a form of arbitrage.

As readers of the financial press know, every merger cycle is characterized by insiders taking advantage of advance knowledge of mergers. Law enforcement has been successful in prosecuting even the most elaborate insider trading rings. One recent case involved New York bankers who bought options over the Internet through an online brokerage account established in Austria in the name of an elderly woman living in Croatia. Despite the complexity of the scheme, the perpetrators were caught and imprisoned.

Penalties for insider trading are up to 10 in years prison, in addition to monetary penalties, rescission of profits, and potential civil liability in shareholder lawsuits.

An arbitrageur who buys the stock on October 30 for $17.00 will receive $17.05 when the transaction closes. The gross profit for the capital gain on this arbitrage is $0.05 on $17.00, or 0.29 percent:

$$R_G = \frac{P_C}{P_P} - 1 = \frac{17.05}{17.00} - 1 = 0.00294 \qquad (1.1)$$

where R_G is the gross return.
        P_C is the cash consideration received in the merger.
        P_P is the purchase price.

This return will be achieved by the closing of the merger. A key component in investments is not just the return achieved but also the time needed. A more useful measure of return that makes comparisons easier is the annualized return achieved. The relevant time frame starts with the date on which the arbitrageur enters the position and ends with the date of the closing. The press release stated that the "transaction is expected to close during the first quarter of 2007." Therefore, the last day of the quarter, March 31, is used as a conservative estimate for the closing of the transaction. Pedantic arbitrageurs would choose March 30 instead because March 31 was a Saturday in 2007. There are 152 days in the period until the anticipated closing. Two methods can be used to annualize the return: simple or compound interest.

Simple interest

$$R_{AG} = \left(\frac{P_C}{P_P} - 1\right) \times \left(\frac{365}{t}\right) = \left(\frac{17.05}{17.00} - 1\right) \times \left(\frac{365}{152}\right) = 0.00706 \quad (1.2)$$

where R_{AG} is the annualized gross return.
       t is the number of days until closing.

Compound interest

$$R_{AG} = \left(\frac{P_C}{P_P}\right)^{\left(\frac{365}{t}\right)} - 1 = \left(\frac{17.05}{17.00}\right)^{\left(\frac{365}{152}\right)} - 1 = 0.00708 \quad (1.3)$$

where R_{AG} is the annualized gross return.
       t is the number of days until closing.

Personal preference determines which method is used. Simple interest is useful if the returns are compared to money market yields that are also computed with the simple interest method, such as the London Interbank Offered Rate (LIBOR) or Treasury bills (T bills). Compound interest is preferable if the result is used in further quantitative studies. If the returns are compared to bond yields, they should be adjusted for semiannual compounding used in bonds. It is an error encountered frequently, even in research by otherwise experienced analysts and academics, that yields calculated on different bases are compared with one another.

An annualized return of 0.71 percent is not enough to excite any investor at a time when money market yields are above 4 percent. Fortunately, there is another source of income in this arbitrage: the dividend that Trustreet pays on its common stock. As a real estate investment trust (REIT), Trustreet is required to distribute at least 90 percent of its income in order to maintain its tax-favored status. Trustreet's quarterly dividends have been $0.33 in the past, and it is fair to assume that it will continue to pay at this level.

The press release states that Trustreet will "pay its quarterly dividend for the quarter ending December 31, 2006, but is not permitted to pay any additional dividends on its common stock thereafter." The last dividend before the announcement of the merger was paid on September 15, so the assumed dividend date for the next payment is December 15. For the first quarter of 2007, no dividend payment should be assumed. A back-of-the-envelope calculation for the net return with dividends is to add the dividend to the merger consideration received. This gives an annualized return of 5.37 percent if simple returns are used:

$$R_{AN} = \left(\frac{P_C + d}{P_P}\right)^{\left(\frac{365}{t}\right)} - 1 = \left(\frac{17.05 + 0.33}{17.00}\right)^{\left(\frac{365}{152}\right)} - 1 = 0.05368 \tag{1.4}$$

where d is the amount of the dividend received.

A more accurate method is the calculation of the internal rate of return (IRR). Spreadsheets have built-in functions to calculate IRRs that require the user to enter each payment with the associated date, as shown in Figure 1.8.

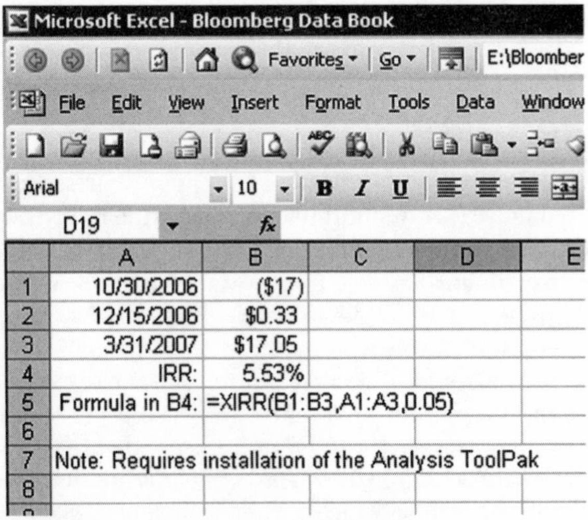
Microsoft Excel - Bloomberg Data Book
Favorites Go E:\Bloomber
File Edit View Insert Format Tools Data Window
Arial 10 B I U
D19
A B C D E
1 10/30/2006 ($17)
2 12/15/2006 $0.33
3 3/31/2007 $17.05
4 IRR: 5.53%
5 Formula in B4: =XIRR(B1:B3,A1:A3,0.05)
6
7 Note: Requires installation of the Analysis ToolPak
8

FIGURE 1.8 IRR Calculation of Annualized Return in Excel

The resulting return is an annualized return of 5.53 percent, slightly higher than in the simplified calculation. The reason for the difference lies in the earlier receipt of the dividend cash flow in the IRR calculation.

It is helpful to look at the actual outcome of this merger arbitrage. The Trustreet acquisition closed earlier than an arbitrageur would have assumed: February 26, 2007. The actual date of the dividend payment was December 26, 2006. Entering these values into the IRR calculation, it can be seen that the actual return on this arbitrage would have been 7.09 percent. Of course, this outcome was not foreseeable on October 30. However, whenever new information becomes known, such as the announcement of the dividend date on November 7, 2006, arbs must update their spreadsheets promptly.

The anticipated annualized return of this arbitrage was 5.53 percent, which may not seem very lucrative. Remember that there are several reasons for this anticipated low rate:

- Several months earlier, the largest buyout ever had closed, that of the REIT Equity Office. An initial acquisition proposal for Equity Office was trumped by a higher bid, and the holder of the stock realized significant extra gains. Some arbs may have hoped for a similar outcome in Trustreet, which is also a REIT. They were willing to settle for a relatively low return for the potential of additional upside should another buyer emerge.
- The timing assumption for the closing on March 31 was very conservative. Had an arbitrageur worked with a closing date of February 28, the annualized return would have been closer to 7 percent.

STOCK-FOR-STOCK MERGERS

Stock-for-stock mergers are more complicated than cash mergers. In stock-for-stock mergers, a buyer proposes to acquire a target by paying in shares rather than cash. Sometimes the consideration paid can be a combination of stock and cash. That case is addressed later.

A good example of a stock-for-stock merger announcement is shown in Exhibit 1.2. It is the $4 billion acquisition of Agere Systems by LSI Corporation, announced in December 2006.

In this case, LSI Logic is the buyer, Agere Systems the target, and the per share consideration is no longer a fixed cash amount but a fixed number of LSI Logic shares. Shareholders of Agere Systems will receive 2.16 shares of LSI Logic for each share of Agere that they hold. The number 2.16 is referred to as the conversion factor.

EXHIBIT 1.2 MERGER ANNOUNCEMENT FOR LSI LOGIC AND AGERE SYSTEMS

MILPITAS, Calif., and ALLENTOWN, Pa., December 4, 2006—LSI Logic Corporation (NYSE: LSI) and Agere Systems Inc. (NYSE: AGR) today announced that they have entered into a definitive merger agreement under which the companies will be combined in an all-stock transaction with an equity value of approximately $4.0 billion. Under the terms of the agreement, Agere shareholders will receive 2.16 shares of LSI for each share of Agere they own. Based on the closing stock price of LSI on December 1, 2006, this represents a value to Agere shareholders of $22.81 per share. . . .

The transaction is subject to the approval of shareholders from both companies as well as customary closing conditions and regulatory approvals. The companies expect the transaction to close in the first calendar quarter of 2007.

The dollar amount of $22.81 mentioned in the press release refers to the value of the merger on the day before the announcement. This amount is calculated simply by multiplying the closing price of LSI's stock of $10.56 on December 1, the last trading day before the announcement, by the conversion factor of 2.16. It is not the value that shareholders will receive at the closing of the merger. The value will vary with the stock price of LSI Logic. This distinction is important, because unlike in the case of a cash merger, arbitrageurs cannot just buy the stock of the target Agere and wait for the merger to close.

A naive strategy would be to purchase Agere stock and wait for the merger to consummate. The investor would receive 2.16 shares of LSI that it would then need to sell at the prevailing market price, which could be higher or lower. There is no arbitrage in such a transaction. Recall that one of the elements of the definition of arbitrage was that a purchase and sale occur simultaneously. Holding a stock and waiting to sell it for a higher price is speculation, not arbitrage.

Instead, arbitrageurs must lock in the value of the transaction through a short sale. For readers new to short sales, a brief explanation is given here. Additional aspects of short sales are discussed in Chapter 13.

SHORT SALES

Most investors will only buy stocks and sell stocks that they bought previously and hold in their portfolio at the time of the sale. Selling short differs from a normal sale mainly through the timing of the purchase. A short sale is done before the stock is acquired. If a stock declines in value, a short seller will make a profit; if a stock increases in value, the short seller will suffer a loss.

An important component in short selling is the delivery of the stock to the buyer. The buyer is unaware that the stock has been sold short and rightfully expects delivery. In order to make delivery of the stock, the short seller must borrow it from someone who owns it. Most brokerages and clearing firms offer their customers the ability to borrow stock. Online discount brokerages generally have fully automated systems to locate stocks that can be borrowed for their customers. If the stock cannot be borrowed, it cannot be sold short, and the brokerage will inform the customer.

The process of closing the short sale—that is, buying back the shares that have been shorted—is a buy-to-cover transaction.

Sometimes the lender of a stock requests its return, for example, if the stock is to be sold. In that case, either the customer must buy to cover or the broker will do a buy-in, meaning that the broker places the buy-to-cover order. If an investor is served with a notice of an upcoming buy-in, it is always better to buy the stock oneself and maintain control over the order than to let the broker execute a buy-in.

Selling short is sometimes portrayed as illegal, dishonest, or un-American. However, in financial markets, arbitrage would not be possible without short selling. Arbitrage involves the simultaneous sale of an asset identical to the one acquired; in many instances, this is possible only through short sales. If there were no arbitrage in financial markets, many products would not be priced correctly, and investors might overpay.

The chief executives of some companies have launched a crusade against naked short selling, which is an illegal activity in which the short seller does not borrow the stock that is sold short.

The graph of the stock prices of LSI and Agere are shown in Figure 1.9. It can be seen that Agere jumped on December 4, the day of the announcement,

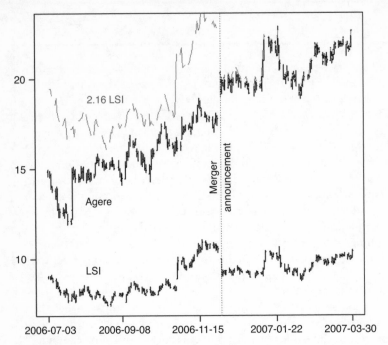

FIGURE 1.9   Stock Prices of LSI and Agere

from under $18.00 to over $20.00 and closed at $19.30. LSI Systems had traded around $10.70 before the announcement and fell to a closing price of $9.12. Articles in the press often attribute such a drop of an acquirer's stock price to skepticism about the merger in the investor community. However, it will be seen that the drop is often the by-product of arbitrage activity.

For simplicity, it will be assumed that an arbitrageur enters the position on December 4 at the closing price. The arbitrageur will execute two transactions:

1. Pay $19.30 per share to buy 100 shares of Agere.
2. Sell short 216 shares of LSI at $9.12 per share.

It helps to examine the cash flows and stock holdings after these two trades. They can be found in Table 1.2. There is an expense of $1,930.00 to acquire the shares of Agere, and proceeds from the short sale amount to $1,970.00.

It can be seen that this transaction leaves the arbitrageur with a net cash inflow of $40.00. At the closing of the merger, the 100 shares of Agere will

TABLE 1.2 Cash Flows in Agere/LSI Merger

	Stock Transaction	Cash Flow
Agere	+100	$(1,930.00)
LSI	−216	$1,970.00
Net	—	$40.00

be converted into 216 shares of LSI. The arbitrageur is then long 216 shares and short 216. The long position can then be used to deliver shares to the counterparty from which the short position was borrowed. As a result, the arbitrageur no longer has a position in stock, long or short, but is left with a profit of $40.00.

The example of 100 shares is useful for illustrative purposes. Rather than looking at the purchase of 100 shares, transactions should be calculated on a per-share basis. Each share of Agere is converted into 2.16 shares of LSI. By multiplying the exchange ratio with the stock price of LSI, it can be seen that per share of Agere an arbitrageur receives $19.70 from the short sale of LSI. The spread is hence $0.40 per share of Agere.

The return calculation is simplified here in that no dividends need to be taken into account. LSI has not paid dividends since 1986, and Agere does not pay dividends either.

$$R_G = \left(\frac{P_S}{P_P}\right) - 1 = \left(\frac{19.70}{19.30}\right) - 1 = 0.0207 \qquad (1.5)$$

$$P_S = r \times P_A$$

where P_S is the proceeds received from the short sale, per share of target stock.

P_A is the price at which the acquirer is sold short.

r is the exchange ratio.

The gross return on this arbitrage is 2.1 percent.

Calculation of the annualized return works as in the example of a cash merger. Only the calculation of compound returns are shown here; simple interest can be calculated analogously. To determine the likely closing date, the arbitrageur will again reference the press release: "The companies expect the transaction to close in the first calendar quarter of 2007." A closing date of March 31 is 117 days from December 4, the day the position was entered.

The number 116 days would be used if March 30, the last business day of the quarter, is used.

Compound interest

$$R_{AG} = \left(\frac{P_S}{P_P} \right)^{\left(\frac{365}{t} \right)} - 1 = \left(\frac{19.70}{19.30} \right)^{\left(\frac{365}{117} \right)} - 1 = 0.00661 \qquad (1.6)$$

The actual closing of this merger occurred on April 2, 2007, so the actual return on this arbitrage was an annualized 6.5 percent.

One of the advantages of stock-for-stock mergers is the simultaneous holdings of a long and a short position. Because of the upcoming merger, the two stocks are highly correlated, so that an increase in Agere's stock price is accompanied by an offsetting increase in LSI's. If the two stocks were no longer to move in parallel, the spread would change, and the annualized return available to arbitrageurs would either compress or expand.

The evolution of the spread of the Agere/LSI merger is shown in Figure 1.10. In the case of a cash transaction, the spread depends on only one variable. In a stock-for-stock merger, it depends on two stock prices. The spread does trend toward zero over time, albeit not very smoothly.

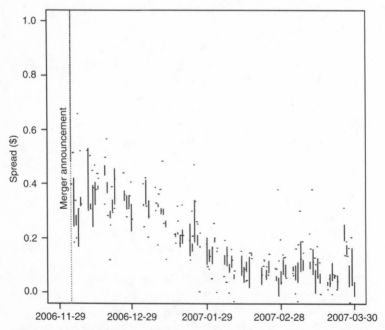

FIGURE 1.10 Evolution of the Agere/LSI Spread

It is clear that short sales from arbitrage activity can lead to significant selling pressure on the stock of a buyer after the announcement of a stock-for-stock merger. Often analysts and journalists attribute the drop of a buyer's stock after a merger announcement to fundamental reasons, such as the prospect for the merged entity. One account of the trading activity following the announcement of the merger of Trane Inc. with Ingersoll-Rand is shown in Exhibit 1.3. The mechanics of this merger are discussed in the next section. Ingersoll-Rand fell over 11 percent following the announcement of the merger. The fundamental reasoning behind this merger appeared solid. Some reports suggested that the combination of the two firms created the number-two air-conditioning company in the United States. The long-term prospects of Ingersoll-Rand clearly were not bad and would not have justified an 11 percent drop. It can be explained only by arbitrage activity. Experienced investment bankers warn company management during merger negotiations of the risk to their stock price and suggest structures with a cash component to a stock-for-stock merger in order to reduce short selling.

EXHIBIT 1.3 ACCOUNT OF INGERSOLL-RAND'S ACQUISITION OF TRANE FOR $10.1 BILLION, CREATING CLIMATE CONTROL BEHEMOTH

TRENTON, N.J. (AP)—In a deal worth a cool $10 billion, Ingersoll-Rand Co. will acquire Trane Inc. and create one of the world's largest makers of commercial and residential home air conditioners, refrigerators for trucks and stores, and other climate control products.

But some Ingersoll-Rand shareholders, who had expected the cash-rich company to pour some money into share repurchases, seemed disappointed with the acquisition announced Monday and sold Ingersoll-Rand stock, driving shares down sharply.

Merger arbitrage is attractive to many investors as a portfolio diversifier because of its long/short components. It is assumed that these positions immunize the portfolio against fluctuations in the overall stock market and leave only uncorrelated event risk to the investor, and therefore, the portfolio is market neutral. This argument is revisited in more detail in Chapter 12. Nevertheless, at this point, a short discussion of one of the pitfalls of long/short positions is necessary. A constant percentage spread can lead to dollar paper losses in an extreme bull market, if both the long and the short position increase, but the percentage spread remains constant. Table 1.3 illustrates this problem with a hypothetical increase of Agere

TABLE 1.3 Losses Suffered at a Constant Percentage Spread in a Rising Market

Agere	LSI	Value of LSI	Spread ($)	Spread (%)	P & L
19.30	9.12	19.70	0.40	2.07	0
20	9.45	20.41	0.41	2.07	−0.01
21	9.92	21.43	0.43	2.07	−0.03
22	10.40	22.46	0.46	2.07	−0.06
23	10.87	23.48	0.48	2.07	−0.08
24	11.34	24.50	0.50	2.07	−0.10
25	11.81	25.52	0.52	2.07	−0.12
26	12.29	26.54	0.54	2.07	−0.14
27	12.76	27.56	0.56	2.07	−0.16
28	13.23	28.58	0.58	2.07	−0.18
29	13.70	29.60	0.60	2.07	−0.20
30	14.18	30.62	0.62	2.07	−0.22
31	14.65	31.64	0.64	2.07	−0.24
32	15.12	32.66	0.66	2.07	−0.26
33	15.59	33.68	0.68	2.07	−0.28
34	16.07	34.70	0.70	2.07	−0.30
35	16.54	35.72	0.72	2.07	−0.32
36	17.01	36.74	0.74	2.07	−0.34
37	17.48	37.77	0.77	2.07	−0.37
38	17.96	38.79	0.79	2.07	−0.39
39	18.43	39.81	0.81	2.07	−0.41
40	18.90	40.83	0.83	2.07	−0.43

and LSI with a constant percentage spread. The losses discussed here are temporary only and will eventually be recovered once the merger closes.

The table starts with the actual spread of 2.07 percent at prices of $19.30 and $9.12 for Agere and LSI, respectively. It shows the profit and loss (P&L) relative to a position entered at $19.30 and $9.12. If both Agere and LSI rise and the percentage spread remains constant, then the spread expressed in dollars must rise (2 percent of $40.00 is more than 2 percent of $19.30). The simulated price rise in Table 1.3 shows that a spread of $0.40 would widen to $0.83 per share if Agere were to double in value to $40.00 per share. Although LSI's stock appreciates by the same percentage as Agere, the difference in dollar terms increases. At $40.00 per share, the arbitrageur's portfolio would record a loss of $0.43 per Agere share.

This scenario does not imply inefficiency in the market. If the hypothetical increase in spreads were to occur on the same day as the position was entered, the annualized return would be unchanged, because the percentage spread is the same whether Agere trades at $40.00 or at $19.30.

It is clear that these losses are only paper losses. As long as the merger eventually closes, the arbitrageur will realize a gain of $0.40. Only those who panic and close their position early will actually suffer a loss. The arbitrageur is short 2.16 shares of LSI for every long position of Agere, and the cash changed hands when the trade was made. Therefore, the eventual profit is certain as long as the merger closes.

Whether an arbitrageur wants to hedge against paper losses is a matter of personal preference. Any hedging transactions will entail costs and will reduce the return of the arbitrage. Because the spread eventually will be recovered, it probably makes little sense to hedge against transitory marked-to-market losses.

It can be extrapolated from this discussion that in the case of a fall in stock prices, the dollar spread will tighten, and the arbitrageur will record a gain even though the percentage spread and the annualized return would remain unchanged.

Sometimes shareholders hold a number of target shares that does not get converted to a round number of buyer shares. For example, a holder of 110 shares of Agere would receive 237.6 shares of LSI. However, the fractional 0.6 shares cannot be traded or issued because corporations have whole shares only. (Note that mutual funds are different even though they are also organized as corporations.) Therefore, companies will liquidate fractional shares and issue only full shares. The investor in our example would receive 237 shares of LSI and a cash payment for the value of the fractional 0.6 shares. The cash payment depends on the share price of LSI at the time of the closing of the merger.

In addition to earning the spread, a stock-for-stock merger has another source of income. When arbitrageurs short a stock, they receive the proceeds of the short sale. In the example from Table 1.2, the arbitrageur received $1,970.00 from the short sale of Agere. These funds are on deposit at the brokerage firm that executed the short sale. Arbitrageurs can negotiate to receive interest on this deposit. This is easier said than done. In the author's experience, most retail brokerage firms do not pay interest on the proceeds of short sales. At the time of writing, one retail brokerage firm advertised that it had paid interest on balances of short proceeds in excess of $100,000.00. Institutions are better off. They are always offered interest on the proceeds. This is referred to as "short rebate" in industry parlance.

The example of the Agere/LSI merger can illustrate the effect of the short rebate on merger arbitrage returns. Assume that the short rebate is 1 percent. This may appear low, but it is quite normal for rates for short rebates to be well below interest rates. In fact, the spread between short rebates and margin rates charged customers who borrow to buy stock is an important source of revenue for brokerage firms. The interest earned on the

$1,970.00 over the 117-day period until the closing of the merger would have been

$$i = \$1,970 \times 0.01 \times \frac{117}{365} = \$6.32 \tag{1.7}$$

This would increase the merger profit from $40.00 to $46.32—an increase of almost 16 percent. For simplicity, simple interest is used in this calculation. Most brokers pay interest monthly, so monthly compounding should be used.

The annualized spread increases by the amount earned on the short rebate:

$$R_{AG} = \left(\frac{P_S \times (1 + r_s)^{\cdot \left(\frac{t}{365}\right)}}{P_P} \right)^{\left(\frac{365}{t}\right)} - 1$$

$$= \left(\frac{19.70 \times (1 + 0.01)}{19.30} \right)^{\left(\frac{365}{117}\right)} - 1 = 0.0767 \tag{1.8}$$

where r_s represents the interest paid on the short rebate.

As discussed in Chapter 13, returns on merger arbitrage tend to be correlated with interest rates as a result of the impact that short rebates have on spreads.

The LSI merger was easy to analyze because neither stock pays any dividends. Stocks paying dividends can be tricky to handle when sold short, because the short seller must pay the dividend on the stock. The long position will generate a dividend; the short position will cost a dividend. A crude calculation to determine the net effect of dividends on the annualized spread is to subtract the dividend yield of the short position from the dividend yield of the long position, and add the result to the annualized return of the merger arbitrage. However, this method can give incorrect results, especially for mergers with a short horizon to closing. The method can be used as a first approximation, but arbitrageurs always must consider the actual dividend dates and dividend amounts.

The gross return in the presence of dividends is calculated for a long/short merger arbitrage in this way:

$$R_G = \left(\frac{P_S}{P_P + d_P} \right) - 1 = \left(\frac{19.70}{19.30} \right) - 1 = 0.0207 \tag{1.9}$$

$$P_S = r(P_A - d_S)$$

where d_S are the total dividends to be paid on the short sale.
        d_P are the total dividends to be received on the purchased (long) stock.

Mixed Cash/Stock Mergers

Many buyers want to limit dilution in the acquisition of a target company or have access only to an amount of cash insufficient to purchase the target entirely for cash. They are structured as the acquisition of a target for a dollar amount plus a shares, or they offer target shareholders the option to choose between cash and stock, typically with a forced proration.

In the former case, every shareholder of the target company is treated equally. Exhibit 1.4 shows the announcement of the merger of Trane, Inc. with Ingersoll-Rand, announced in December 2007. This merger was mentioned briefly earlier to illustrate the effect that arbitrage-related short selling can have on a company's stock price immediately following the announcement of a merger.

EXHIBIT 1.4 ANNOUNCEMENT OF ACQUISITION OF TRANE INC. BY INGERSOLL-RAND

HAMILTON, Bermuda, and PISCATAWAY, N.J.—(BUSINESS WIRE)—Ingersoll-Rand Company Limited (NYSE: IR) announced today that it has executed a definitive agreement to acquire Trane Inc. (NYSE: TT), formerly American Standard Companies Inc., in a transaction valued at approximately $10.1 billion, including transaction fees and the assumption of approximately $150 million of Trane net debt. Trane is a global leader in indoor climate control systems, services and solutions with expected 2007 revenues of $7.4 billion.

Under the terms of the merger agreement, which has been approved by the Boards of Directors of both companies, Ingersoll Rand will acquire all outstanding common stock of Trane. Holders of Trane's approximately 200 million common shares will receive a combination of $36.50 in cash and 0.23 Ingersoll Rand shares of common stock per each Trane share. The total value for this transaction was $47.81 per Trane share based on the closing price as of December 14, 2007. The transaction which is expected to close late in the first quarter or early in the second quarter of 2008, is subject to approval by Trane shareholders, regulatory approvals and customary closing conditions.

Trane's shareholders will receive $36.50 plus 0.23 share of Ingersoll-Rand. Trane's shares closed on December 17 at $45.24, whereas those of

Ingersoll-Rand closed at $43.60. An arbitrageur entering a position at these prices would make a gross return of 2.85 percent:

$$R_G = \left(\frac{P_S + P_C}{P_P} \right) - 1 = \left(\frac{0.232 \times 43.60 + 36.50}{45.24} \right) - 1 = 0.00285$$

(1.10)

where $\quad P_S = r \times P_A$ as before.

$\quad\quad P_C$ is the cash component received in the merger.

This gross return should be annualized by one of the methods explained earlier.

Another form of mixed cash/stock transactions does not specify a set dollar amount to be received per share but instead sets a fraction of the total consideration to cash. Frequently used ratios are 50/50 cash/stock, 40/60, or 20/80.

The acquisition by Vulcan Materials Company of Florida Rock Industries, Inc. had 70 percent cash and 30 percent stock. The press release is shown in Exhibit 1.5.

Mixed transactions with election rights can be difficult to calculate because they require some guesswork. Shareholders can choose to receive either cash or stock. Arbitrageurs and many shareholders will pick the option that is worth the most. In this case, if Vulcan's shares trade above $67.00 at the time of the merger, profit-maximizing shareholders will want to receive shares. If Vulcan's shares trade below $67.00, shareholders will prefer $67.00 in cash. For this reason, these transactions have a proration provision, so that the buyer of the firm can make the blended cash/stock payment of 30 percent stock and 70 percent cash. However, not all shareholders will seek to be paid in cash when the shares are below $67.00. Some shareholders fail to make a selection and will be allocated the less valuable consideration by default. Many long-term shareholders will select shares even though they could get a higher cash payment because they intend to continue to hold the shares. Strategic investors or managers will hold on to their shares. Some asset allocators may find it easier to roll their shares into the buyer's stock than reinvest themselves. Finally, the most important group selecting stock rather than cash are long-term holders who have significant appreciation in their holdings of target stock. They would be faced with an immediate tax bill if they realized a gain in the merger. By selecting stock, they can defer realization of a taxable gain into the future. Because these investors have a preference for stock even if the cash component is worth more at the time of the merger, slightly more cash will be paid to shareholders who select cash than if proration were applied at the stated ratio.

In the case of Florida Rock, 85.7 percent of shareholders elected to receive cash, 10.7 percent elected stock, and the remaining 3.6 percent did not make a selection. Because the cash election was oversubscribed, the

EXHIBIT 1.5 ACQUISITION OF FLORIDA ROCK BY VULCAN MATERIALS

Birmingham, AL, and Jacksonville, FL—February 19, 2007—Vulcan Materials Company (NYSE: VMC), the nation's largest producer of construction aggregates and a major producer of other construction materials, and Florida Rock Industries Inc. (NYSE: FRK), a leading producer of construction aggregates, cement, concrete, and concrete products in the Southeast and Mid-Atlantic states, today announced that they have signed a definitive agreement for Vulcan Materials to acquire Florida Rock in a cash and stock transaction valued at approximately $4.6 billion.

The acquisition, which has been unanimously approved by both companies' boards of directors, will significantly enhance Vulcan Materials' strategic position and long-term growth opportunities by greatly expanding its presence in attractive Florida markets and in other high-growth Southeast and Mid-Atlantic states. The combined company will have aggregate reserves totaling approximately 13.9 billion tons, an increase of more than 20% over Vulcan Materials' stand-alone aggregate reserves, and 2006 pro forma aggregate shipments of 300 million tons, an increase of approximately 18% compared to Vulcan Materials' stand-alone shipments.

Under the terms of the agreement, Vulcan Materials shareholders will receive one share of common stock in a new holding company (whose subsidiaries will be Vulcan Materials and Florida Rock) for each Vulcan Materials share. Florida Rock shareholders can elect to receive either 0.63 shares of the new holding company or $67.00 in cash for each Florida Rock share, subject to proration, to ensure that in the aggregate 70% of Florida Rock shares will be converted into cash and 30% of Florida Rock shares will be converted into stock. The transaction is intended to be non-taxable for Vulcan Materials shareholders and non-taxable for Florida Rock shareholders to the extent they receive stock. The total blended cash and stock consideration of $68.03 per share, based on the closing price of Vulcan Materials' stock on Friday, February 16, 2007, represents a premium of 45% for Florida Rock shareholders based on Friday's closing price of each company's stock.

shareholders who did not select cash received all stock. Shareholders who elected to receive cash received cash for 81.6 percent of their shares and stock for the other 18.4 percent.

Arbitrageurs must use experience and guesswork to determine the ratio that is most likely to apply. In the next discussion, it is assumed for simplicity that the ratio of cash/stock that the arbitrageur will receive is that of the stated proration factor.

To calculate the gross return,

$$R_G = (R_S \times P_S + R_C \times P_C) \div P_P - 1 \qquad (1.11)$$

where R_S is the ratio of stock to be received.

R_C is the ratio of cash to be received (obviously, $R_S + R_C = 1$).

P_S is the proceeds received from the short sale, per share of target stock.

As before, $P_S = r \times P_A$

This gross return can be annualized by analogy with the previous examples.

Mergers with Collars

The Agere/LSI merger had a fixed exchange ratio of 2.16. This exposes both Agere and LSI to a certain market risk: If the value of LSI's stock increases significantly, then the 2.16 shares that Agere shareholders will receive for each share will also increase in value. In this case, the value of the transaction will be much higher than $4 billion. While Agere shareholders will be happy with this outcome, the investors in LSI will wonder whether they could have acquired Agere by issuing fewer shares. Conversely, if LSI's stock falls, then Agere's shareholders will receive less valuable shares for each Agere share. They would have been better off with a higher exchange ratio.

For this reason, many merger agreements include provisions to fix the value of stock received by the target company's shareholders at a set dollar amount or at a fixed exchange ratio. The exchange ratio is adjusted as a function of the share price of the acquirer. Two reference prices are determined.

Two types of collars are common:

1. *Fixed value collars*. Target shareholders will receive a set dollar value's worth of shares of the acquirer as long as the acquirer's share price is within a certain collar. This collar is buyer-friendly. The exchange ratio can change within the collar range. This type of collar is so common that the term "fixed value" is often dropped. References to a generic "collar" relate to fixed value collars.
2. *Fixed share collars*. A set number of shares is given to the target shareholders as long as the acquirer's share price is within a certain range. If

the acquirer's share price rises above the maximum, the exchange ratio declines. This collar is seller-friendly. The exchange ratio is fixed within the collar range.

The September 2006 acquisition of Windrose Medical Properties Trust by Health Care REIT, Inc. contained a fixed value collar, shown in the press release in Exhibit 1.6.

EXHIBIT 1.6 ACQUISITION OF WINDROSE MEDICAL PROPERTIES BY HEALTH CARE REIT

Toledo, Ohio, and Indianapolis, Indiana, September 13, 2006—Health Care REIT, Inc. (NYSE: HCN) and Windrose Medical Properties Trust (NYSE: WRS) announced today that they have entered into a definitive merger agreement pursuant to which Health Care REIT will acquire Windrose for approximately $877 million, including the assumption of Windrose's outstanding debt which totaled approximately $426 million as of June 30, 2006. The merger will create a company with investments throughout the health care delivery system with more than 550 properties in 37 states. The combined entity would have gross real estate assets of approximately $4 billion and an enterprise value of approximately $5 billion based on the closing prices of both Health Care REIT and Windrose's stocks on September 12, 2006....

Under the terms of the agreement, each outstanding share of Windrose will be exchanged for 0.4509 shares of Health Care REIT common stock. At yesterday's closing prices, this represents a price of $18.06 for each Windrose share. The actual exchange ratio at closing will be based upon the volume-weighted average price per share of Health Care REIT common stock on the New York Stock Exchange for the 10 trading days selected by lot from the 15 trading day period, ending on and including the fifth trading day prior to the closing of the transaction. The exchange ratio will be subject to increase up to a maximum of 0.4650 in the event of a decrease in Health Care REIT's common stock price prior to the end of such period. Upon closing, Windrose stockholders will own approximately 15% of Health Care REIT, assuming conversion of all of the outstanding Windrose convertible preferred stock. The transaction is expected to close on or about year-end 2006, subject to the approval of the stockholders of Windrose and other customary conditions and consents. Completion of the transaction does not require approval of Health Care REIT stockholders.

Exhibit 1.6 also illustrates that arbitrageurs sometimes need to reverse-engineer merger announcements to understand the terms. Nowhere in the press release is the expression "fixed value collar" used, and the reference prices are also missing. The merger agreement is sometimes of help. It is shown in Exhibit 1.7.

Unfortunately, the merger agreement has similar wording as the press release. In addition, it was not filed with the SEC until the afternoon of September 15, two days after the press release. A merger arbitrageur would have lost valuable time in which a position could have been established.

EXHIBIT 1.7 ACQUISITION OF WINDROSE MEDICAL PROPERTIES BY HEALTH CARE REIT

Merger agreement, section 2.2

(c) Conversion of Shares. Each Share issued and outstanding immediately prior to the Merger Effective Time (other than Shares to be cancelled in accordance with Section 2.2(b)) shall be converted into a fraction of a duly authorized, validly issued, fully paid and non-assessable share of common stock, par value $1.00 per share, of Parent (a "Parent Share" and collectively, the "Parent Shares") equal to the quotient determined by dividing $18.06 by the Parent Stock Price (as defined below) and rounding the result to the nearest 1/10,000 of a share (the "Exchange Ratio"); provided, however, that if such quotient is less than 0.4509, the Exchange Ratio will be 0.4509 and if such quotient is greater than 0.4650, the Exchange Ratio will be 0.4650. For the purposes of this Section 2.2, the term "Parent Stock Price" means the average of the volume weighted average price per Parent Share on the NYSE, as reported on Bloomberg by typing "HCN.N <EQUITY> AQR <GO>", for ten (10) trading days, selected by lot, from among the fifteen (15) consecutive trading days ending on (and including) the date that is five trading days prior to the Effective Times.

An arbitrageur can calculate the reference values for the collar from the information in the press release. The value is fixed at $18.06 per share in the collar, and the exchange ratio can fluctuate between 0.4509 and 0.4650. The two reference prices are calculated as

$$\$18.06 \div 0.4650 = \$38.84 \quad \text{and} \quad \$18.06 \div 0.4509 = \$40.05$$

This is a very narrow collar. As long as Health Care REIT's stock price remains between $38.84 and $40.05, Windrose's shareholder will receive $18.06 worth of Health Care REIT's stock. The range for this collar is less than 5 percent of the buyer's stock price. Typical are ranges of 10 or 15 percent. It can be seen from the chart in Figure 1.11 that Health Care REIT was fluctuating quite wildly during the merger period and exceeded the upper limit of the collar by the time of the closing on December 20, 2006.

Arbitrageurs must hedge mergers with collars dynamically. If the merger is hedged with a static ratio and the stock price of the acquirer moves, the arbitrageur will incur a loss. For example, if Health Care REIT trades at $40.05 and the arbitrageur hedges with a ratio of 0.4509, there will be an insufficient number of shares sold short if the price falls to $38.84, where the correct number of shares sold short would be 0.4650. This underhedging results in the short position's not generating enough return to offset losses on the long position of the arbitrage. Similarly, if 0.4650 shares of Health Care REIT are sold short when it trades at or below the lower end of the

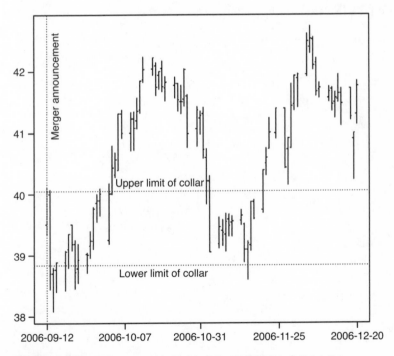

FIGURE 1.11 Fluctuation of Health Care REIT's Stock Price Prior to the Merger

collar, the arbitrageur will be short too many shares if it subsequently rises. The overhedged short position then will generate losses that are too high. The correct way to hedge a collar is dynamically, in the same way that an option collar is hedged by an option market maker.

In the case of the Windrose/Health Care REIT merger, the collar is very tight and the hedge ratio does not change very much. It would be possible to enter an arbitrage position with a static hedge ratio and assume the modest risk that the position needs to be adjusted once the exact conversion ratio is known. An arbitrageur will weigh the potential transaction costs of such a strategy against the spread that can be earned.

A more accurate method for hedging transactions with collars is delta hedging. Both discontinuities in the payoff diagram of collars lead to optionality (see Figure 1.12). The discontinuity to the left of a fixed value collar resembles the payoff diagram of a short put position, whereas the discontinuity to the right resembles a long call position. In a delta-neutral hedge, the arbitrageur calculates the sum of the deltas of these two options and shorts the number of shares given by that net delta. A drawback of delta-neutral hedging is that it requires constant readjustment with fluctuations in the stock price and as time passes. However, for wide collars with

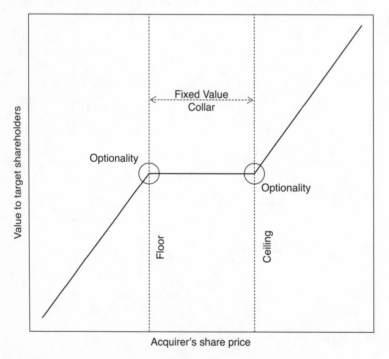

FIGURE 1.12 Optionality in Mergers with a Fixed Value Collar

exchange ratios that change significantly, delta-neutral hedging is the best method to hedge. For further details on the concept of delta hedging, the reader should consult texts dealing with options.

Fixed share collars are less common. One example is shown in Exhibit 1.8. It is the May 2007 acquisition of East Penn Financial Corporation by Harleysville National Corporation. This merger is relatively complex because it combines a collar with a cash/stock proration formula, as discussed earlier. Collars are very common in mergers of small banks.

EXHIBIT 1.8 ACQUISITION OF EAST PENN FINANCIAL CORPORATION BY HARLEYSVILLE NATIONAL CORPORATION

HARLEYSVILLE, Pa., May 16 /PRNewswire-FirstCall/—Harleysville National Corporation (HNC) (NASDAQ: HNBC) and East Penn Financial Corporation (NASDAQ: EPEN) jointly announced today that they have reached a definitive agreement for East Penn Financial Corporation to merge with and into HNC and East Penn Financial's wholly owned subsidiary, East Penn Bank, a $451 million bank offering deposit and lending services throughout the Lehigh Valley, PA, to merge with and into Harleysville National Bank and Trust Company, HNC's banking subsidiary (HNB)....

The total value of the transaction if it closed currently under the agreement is estimated at $92.7 million or approximately $14.50 per share of East Penn Financial stock, although actual value will depend on several factors, including the price of Harleysville National Corporation stock, but will not be less than $13.52 per share ($86.3 million) or greater than $15.48 per share ($99.1 million). Under terms of the Merger Agreement, each shareholder of East Penn Financial Corporation may elect to receive either cash only or HNC shares only for each share of East Penn Financial Corporation stock, but may receive a combination of both in the aggregate for all East Penn Financial Corporation shares the shareholder owns. The amount of final per share consideration is based on a formula that is determined by the average per share value of HNC stock during the twenty-day period ending eleven days prior to closing. The consideration is subject to election and allocation procedures designed to provide that the cash portion is $50,284,000 but in any event not greater than 60% of the dollar value of the merger consideration.

EXHIBIT 1.9 MERGER AGREEMENT FOR THE ACQUISITION OF EAST PENN FINANCIAL CORPORATION BY HARLEYSVILLE NATIONAL CORPORATION

Section 2.2 Exchange of and Consideration for East Penn Financial Shares. Upon the Effective Time, all of the East Penn Financial Shares issued and outstanding immediately prior to the Effective Time, shall, at the Effective Time, by reason of the Merger and without any action on the part of the holder thereof, cease to be outstanding and shall be converted into the "Merger Consideration," which shall be comprised of:

(i) the "Cash Consideration," which shall be the sum of $50,284,464.00 (or $14.50 per "Cash Election Share" as defined below assuming 6,305,262 East Penn Financial Shares are outstanding at the Effective Time) plus $7.97 per share for each of the Converted Option Shares (the "Aggregate Converted Share Cash"); plus

(ii) shares of HNC Common Stock as more fully provided below (the "Stock Consideration").

Holders of East Penn Financial Shares shall be entitled to receive, for each East Penn Financial Share, either HNC Common Shares only (a "Stock Election Share") or cash only (a "Cash Election Share"), based on an allocation of the Cash Consideration identified above and the "Stock Consideration" shown below according to the provisions of this Article II, including without limitation Section 2.4:

(a) If the "Indicated HNC Share Price" (as defined in Section 2.4(b)) is equal to or less than $19.84 and equal to or greater than $14.66, the "Stock Consideration" shall be (I) 2,385,172 shares of HNC Common Stock, plus (II) 0.3782 shares of HNC Common Stock for each of the Converted Option Shares.

For example:

Under subsection (a), if the Indicated HNC Share Price is $17.25 and 6,305,262 East Penn Financial Shares are outstanding, an East Penn Financial shareholder will receive 0.8406 shares of HNC Common Stock for each Stock Election Share and $14.50 in cash for each Cash Election Share.

(b) If the Indicated HNC Share Price is less than $14.66, the "Stock Consideration" shall be (I) that number of HNC Common Shares equal to the result obtained by dividing $34,970,559.00 by the Indicated HNC Share Price, plus (II) for each of the Converted Option Shares, that number of HNC Common Shares equal to the result obtained by dividing $5.55 by the Indicated HNC Share Price.

For example:

Under subsection (b), if the Indicated HNC Share Price is $14.50 and 6,305,262 East Penn Financial Shares are outstanding, an East Penn Financial shareholder will receive 0.8500 shares of HNC Common Stock for each Stock Election Share and $14.50 in cash for each Cash Election Share.

(c) If the Indicated HNC Share Price is greater than $19.84, the "Stock Consideration" shall be (I) that number of HNC Common Shares equal to the result obtained by dividing $47,313,110.00 by the Indicated HNC Share Price, plus (II) for each of the Converted Option Shares, that number of HNC Common Shares equal to the result obtained by dividing $7.51 by the Indicated HNC Share Price.

For example:

Under subsection (c), if the Indicated HNC Share Price is $20.00 and 6,305,262 East Penn Financial Shares are outstanding, an East Penn Financial shareholder will receive 0.8337 shares of HNC Common Stock for each Stock Election Share and $14.50 in cash for each Cash Election Share.

This collar is easier to understand because the reference prices are stated clearly. If Harleysville's share price falls below $13.52, shareholders of East Penn will receive more shares so that the value they receive remains $13.52. This is a very risky transaction to enter for a seller, and probably one of the reasons for its rarity. If Harleyville's share price were to suffer a sudden sharp drop, it would have to issue more shares in the merger. The additional issuance dilutes existing shareholders and leads to a drop in the share price with the issuance of even more shares. It risks triggering a downward death spiral in the share price. As discussed earlier, arbitrage activity always exerts some selling pressure on an acquirer's stock, so that the possibility of this effect should not be ignored. Only buyers who acquire target companies that are small relative to their own size should use fixed share collars, because the dilution would remain insignificant even for a sharp drop in share prices, and no death spiral would be triggered. If Harleysville accepted a fixed share collar, it must have been very confident that its share price would remain strong.

The ratios can be found in the merger agreement, an extract of which is shown in Exhibit 1.9. The fact that this information is also contained in section 2.2, as in the Windrose merger agreement, is pure coincidence. There is no standardized numbering of the sections of merger agreements.

Subsection (a) fixes the number of shares to be issued as long as Harleyville's share price is in the collar. Subsections (b) and (c) have a set dollar amount for the value of the consideration, so the exchange ratio varies.

This transaction is difficult to hedge. The banks are so small that no options are traded that could help in the hedging—Harleysville has a market capitalization of only $400 million. The only way to hedge this merger is by running a delta-neutral hedge.

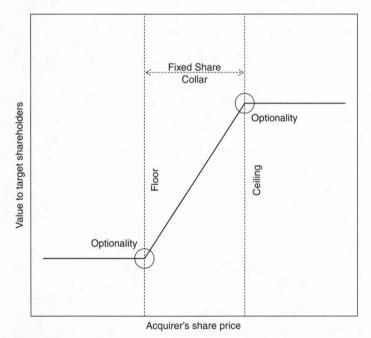

FIGURE 1.13   Optionality in Mergers with a Fixed Share Collar

Figure 1.13 shows the implied options in a fixed share collar. The combination of a long call with a low strike price and a short call with a higher strike price yields such a payoff diagram. This combination is also known as call spread or bull spread. An arbitrageur who wants to hedge a fixed share collar needs to calculate the delta for each option, sum the deltas, and then short the net delta in the form of shares of the target firm.

CHAPTER 2

Incorporating Risk into the Arbitrage Decision

So far, all arbitrages were analyzed under the assumption that the merger would close. Unfortunately, life is not that easy for an arbitrageur. A small number of mergers are not completed. In rare instances, the collapse of a merger can lead to an increase in a stock's price. This happens very rarely. One of the few cases that I have seen was the attempted acquisition of Unisource Energy by Kohlberg Kravis Roberts & Co. Even in this case, the increase did not happen instantly after the announcement that the Arizona Corporation Commission voted to reject the buyout. On the day of the announcement, Unisource fell (see Figure 2.1). However, over the next month, Unisource rose and eventually exceeded the price that shareholders would have received in the merger. This is the one exception that proves the rule that collapsing mergers lead to a loss.

Most acquisitions are made at a significant premium to the most recent market price because buyers anticipate cost savings. At a minimum, this premium should be given back when a merger is canceled. Bigger losses are often possible because the composition of a company's shareholder base changes during the merger process. The interaction between long-term holders and arbitrageurs is an important factor that determines the extent of a drop. Long-term holders often sell their holdings, and arbitrageurs acquire these shares. If the merger collapses, arbitrageurs have little interest or incentive to hold the position much longer. They want to take their loss and move on to the next merger. Therefore, a large amount of merger arbitrage involvement in a collapsing transaction can exacerbate losses.

In finance, the analysis of losses separates then into two dimensions:

1. The probability that a loss will happen.
2. The extent of the losses. Credit analysts refer to this as "severity" or "loss given default."

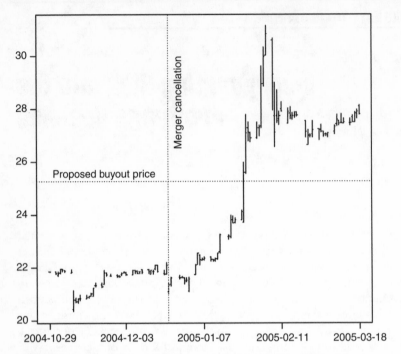

FIGURE 2.1   Stock Price of Unisource after the Collapse of the Merger

There are many analogies between merger arbitrage and credit management.

Arbitrageurs also estimate the probability of a merger's collapsing and the severity of the loss separately. The two are combined to give the expected loss:

$$E(L) = Pr(L) \times L \qquad (2.1)$$

where L is the severity of the loss.

$Pr(L)$ is the probability of suffering a loss.

$E(L)$ is the expected value of the loss.

The expected loss is also called a probability-weighted loss. It represents the loss that an arbitrageur would expect to suffer on average if positions in a large number of identical mergers were taken.

In terms of the probability of success, this can be rewritten as

$$E(L) = (1 - P_{success}) \times L \qquad (2.2)$$

PROBABILITY OF CLOSING

The vast majority of merger transactions are completed without problems. It is my experience that even among the transactions that do run into problems, the eventual completion rate is high.

Academic research has been trying for the past 25 years to examine the probability of successful completion of mergers. Many of these studies are directly related to the returns that can be achieved through merger arbitrage. These studies have identified a number of factors that drive the completion of a merger:

- Hostile transactions generally have a lower probability of success than friendly transactions. This comes as no surprise to anyone reading the newspaper headlines.
- One recurring factor that increases the likelihood of a successful merger closing is the market size of the target. However, there is no agreement on the direction in which this variable influences the outcome. Early studies show that larger transactions are less likely to close than smaller ones.[1] More recent studies[2] indicate that large transactions are more likely to fail than smaller ones.
- The impact of the bid premium is similarly uncertain for the probability of completion.
- Tender offers are less likely to close than mergers.[3] However, this could be another manifestation of the size effect, because cash tender offers are smaller on average than stock-for-stock mergers.
- Index membership. One study[4] finds that mergers are more likely to be completed if the buyer is a member of the S&P 500.
- If the acquirer owns a larger percentage of the target firm prior to the announcement, the merger is more likely to close.

Ben Branch and Taewon Yang[5] find that 89 percent of all mergers were completed in the period from 1991 to 2000. They find that the type of payment impacts the probability: Collar mergers have the highest success rate with 93 percent, whereas stock-for-stock mergers without collar provisions come to only 88 percent. Cash tender offers are the least successful types of mergers, with a completion rate of only 87 percent. In their study regarding mergers of S&P 500 members, Fich and Stefanescu[6] find failure rates shown in Table 2.1.

As most of these studies rely heavily on data from the 1990s, a model with more recent merger data was built.[7] For convenience, only cash mergers were considered. Information about mergers for the three years from

TABLE 2.1 Failure Rates of Mergers According to Fich and Stefanescu

	Cash Merger	Stock-for-Stock Merger
In S&P	7.45%	10.29%
Not in S&P	27%	25.7%

Based on analysis by Eliezer M. Fich and Irina Stefanescu, "Expanding the Limits of Merger Arbitrage," University of North Carolina Working Paper, May 18, 2003.

January 1, 2002, until December 31, 2004, retrieved from Bloomberg consists of 797 transactions announced in that period, of which 648 had closed. After eliminating mergers of questionable data quality, the ultimate data set consisted of 528 cash mergers. No minimum transaction size was imposed, and therefore, the distribution of this dataset is weighted heavily toward small mergers of less than $50 million. Many studies consider only "investable" mergers above $50 million. In this model, 468 mergers closed and 60 were terminated, giving a failure rate of 11.5 percent. This is in line with the results of the studies just mentioned.

The probability of success of a merger can be estimated through logistic regressions. This type of regression relates a binary variable, such as the merger closes (1) or fails (0), to continuous variable, such as the size of the firm. Several models have been developed in the literature. Based on the Bloomberg data set of 528 cash mergers, the author developed a logit estimator of the probability of success:

$$Pr_{success} = \frac{\exp\left(2.06 + 0.71 \times DealSize - 0.31 \times Owned\right)}{1 + \exp\left(2.06 + 0.71 \times DealSize - 0.31 \times Owned\right)} \qquad (2.3)$$

where   *DealSize* represents the size of the acquisition in $billions.
Owned is the percentage of the target firm owned by the acquirer prior to the announcement of the transaction, represented as a number between 0 and 1.

The sparse nature of the model illustrates the problem in the estimation of models that can be used in merger arbitrage. Despite the wealth of studies on the completion of mergers, it is difficult to build statistical models to calculate probabilities accurately. Factors determining the likelihood of successful completion vary from transaction to transaction. In statisticians' language, mergers have too many degrees of freedom. The first hurdle to overcome is data collection. Unlike financial variables used in most models, the information relevant to merger arbitrage is only partially quantitative. Some of the factors that are not amenable to incorporation into models are subtleties in the wording of merger agreements, such as material adverse change clauses; in a contested merger, the skill of an acquirer in building alliances; and in the case of transactions challenged on antitrust grounds, the ability of companies to divest divisions and thereby become compliant with antitrust regulations. At best, a statistical model can be used as a starting point, and its results then must be adjusted subjectively.

The rest of this section discusses a number of factors that frequently lead to the cancellation of mergers. It should be remembered that often the confluence of several problems is necessary to lead to the cancellation of a merger. Buyers have different reasons to try to void a merger from target companies. Separation is more likely to happen when both buyer and target have good reasons to walk away from the merger.

The most important pitfalls that can lead to the cancellation of a merger are discussed in future chapters in great detail. The next sections give an overview of factors that arbitrageurs should be mindful of.

Inability to Obtain Financing

In cash transactions, the ability of the buyer to obtain financing is one of the key determinants of a successful completion. This is of particular concern for highly leveraged transactions, such as those involving private equity funds as buyers. Financing is discussed in more detail in Chapter 3.

Changes in Business Conditions

Market, sector, and company risk are not normally associated with market-neutral investment strategies such as merger arbitrage. For merger arbitrage, event risk is the principal risk faced by arbitrageurs, namely the risk that the transaction will not occur. However, it would naive to assume that none of the risks associated with traditional investment styles apply to arbitrage. These traditional forms of investment risk are second-order effects.

- The first-order risk is the event risk, the risk that the transaction fails.
- Market, sector, and company risk are second-order risks that can contribute to event risk.

Event risk is not completely independent of market movements. For large drops in the stock market, the risk of failure increases if the acquirer thinks it overpaid. For large increases in the stock price, shareholders may vote against the deal if they think they are not receiving a high enough price.

A significant deterioration in business climate is referred to as a "material adverse change" (MAC) in legal terms. Whether a buyer can walk away from a merger or not depends on the exact provisions of the merger agreement. MAC clauses have become more restrictive over time, and it is becoming increasingly difficult for buyers invoke them. Doing so will inevitably lead to litigation, which has a negative effect on the share prices of the buyer and the target. The current status of MAC jurisprudence is driven by the IBP/Tyson Food decision in 2001.[8] Tyson Foods had entered into a merger agreement to acquire IBP for $30 per share after winning a bidding war with Smithfield Foods but tried to cancel the acquisition when IBP reported poor results for the fourth quarter of 2000 as a result of harsh winter conditions. Tyson claimed that IBP's business had suffered a material adverse change. The judge in the case ruled that one bad quarter does not constitute a material adverse change and that IBP's business would have to be affected permanently in order to constitute MAC.

IBP was awarded "specific performance" by the court. This means that Tyson was forced to implement the merger agreement and complete the acquisition. It was the best outcome that IBP shareholders could have hoped for, and the merger closed in the middle of 2001.

Unfortunately, the remedy of specific performance is not available to shareholders in all states. While Delaware courts can impose specific performance, New York courts will not do so. Instead, they will force the buyer, should it lose the case, to pay monetary damages to the target rather than complete the merger. Although these damages will increase the value of the target, it is uncertain whether this will be sufficient to offset losses suffered by target's shareholders.

Today, lawyers write MAC clauses to exclude certain events that affect the economy in general but do not affect the target firm disproportionately. As a result, it is difficult for an acquirer who experiences buyers' remorse to back out of a transaction solely on the basis of MAC. Other loopholes must be invoked instead.

Public Intervention

Fortunately for arbitrageurs, politicians and the general public rarely show much interest in merger activity. Most concerns that arise are related to monopoly pricing power and affect antitrust issues. In some instances, however, public opposition to mergers falls outside of the narrow scope of an antitrust review.

One type of transaction particularly susceptible to political intervention is utility mergers. The long time period required to close such a merger is partly a reflection of the involvement of multiple state regulators. However, the number of regulators involved does not yet explain the low success rate of such mergers. After all, bank mergers also often involve several states and nevertheless have a high completion rate. Instead, the monopoly pricing power for the indispensable services provided by the utility triggers added interest by state regulators, the general public, and hence also politicians.

The federal government tends to take a hands-off approach to mergers with the exception of some high-profile areas (media, airlines, national security), so that the field of government interference is left wide open to state regulators. States always get involved in mergers of public utilities and sometimes in mergers of state-chartered banks. Utilities are a particular minefield because politicians are sensitive to allegations that any future price increases in rates are due to the state's failure to block a merger, potentially ending the careers of many local politicians.

Relative Size of Buyer and Target

A merger is more likely to close if the buyer is much larger in size than the target. This is discussed in more detail in Chapter 3.

Antitrust Problems

Antitrust problems are primarily concerns for strategic mergers but may become more prevalent in leveraged buyouts as large private equity firms acquire an increasingly large share of businesses. Antitrust issues are discussed in Chapter 10.

Shareholder Opposition

It happens frequently that long-term shareholders of a target company oppose a merger as providing too little value.

Similarly, shareholders of a buyer may also oppose an acquisition if they feel that the company overpaid.

Successful shareholder opposition is relatively rare, as it can be difficult to oppose a transaction if the premium paid relative to the last trading price is high. Most shareholders will take the certain money rather than live with the uncertainty of having the firm continue to be run by managers who may not have added much value. The lack of value addition is often the principal reason why a company becomes a takeover target in the first place.

Shareholder opposition is often a fruitless exercise, but it can wreak havoc on an arbitrageur's position. It takes a very well organized shareholder campaign to derail a merger. The typical reasoning of a shareholder is the argument that the company is worth more than what shareholders will receive in the merger, and so the firm should be sold to another buyer at a higher price. However, absent other buyers with a compelling higher offer, other shareholders have no incentive to follow this reasoning. In fact, once the merger was announced, the shareholder base began to change: Long-term shareholders sell their shares to arbitrageurs, who provide those shareholders with the liquidity they need. The arbitrageurs, in turn, are interested in a prompt closing of the merger rather than a lengthy search process. Even worse for an arbitrageur is a collapse of the deal without a competing higher offer; this situation leaves the arbitrageur open to market risk. In a stock-for-stock merger, this event can lead to the worst-case scenario where the target drops and the acquirer rises in a short squeeze due to the sudden simultaneous unwinding of arbitrage positions. The mere threat of a cancellation of a merger is often sufficient to induce arbitrageurs to reduce their exposure to the deal, which will lead to a widening of the spread and a mark-to-market loss for existing arbitrage positions. If a shareholder wants to mount a successful campaign to undo a merger, it must be done in a way that comforts arbitrageurs that they will not sit on a losing position at risk of market movements if the deal collapses.

It is easier for shareholders to oppose mergers than tender offers. A merger has a long time frame, giving activists a better opportunity to convince shareholders to vote against. In a tender offer, with a much shorter time frame, shareholders may have tendered their shares already by the time they receive word of opposition. In addition, they will get the consideration much sooner from the tender offer than any better deal in the future. Each shareholder faces a prisoner's dilemma: If all shareholders oppose the transaction, they may eventually be better off. However, a shareholder not tendering must wait until the completion of the second step, the short-form merger, to get paid. Because most investors, professional or retail, have high subjective discount rates, the immediate payoff in a tender offer is much more attractive than the same consideration after the second step or even hope for a better transaction down the road. Two transactions illustrate the difference.

In the acquisition of VistaCare, health care hedge fund Accipiter Capital Management opposed the acquisition by VistaCare's competitor Odyssey HealthCare. Accipiter encouraged shareholders not to tender their shares and to seek appraisal rights. Accipiter had a solid case to make: VistaCare was in the middle of a turnaround that was beginning to show fruit. This is an uncommon event in itself. Many companies appear to drift from one turnaround to another without ever having any success. Margins were beginning to improve. In addition, the earnings yield of the firm was depressed artificially because the $8.60 stock had a cash balance of $1.40 per share. VistaCare's gross margins were almost half those of Odyssey. Nevertheless,

84 percent of shareholders tendered their shares in Odyssey's offer during the first offer period, which lasted almost one month. Odyssey extended the tender period for four more days, after which it had obtained 94 percent of all shares and was able to close the merger.

Even long proxy fights are insufficient for shareholders to block some mergers. When SCPIE, a California medical insurance firm, was acquired by The Doctors' Company, long-term shareholder Stilwell attempted to block this transaction in favor of a higher bid by one of SCPIE's competitors, American Physicians Capital (ACAP). ACAP had also been bidding to acquire SCPIE and offered $28.00 in stock, whereas The Doctors' Company, as a private firm, offered $28.00 in cash. Much of the public disagreement between Stilwell and the SCPIE's board concerns the question whether ACAP's bid was better or not. The board points to the certain value of cash and the absence of a firm bid from ACAP. However, ACAP was prevented from making a bid under a standstill agreement that it had previously signed in order to conduct due diligence. Unfortunately, Stilwell's many shareholder communications never made clear where the problem was, and SCPIE was eventually sold to The Doctors' Company.

The acquisition of Pinnacle by Quest Resources is one of the rare examples where shareholder activism can succeed in derailing a merger. However, it succeeded only against a backdrop of unhappy investors. The effects of this merger gone bad are discussed in Chapter 3.

Management Opposition

Hostile merger transactions are hostile by definition because the management of the target company is opposed to the merger. The nature of hostile transactions has changed significantly in the last decade.

Hostile mergers became a widespread phenomenon in the 1980s when corporate raiders sought to undo the effects of the conglomerate boom of the preceding decade. At the time, it was the raiders themselves who sought to acquire a company against the wishes of management. Managers of the target firms frequently were opposed to these buyouts because they would have lost their lucrative jobs. Shareholders, however, would have benefited from a sale of the company at a premium. One of the effects of management opposition was the justification of stock options by the buyout argument: If managers will gain wealth from a premium offered for shares by a buyer, their interests are more aligned with those of shareholders. An analogous argument can be made to justify golden parachutes: They compensate managers for the loss of their employment and make them less likely to oppose transactions that are favorable for shareholders.

Today, buyouts have changed; raiders rarely acquire firms anymore. Modern raiders are activist shareholders who agitate to get a company to sell itself, but the activists are not normally the ones who want to buy the firm.

An interesting and ultimately successful attempt to block a sale of itself was implemented by Sovereign Bancorp. Hedge fund Relational Investors had agitated to get Sovereign to sell itself. An opportunity to frustrate share-holders' push for a sale came in 2005, when Sovereign's management convinced Spanish bank Grupo Santander to acquire 19.8 percent of Sovereign through the issue of new shares and used the proceeds from the investment to purchase Independence Community Bank. Santander was seen as a management-friendly shareholder that was unlikely to sell out to any potential acquirer. In the words of the chief executive officer of Ryan Beck & Co., the firm that advised Sovereign: "Obviously, some shareholders don't like the Santander transaction, because it effectively means Sovereign won't be selling out in the short term."[9] Santander took on the role of a "white knight" typical of takeover defenses (see Chapter 6). Unlike in most such scenarios, however, Sovereign continued to exist as an independent bank. Usually a white knight takes complete control of the target. Therefore, the Santander/Sovereign transaction stands out as a particularly shareholder-unfriendly management coup. Santander acquired the remainder of Sovereign during the banking crisis of 2008 at a much reduced price compared to the value of Sovereign in 2005.

Due Diligence and Fraud

In rare instances, fraud is discovered after the signing of a merger agreement. Typically, fraud is a good enough reason to call off a deal.

After the signing of the merger agreement between Enron and Dynegy, it became known during Dynegy's due diligence process that Enron had engaged in a number of fraudulent activities. Readers will be familiar with the Enron saga given the press coverage it received at the time. The attempt by Dynegy to acquire Enron was only one short episode in the collapse. Dynegy had speculated that Enron would not collapse and that it might be able acquire a valuable business that had been battered excessively. Therefore, Dynegy bid $9.5 billion in cash and stock for Enron. Dynegy had completed due diligence prior to signing the merger agreement but decided to conduct additional due diligence after the announcement of the transaction. Enron's situation continued to deteriorate, and Dynegy attempted to renegotiate the price. Eventually, the true state of Enron's business began to emerge, and credit agencies downgraded Enron, thereby triggering immediate repayment of much of its debt. Dynegy use this to call a "material adverse effect" and exited the merger agreement. The spread on this transaction had been unusually wide, which could have been an indication either that few in the market believed that the transaction was likely to be completed or, more likely, that the downside risk in the event of a collapse of the deal was a complete loss on the long position in Enron. It turned out that the latter was the case for any arbitrageur who attempted to profit from this transaction.

As an aside, Dynegy had provided Enron with emergency funding in the amount of $1.5 billion to prevent an immediate cash crunch. Fortunately, Dynegy had this loan secured by pipeline assets, which it recovered in the bankruptcy. It is common to see emergency funding for troubled businesses by acquirers as soon as a merger is announced. Absent fraud as in Enron, these transactions tend to be very likely to be completed, because a collapse of the target can make it impossible for the acquirer to retrieve assets that secure the funding. In fact, the loan can even be subordinated to prior debt under certain circumstances during bankruptcy. Partly for this reason, Dynegy settled by paying Enron $25 million after lengthy litigation over the pipeline assets.

Breakup Fees

Merger agreements contain breakup fees that the target company has to pay the buyer if it wants to cancel the merger. Less common are reverse-breakup fees, which the buyer has to pay the target company if it decides not to proceed with the transaction. Two types of breakup fees can be distinguished:

1. *Target breakup fees.* These are the fees that the target firm must pay to the buyer if it cancels the merger. Triggers for the payment of breakup fees can be a negative shareholder vote, a change of mind by the board of directors, or the acceptance of a better proposal from another buyer. Generally, when the term "breakup fee" is used generically without further qualification, it refers to target breakup fees.
2. *Buyer breakup fees, more commonly known as reverse breakup fees.* These fees are less common and are paid by the acquirer if it changes its mind. Reasons could be the unavailability of financing or negative shareholder votes.

Typical values are between 3 and 7 percent of the value of the merger. For smaller transactions, breakup fees of a larger percentage of the deal value are the rule. Figure 2.2 shows average target and buyer breakup fees for mergers of different sizes overall, including those transactions that have no breakup fees. However, when only transactions with breakup fees

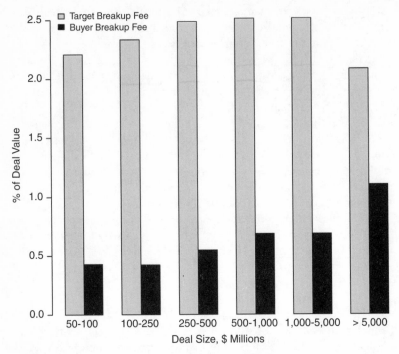

FIGURE 2.2 Typical Breakup Fees for Targets of Different Sizes across All Transactions

are considered, smaller transactions indeed have higher breakup fees as a percentage of the transaction value, as can be seen in Figure 2.3. The prevalence of breakup fees has increased over the last decade. In 2007, 90 percent of all announced mergers had target breakup fees and almost one third had buyer breakup fees (see Figure 2.4).

Arbitrageurs must read the merger agreement carefully to understand the circumstances under which breakup fees are payable. In some instances, staggered breakup fees are imposed, so that a higher or lower amount has to be paid depending on the reason for the cancellation of the merger. Breakup fees sometimes carry other monikers, such as in the case of the failed acquisition of movie and music distributor Image Entertainment by producer and financier David Bergstein. In this buyout, the buyer breakup fee was referred to as a "business interruption fee." Breakup fees are generally not payable when a merger agreement is terminated due to a material adverse effect. Any other exceptions are spelled out in the merger agreement.

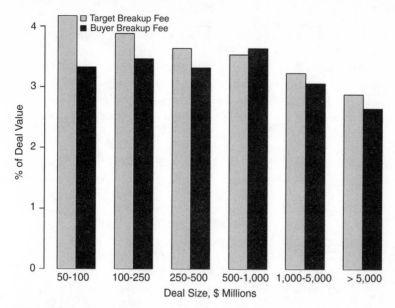

FIGURE 2.3   Typical Breakup Fees for Targets of Different Sizes Only for Transactions that Have Breakup Fees

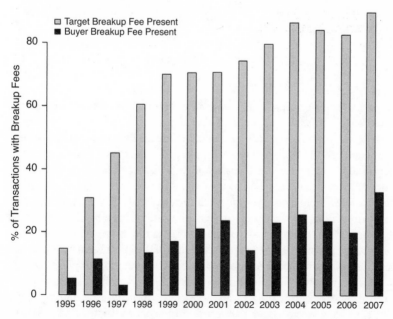

FIGURE 2.4   Percentage of Transactions with Breakup Fees

Breakup fees make the consummation of a merger more likely. A drawback is that if another buyer wanted to make a bid for the target firm, it would incur the breakup fee as a cost. Although the breakup fee is first an obligation of the target firm, no firm will enter into a new agreement unless the other buyer is willing to shoulder the fee. Otherwise, in a worst-case scenario, the second merger could collapse, and the target firm may find itself without a merger but with the obligation to pay the breakup fee.

The recent buyout boom has seen a number of cancellations of leveraged acquisitions by private equity funds. Transactions involving private equity firms normally have not had reverse breakup fees in the past. One well-known case is that of the acquisition of student loan provider Sallie Mae by private equity firm JC Flowers. Sallie Mae was facing potential changes to its regulatory environment. When credit markets worsened and it became more difficult for JC Flowers to borrow the funds needed for the acquisition, the government simultaneously adopted regulatory changes that were different from those proposed at the time of the signing of the agreement, and JC Flowers sought to cancel the agreement under its MAC clause. Sallie Mae argued that no material adverse change had taken place and sued JC Flowers for the breakup fee: $900 million. Sallie Mae had to drop the lawsuit against Flowers when it needed funding for its business and the lenders made settlement of the litigation a condition to providing the loans. If this breakup fee had been paid, it would have set a record unlikely to be overtaken for quite some time.

It remains to be seen whether the experience of some high-profile cancellations will lead to a more widespread adoption of reverse breakup fees. It would be in the interest of arbitrageurs to see reverse breakup fees of some significance.

The data in the Mergerstat database show the impact of breakup fees on the likelihood of the closing of a merger very clearly. On average, completed deals have a breakup fee of 2.38 percent whereas deals that are canceled have a fee of only 1.07 percent. Buyer breakup fees have significantly lower averages of 0.57 percent for all deals and 0.38 percent for canceled deals (see Table 2.2).

The large difference in average breakup fees between completed and canceled transactions is due mainly to the absence of breakup fees in many canceled deals. For those deals that have breakup fees, their averages are almost identical for successful and canceled deals: 3.64 percent versus 3.62 percent in the case of target breakup fees, and 3.23 percent for buyer breakup fees in both completed and canceled mergers. This finding suggests that the presence of breakup fees is a much stronger indicator of management determination to close the deal than their higher or lower level. Managers of target firms should insist in their negotiations on a buyer breakup fee; however, this is not always done.

TABLE 2.2 Average Breakup Fees for Completed and Canceled Mergers with an Announcement Value of at Least $50 Million

	Target Breakup Fees		Buyer Breakup Fees	
Industry	All Deals (%)	Canceled Deals (%)	Buyer (%)	Canceled Deals (%)
Aerospace, Aircraft, and Defense	1.95	0.44	0.24	0.00
Agricultural Production	1.54	0.00	0.96	4.65
Apparel	2.50	0.66	0.60	0.00
Automotive Products and Accessories	1.33	0.00	0.44	0.00
Autos and Trucks	1.29	0.00	0.00	0.00
Banking and Finance	1.83	1.45	0.36	0.54
Beverages	3.79	2.68	0.42	0.00
Broadcasting	2.51	0.41	0.63	0.00
Brokerage, Investment, and Management Consulting	2.53	1.04	0.52	0.44
Building Products	2.46	2.45	0.64	1.49
Chemicals, Paints, and Coatings	2.38	0.89	0.35	0.00
Communications	1.95	0.40	0.78	0.23
Computer Software, Supplies, and Services	2.90	1.10	0.71	0.44
Construction Contractors and Engine Services	2.39	1.33	0.38	0.00
Construction Mining and Oil Equipment and Machinery	2.54	0.00	0.59	0.00
Drugs, Medical Supplies, and Equipment	2.62	1.04	0.50	0.55
Electric, Gas Water, and Sanitary Services	2.41	2.29	0.96	0.79
Electrical Equipment	2.40	0.70	0.38	0.00
Electronics	2.83	1.73	0.85	1.29
Energy Services	2.45	1.23	1.06	2.7
Fabricated Metal Products	2.21	0.00	0.69	0.00
Food Processing	2.58	2.7	0.87	0.73
Furniture	1.91	0.00	0.10	0.00
Health Services	2.35	2.6	0.66	0.43
Household Goods	2.17	0.91	0.72	0.36
Industrial and Farm Equipment and Machinery	2.68	0.69	0.26	0.00
Instruments and Photographic Equipment	2.89	1.91	0.72	0.90

(*Continued*)

TABLE 2.2 (*Continued*)

Industry	Target Breakup Fees		Buyer Breakup Fees	
	All Deals (%)	Canceled Deals (%)	Buyer (%)	Canceled Deals (%)
Insurance	2.33	1.41	0.32	0.08
Leisure and Entertainment	2.37	1.04	0.45	0.39
Mining and Minerals	1.21	1.50	0.08	0.00
Miscellaneous Manufacturing	1.91	0.42	0.60	0.00
Miscellaneous Services	2.79	1.32	0.86	0.16
Office Equipment and Computer Hardware	2.84	2.22	0.92	0.61
Oil and Gas	2.48	0.26	0.82	0.26
Packaging and Containers	2.76	2.6	0.45	0.00
Paper	2.49	0.78	0.71	0.00
Plastics and Rubber	2.65	1.70	0.22	0.25
Primary Metal Processing	2.21	0.46	0.41	0.00
Printing and Publishing	2.85	1.41	0.62	0.00
Real Estate	2.46	0.91	0.41	0.00
Retail	2.33	0.62	0.66	0.00
Stone, Clay, and Glass	2.09	0.00	0.37	0.00
Textiles	2.88	2.42	0.00	0.00
Timber and Forest Products	2.46	0.00	0.00	0.00
Toiletries and Cosmetics	1.09	0.00	0.00	0.00
Toys and Recreational Products	1.90	0.59	0.27	0.39
Transportation	2.06	0.79	0.34	0.10
Valves, Pumps, and Hydraulics	2.72	3.89	0.00	0.00
Wholesale and Distribution	2.15	1.01	0.54	0.89
Average Overall Transactions	**2.38**	**1.07**	**0.57**	**0.38**

Source: Analysis based on Mergerstat data.

Over the last 12 years, average breakup fees have increased significantly. Figure 2.5 shows the evolution of average target and buyer breakup fees. The increase of buyer breakup fees is particularly striking. Much of the increase is driven by the larger percentage of mergers that contain breakup fee clauses, as can be seen in Figure 2.4. It shows that target boards are seeking some recourse from the buyer in case the deal falls through.

Breakup fees themselves are often overrated as a reason for closing a merger transaction. Their principal benefit is to the buyer, who gets a nice

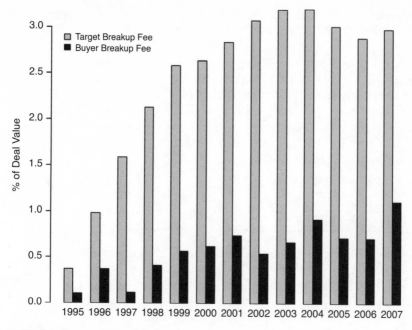

FIGURE 2.5 Evolution of Breakup Fees

payoff when a higher bidder comes along and acquires the target. In the rare cases where buyers must pay breakup fees, lengthy litigation is begun, and buyers try any means available to get out of their payment obligation. The collapse of the recent private equity–buyout boom provides many examples of busted mergers where private equity firms escape the payment of breakup fees that could have crippling effects on their businesses. Private equity firm JC Flowers was potentially on the hook for a record $900 million breakup fee after it pulled out of the acquisition of student loan provider Sallie Mae. Even thought part of the breakup fee was to have been paid by the banks that had committed to providing the financing for the buyout, it would have affected Flowers's ability to raise funds for future deals among investors if such a large sum had been used to pay for the nonconsummation of a buyout rather than actually invested. Sallie Mae, Flowers, and the banks settled the litigation within only three months through a deal in which J.P. Morgan, Bank of America, and a syndicate of other banks provided Sallie Mae with $31 billion of financing.

A similar arrangement helped Goldman Sachs Group and Kohlberg Kravis Roberts avoid paying a $225 million breakup fee when they pulled out of the $8 billion acquisition of Harman International Industries. They acquired $400 million in convertible bonds from Harman instead, paying 1.25 percent interest. The proceeds of the bond were used to repurchase shares. Harman would have been better off receiving the breakup fee rather than a loan that must be paid back in one way or another—either in cash or by dilution of existing shareholders. Harman could have used the breakup fee to repurchase stock and then borrowed another $175 million to retire additional stock. It would have left its balance sheet in much better shape with less debt. It is unclear why the board accepted a transaction that was so unfavorable to shareholders.

SEVERITY OF LOSSES

After probabilities, the second dimension to losses is severity. Severity is the extent of a loss on a given merger if it were to fail. To illustrate the difference between expected losses and severity, assume that arbitrageurs were to take positions in a large number of mergers that are exactly identical. A small fraction of these mergers will collapse, whereas the rest of the mergers are closed. Assume that the arbitrageur suffers a loss of 25 percent on each of the mergers that collapses. The 25 percent loss is the severity. Assume that 5 percent of the mergers collapse. The probability of collapse is 5 percent. The expected loss is $0.25 \times 0.05 = 0.0125$. This means that the arbitrageur would expect to lose on average 1.25 percent due to mergers that collapse. Severity is analogous to the quantity known as loss given default in credit analysis.

It was shown in the previous section that the determination of probabilities involves much guesswork. The determination of severities does even more so. The principal method available to arbitrageurs is a chartist approach, coupled with subjective adjustments. Valuation techniques, such as fundamental valuation or comparables analysis, can be helpful also.

Fundamental techniques can be helpful by giving a point of reference where the stock price should trade absent the merger. But for a variety of reasons, stocks rarely trade where fundamental methods suggest they should trade. When a merger fails, the last thing in arbitrage investors' minds is the theoretical, fundamental value of a company. Most seek to exit their holdings immediately. Therefore, in the short run, technical trading considerations outweigh any fundamental value that stock may rightfully have. For mergers that fail to close over a longer period of time, or where industry conditions are changing, a fundamental approach may yield better estimates.

Nevertheless, the problem with both fundamental and technical methods is that they fail to capture the primary driver of the fall in the target's stock price: the sudden overhang of sell orders by arbitrageurs who want to liquidate their positions when a merger collapses. Fundamental methods are least able to account for this effect. Chart-based methods are generally a little more useful in trading scenarios where fundamental methods cannot be used. The problem underlying the collapse of a target company's stock price has two sources:

1. *The merger premium.* The purchase of a stock is done at a premium to its trading price before the merger. Once the merger is no longer an option, the stock should return to its regular nonmerger trading level.
2. *The change in the composition of a company's shareholder base.* With the announcement of a merger, many long-term investors sell to arbitrageurs. Long-term investors are happy to capture the premium at which the company is acquired but are unwilling to assume the risk that the merger collapses. Arbitrageurs take the opposite position and provide sellers with liquidity. If a merger collapses, arbitrageurs no longer want to hold the target company's stock, and sell it. Long-term investors, however, do not buy back the stock immediately, so the overhang of sell orders leads to a drop in the stock price. In some instances, the price can even drop below the level it traded when the merger was announced.

Returning to the acquisition of Trustreet by GE, an arbitrageur looks at the price range in which the stock traded prior to the proposal by GE. Figure 2.6 is a subset of the chart in Figure 1.6. A shorter time frame has been chosen to highlight the critical period just prior to the announcement of the merger. This chart shows that Trustreet traded between $12.44 and $12.71 on the day before the announcement of the merger. However, focusing only on the last day before the announcement is not sufficient. The chart reveals that Trustreet traded as low as $10.69 on August 10 and as high as $13.28 on August 4. Most of the trading in the two months prior to the announcement occurred between $11.75 and $12.50.

Because no scientific approach exists to determine an exact level to where the price could fall to if the merger had collapsed, guesswork is needed to make sense of the chart. By observing the past trading range of the stock, an arbitrageur would take a price near $12.00 as a reasonable assumption of the level to which the stock could fall back. If the arbitrageur had bought the stock at a price of $17.00, as was assumed in the earlier example, then the severity amounts to $5.00 per share:

$$L = P_P - P_S = 17.00 - 12.00 = 5 \qquad (2.4)$$

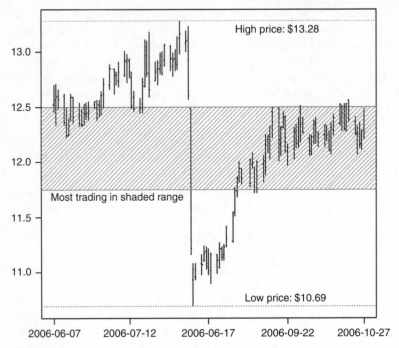

FIGURE 2.6 Trustreet Prior to Its Acquisition by GE

where L is the severity of the loss.

P_S is the postcollapse price at which the stock can be sold.

P_P is the purchase price.

In other instances, a more conservative or more aggressive assumption could be made. These factors should be considered:

- Was there rampant takeover speculation prior to the announcement of the deal? If so, the stock may have traded higher than it would have otherwise. The downside risk should be adjusted accordingly. The arbitrageur should try to determine when rumors first started circulating and at what price the stock traded then.
- What could be the reason for the collapse of the merger? If a material adverse event occurs, the stock will drop well below the preannouncement price. If the fundamentals underlying the business have deteriorated, then the stock would trade lower absent a merger. Conversely, if the

fundamentals of the sector are improving, then a deal failure may not have too severe an impact.

- How is the economic environment developing? If there is a deterioration of the stock market in general or the industry in which the firm operates, then a drop to below the announcement price is likely. Note that not only the severity is affected by such deterioration. The probability of deal failure increases also, so that an arbitrageur takes a hit on two fronts simultaneously.

As an aside, consideration of the last point by many arbitrageurs simultaneously can introduce a correlation with the overall stock market in merger arbitrage returns. If merger arbitrageurs reassess the downside risk of a position, they will reduce their holding in that stock. If a sufficiently large number of arbitrageurs reduces their exposure at the same time, the spread will widen, which in turn leads to a drop in the performance of merger arbitrage just at the same moment the market corrects. Some of the put option–like characteristics of merger arbitrage can be explained by this effect.

In stock-for-stock mergers, the calculation of loss severities is complicated by the simultaneous exposure to two stocks: a long position on the target firm and a short position on the acquirer. Estimation of the total severity is more complex due to the short leg of the trade. When a large number of arbitrageurs are involved in a stock-for-stock merger, the short side of the arbitrage will undergo a short squeeze if the deal collapses as all arbitrageurs seek to cover their short positions at the same time. This effect will aggravate loss severities. The arbitrageur will lose not only from the drop of the price of the stock held long but also will suffer a loss from the short squeeze. In other word, a stock-for-stock merger yields twice as many opportunities to lose money as a simpler cash merger.

The loss severity on the target is calculated in the same manner as for cash transactions. In principle, an analogous method for the long leg can be used to determine the loss severity of the short leg: By looking at the trading level before the announcement of the merger, a level can be estimated. However, a judgment must also be made about the likelihood of a short squeeze and the potential price that the stock can reach as a result of the squeeze.

The acquisition of Pinnacle Gas Resources by Quest Resource Corp. is a good example of how arbitrageurs can be hit on both sides of the arbitrage in a stock-for-stock merger. Quest proposed on October 16, 2007, to acquire Pinnacle by exchanging each Pinnacle share with 0.6584 of its own shares. Some Quest shareholders were unhappy with this transaction and felt that they would be subject to an unacceptable level of dilution. But the filing by Advisory Research, shown in Exhibit 2.1, contained another hint that Quest

EXHIBIT 2.1 LETTER TO THE MANAGEMENT OF QUEST RESOURCES BY ADVISORY RESEARCH

It is incumbent upon each of you as Board members and fiduciaries to preserve and maximize value for the Company's stockholders. By any meaningful objective measure, your issuance of substantially undervalued shares of Common Stock in the Pinnacle transaction would accomplish the very opposite of those objectives. As the Company's largest stockholder, we cannot understand why the Board would pursue this course of action in the face of such tangible evidence of stockholder harm.

Should the Board elect to proceed with the Pinnacle merger, we will regrettably find ourselves in the position of having to consider alternatives to preserve the value of our investment. To that end, and in accordance with Section 78.438 of the Nevada General Corporation Law (the "Nevada Corporation Law"), we hereby request that the Board approve purchases by ARI, its clients, Advisory Research Micro Cap Value Fund, L.P. and Advisory Research Energy Fund, L.P., of additional shares of Common Stock in a transaction or series of transactions such that, subsequent to all such transactions, such persons will beneficially own in the aggregate up to 14.99% of the outstanding shares of Common Stock.

We are requesting Board approval of all such transactions, as we may elect to pursue a "combination" (as defined in Section 78.416 of the Nevada Corporation Law) with the Company after we beneficially own 10% or more of the outstanding shares of Common Stock and thereby are deemed an "interested stockholder" under Section 78.423 of the Nevada Corporation Law. As you are aware, this Nevada statute stipulates that unless the Board approves the transactions in advance, stockholders that surpass 9.99% ownership of the Company become subject to a three-year moratorium on pursuing a "Combination" with the Company. Though it is not currently the intention of ARI to independently, or with a third party, pursue an acquisition of QRCP, we may soon determine that it is in best interest of QRCP's stockholders to solicit third parties that have an interest in acquiring the Company for fair consideration—which we believe would be significantly in excess of the current share price. Though we do not currently have any

intention of doing so, we would like to preserve our ability to participate in any ensuing transaction with a third party.

Source: Letter to Quest Resources board of directors, filed with the Securities and Exchange Commission on February 4, 2008, http://sec.gov/Archives/
edgar/data/775351/000090258408000006/qrcp13d.txt.

would have significant upside should the transaction collapse, and hence
that a short squeeze might be possible.

Advisory Research suggested not only that it may purchase more shares
but also that it would try to find an acquirer to buy the company, presumably
at a premium to its trading price. Some of the technical details about sections
78.416 and 78.423 concerns freeze-out provisions under state law, which
are discussed in Chapter 9.

As a result of the opposition to the merger, Quest's management renegotiated the terms of the transaction in order to make it more palatable to
its shareholders. The exchange ratio was lowered from 0.6584 to 0.5278
only two days after Advisory Research filed its letter with the Securities
and Exchange Commission. Nevertheless, approval of the transaction remained difficult for Quest, and the transaction eventually was canceled on
May 19, 2008.

The result of the undoing of this merger can be seen in the stock charts of
Pinnacle and Quest in Figure 2.7. The spread had been widening for some
time. This can be inferred quite clearly through visual inspection of the
Pinnacle and Quest charts. Pinnacle's stock price was falling while Quest's
was rising. On May 19, Pinnacle's stock dropped severely to under $3.00
and settled near $2.50 over the next few days. Quests stock price, however,
was rising inexorably, from $8.91 on the day before the announcement
to $10.81 after the announcement. It even reached $11.99 the following
day—a 34.6 percent jump over the closing before the announcement.

The increase in Quest matches its trading level before the merger announcement quite closely. It had traded between $9.50 and $11.00 before
the merger was announced in October 2007. For Pinnacle, however, the drop
to $2.50 was not easily predictable from a chart alone. The steep drop in the
months before the transaction with Quest was a sign that further downside
was to be expected if the merger were not to happen. A fundamental analysis
would have yielded more reliable target levels than a chartist approach.

Another method to determine loss severities is the quantitative analysis
of past transactions that have failed. This method should be more reliable

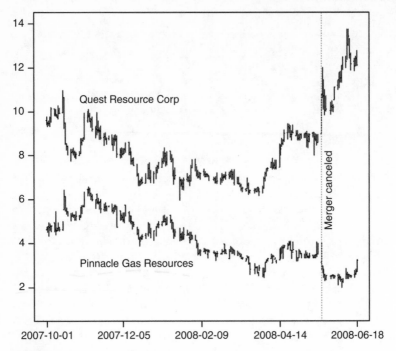

FIGURE 2.7 Pinnacle Resources and Quest Resource Corp. after the Canceled Merger

if applied to a large number of transactions. It also has appeal with arbitrageurs grounded in quantitative analysis and also has value in larger organizations, where statistical inferences are preferred over judgment for decision making. However, at any given time, only few transactions fail, so statistical inferences can be misleading.

Historical information about the premia paid in mergers gives some indication to the downside risk on the target. Table 2.3 shows average premia paid by acquirers over the 1-day, 5-day, and 30-day prior trading prices. These numbers are based on Mergerstat's database for transactions between 1995 and early 2008.

TABLE 2.3 Average Acquisition Premia

	1-Day	5-Day	30-Day
Average premium	29.8%	34.8%	52.7%

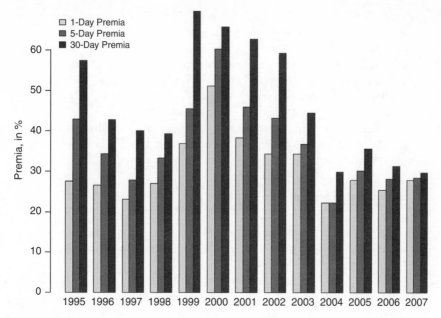

FIGURE 2.8 Evolution of Acquisition Premia

Figure 2.8 shows that acquisition premia change over time. In general, the 30-day premia are higher than 5- and 1-day premia. There are two possible explanations for the difference: It indicates either rampant insider trading or that most mergers are anticipated by the market. In both cases, a stock will trade up to the acquisition price as time approaches the announcement of a transaction. An alternative explanation would be the natural uptrend of markets. Over the period of 1995 to early 2008, the market has generally traded up. The difference between 30-day and 1-day premia could simply reflect this natural trend. However, the difference is by far greater than what one would expect from a trending market over a short period of 25 or 29 days. It should also be noted that the difference between 1-day and 30-day premia has declined since 1995. This confirms the insider trading hypothesis. Regulatory enforcement against insider trading has increased over the last decade, and the numbers suggest that it appears to have a positive effect.

For an arbitrageur, the significance of this data is that downside risk in the portfolio overall varies over time. Even if each merger is examined on its own merits for the potential loss severity from a collapse in the deal, it can be assumed that premia are somewhat correlated with downside risk.

These numbers can give some guidance to how much downside an arbitrageur might expect on a typical merger. However, it still is worth the effort to examine each transaction individually to get a more accurate sense of the severity that an arbitrageur can expect.

Compared to other analysts of downside risk, in particular participants of the credit derivative markets, merger arbitrageurs tend to have a more sophisticated approach to severity. It is not uncommon to see the pricing of credit derivatives performed with a standard severity (or loss given default) assumption of 40 percent, sometimes with industry-specific variations. Few credit derivative participants will go to the trouble of making a more careful estimation of loss severities. In contrast, merger arbitrageurs routinely estimate separate severities for each of their investments.

EXPECTED RETURN OF THE ARBITRAGE

After an arbitrageur has determined the loss severity and probability of that loss, the risk-adjusted return on the arbitrage is calculated. It will be referred to as the annualized "net return":

$$R_{AN} = \left(\frac{Pr_{Success} \times P_C + (1 - Pr_{Success}) \times (P_C - L)}{P_P} - 1 \right) \times \left(\frac{365}{t} \right) \tag{2.5}$$

The principal difference between the gross returns calculated earlier and the net return shown here is that the latter incorporates the possibility of a loss. The gross return in itself is not a very meaningful measure, because it assumes that the merger will be consummated. Naturally, large gross returns are associated with higher risks of deal failure. Therefore, net returns are better measures of potential profitability than just gross returns, because they incorporate risk.

Net returns make most sense when used in the context of a portfolio of merger arbitrage transactions. Even though it is possible to make a net return calculation for a single merger, it is clear that the net return will never be achieved. As a stand-alone number, net returns are not very useful because the outcome of a single merger is a binary one: Either the merger will be consummated and the arbitrageur will earn the gross return, or the merger will fail and the arbitrageur will suffer a loss in the amount of the severity. What I refer to as net returns are also referred to by statisticians as probability-weighted returns or expected returns. The term "expected" in "expected return" is somewhat of a misnomer. It is highly unlikely that the "expected return," or net return, actually is achieved in any single arbitrage transaction. If one were to invest repeatedly in identical mergers, then on average the investor would achieve the net return. Of course, no two mergers are alike, and in practice, a net return calculation is no more than a decision tool. Too much reliance on this number can be dangerous because most of the time either it will be exceeded or the arbitrageur will suffer a loss.

It is possible to calculate net returns for more than one scenario. For example, a merger may either go through without difficulties or be challenged by antitrust authorities. If it is challenged, there are two possible outcomes: The transaction fails or is approved. Multiple scenarios such as these can also be computed with the previous formula, albeit with minor modifications:

$$R_{AN} = \left(\frac{Pr_{Success} \times P_C + Pr_1 \times L_1 + Pr_2 \times L_2 + \ldots}{P_P} - 1 \right) \times \left(\frac{365}{t} \right)$$

$$(2.6)$$

or

$$R_{AN} = \left(\frac{Pr_{Success} \times P_C + \sum_{i=1}^{n} Pr_i \times L_i}{P_P} - 1 \right) \times \left(\frac{365}{t} \right) \qquad (2.7)$$

where Pr_1, Pr_2, and so on signify the probability of each outcome other than a straight passage of the merger.

It should be remembered that $Pr_{success} + Pr_1 + Pr_2 + \ldots = 1$

The various other methods for calculating annualized returns discussed in Chapter 1 can also be used with this formula. It is left as an exercise to the reader.

Some arbitrageurs use decision trees to calculate net returns for mergers with multiple outcomes. Decision trees are a tool that will yield the same result as the last calculation, if done correctly. Which method to use is a question of personal preference. Readers interested in decision trees are encouraged to review the extensive existing literature on that topic. Its application to merger arbitrage should be clear from the techniques discussed in this chapter, and is left as another exercise to the reader interested in the matter.

It is tempting to assign too much significance to net returns as a measure of risk and return. Although they represent probability-weighted returns, the inputs are mostly subjective. Even if quantitative methods are used to determine probabilities, it is difficult to say for sure how much credibility they have. Mergers are subject to a large number of variables that behave very differently under varying economic circumstances. Moreover, most arbitrage portfolios tend to have a limited number of positions because only a limited number of companies merge at any one time. An overreliance on probabilities in such portfolios can be dangerous.

CHAPTER 3

Sources of Risk
and Return

The two most important drivers of returns on merger arbitrage are the deal spread and timing of the closing. Both are discussed briefly in Chapter 2 but are examined more systematically here. For dividend-paying stocks, dividends are also an important element of return and can, in some instances, even be the only return, as in the case of a preferred stock. Additional ways that arbitrageurs can generate returns are interest on the proceeds of short sales and leverage.

DEAL SPREAD

In Chapter 2, we discussed how to calculate the spread and factored the risk of a collapse into the equation. In a way, the spread calculation is a chicken-and-egg type of situation: The spread exists because there remains risk, and the risk is explained by the existence of a spread.

Some terminology related to spreads has already been introduced in the discussion of Chapter 1. We will clarify some of the terms here.

Spreads can be *wide* or *tight* and can become more so if they *widen* or *tighten.* "Narrow" is less commonly used to describe tight spreads.

Gross spreads exclude dividends, whereas *net spreads* are supposed to include dividends and all other costs.

Merger arbitrage spreads are typically very tight in absolute terms. A merger arbitrageur rarely makes large returns. However, the seemingly low returns must be viewed against the short time frame in which the returns can be achieved. Typical merger arbitrage spreads are in the range 2 to 4 percent for transactions with little risk of completion. Uninitiated observers may consider merger arbitrage unattractive because of the apparently low returns that can be achieved by the strategy. A return is meaningful only in the context of the time period over which it can be achieved. For merger

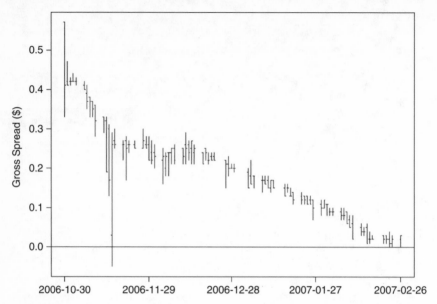

FIGURE 3.1 Evolution of the Spread of the Trustreet Merger

arbitrage, returns typically are achieved in a very short time frame of three to six months. As we discuss later in this chapter, the average time frame for the closing of a merger is 135 days, or four to five months. On the back of an envelope, returns of 2 to 4 percent achieved over four months amount to 6 to 12 percent on an annualized basis. This compares favorably to a long-term return on the stock market of 10.7 percent.[1] A better comparison of general equity and merger arbitrage returns will take the riskiness of this return into account, as we do in Chapter 12.

A spread is expected to narrow over time and finish at zero at the closing of the merger, as we saw in the idealized diagram in Figure 1.7. Naturally, this does not happen in a straight line. The evolution over time of an actual spread, that of Trustreet Properties, is shown in Figure 3.1. The spread fluctuates, albeit less so then the equity market in general, as we discuss in Chapter 12. For now, it is sufficient to say that the principal driver in fluctuations in the deal spread have to do with events that are specific to the completion risk of the transaction. A secondary driver depends on general trading activity. Many shareholders want to exit their investment once a firm has announced that is going to be acquired, because there is little upside left and they are unwilling to assume the completion risk. A large sell order, or several smaller orders that happen to arrive at the same time, can lead to a temporary widening of the spread even though no fundamental news has arrived. In those situations, arbitrageurs are faced with the difficult decision of whether to take advantage of the temporarily widened spread and increase their holdings or to join the selling. After all, it is possible that some real information pertaining to an increased risk of deal failure has leaked into the market.

The level of interest rates is one of the principal determinants of overall merger arbitrage spreads. If interest rates are high, merger arbitrage spreads must be wide to provide an attractive investment alternative to other short-term investments. When interest rates are low, capital will be allocated to merger arbitrage, driving down returns available to arbitrageurs.

Other factors influencing deal spreads are, among others:

- *Short rebate*. The short rebate, discussed later in this chapter, is a big contributor to returns for merger arbitrageurs.
- *Cash mergers versus stock-for-stock mergers*. Spreads tend to be wider for cash mergers due to the higher risk that financing may not be available at the anticipated closing. A pure stock-for-stock merger does not have financing risk and will have a smaller spread. However, stock-for-stock mergers provide extra income through the short rebate, which is not available to pure cash mergers.

TWO ASPECTS OF LIQUIDITY

"Liquidity" is a term that describes the ease with which a trader can enter and exit positions in a stock. A liquid stock is one that can be traded easily without any impact on the stock price. Trading volume and bid/offer spreads are the two principal characteristics of liquidity. A high volume and tight bid/offer spreads usually go hand in hand.

Liquidity drives merger arbitrage returns in two ways:

1. Merger arbitrageurs provide liquidity to sellers.
2. Arbitrageurs can earn a liquidity premium on illiquid stocks.

Most mergers are done at a significant premium to the last trading price of the stock. Following the announcement, the stock jumps to a level that is very close to the eventual buyout value. At this point, many long-term holders will try to sell in order to capture most of the acquisition premium. They probably acquired the stock as a value or growth investment, and now that their investment thesis has played out successfully, they have no more interest in holding the stock. Their business in not assuming the completion risk of the merger, but it was the original value or growth strategy. Therefore, they will try to sell.

So who is buying? Other long-term investors will have no interest in a stock that provides limited upside and much downside in the event that the deal collapses and will be taken off the market shortly. Arbitrageurs are the only buyers of such stocks. The liquidity they provide to the sellers allows them to move on to their next investment. If there were no arbitrage buying, the market would face an overhang of sell orders, and the stock would trade at a wide spread to its buyout price. By providing liquidity under unusual circumstances such as a merger, merger arbitrage contributes to the efficiency of the stock market. In economic terms, it is the provisioning of the liquidity to the market that generates returns for merger arbitrageurs. And because liquidity is limited with an overhang of sell orders after a merger announcement, those who provide liquidity should earn a premium return. Arbitrageurs are liquidity providers; those who sell are liquidity takers.

Trading volumes always spike on the first trading day following the announcement of a merger. The Trustreet example illustrates this point well. Figure 3.2 shows the stock price and volume for the common stock of Trustreet. On the day of the buyout announcement, when Trustreet stock jumped almost $4.50 to just under $17.00, volume spiked and almost 10 million shares were traded. On each of the following two days, volumes were above 2 million but soon dropped to below 1 million. Most days

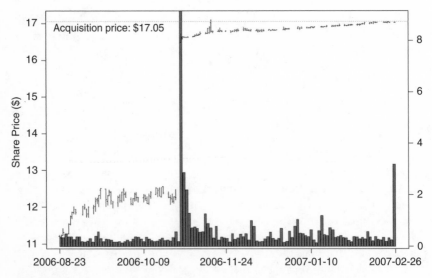

FIGURE 3.2   Price and Volume Chart of Trustreet Common Stock

saw volumes of over 400,000 shares. This compares to trading volumes of 200,000 to 400,000 shares on most days in the two months before the merger announcement. The only way that such high volume can be absorbed in a stock that has little interest as a going concern is because arbitrageurs provide sufficient liquidity through their buy orders.

Another form of liquidity that can help arbitrageurs, or any investor for that matter, earn additional return is the trading volume of the stocks involved in the merger. Liquidity describes the trading volume of a stock and the ability of an arbitrageur to take a position. An arbitrageur will find it difficult to establish a position in a stock with a low trading volume. Typically, these are companies with a small market capitalization, or companies where only a small fraction of the outstanding stock is held by the public and large blocks are controlled by long-term investors who do not buy or sell. This liquidity is somewhat related to the liquidity just discussed, because the overhang of sell orders can have a larger impact on spreads for stocks that do not trade large volumes than for large blue chips.

Low levels of liquidity prevent many large arbitrageurs from taking positions in smaller mergers, even if the annualized return appears attractive. Low trading volumes can make it difficult to build up holdings of even just a few million dollars. For an arbitrageur with an investment book in the billion-dollar range, it is not worth the effort to analyze such a small merger. As a result, spreads can remain attractive for a long period of time for those arbitrageurs small and humble enough to get involved in the transaction.

This is another manifestation of the small-cap premium that has been observed in the investment literature. Small caps delivered returns 4 percent larger than large-cap stocks over the 50 years through 1981, but the small-cap premium has been more difficult to observe since then. Merger arbitrage may be the one area where it has managed to survive until today.

Low liquidity can also affect mergers of large companies that have an illiquid class of securities outstanding in addition to a liquid one. One opportunity that I have encountered frequently in large mergers is preferred stock issued by companies that have a liquid common stock. The preferred stock is typically a supplemental element in the firm's capital structure and has a much smaller capitalization than the common stock. As a result, its liquidity is much lower. The spread of the preferred stock is therefore much wider than that of the common stock. Preferred stocks are often liquidated in a merger. However, there is one caveat with preferred shares that arbitrageurs must be mindful of: Before trying to arbitrage a preferred stock, an arbitrageur must make sure that the preferred stock actually will be liquidated in the merger. An example of a merger in which only the common stock was acquired but several classes of preferred stock remained outstanding is the acquisition of Duquesne Light Company by Macquarie

Infrastructure Partners and The DUET Group that closed at the end of May 2007. After the merger, six series of preferred stock remain outstanding:

Duquesne Light Co. $2.10 Series Cumulative Preferred Stock
                     3.75% Series Cumulative Preferred Stock
                     4.10% Series Cumulative Preferred Stock
                     4.15% Series Cumulative Preferred Stock
                     4.20% Series Cumulative Preferred Stock
                     6.50% Cumulative Preferred Stock

All of these preferred shares continue to trade at the time of writing, albeit with little liquidity on the pink sheets. On many trading days, not a single transaction takes place in these stocks.

The scenario that arbitrageurs are more interested in is when a preferred stock is liquidated in a merger. Trustreet Properties, which was already discussed in Chapter 1, had a Series C Preferred stock traded on the New York Stock Exchange (NYSE) with much smaller trading volume than its common stock. Trading volume of the preferred stock is much more erratic than that of the common stock. The volume chart is shown in Figure 3.3. Before the announcement of the merger, only a few thousand shares changed hands every day, and the occasional day with large trades of 20,000 or more shares is easily identifiable. Following the announcement of the merger,

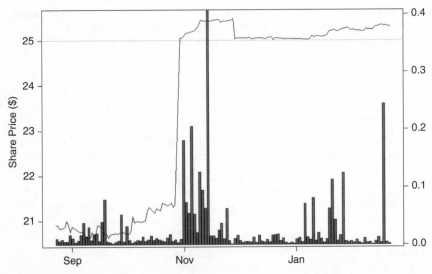

FIGURE 3.3   Volume Chart of Trustreet Series C Preferred Stock

trading volume remains low on most days, amounting to only a few thousand shares. However, large trades generate much more volume now with spikes of up to 100,000 shares. At a price of $25.00 per share, that amounts to a mere $2.5 million of trading volume. For days on which only a few thousand shares traded, the dollar value is of the order of magnitude of only $100,000. By comparison, Trustreet's common stock traded volumes north of 400,000 shares with a value of around $17.00 per share, or a total trading volume of $6.4 million on most days. Clearly, it is difficult for a large arbitrageur to establish a meaningful position in Trustreet's preferred stock, and as a result, the common stock had a tighter spread than the preferred.

As discussed previously, trading volume and bid/offer spreads are closely related. Stocks with low trading volumes have wider bid/offer spreads than those with good liquidity. Bid/offer spread, also known as bid/ask spread, sometimes can be one of the sources of returns. Stocks are quoted with two prices: a bid price at which a buyer in the market is willing to acquire a stock, and an ask (offer) price at which someone is willing to sell. These quotes are placed by either other investors or market makers. In the case of electronic communication networks (ECNs), the quotes come from other investors. In organized exchanges or Nasdaq, the quotes are placed by market makers or specialists, who manage an inventory of stocks and provide buyers and sellers with liquidity.

Bid/offer spreads are related to liquidity. Stocks with low trading volumes tend to have tighter bid/offer spreads. Figure 3.4 shows the screenshot of a level 2 quote of Wilshire Enterprises (ticker symbol WOC), a company with a market capitalization of only $29 million. Wilshire Enterprises was going through an acquisition by a private company run by real estate operator Nickolas W. Jekogian III. Level 2 quotes provide information on different market makers and their posted bid and offer prices and volumes. For example, it can be seen that UBS, whose abbreviation is UBSS, has a bid of $3.50 and offer of $3.80. The lack of liquidity can be seen from the low trading volume of only 3,900 shares at half an hour before the market closes and also from the wide bid/offer spread. The three-month average daily trading volume was only 4,969 shares, which is $17,600. It is difficult for an arbitrageur managing several hundred million dollars in assets to build a position in this stock that can have an impact on the portfolio.

The best bid and offer available are $3.51 and $3.58, respectively. The bid/offer spread is $0.07, or almost 2 percent. For a company with a small market capitalization, such wide bid/offer spreads are common. An arbitrageur must place buy and sell orders in such an illiquid security carefully. After all, arbitrage spreads are very narrow to begin with. If an arbitrageur pays the full 7-cent bid/offer spread, then much of the arbitrage spread is forgone. Conversely, the arbitrage spread can be improved if limit orders

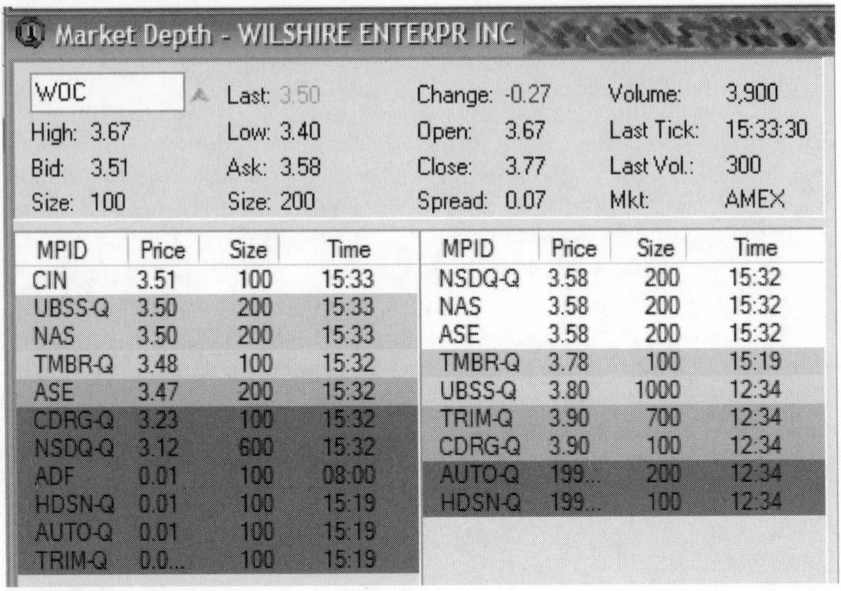
Market Depth - WILSHIRE ENTERPR INC

WOC		Last:	3.50	Change:	-0.27	Volume:	3,900
High:	3.67	Low:	3.40	Open:	3.67	Last Tick:	15:33:30
Bid:	3.51	Ask:	3.58	Close:	3.77	Last Vol.:	300
Size:	100	Size:	200	Spread:	0.07	Mkt:	AMEX

MPID	Price	Size	Time	MPID	Price	Size	Time
CIN	3.51	100	15:33	NSDQ-Q	3.58	200	15:32
UBSS-Q	3.50	200	15:33	NAS	3.58	200	15:32
NAS	3.50	200	15:33	ASE	3.58	200	15:32
TMBR-Q	3.48	100	15:32	TMBR-Q	3.78	100	15:19
ASE	3.47	200	15:32	UBSS-Q	3.80	1000	12:34
CDRG-Q	3.23	100	15:32	TRIM-Q	3.90	700	12:34
NSDQ-Q	3.12	600	15:32	CDRG-Q	3.90	100	12:34
ADF	0.01	100	08:00	AUTO-Q	199...	200	12:34
HDSN-Q	0.01	100	15:19	HDSN-Q	199...	100	12:34
AUTO-Q	0.01	100	15:19				
TRIM-Q	0.0...	100	15:19				

FIGURE 3.4 Level 2 Quote of Wilshire Enterprises

are placed carefully between the bid and ask. The drawback of that strategy is that the limit orders may not be filled.

For comparison, the level 2 quotes of highly liquid Anheuser-Busch (ticker symbol BUD) is shown in Figure 3.5. Anheuser-Busch had a market capitalization of $49 billion and was to be acquired by InBev SA for $70 per share at the time. The daily trading volume at about the same time of day was 4.7 million shares, or by a factor of 1,000 higher than that of Wilshire Enterprises. Similarly, the bid/offer spread is only $0.01, or 0.01 percent. The daily trading volume represents $322 million worth of stock. With so much trading, it is easy for an arbitrageur to build a position worth many millions of dollars in this stock.

Unfortunately, with improvements in technology, posted bid/offer prices are becoming less and less relevant. Many market participants use computerized trading systems that show only a small fraction of the true volume that they are willing to buy or sell. When a fraction of an order is executed, the trading software automatically places another order. These systems allow for better execution of larger orders. If a large order were shown in its entirety, other investors would realize that they stand a small chance of getting executed at this price and will drive the price up (buy order) or down (sell order). By placing the large order tactically in smaller pieces, an

Market Depth - ANHEUSER BUSCH							

BUD   ▼ Last: 68.03   Change: 0.26   Volume: 4,740,162
High: 68.08   Low: 67.75   Open: 67.75   Last Tick: 15:35:38
Bid: 68.03   Ask: 68.04   Close: 67.77   Last Vol.: 100
Size: 2,800   Size: 4,100   Spread: 0.01   Mkt: NYSE

MPID	Price	Size	Time	MPID	Price	Size	Time
ISE	68.03	1800	15:35	NYS	68.04	700	15:35
PSE	68.03	2400	15:35	PSE	68.04	4100	15:35
CIN	68.03	600	15:35	NAS	68.04	4000	15:35
NAS	68.03	2200	15:35	ISE	68.04	3600	15:35
NSDQ-Q	68.03	2200	15:35	NSDQ-Q	68.04	4089	15:35
NYS	68.03	2800	15:35	CIN	68.04	800	15:35
BOOK-Q	67.86	100	11:19	UBSS-Q	68.09	100	15:33
UBSS-Q	67.85	800	15:28	MADF-Q	68.10	100	15:32
MSCO-Q	67.75	200	15:28	MSCO-Q	68.34	200	15:33
MADF-Q	67.40	100	15:32	ADF	68.45	400	15:33
CDRG-Q	62.70	100	10:17	RBCM-Q	70.00	100	15:33
SUSQ-Q	62.34	100	10:18	CDRG-Q	72.99	100	10:17
RBCM-Q	62.00	100	11:35	SUSQ-Q	73.24	100	10:18
ADF	56.50	100	15:31	BARD-Q	75.00	100	13:01
DOMS-Q	35.00	100	11:35	DOMS-Q	95.00	100	13:01
BARD-Q	25.00	100	09:59	TMBR-Q	255...	100	10:27
WBLR-Q	1.00	100	10:12	CBOE	999...	100	09:15
CBOE	0.01	100	09:15	WBLR-Q	100...	100	10:01
AUTO-Q	0.01	100	10:02	AUTO-Q	199...	200	10:01
TMBR-Q	0.01	100	10:03	TRIM-Q	199...	100	10:02
COWN-Q	0.01	100	10:13	COWN-Q	199...	100	10:13
HDSN-Q	0.01	100	10:19	ETMM-Q	199...	100	10:13
TRIM-Q	0.0...	100	10:02	OCTG-Q	199...	100	15:24
OCTG-Q	0.0...	100	15:29	HDSN-Q	199...	100	15:24
ETMM-Q	0.0...	100	15:29				

FIGURE 3.5   Level 2 Quote for Anheuser-Busch

investor can improve her execution quality. In addition, "dark" pools of liquidity are available to participants of certain ECNs. These are orders that are not shown at all in the market but are matched if an order is placed with the same ECN. This has led to a paradox. Although technology has made stock price information much more available and easier to process, it has also made the information that can be seen much less relevant. If posted order books represent only a fraction of actual order books, it is much more difficult for market participants to gauge the state of the market.

Liquidity also determines indirectly the outcome of mergers. The more liquid a stock, and the easier it is for arbitrageurs to build positions, the greater the proportion of stock held by arbitrageurs when the merger is voted on. Because arbitrageurs have a strong interest in seeing the merger close, they will vote in favor. Therefore, mergers sometimes are structured to appeal to arbitrageurs. Table 3.1 shows arbitrageurs' holdings as a percentage of outstanding shares for a number of large mergers since 1985. The importance of arbitrageurs has increased over time. While through 1996 arbitrageurs rarely held more than 30 percent of a stock, their holdings are sometimes around 50 percent for more recent mergers. Companies that want to improve the chances of closing their mergers should structure them in a way that is appealing to arbitrageurs.

Finally, liquidity also has an impact on a less obvious aspect of merger arbitrage: short selling. The ability to borrow a stock to sell short is linked to its liquidity and free float. More on short selling follows later in this chapter.

TIMING AND SPEED OF CLOSING

After the deal spread, the second crucial aspect to the profitability is the time a merger takes to complete. A small spread earned in a short period of time can yield a higher annualized return than a large spread in a merger that drags on for a several years. Arbitrageurs will pay particular attention to the question of timing.

Mergers can be structured in two different ways: as classic mergers, which require a vote by shareholders, or as tender offers, which do not require a vote and where shareholders simply sell their shares to the buyer through a tender process. The difference between the two mechanisms is described in more detail in Chapter 4.

As a general rule, tender offers can be completed much faster than mergers because there is no need to hold a shareholder meeting with the associated advance notice requirements. Tender offers can close in as little as 30 to 60 days. In a tender offer, shareholders can decide whether to tender their shares directly to the acquirer. The buyer will try to obtain all shares, but in practice, some shareholders will not tender their shares. Shareholders are not necessarily opposed to the merger but may simply fail to tender for a variety of other reasons. To allow the buyer to acquire the entire target despite not obtaining 100 percent of the shares in the tender offer, tender offers are structured in two steps:

1. A tender offer is launched.
2. A short-form merger is completed to squeeze out any remaining shareholders.

TABLE 3.1 Arbitrageurs' Holdings of Target Company Stock in Selected Mergers

Year	Announcement Date	Bidder Name	Target Name	Target Market Value ($000s)	Arbitrageurs' Holding (%)	Deal Outcome
1985	4/8/1985	Investor Group	Unocal Corp.	15,172,254	16.96	Withdrawn
1986	10/20/1986	Tri-Star Pictures Inc.	Loews Theaters Corp.	9,130,790	–	Completed
1987	3/26/1987	BP America	Standard Oil Co.	27,853,840	16.85	Completed
1988	10/20/1988	Investor Group	RJR Nabisco Inc.	27,795,615	21.63	Withdrawn
1989	7/27/1989	Bristol-Myers Co.	Squibb Corp.	16,641,443	31.56	Completed
1990	7/12/1990	GTE Corp.	Contel Corp.	8,021,125	31.65	Completed
1991	8/12/1991	BankAmerica Corp.	Security Pacific	5,555,271	25.10	Completed
1992	5/27/1992	Sprint Corp.	Centel Corp.	4,861,927	27.11	Completed
1993	10/13/1993	Bell Atlantic Corp.	Tele-Communications Inc.	15,720,005	36.89	Withdrawn
1994	11/10/1994	Shareholders	Allstate Corp.	13,835,660	9.24	Completed
1995	7/31/1995	Walt Disney Co.	Capital Cities/ABC Inc.	22,179,509	28.29	Completed
1996	4/22/1996	Bell Atlantic Corp.	NYNEX Corp.	26,143,261	29.16	Completed
1997	10/1/1997	WorldCom Inc.	MCI Communications Corp.	23,294,576	47.07	Completed
1998	4/6/1998	Travelers Group Inc.	Citicorp	94,508,038	45.36	Completed
1999	1/18/1999	Vodafone Group PLC	AirTouch Communications Inc.	60,079,773	36.76	Completed
2000	1/10/2000	America Online Inc.	Time Warner	116,513,913	50.72	Completed
2001	3/12/2001	Prudential PLC	American General Corp.	20,812,206	42.60	Withdrawn
2002	7/15/2002	Pfizer Inc.	Pharmacia Corp.	53,294,077	46.87	Completed
2003	10/27/2003	Bank of America Corp.	FleetBoston Financial Corp.	42,347,745	37.85	Completed
2004	2/11/2004	Comcast Corp.	Walt Disney Co.	56,476,998	40.79	Withdrawn

Source: Micah S. Officer, "Are Performance-Based Arbitrage Effects Detectable? Evidence from Merger Arbitrage," *Journal of Corporate Finance* 15, No. 5 (2007), 793–812. Reprinted with permission by Elsevier.

Under the laws of most states, once a shareholder reaches a certain threshold of ownership, usually 90 or 95 percent, it can force the minority shareholders to sell it their shares. This provision is often called a squeeze-out of minority shareholders. The threshold depends on the state of incorporation. It is over 90 percent in most states but can be as low as 85 percent. In Delaware, the threshold is 90 percent. Following a tender offer, the buyer will take advantage of a squeeze-out to obtain control of the target from the last few remaining shareholders.

It is normal that buyers do not get to the requisite 90 percent threshold at the expiration of the first tender offer period. Multiple extensions of tender offer periods are not unusual. In some instances, shareholders do not tender out of ignorance or for other reasons that can be difficult to pinpoint. In those scenarios, tender offer extensions typically work.

The situation is different when shareholders refuse to tender because they believe that the price is insufficient. In these cases, a new sweetened tender offer with a higher price is necessary. This was the case when Lafarge S.A. wanted to acquire the publicly held 46.8 percent of its NYSE-traded subsidiary Lafarge North America (see Figure 3.6). Lafarge S.A. first offered $75.00 per share price on February 6, 2006, for Lafarge North America, a proposal that few shares were tendered into. Shares of Lafarge North America traded well above $75.00, indicating that the market expected a substantial price improvement. A subsequent $82.00 tender offer on April 4 received a similarly lukewarm reception. Only following the third sweetened offer of $85.50 per share were sufficient shares tendered to bring Lafarge above the 90 percent threshold: At the expiration of the offer on May 15, it held 92.37 percent of Lafarge North America and was able to squeeze out the minority shareholders.

It is also possible for a buyer who cannot get to the 90 percent squeeze-out threshold to increase its holdings by acquiring newly issued shares of the target. This is referred to as a top-up option.

Mergers are different because they require shareholder approval. The notice periods prior to the annual meeting can be longer than the entire process for a tender offer. The pros and cons of acquiring a company through a merger or tender offer are discussed in Chapter 4. For now, suffice it to say that mergers are more complex and tend to be drawn out for a longer period of time.

The statistics of time period required to complete an acquisition reflect this. Table 3.2 shows the average and maximum time periods required to close a merger for a range of industries. Overall, mergers close on average in 4.5 months. Companies in the energy and power industry along with

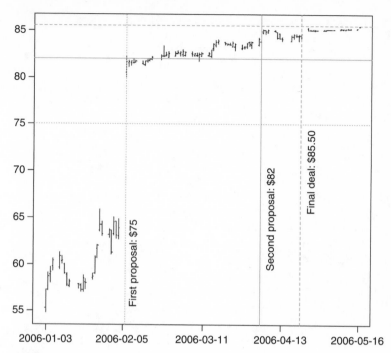

FIGURE 3.6 Lafarge North America

financials take the longest to complete their mergers. This finding reflects the high level of regulation of these sectors and the multiple state regulatory bodies that have to give their consent before the closing. Smaller mergers with a value below $500 million close half a month faster than those with a value in excess of that level.

Interestingly, mergers that fail to close do so a little faster on average than those that close successfully, as shown in Table 3.3. Intuition would suggest that mergers that fail should do so more slowly than those that are successful. One would expect that it takes multiple delays and extensions until it becomes clear that a merger is beyond hope. This appears to be the case in some individual mergers. Several industries show outliers of mergers that drag on for an extremely long time until they fail. For example, a merger in the financial industry took 2,031 days until it fell apart for good. For most mergers, however, the opposite effect is at work. If a merger runs into obstacles, the parties involved make multiple attempts to rescue the transaction, and eventually succeed. As a result, successful mergers take longer on average.

TABLE 3.2　Time Periods Required to Close a Merger, by Industry and Company Size

	50–500 Million		>500 Million		All
	Average	Maximum	Average	Maximum	Average
Consumer Products and Services	97.9	316	115.0	434	103.2
Consumer Staples	115.2	429	133.3	298	122.5
Energy and Power	172.3	893	236.3	906	207.0
Financials	169.4	990	163.2	764	167.6
Health Care	111.5	498	120.1	430	115.2
High Technology	98.5	1162	105.0	581	100.9
Industrials	99.0	442	119.9	676	106.1
Materials	125.7	1065	132.6	552	128.9
Media and Entertainment	146.6	821	172.9	483	160.8
Real Estate	148.6	583	124.4	386	138.5
Retail	111.9	370	119.2	348	114.5
Telecommunications	111.0	405	181.3	703	147.3
Total Average	129.7		145.4		135.7

Source: Author's calculations based on Mergerstat data.

Smaller mergers both fail and close faster than larger ones. This finding reflects the complexity of large mergers that are more likely to require antitrust approvals and thus take longer, whether they succeed ultimately or not.

For both collapsed and successful mergers, a few outliers lie at a multiple of the average. These rare events skew the average values to the upside. It should also be remembered that these tables show averages of mergers and tender offers. Tender offers, however, take much less time to close than mergers. Therefore, the distribution of closing times underlying both tables is binomial rather than bell shaped.

Arbitrageurs will analyze the timing for each transaction individually rather than work with averages. However, averages can be useful as a point of reference. Companies indicate most of the time in the press release announcing the merger an anticipated time frame. This time frame always should be an arbitrageur's principal data point. It can be adjusted if, based on analysis and experience, the transaction is likely to take longer. Reasons for extending the time frame can be antitrust issues, uncertain financing, shareholder opposition, or any other potential problem.

TABLE 3.3 Time Periods Required to Close a Merger, by Industry and Company Size

	50–500 Million		>500 Million		All
	Average	Maximum	Average	Maximum	Average
Consumer Products and Services	124.2	405	123.3	347	123.9
Consumer Staples	131.2	257	119.6	588	125.6
Energy and Power	150.2	797	281.7	1361	237.8
Financials	148.8	2031	127.7	329	141.1
Health Care	106	774	138.2	419	120.5
High Technology	116.1	1063	121.5	510	117.7
Industrials	90.5	292	126.6	430	103.2
Materials	118.3	507	102.6	410	112.3
Media and Entertainment	118.7	585	124.4	396	121.3
Real Estate	185.8	809	84.5	279	149.9
Retail	97.5	343	146.1	301	108.4
Telecommunications	111.8	386	137.5	491	124.3
Total Average	121.7		144.1		130.3

Source: Author's calculations based on Mergerstat data.

Over time, as the merger progresses and new information becomes available, the closing date of the merger must be adjusted if necessary. I have found that in the majority of cases, mergers close faster than the initial indication given in the company's press release. However, as soon as a closing date is extended, the annualized return of a merger drops. Therefore, finding an estimate of the closing date that approaches the actual date reasonably well is critical.

Extension risk affects returns for arbitrageurs in a twofold manner:

1. The annualized return on existing arbitrage positions is depressed.
2. Spreads will widen, which leads to losses.

Let us return to the acquisition of Trustreet Properties, Inc. by GE Capital Solutions discussed in Chapter 1 and assume that instead of March 31, the closing date were to be delayed to May 30. The reason for such a delay is of no interest for the purposes of this discussion. There would be an extra 61 days until the closing if such a delay were to occur. The total time period for the merger is now 213 days instead of 152, and the annualized return under the simple interest method falls from 5.4 to 3.86 percent:

$$R_{AN} = \left(\frac{P_C + d}{P_P}\right)^{\left(\frac{365}{t}\right)} - 1 = \left(\frac{17.05 + 0.33}{17.00}\right)^{\left(\frac{365}{213}\right)} - 1 = 0.038609$$

(3.1)

If, however, the annualized spread were to remain constant at 5.4 percent, the price of the stock would have to decline so that

$$\left(\frac{17.05 + 0.33}{P_P}\right)^{\left(\frac{365}{213}\right)} - 1 = 0.05368$$

(3.2)

$$\text{This yields } P_P = \frac{17.38}{1.05368^{\frac{213}{365}}} = 16.86$$

(3.3)

Therefore, the gross spread would widen by $0.14 to $0.19. Given that the initial spread was only $0.05, this is almost a quadrupling. Arbitrageurs will suffer losses as a result of the extension. Of course, these losses are only temporary and occur only for those arbitrageurs who are forced to mark to market. Arbitrageurs who report their results only monthly or even less frequently may not even show these losses. If the merger is consummated, the spread will narrow again, and eventually arbitrageurs will recover the marked-to-market losses.

When a deal is extended, both the first and second effect happen simultaneously. However, the spread is likely to widen much more than a simple mathematical parity of a constant annualized spread suggests. The market perceives the extension of a merger as a signal that the deal may be in trouble. In this case, arbitrageurs will require a higher annualized spread to compensate for the higher perceived risk.

Sometimes the widening can be large briefly intraday and provide trading opportunities. This temporary widening can be caused by sudden selling pressure coming from the uncertainty created by the announcement of the deal extension. If arbitrageurs themselves are sellers, market movements can be swift because the very providers of liquidity have turned into liquidity takers.

Extensions of the time a merger takes to close can also provide additional return if shareholders receive an extra dividend payment. Whether a dividend can be expected is stipulated in the merger agreement. Sometimes merger agreements restrict a company's ability to make dividend payments. In the case of real estate investment trusts (REITs) discussed in the next section, merger agreements often specify that dividends will continue to be paid in amounts sufficient to maintain REIT status until the closing. If an additional dividend is received, it will at least partially offset the reduction in net annualized return that the arbitrageur suffers from the delay. In rare instances, if a company pays very high dividends, or in cases of preferred stock, additional dividend payments actually can boost the net annualized return.

DIVIDENDS

Historically, dividends have made a large contribution to the returns achieved by investors in the stock market. With the multiple expansion in the bull market since 1981, the unfavorable tax treatment of dividends relative to capital gains, the widespread use of stock options in management compensation,[2] and the widespread acceptance of theories promulgated by two academics, Franco Modigliani and Merton Miller, dividend yields of most indices have fallen to around 2 percent. Modigliani and Miller show that in a hypothetical world without taxes, investors are indifferent between receiving capital gains and dividends.

Dividends historically were an important driver of returns earned on stocks until the Modigliani-Miller paradigm became widely accepted and capital gains replaced the role of dividends. For merger arbitrageurs, dividends remain an important element of return.

It was shown in Chapter 2 that merger spreads are usually very small and amount to only a few percentage points. Therefore, dividends that amount to 2 percent per year on average can make a difference; in cases of income-producing stocks, they can present the bulk of the return. In the example of Trustreet, the annualized return without dividends was only 0.71 percent but amounted to 5.53 percent when dividends are taken into account.

It was also shown in Chapter 1 that dividends complicate stock-for-stock mergers, because an arbitrageur must pay the dividend on the stock sold short. Dividends on the long leg of an arbitrage increase returns; dividends paid on the short leg diminish returns.

In addition to providing additional income, dividends can also alter the tax effect of an arbitrage strategy. Until recent changes in tax rates, dividends were taxed as ordinary income, whereas most investors held stocks for long periods of time, so that their capital gains were taxed at a lower tax rate applicable to long-term capital gains. This changed with the Jobs and Growth Tax Relief Reconciliation Act of 2003, which introduced a new lower "qualified" tax rate of 15 percent as long as the stock has been held for more than a 60-day period that includes the dividend date. With the Tax Increase Prevention and Reconciliation Act of 2005, this 15 percent tax rate for dividends has been extended to 2010. The effect of this change in the tax treatment of dividends is that for long-term holders of a stock, there is no difference in the tax treatment between dividend payments and capital gains (other than second-order effects, such as a potential deferral of the tax payment, or compounding).

However, arbitrageurs are not long-term holders of stocks and therefore experience more complex tax effects. Arbitrageurs have two sources of income: capital gains earned from the spread of the merger and dividends. Most mergers close in less than one year, and under current U.S. tax laws, short-term capital gains are taxed as ordinary income. Under the old tax regime, short-term capital gains and dividends were awarded the same tax treatment, and arbitrageurs were indifferent between generating capital gains or dividend income.

Since the introduction of the favorable tax rate on "qualified" dividends, the situation has changed. Many mergers take longer than 60 days to close, and often arbitrageurs find themselves holding a dividend-paying stock for more than 60 days. These dividends are taxed at a lower "qualified" rate of 15 percent as long as the arbitrageur meets the 60-day holding period requirement. Capital gains continue to be taxed as ordinary income. Therefore, arbitrageurs often have a preference for dividends over capital gains.

When a dividend-paying stock is expected to be held for a long enough period to qualify for the 15 percent tax rate, an arbitrageur will be better off after taxes than with an otherwise identical spread that consists only of capital gains.

In the case of Trustreet Properties, the impact of different holding periods has a significant impact on after tax returns. In the next example, it is assumed that the arbitrageur (or its customer) has a tax rate of 40 percent. This is a reasonable assumption if the client is in the highest federal tax bracket of 35 percent and also pays state and local taxes and possibly also Medicare taxes. If the shares are held for less than 60 days, the entire net spread will be subject to income taxes at 40 percent:

$$T = (17.05 + 0.33 - 17.00) \times (0.4) = 0.15 \tag{3.4}$$

The annualized after-tax return becomes

$$R_{ANT} = \left(\frac{P_C + d - T}{P_P} \right)^{\left(\frac{365}{t} \right)} - 1 \tag{3.5}$$

$$= \left(\frac{17.05 + 0.33 - 0.15}{17.00} \right)^{\left(\frac{365}{152} \right)} - 1 = 0.023296$$

where: $T =$ is the amount of taxes dues.

$R_{ANT} =$ is the annualized net after-tax return.

If the shares are held for 60 days and dividends are eligible for taxation at the qualified rate of 15 percent, then the tax impact is reduced by more than half:

$$T = (17.05 - 17.00) \times (0.4) + 0.33 \times 0.15 = 0.07 \tag{3.6}$$

$$R_{ANT} = \left(\frac{P_C + d - T}{P_P} \right)^{\left(\frac{365}{t} \right)} - 1 \tag{3.7}$$

$$= \left(\frac{17.05 + 0.33 - 0.07}{17.00} \right)^{\left(\frac{365}{152} \right)} - 1 = 0.031451$$

If a client pays taxes at the rate for the alternative minimum tax, the difference will be less. Many arbitrageurs have tax-exempt clients, such as university endowments or pension funds. In these cases, tax considerations obviously are irrelevant.

Arbitrageurs have to be careful to follow the ex-dates and record dates of dividends correctly. Dividends are paid only to the holders of record on the record date. The payment date is usually two to four weeks after the record date. Shares acquired before the payment date of the dividend, but after its record date, are not eligible to receive a dividend payment.

REIT dividends are a special case: REITs are required to pay out 90 percent of their income to their investors in order to maintain their status as pass-through entities that distribute substantially all income and need not pay taxes at the entity level. REITs are governed by subchapter M of the Internal Revenue Code, which also regulates mutual fund taxation. When a REIT is acquired, it will make a final dividend payment on the day of the closing that is large enough to satisfy the requirement of subchapter M. Shareholders do not normally know the exact amount of the final dividend payment that they can expect. Management guidance often underestimates the actual payment. It also varies with the timing of the merger. The longer the merger takes, the more dividends must be paid out so that the REIT can maintain its status as a pass-through entity. Merger agreements will stipulate whether dividends will continue to be paid. A typical clause specifies that dividends will be paid until the closing in amounts sufficient to maintain REIT status.

Finally, there is one caveat on the availability of the 15 percent rate for dividends on stocks that have been held for more than 60 days: It does not apply to a stock that was acquired from a short seller. Because the short seller pays the dividend on the shorted stock, it is considered a payment in lieu of a dividend, not a dividend paid by the company. Only dividends paid by the company are eligible for the 15 percent rate; payments in lieu of dividends are not. Buyers of heavily shorted stocks must be careful about the nature of their purchase. Fortunately, there is a trick that a buyer can use to convert a long position in borrowed shares into a long position of unencumbered shares: Request the issuance of a physical certificate. There is a cost involved, not to mention the risk of loss and the effort required to handle certificates. More important, it can be difficult to sell the shares (short sales are a temporary fix, though). However, if an arbitrageur has a sufficiently large holding of a stock, it may be worthwhile taking the extra step to optimize taxes.

SHORT SALES AS A HEDGE AND AN ELEMENT OF RETURN

Short sales are one of the trickier aspects of merger arbitrage that warrant special consideration. Short sales are performed as one leg of a stock-for-stock merger arbitrage. It was described in principle in the example of the Agere/LSI merger in Chapter 1. It is often said that shorting requires special skill; whether we call it a skill or not, it is true that shorting requires special attention and is one of the most regulated aspects of stock trading.

In the sense that shorts are entered as part of a two-legged position, merger arbitrage short positions can be said to be hedged. But the hedge works only while the merger is on track to close. If uncertainty about the closing increases, the short will no longer be hedged and will take on a life of its own.

In order to sell a stock short, an arbitrageur must be able to deliver it. Since the arbitrageur does not own the stock, it must be borrowed from an owner. To borrow shares, an arbitrageur or its broker contacts some of the large clearing firms, which will lend their customers' securities. Institutions that custody their assets with a bank custodian often have their own stock lending desk in order to generate additional revenue. Retail investors can short out of the inventory of their broker's clearing firm.

The cost of borrowing is generally included in the short rebate paid by the broker that handles the short. In the event that an arbitrageur borrows stock elsewhere, it may have to pay a separate fee. The short rebate was discussed earlier in Chapter 1 in the Agere/LSI stock-for-stock arbitrage.

The short rebate makes an important contribution to arbitrageurs' returns. Short rebates vary slightly from broker to broker. Large arbitrageurs will obtain higher short rebates than smaller ones. Many retail brokerage firms do not pay their customers a short rebate at all. The example of the Agere/LSI stock-for-stock arbitrage from Chapter 1 will be used to illustrate how returns can be affected by different levels of the short rebate.

In the example given in Chapter 1, it was assumed that the arbitrageur would earn a short rebate of only 1 percent, amounting to $6.32 over a period of 117 days on $1,970 of short proceeds. This represented an increase of almost 16 percent over the annualized net spread excluding the short rebate. In early 2007, interest rates were very low, and a low rate of 1 percent is a reasonable assumption. When interest rates are higher in more normal times, short rebates paid by brokerage firms will also be higher and make a larger contribution to an arbitrageur's annualized return.

To calculate the impact of the short rebate in a pure stock-for-stock merger, the rate of the short rebate can simply be added to the annualized net return as a shorthand calculation. In a mixed cash/stock merger, the short rebate must be reduced by the ratio of cash to stock and then added to the annualized return. These two calculations are not accurate but are good enough for most purposes.

For a more accurate calculation, the short rebate must be calculated on the dollar amount sold short, as was done in the Agere/LSI example in Chapter 1. Table 3.4 shows how the annualized return on the arbitrage would have improved for different levels of the short rebate. The interest earned is based on the amount of $1,970 sold short and the annualized return without incorporation of the short rebate is 6.61 percent. For a short rebate of 6.2 percent, the annualized return doubles compared to the return without a short rebate.

In mergers that pay a combination of cash and stock, the dollar amount sold short is much smaller than in a pure stock-for-stock merger. If the cash component is very large, the transaction will provide almost no short rebate.

The gross spread reflects the ability of arbitrageurs to earn additional income through the short rebate. Cash mergers have wider spreads in part because arbitrageurs cannot earn a short rebate and in part because the risk profile is higher due to the risk associated with financing the cash consideration.

A high risk with borrowing shares is due to the propensity of the original owners to ask for the return of their shares at a time that is inopportune for the borrower. The owners may ask for their shares back, for example, because they want to sell their position. When they sell, they will have to

TABLE 3.4 Improvement in the Arbitrage Spread of the Agere/LSI Stock-for-Stock Merger for Different Levels of Short Rebates

Short Rebate (%)	Interest Earned ($)	Increase in Spread (%)	Annualized Return (%)	Increase in Annualized Return (%)
0.00	0.00	0.00	6.61	0.00
0.50	3.16	7.89	7.14	8.07
1.00	6.31	15.79	7.67	16.13
1.50	9.47	23.68	8.21	24.20
2.00	12.63	31.57	8.74	32.26
2.50	15.79	39.47	9.27	40.33
3.00	18.94	47.36	9.81	48.39
3.50	22.1	55.25	10.34	56.46
4.00	25.26	63.15	10.87	64.53
4.50	28.42	71.04	11.41	72.59
5.00	31.57	78.93	11.94	80.66
5.50	34.73	86.83	12.47	88.72
6.00	37.89	94.72	13.01	96.79
6.20	39.15	97.86	13.22	100.00
6.50	41.05	102.62	13.54	104.85
7.00	44.2	110.51	14.07	112.92
7.50	47.36	118.40	14.60	120.99
8.00	50.52	126.30	15.14	129.05

deliver their shares to the new owner. The arbitrageur then has only two choices: find another counterparty from which the shares can be borrowed, or cover the short. When many short sellers are required to close their position at the same time, a short squeeze ensues. In a short squeeze, a heavily shorted stock suddenly rallies abruptly. A good sign that a rally is a short squeeze rather than an upside revision by the market of the intrinsic value of a stock is the absence of any fundamental information.

The short seller of a stock must make dividend payments to the buyer. When a short seller borrows shares and sells them short, there are now two owners of the stock: the original owner who has lent the shares, and the counterparty to the short sale. Both are long stock and expect to receive dividends. However, only one dividend payment is made by the company underlying the stock. The dividend payment going to the counterparty of the short sale must be made by the short seller. For most investors, the clearing broker that holds the short position will administer the payment and debit the account directly. We mentioned earlier that this payment in lieu of a dividend is not eligible for the "qualified" tax rate of 15 percent on dividends. Instead, it is taxed as ordinary income even if the shares were held for more than 60 days.

Paying dividends on shorted stock is a cost of carry of the position. The higher the dividend yield, the higher the cost of carry. In theory, stocks respond to the payment of a dividend by dropping by the dividend amount on the ex-date. However, dividends are paid out of income, so that companies with large dividend payments tend to be profitable and do not drop as much, certainly not in the long run.[3] A quick way to estimate on the back of an envelope the carry for a stock-for-stock merger arbitrage is by comparing the dividend yields of the two stocks.

- If the long position has a higher dividend yield than the short, the position has a negative carry and dividends improve the spread. If the spread were to remain constant, the arbitrageur would earn the differential in dividend yields.
- If the long position has a lower dividend yield than the short, then the position has a positive carry. If the spread were to remain constant, the arbitrageur would have to pay the differential in dividend yields.

This method is a rough estimate only. A more careful estimation of the carry needs to take the exact timing of the dividends into account as well as the anticipated closing of the merger. Future dividend dates and amounts can be extrapolated from historical dividends.

A more extensive discussion about short selling can be found in Chapter 13.

LEVERAGE BOOSTS RETURNS

Merger arbitrageurs are no different from other investors in their desire to boost returns by borrowing. It is appropriate and safe to use leverage when the investments financed have low volatility, such as real estate, fixed income, or private equity. Merger arbitrage is also a low-volatility strategy.

There are two principal ways that allow arbitrageurs to use leverage: through the use of margin or other borrowings, or via derivatives. The two ways differ not only in economic terms but also in the approach taken to evaluate their effect. Derivatives are acquired in connection with specific investments and provide leverage on those investments only, whereas margin or other borrowings are taken against the portfolio as a whole and cannot normally be attributed to a specific arbitrage opportunity.

Margin borrowing is the classic but expensive way to leverage a portfolio. In margin borrowing, an arbitrageur borrows money from a broker and pledges the securities acquired as collateral. In most cases, arbitrageurs obtain this form of financing from their prime broker. The prime broker borrows funds in the money market, or uses funds deposited by other customers, and lends them to arbitrageurs. Proceeds from customers' short sales are another source of funds. Prime brokers effectively are acting as banks for securities traders. Like a bank, the prime broker makes a profit because it lends for a higher rate than it borrows at.

Due to the more volatile nature of securities markets, the Federal Reserve has imposed capital requirements not only on the brokers but also on the customers who borrow on margin. Under Regulation T, a customer must have at least 50 percent equity when acquiring a security. This criterion is also known as the initial margin requirement. Because securities prices fluctuate so much, the capital requirement for ongoing borrowings is much lower than for the initial margin. After the security has been acquired, a customer must maintain at least 25 percent of the account value in equity, the maintenance margin. This allows for a significant drop in the value of a portfolio. If the equity falls below the maintenance margin requirement, the broker will issue a margin call that forces the customer either to sell securities or to inject additional funds into the account. If a customer fails to do either, the broker will liquidate positions until the maintenance margin is restored. Brokers are free to set more stringent margin requirements, and many do so to protect themselves and their customers from volatility.

The use of borrowings other than through margin is open only to some of the larger arbitrageurs. Investment banks that run arbitrage books can borrow at a small spread to the London Interbank Offered Rate (LIBOR). Their cost of capital typically is allocated on a corporate level under a blended rate of one form or another to each business unit, and the arbitrage desk will be assigned a cost of capital. Imitating investment banks, some large hedge funds recently have tapped the capital markets and issued bonds in order to have access to permanent capital independently of the availability of margin borrowing from brokerage firms. It is clear that the economics of leverage is much more favorable for large operations with access to such a varied array of funding sources at attractive spreads.

Funding arbitrage and other hedge funds has become a very profitable business for prime brokers. Many brokers make more than half of their income from the funding spread between their cost of capital and the margin rate. The other half is made through commissions. The high profitability of margin borrowing to prime brokers is a corollary of the method's expensive nature.

In addition to its high cost, arbitrageurs using margin also make themselves dependent on the business prospects of their prime broker. During the credit crisis of 2007–2008, many hedge funds were forced by their prime brokers to reduce leverage because the brokers themselves suffered losses and needed to reduce their exposure to risky customers. When many customers, including merger arbitrageurs, were forced to sell their holdings, spreads widened on a wide variety of arbitrage strategies, not just merger arbitrage. This had nothing to do with the inherent risk of these transactions increasing; it was caused only by the actions of the arbitrageurs, who are normally liquidity providers. In this case, they became liquidity takers.

COVERED CALL WRITING

A popular technique for enhancing returns on stock positions is the writing of covered calls. The idea is that an investor holds a stock and by writing a call option against that stock, additional income can be generated. I have come across several financial advisers who recommend this strategy to their customers.

Covered call writing is more complex than many of its proponents admit. Owning a stock and writing a call against it limits the upside: If at expiration the stock price rises above the strike price of the option, the stock will be called (see Figure 3.7). Conversely, if the stock price drops, the option will expire worthless, so that the investor can keep the premium as a profit. But the holder of this position will suffer a loss on the stock that probably will exceed the premium income. This payout profile resembles that of a short put position. When an investor writes a put, the upside is limited to the premium received. However, the downside is practically unlimited. The only limitation is that the underlying stock cannot fall below zero. Many investors are not aware that by writing a covered call, their effective position is identical to writing a naked put. Nevertheless, covered call writing is peddled as a conservative strategy. Most conservative investors would never write a naked put if asked to do so by their financial adviser.

For a merger arbitrageur, covered call writing makes more sense than for a buy-and-hold investor. In a cash merger, the upside is limited anyway to the buyout price. Further limiting the upside through a written call will not affect the payoff profile in any way. Readers are reminded of Figures 1.4 and 1.5, which show that merger arbitrage has a payoff pattern that resembles that of a put option. If the long stock position is supplemented with a covered call, the arbitrageur creates a parallel put exposure in addition to the implicit put created by the arbitrage. However, the risk is not cumulative. The downside risk comes only from the long position in the stock. The written call limits only the upside, which is already limited by the presence of an acquisition proposal.

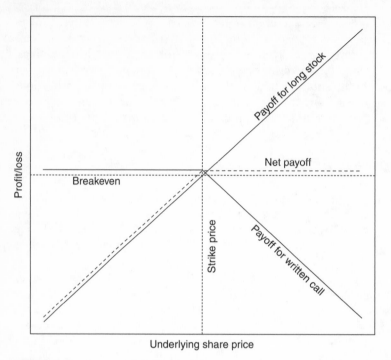

FIGURE 3.7   Covered Call Writing

Covered call writing should be considered only for cash mergers. If the long leg of a stock-for-stock merger were to be used as cover for a call, the stock price of both the long and short might rise. But the long leg of the arbitrage will be called when it rises above the strike price of the written call. This would expose the arbitrageur to losses from the short position. Both the long and short leg are supposed to move in sync when their prices increase, and covered call writing disrupts this principle.

So can covered call writing add extra income to an arbitrage position? Unfortunately, there is no such easy way to make money. First, option premia tend to drop significantly once a merger has been announced. Second, by writing a covered call, the arbitrageur limits the ability to participate in any increase in the acquisition price if, for example, another buyer were to emerge offering a higher price.

Options are priced based on the fluctuation of the underlying stock—its volatility. The higher the volatility, the higher the time value of the option. Once a merger is announced, volatility tends to drop significantly. This effect is discussed in more detail in Chapter 12. Market makers for options

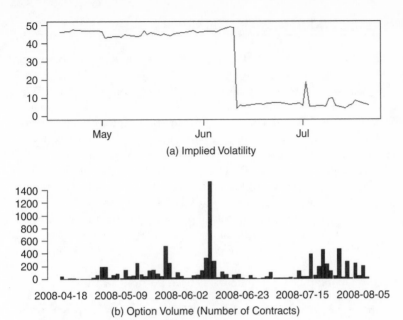

FIGURE 3.8 Implied Volatility and Option Trading Volume of Superior Essex Inc.

are aware that the underlying stock will soon cease to exist and price the options accordingly. Figure 3.8(a) shows the implied volatility of options of Superior Essex Inc., which was acquired by Seoul-based LS Cable in August 2008, for a period of one year prior to the acquisition. For the time leading up to the June 11, 2008, announcement of the merger, Superior Essex call and put options traded at implied volatilities mostly between 40 and 50 percent, temporarily shooting up to 60 percent. After the merger agreement was announced publicly on June 11, implied volatility dropped to between 5 and 20 percent. The associated option volume is shown in Figure 3.8(b).

As a result of the sharp drop in option volatility, premia drop to levels that make covered call writing unattractive. Only the writing of long-dated call options can in some instances generate noticeable additional returns, because the additional time value increases the premium.

It should also be noted from Figure 3.8(a) that implied volatilities for call and put options track each other very closely. Due to call-put parity, implied volatilities should be close for calls and puts. This shows that the option markets remain efficient even when a company is about to be delisted.

COMMISSIONS AND PORTFOLIO TURNOVER

Since fixed commissions were abolished in 1975, the cost of executing stock trades has dropped almost every year. The "May Day" of 1975 may have been the trigger, but the biggest enabler of the drop in commission has been technology. The securities markets are becoming increasingly disintermediated. While it was common during the 1990s to place trades via a telephone with a broker, software applications provide today's investors direct access to the various execution venues with split-second order transmission.

The average commission in 1980 was close to $0.40 per share and has dropped to roughly $0.05 per share in 2003, according to data by Greenwich Associates. Today, low-cost commissions of direct access providers are even lower, amounting often to less than $0.01 per share. Some brokerage firms offer flat-rate tickets for low-priced shares, where $0.01 would constitute a larger percentage of the stock's price than for a typical stock priced at $20.00.

For arbitrageurs, this development has been positive for two reasons:

1. The drop in the price of commissions has helped to maintain profitability of merger arbitrage spreads.
2. Technological improvements have improved the placement of orders and decreased the risk of trading errors.

In the examples of merger arbitrage investments discussed in Chapter 1, the dollar amounts and percentages of spreads were always very small. An overview of the spreads is shown in Table 3.5.

If an arbitrageur were to pay commissions at the level of 1980, the Trustreet merger would generate a loss and Agere/LSI would be uneconomical. Even at 2003 commission levels, the Trustreet merger would not be profitable. Fortunately, commissions are now at $0.01 per share and below, so their impact on profitability is less significant. In stock-for-stock mergers, arbitrageurs must pay two commissions: one for the long leg and another for the short leg of the arbitrage. The impact of the level of commissions is twice as large for these transactions as for cash mergers.

TABLE 3.5 Overview of Spreads from Examples in Chapter 1

Transaction	$ Spread	% Spread	Annualized Return (%)
Trustreet	0.05	0.29	0.71
Agere/LSI	0.40	2.07	6.61
Trane/Ingersoll Rand	1.64	2.85	

Improvements in trading technology have also helped arbitrageurs handle narrow spreads more efficiently. In stock-for-stock mergers, the arbitrageur must acquire and sell short two securities simultaneously. This can be difficult to do if the arbitrageur enters separate orders for each side manually. If the market moves quickly, the arbitrageur may get a fill on one side but not the other. The market is then moving against the filled side, but the other side is not yet offsetting the executed one. For example, if the market rises after an arbitrageur has been filled on the short sale, the order for the long leg of the arbitrage may not get filled, and the arbitrageur will have to pay a higher price, which reduces the spread that can be earned. Using market orders instead of limit orders can mitigate this risk somewhat, but market orders also risk reducing the spread.

Fortunately, a number of software providers have developed trading applications that allow arbitrageurs to enter spread orders. The arbitrageur defines a spread and a ratio at which an arbitrage is to be executed; the broker's computer then places orders so that the defined spread is locked in, and the right number of shares is purchased and sold short. The arbitrageur can also select which leg should be executed first and how many shares of the order should be shown at any one time (reserve order).

Some brokerage firms offer their customers so-called soft-dollar payments. These are arrangements whereby some of the commission paid for the execution of trades is used to pay for research services or certain eligible software products, such as Bloomberg terminals. Arbitrageurs who use soft dollars will pay higher commissions than those who choose execution-only services. Due to the short holding periods of mergers, arbitrageurs trade frequently and incur significant commission expenses, and hence soft-dollar credits, if they use these facilities. Therefore, soft dollars can have a large impact on performance. If an arbitrageur trades with client funds, soft dollars are clearly not in clients' best interests. Nevertheless, some arbitrageurs use soft dollars to help offset many of the arbitrageurs' expenses. In my opinion, these expenses are supposed to be covered by the management fee. Some arbitrageurs, such as my firm, have decided to forgo soft-dollar arrangements in order to avoid their negative impact on performance.

Commentators cite portfolio turnover as a negative factor in evaluating investment managers. Merger arbitrageurs generate large portfolio turnover, not infrequently of 300 percent and more, due to the short time frame for mergers to close and the long/short nature of many investments. The negative influence of high portfolio turnover on traditional investment strategies is based on two effects of frequent trading:

1. Frequent trading generates commissions and other transaction costs, such as bid/offer spreads.
2. Frequent sales of stock generate short-term capital gains.

Both arguments are valid in the context of traditional investment strategies but are inapplicable for merger arbitrage. For a start, any strategy that uses a long/short approach to investing will have a higher portfolio turnover than a buy-and-hold strategy. The simultaneous purchase and sale of stock generates additional turnover that a long-only investor does not incur. Of course, the risk profiles of long/short and long-only investments are drastically different, so portfolio turnover is not a good metric to compare the strategies. Similarly, commissions incurred will be higher in a long/short than in a long-only portfolio. The higher cost of executing the trade is a necessary condition for achieving the desired risk profile of the long/short strategy as opposed to a long-only one.

Taxes are more valid as a concern. Merger arbitrage for the most part generates short-term capital gains. But as with transaction costs, the tax effect of merger arbitrage is a side effect of the strategy that cannot be avoided. Mergers close on a short time frame, and it is impossible to devise a merger arbitrage strategy that invests for the long run. An investor who seeks the risk profile associated with merger arbitrage must be willing to incur the tax effects of the strategy. Fortunately, many investors in merger arbitrage vehicles are tax-exempt institutions for whom the tax effects are irrelevant.

BIDDING WARS AND HOSTILE BIDS

Hostile bids and bidding wars can be among the most profitable mergers, yet they also present the most risk of loss. The risk of noncompletion is very high.

Hostile bids occur when a potential buyer wants to acquire an unwilling target. A recent example is the bid by Belgian-Brazilian beverage giant In-Bev SA for Anheuser-Busch Cos. (see Figure 3.9). InBev first bid $65.00 per share on June 11, valued at $46 billion. Anheuser-Busch rejected the bid and announced a cost-cutting initiative instead. InBev threatened to take its proposal directly to shareholders. This would most likely have meant a tender offer or a proxy fight to obtain control of the board. For a while, it looked like Mexico's Grupo Modelo might enter the race to acquire Anheuser-Busch. This would have turned the hostile bid into a full-fledged bidding war. By late June, InBev had secured financing for its bid and indicated that it would go forward with a its hostile bid. However, on July 11, it became clear that both firms had entered friendly negotiations. Three days later, both companies announced a friendly merger for $70.00 per share.

It can be seen from the stock chart that Anheuser-Busch traded below the $65.00 offered by InBev. In other cases, the stock of the target trades above the offer price because market participants expect that the final price

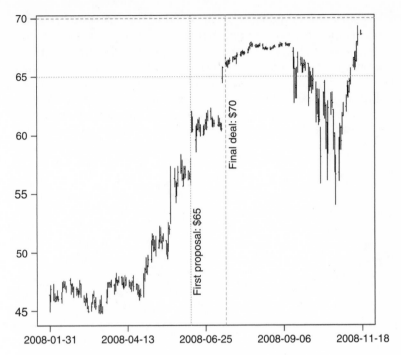

FIGURE 3.9 Stock Price of Anheuser-Busch Cos.

will be higher yet. The potential loss on a hostile transaction is even larger in those cases. Many arbitrageurs stay away from hostile transactions.

Few hostile bids go as smoothly as the Anheuser-Busch merger. The sheer size of the transaction, almost $50 billion, limited the circle of other acquirers that were large enough to make a serious bid. This explains why the stock traded at a discount to the $65.00 offer. A serious risk is also the possible abandonment of the hostile bid by the hopeful buyer once it faces heavy opposition. Some firms shun headlines that make them appear as ruthlessly aggressive corporate raiders.

Had Grupo Modelo become involved in the bidding, a bidding war would have broken out. Bidding wars come about for a variety of reasons. Sometimes they are the result of an unwilling target that seeks a white knight. This is a buyer who is friendly to management. At other times, a target may have a unique strategic value that its competitors do not want to see fall into the hands of each another.

Bidding wars in stock-for-stock mergers present a special risk for arbitrageurs. Most of the time, it is best to stay out of these transactions until the dust has settled. The problem is that an arbitrageur needs to establish a long/short position between a target and a bidding acquirer. However, it is not clear which of the bidders to short. The highest bidder changes in each round of bidding. When an arbitrageur is short one bidder and another wins, there could be a short squeeze on the bidder that was shorted. Like hostile bids, bidding wars are too speculative for most arbitrageurs. It is best to stay away from bidding wars, or build small positions carefully with limited exposure and partial hedging.

CHAPTER 4

Deal Structures: Mergers and Tender Offers

The preceding chapters mostly ignored the structure of the deal. When the timing of the closing of a merger was discussed, I alluded briefly to the difference in speed with which tender offers or mergers are completed. Differences between tender offers and mergers run deeper, and this chapter describes the structure of mergers in more detail.

A merger is a structure where two companies are integrated into a single entity. The buyer is normally the surviving corporation, and the target ceases to exist as it is integrated into the buyer. Target shareholders receive cash, stock of the acquirer, or a mix of both. The acquirer buys the target firm directly.

In contrast, in a tender offer, the acquirer buys the shares of the target firm from the target shareholders. Therefore, a second step is needed to complete the transaction: a merger in which the target is merged into the acquirer.

MERGERS

In a direct merger (see Figure 4.1), the target firm merges directly into the acquirer. Shareholders of the target receive the merger consideration. To the extent that they receive stock of the acquirer, they become shareholders of the buyer. Direct mergers are not very popular because they require the approval of the shareholders of both target and acquirer. Therefore, a more common merger structure is an indirect merger in which the acquirer forms a wholly owned subsidiary that merges with the target. These structures involve three firms and are known as triangular mergers. The merger subsidiary (or merger sub) is a corporation that is created only for the purpose of effecting the merger.

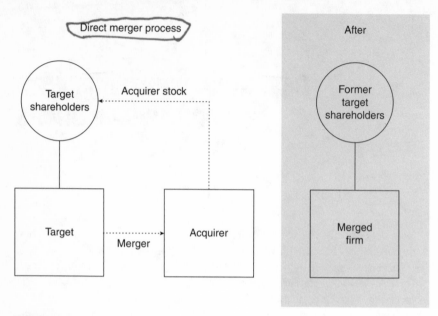

FIGURE 4.1 Direct Merger

Two types of triangular mergers are possible. In a forward triangular merger, the merger sub merges with the target, and the merger sub is the surviving entity, as shown in Figure 4.2(a). In a reverse triangular merger shown in Figure 4.2(b), the target is the surviving corporation. Reverse triangular mergers are by far the most favored transaction structures.

The choice between direct mergers or the two types of triangular mergers is driven by tax and legal considerations. In a direct merger, the buyer acquires all assets and also all liabilities of the target.

When the target is the surviving corporation, all its contracts and licenses are maintained. This can be particularly important when complex licensing applications have to be maintained in heavily regulated industries, such as financial services, air transportation, or casinos. If the target company is merged out of existence through a direct or forward triangular merger, all contracts and licenses must be assigned to the surviving corporation. Similarly, debt may not have to be refinanced when the borrower continues to exist. Assignment of contracts and refinancing of debt can take a considerable amount of time for larger firms.

The tax treatment of mergers is governed by Section 368 of the Internal Revenue Code. As a general principle, stock-for-stock mergers are tax-free.

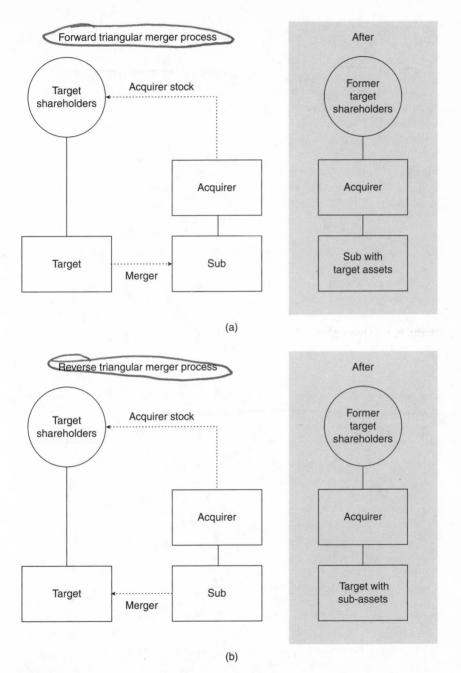

FIGURE 4.2 (a) Forward Triangular Merger, (b) Reverse Triangular Merger

In mixed cash and stock mergers, the stock portion is tax-free. The cash portion of the merger is referred to as boot.

In reverse triangular mergers, the stock portion is tax-free only if it is not less than 80 percent of the consideration received. In a forward triangular merger, only 50 percent of the consideration needs to be stock. In a direct merger, any combination of stock and cash or other property can be used to maintain the tax-free status of the stock portion. The relevant date for the determination is the closing date of the merger.

Even if merging companies chose a triangular merger structure, they can combine later into a single firm. Such later combinations, known as upstream mergers, are subjected to the tax treatment as if they were completed at the time of the original transaction. Therefore, it is possible to perform a reverse triangular merger with a cash consideration of more than 20 percent if it is followed shortly by an upstream merger. The two transactions will be collapsed into one by the Internal Revenue Service and considered a direct merger for tax purposes.

Arbitrageurs can identify the type of merger from the disclosures in the Securities and Exchange Commission (SEC) filings. Exhibit 4.1 is an excerpt from the merger agreement of Wilshire Enterprises, Wilshire was hoping to be acquired for cash only in a forward triangular merger that eventually collapsed.

EXHIBIT 4.1 DESCRIPTION OF A FORWARD TRIANGULAR MERGER IN ARTICLE I OF THE MERGER AGREEMENT OF WILSHIRE ENTERPRISES

Section 1.1 The Merger. Upon the terms and subject to the conditions of this Agreement and in accordance with the DGCL, at the Effective Time (as defined herein), Merger Sub shall be merged with and into the Company. As a result of the Merger, the separate corporate existence of Merger Sub shall cease and the Company shall continue as the surviving corporation of the Merger (the "Surviving Corporation") and a wholly owned subsidiary of Parent.

Source: PREM14A of Wilshire Enterprises filed on July 22, 2008.

The proxy statements also contain descriptions of the type of merger. Exhibit 4.2 shows excerpts of the proxy statement of the acquisition of

Celebrate Express by Liberty Media. This merger was structured as a reverse triangular merger, which is described in the last sentence. Celebrate Express was acquired for cash only.

EXHIBIT 4.2 REVERSE TRIANGULAR MERGER IN THE ACQUISITION OF CELEBRATE EXPRESS BY LIBERTY MEDIA

Celebrate Express, Inc.

Celebrate Express is a Washington corporation that was formed in June 1994. Celebrate Express is a provider of celebration products serving families with young children, via the Internet and catalogs. We currently operate two brands, Birthday Express and Costume Express, which respectively offer high-quality children's party products and children's costumes and accessories.

Our principal executive offices are located at 11232 120th Avenue NE, Kirkland, Washington 98033 and our telephone number is (425) 250-1064. Our common stock is publicly traded on the Nasdaq Global Market under the symbol "BDAY."

Liberty Media Corporation and Washington Merger Sub, Inc.

Liberty is a holding company which, through its ownership of interests in subsidiaries and other companies, holds interests in a broad range of electronic retailing, media, communications and entertainment businesses, attributed to three tracking stock groups: (1) the Liberty Interactive Group, (2) the Liberty Entertainment Group, and (3) the Liberty Capital Group. Shares of the tracking stock groups trade on Nasdaq under the symbols LINTA, LINTB, LCAPA, LCAPB, LMDIA and LMDIB. Liberty's wholly owned subsidiary, BuySeasons, Inc., has entered into a distribution agreement with Celebrate Express in connection with the merger agreement.

(Continued)

EXHIBIT 4.2 REVERSE TRIANGULAR MERGER IN THE ACQUISITION OF CELEBRATE EXPRESS BY LIBERTY MEDIA (*Continued*)

Liberty's principal executive offices are located at 12300 Liberty Boulevard, Englewood, Colorado and its telephone number is (720) 875-5400.

Merger Sub is a Washington corporation and was organized solely for the purpose of entering into the merger agreement and consummating the transactions contemplated by the merger agreement. It has not conducted any activities to date other than activities incidental to its organization and in connection with the transactions contemplated by the merger agreement. Merger Sub is an indirect wholly owned subsidiary of Liberty.

Under the terms of the merger agreement, Merger Sub will merge with and into Celebrate Express. Celebrate Express will survive the merger and Merger Sub will cease to exist.

Source: DEF14A proxy statement filed by Celebrate Express on August 7, 2008.

TENDER OFFERS

In a tender offer, the buyer purchases the target indirectly. The buyer asks the shareholders of the target company to tender their shares into the offer. Most tender offers are friendly and are done after an agreement has been negotiated between the target and the acquirer. However, because no agreement between the target and the acquirer is necessary, a tender offer is the vehicle used in hostile acquisitions. The acquirer simply asks the shareholders to tender their shares directly to the acquirer. The transaction takes place between shareholders and the acquirer, so that it can occur even when the target firm is opposed to the acquisition. In such a hostile transaction, the acquirer replaces the board of the target once it has sufficient shares and then acquires control.

The advantage of a tender offer is the speed with which it can be executed and the absence of a shareholder vote with the associated proxy solicitation. Shareholders vote with their feet in that they can tender their shares or not.

It is impossible to obtain full control of a public company with a shareholder base of thousands, possibly millions, of small holders through a tender offer. There will always be some shareholders who do not tender. This is why tender offers are structured as two-step transactions.

Step 1. The acquirer seeks to get as many shares as possible in the tender offer.

Step 2. Once a certain threshold is reached, the acquirer squeezes out the remaining shareholders through a short-form merger.

A short-form merger allows the acquirer to cash out remaining shareholders if it holds more than a threshold percentage of a firm. The level of the threshold depends on the state of incorporation and lies between 85 and 95 percent. In Delaware, it is 90 percent.

Tender offers often are extended to allow shareholders who have not yet tendered to do so when an acquirer does not reach the requisite ownership level for the short-form merger. As the offer is extended, the shareholder base turns over, and more arbitrageurs will hold stock in the target. Arbitrageurs are more likely to tender their shares than other investors. In case several extensions still are insufficient, buyers include top-up options in their offers: The target agrees to issue sufficient shares to the buyer to bring the ownership to the level where a short-form merger can be completed. The number of shares that must be issued is calculated in this way:

$$T = \frac{P \times N - O}{1 - P} \tag{4.1}$$

where T is the number of shares to be acquired through the top-up option.
        N is the total number of outstanding shares.
        O is the number of shares owned.
        P is the percentage required by state law to perform a short-form merger.

A problem with the top-up option is that a large number of shares must be issued to increase the ownership of the acquirer. This is possible only if a sufficient number of shares has been authorized. In addition, if more than 20 percent of the shares are issued, most exchanges require shareholder approval. Arbitrageurs can estimate the probability of completion of the deal from the number of shares that must be issued.

COMPARISON OF MERGERS AND TENDER OFFERS

The speed of completion works in favor of tender offers, which are much faster to complete than mergers. The SEC reviews tender offer documents while the offer is open; in a merger, the SEC must approve the merger's proxy materials before they can be distributed to shareholders. A tender offer must be open for as little as 20 days, whereas the advance notice period for the shareholder meeting to approve a merger is at least 30 days. Further time may be required if the buyer must register new shares. Moreover, the waiting period under the Hart-Scott-Rodino Act (see Chapter 10) for a cash tender offer is shortened to 15 days compared to 30 days in a merger, which makes it possible to close the transaction earlier. All these facts suggest that the default acquisition method should be a tender offer.

The difference in speed at which mergers and tender offers can be completed can be seen in statistics of actual transactions. Table 4.1 shows the timing of mergers and tender offers in the years from 1980 to 2005. It can be seen that for public targets, tender offers always close faster than mergers. For private targets, however, mergers are faster. This difference reflects the delay that public companies experience due to the filing of proxy

TABLE 4.1   Timing in Mergers and Tender Offers, 1980 to 2005

| | | | | Trading Days from Initial Control Bid to Effective Date (*) | | | |
| | | Public Status | | | Quartiles | | |
	Target	Bidder	No. of Observations	Mean	Median	Lowest	Highest
Entire Sample			25,166	64.62	42	0	100
Merger			22,030	62.42	39	0	100
	Public	Public	5,147	107.92	96	63	136
	Public	Private	1,766	97.84	86	42	136
	Private	Public	11,131	48.42	19	0	73
	Private	Private	3,986	27.09	0	0	28
Tender			3,136	80.06	52	30	98
	Public	Public	1,257	71.44	49	31	85
	Public	Private	1,030	97.8	67	34	123
	Private	Public	533	73.61	43	21	84

* "Effective date" is defined here as the day of the shareholder vote approving the transaction, not the closing date, which is the relevant date used in this book for the most part.

Source: S. Betton and K. S. Thorburn, "Corporate Takeovers," in B. E. Eckbo, ed., *Handbook of Empirical Corporate Finance*, Vol. 2 (Amsterdam: Elsevier, 2008), 304. Reprinted with permission of Elsevier.

statements. Private companies do not have to go through an SEC review of proxy statements and therefore can close their transactions faster.

A corollary of the increased speed of the tender offer is the lower likelihood of the emergence of a competing bid from another buyer. A potential acquirer needs a certain amount of time to conduct due diligence, and the time frame of a tender offer is simply too short for thorough research. In addition, if the competing bidder needs to raise additional capital to make the acquisition, it is unlikely to find sources of capital quickly enough to beat the original tender offer's deadline. This is definitely a plus from the acquirer's point of view; for investors and arbitrageurs, however, it reduces the probability of getting a higher value for their shares.

Shareholder acceptance is easier to obtain in a tender offer than in a merger. In a merger, shareholders can vote if they owned shares on the record date. The record date is four to eight weeks before the vote takes place. Many shareholders sell their holdings after the record date and before the date of the shareholder meeting. They have the right to vote at the shareholder meeting but no longer have an interest in voting shares of a company that they do not own. The new owners of the shares, who would have an interest in voting, do not have the right to vote because they did not own the shares on the record date. The result is that these shares are not voted at all. Shares that do not vote in favor are counted as voting against the merger. Therefore, a large turnover in the investor base after the announcement of a merger makes it more difficult for the target company to obtain shareholder approval. One way to improve the odds is to set the record date at a longer interval after the announcement of the merger. This gives shareholders time to sell and arbitrageurs time to accumulate shares. Arbitrageurs naturally have an interest in the closing of the merger and will vote their holdings in favor. If a large premium is paid in a merger, then long-term holders are more likely to sell to arbitrageurs than when the premium is modest. Therefore, the period between the announcement of a merger and the record date should be longer for mergers with larger premia than for those with smaller premia.

Tender offers have one major drawback that limits their use: the best price Rule 14d-10. This rule means that all shareholders must receive the same merger consideration no matter when they tender their shares. The price paid to all must be the highest that is paid to any shareholder. Courts interpreted this rule in a very broad sense. Until November 2006, consideration received in a merger was interpreted by some courts to include also bonuses paid to management, noncompete payments, and golden parachutes and other executive compensation if it becomes due as a result of the acquisition. A tender offer had to pass an "integral part of the tender offer" test in order to avoid violating the best price rule. Under this test, if a payment is connected with the transaction, such as a change of control payment that is triggered by the transaction, then it is part of the price paid and violates Rule 14d-10. As a result, transactions in which large golden parachutes are made, or where executives continue to own shares—for example, as part of a co-investment with a private equity fund—had to be structured as mergers rather than tender offers. Other courts used a more lenient standard, the "bright line" test. Under this test, the best price rule applied only to transactions that occurred while the tender offer was pending. The legal uncertainty created by these divergent interpretations limited the use of tender offers.

In November 2006, the SEC issued a clarification to Rule 14d-10 that made tender offers more attractive. Under the new and current standards, compensation paid to employees is no longer considered "integral part of the tender offer" if two conditions are met:

1. The compensation is related to services rendered in the past or future, or related to noncompete agreements (i.e., services that are not rendered).
2. This compensation cannot be based on the number of shares tendered by the employee.

This change was done through the addition of only a few words to one sentence in the rule. The original Rule 14-d10 read:

> The consideration paid to any security holder *pursuant to the tender offer* is the highest consideration paid to any other security holder *during such tender offer*. [Italics added.]

The amended Rule 14-d10 reads:

> The consideration paid to any security holder *for securities tendered in the tender offer* is the highest consideration paid to any other security holder *for securities tendered in the tender offer*. [Italics added.]

A direct consequence of the update of Rule 14d-10 has been an expanded use of tender offers, including by private equity firms. The incentive structure of private equity firms previously prevented them from using tender offers. During the first six months of 2007 at least 29 tender offers for U.S. targets with a market cap in excess of $200 million were announced, compared with just 5 for the same period in 2006. This trend is expected to continue.

A remaining problem with tender offers is the financing of the shares that are acquired in the tender. Because the company remains public between the completion of the first step, the tender offer, and the second step, the short-form merger, the investment bank financing a tender offer is subject to the margin requirements of Regulation T (Reg. T). Under Reg. T, customers must have at least 50 percent equity in their account at the time of the purchase of a security on credit.

Overall, tender offers remove many of the protections for investors that mergers provide. For a start, appraisal rights are not available in a tender offer. Only in the subsequent short-form merger can shareholders exercise their appraisal rights. Appraisal rights are discussed in Chapter 11.

For investors, another big disadvantage of tender offers over mergers is the lower fiduciary standard to which boards of directors are held in a tender offer. As we discuss in Chapter 6, courts apply a high standard of entire fairness in a merger. In a tender offer, however, courts only evaluate whether the tender offer was coercive. As long as there is no coercion, a tender offer will pass legal muster. In addition, there is no obligation for the board of the target to seek a maximum price for shareholders. We discuss this in more detail in Chapter 9, when we look at the use of tender offers to squeeze out minority shareholders.

The absence of a shareholder vote is also a drawback, in particular for institutional investors. Many institutions rely in their voting on the advice of the major proxy advisory services. These services do not provide recommendations on tender offers because no shareholder vote is involved. As a result, many institutions simply go with the default decision of tendering their shares. Institutional investors may not have as sound a basis for tendering their shares as they would if they were voting on a merger.

Courts take a somewhat naive position when they assume that tender offers are voluntary and that shareholders have a choice whether to tender or not. Most institutional investors will not make a careful evaluation of a tender offer but simply follow the management recommendation to tender. It takes the initiative of an aggressive activist investor to stop institutions from tendering their shares. It is easier for shareholders opposed to a buyout to solicit proxies against the transaction in a merger than to convince investors not to tender their shares.

Moreover, extension risk introduces a strong incentive to tender rather than withhold shares. An investor who does not tender shares eventually will be cashed out at the same price in the second step when the short-form merger closes. This delay can last anywhere from a few days to several months. The investor loses the time value of money in this period, because the ultimate payment after the short-form merger must be the same as that in the tender and cannot pay interest for the forgone period of time. Therefore, it is always optimal to tender unless opposition to the transaction is so strong that the probability of the deal not closing, or the price being increased, is very high.

Even companies that are not current on their financial statements can be acquired through a tender offer. If the company were to be acquired through

TABLE 4.2 Cumulative Abnormal Stock Returns to Targets and Bidders (Individually and Combined) Relative to the Initial Bid Date

		Target CAR			Initial Bidder CAR			Combined CAR	
	Number	Run-up (−41,−2)	Announcement (−1,1)	Number	Run-up (−41,−2)	Announcement (−1,1)	Number	Run-up (−41,−2)	Announcement (−1,1)
Merger	6,836			13,995			3,939		
Mean		0.0619	0.1338		0.0050	0.0069		0.0071	0.0060
Median		0.0481	0.1134		−0.0024	−0.0008		0.0070	0.0037
Z-Score		20.7051	88.2153		−2.2479	−3.8858		3.5536	7.7429
% positive		0.6181	0.8212		0.4921	0.4920		0.5268	0.5380
Tender Offer	2,320			1,468			837		
Mean		0.0868	0.1881		0.0060	0.0076		0.0090	0.0335
Median		0.0693	0.1707		0.0006	0.0011		0.0073	0.0232
Z-Score		14.9492	52.7321		0.5420	0.9110		2.6312	18.4987
% positive		0.6427	0.8573		0.5014	0.5123		0.5245	0.6941

Source: S. Betton, and K. S. Thorburn, "Corporate Takeovers," in B. E. Eckbo, ed., *Handbook of Empirical Corporate Finance*, Vol. 2 (Amsterdam: Elsevier, 2008), 363–364. Reprinted with permission of Elsevier.

a merger, it would have to update its financial statements to become current on its SEC filings before it could solicit proxies for a merger. In a tender offer, however, an acquirer can purchase a target company even if shareholders have no basis to evaluate the offer or determine whether the price paid is reasonable. A company that is delinquent on its SEC filings usually trades at a distressed price; it may even be delisted from an exchange and be relegated to the pink sheets if it cannot update its filings promptly. This uncertainty about the company's financial condition leads to significant selling pressure and a steep drop in its share price. Such a firm can be bought at a price that is much lower than what shareholders would have accepted if they were informed fully about the company's value and prospects. Shareholders will accept cash, even if they think it is less than the value of the firm, rather than hold a pink sheet company that is delinquent in its filings.

Finally, an interesting difference between mergers and tender offers can be seen in the returns earned by shareholders of target and acquirer before and after the announcement of the transaction. Table 4.2 shows the cumulative abnormal returns (CARs) earned in the run-up to an announcement of a transaction between days 41 and 2 prior to the announcement, as well as from the day prior to the announcement until the day after. It can be seen that the abnormal returns are higher in tender offers than mergers. This is true for both the target and the acquirer. Abnormal returns are defined by the authors of this study as the excess return over the expected return $\alpha + \beta \times r_{market}$. This is a standard method for estimating excess returns used widely in the financial literature.

The conclusions that can be drawn from these results are not only that abnormal returns are higher for tenders than mergers but also, just as interestingly, that both transaction structures generate positive abnormal returns for the combination of target and acquirer. In layman's terms, on average, mergers are win-win situations for investors in all firms involved.

Pitfalls of
Merger Arbitrage

Financing

The most critical aspect an arbitrageur faces in assessing the probability of whether a merger will go through is the question of financing. This is primarily a concern for cash deals or mixed cash and stock deals. As soon as a deal has a cash component, the source of the funding becomes a potential source of trouble.

In a stock-for-stock merger, financing can also be a problem. This is less obvious, because this detail is buried deep inside the covenants for the target's bonds or loans. Target companies that have debt are often required by covenants in the loan or bond documentation to redeem their debt if a merger happens. These clauses are called "change of control covenants." If a target company has large amounts of debt outstanding, it may be difficult for a buyer to redeem the outstanding debt. This is especially true if the buyer is not very strong financially.

Merely from a net return point of view, some of the transactions least attractive for arbitrageurs are the purchases of small-cap firms by large corporations. In these cases, the buyer can often pay for the acquisition out of its cash on the balance sheet. The low risk is obvious to all market participants, and the spread reflects the low risk very quickly. The acquisition of Neoware by HP is a good example. The tender offer was announced on July 23, 2007, with an anticipated closing "in the fourth quarter of 2007." The transaction had a value of only $214 million. HP's quarterly report for April 30, 2007, showed a cash balance of $12 billion, and HP's quarterly cash flow from operations amounts to $4 billion. Not only did HP have more than enough cash on its balance sheet to pay for the acquisition, it had more than enough cash flow to pay for it in about one week. An arbitrageur can conclude safely that this deal has no financing risk. In such a simple transaction, the rest of the market came to the same conclusion very quickly, as the chart of Neoware's stock price shows (see Figure 5.1). Neoware traded at no meaningful discount to HP's buyout price of $16.25 per share.

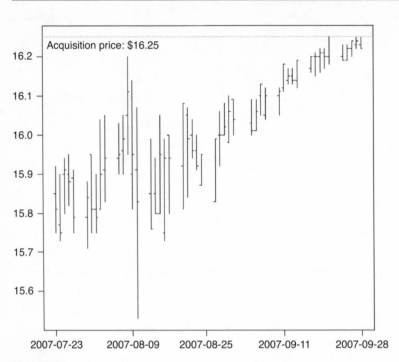

FIGURE 5.1   Neoware's Stock Price after HP's Acquisition Proposal

In the absence of any real risk, the spread narrowed very quickly and amounted to only $0.38 on August 23, 2007. An arbitrageur would assume a closing on December 31 and calculate an annualized spread of only 5.9 percent, not attractive to any arbitrageur. The actual outcome was an earlier closing that took place on September 30, so that the annualized spread would have amounted to 8.5 percent. Of course, the actual timing of the closing was still uncertain on August 23, when an arbitrageur could have locked in the spread of $0.38.

An arbitrageur always should understand the rationale behind such an acquisition. Several scenarios can be distinguished when a large company buys a smaller one:

▪ *A buyer acquires a target firm in order to acquire its technology.* These acquisitions are examples of vertical integration.

  These transactions tend to be safe because strategic considerations matter more than price. Investors tend to think in terms of earnings and consider loss-making firms as very risky. A strategic buyer, however, is thinking in terms of unique intellectual property, strategic fit, timeliness, cutting off competitors from technology, and at best replacement cost as far as financial aspects are concerned. It is not unusual to see unusually high multiples in this type of transaction. Moreover, some technology companies have more or less outsourced their research and development departments to venture capital firms; rather than having to expense their development cost when they do their own research, they can record goodwill if instead they acquire the technology through the purchase of another firm. This will boost their own earnings and allows them to benefit from significant leeway in the timing of the eventual write-off of the goodwill.

- *A buyer acquires a profitable firm in a multiple arbitrage.*

If a buyer's stock trades at a high multiple and it acquires a firm that trades at a lower multiple, it will boost its own valuation because its multiple will now be applied to the earnings of the combined entity. WorldCom was a prime example of this type of strategy and illustrates the inherent risks. As far as merger arbitrage is concerned, multiple arbitrage tends to be a safe bet. Roll-ups and similar forms of horizontal integration are usually examples of multiple arbitrage.

The usual rationale for a merger is either growth or synergies. This rationale also applies when a large firm buys a smaller one but is less relevant. The addition of the small firm will not yield cost savings through synergies or additional growth that are noticeable. Most likely, these effects will be diluted by the large firm's other activities. Diversification was a popular reason for merging during the conglomerate boom in the 1960s and 1970s but has since been discredited with some notable exceptions, such as General Electric.

The analysis of financing risk becomes more complex when a buyer must raise funds to consummate the purchase of a target. The analysis often can again be rather simple when a large firm buys a smaller one and has more than enough cash flow to cover the interest expense and repayment. As the size of the acquisition grows relative to the size of the acquirer, financing will become a critical component of the risk.

The biggest financing risk is found in leveraged buyouts (LBOs). Frequently they are management buyouts (MBOs) backed by private equity. Almost always, private equity buyouts have strong management involvement, and the line between MBOs and private equity buyouts has become somewhat blurred. In these transactions, the size effect is inverted. A small equity contribution by the sponsor of the acquisition is used to buy firms that are a multiple of the size of the acquirer. In an MBO, the acquirers ultimately are individuals. No bigger discrepancy in size can be found elsewhere.

These transactions have in common that the buyer uses very little equity to buy the target and borrows most of the funds required for the transaction from banks. In addition to bank loans, bonds are often issued, and the period until the issuance of the bonds is funded through bridge loans. Banks resell the loans in the secondary market.

TYPES OF DEBT FUNDING

In the vast majority of cases, debt used in the acquisition of a company is underwritten by a bank. The debt is structured into several different tranches until the transaction is consummated. It is expected that some bank debt will be repaid immediately after the completion of the merger; other debt will be replaced by bonds later on. There are three principal uses for the debt:

1. *Repayment of existing debt that becomes due under change of control provisions.*

   A common form of protection for lenders against the risk of an increased debt load after a buyout is change of control clauses. If the ownership changes, the debt becomes due immediately. The lender can waive this provision in circumstances where the debt load is not overly burdensome, and the debt remains outstanding. However, in most mergers, lenders seek repayment. This is even more so the case in leveraged buyouts because creditors can get higher interest from new, more risky debt issued under buyout conditions. High-yield bonds often require redemption at a premium if a change of control occurs. If a bond would normally be redeemed at par, the redemption price under a change of control provision is often 101 percent, of course plus accrued interest. Sometimes early redemption under change of control clauses is subject to a sliding scale, where the premium is higher in early years and declines later. Change of control covenants are used widely in debt of U.S. companies and have been introduced only recently into European bonds after bondholders suffered losses when issuing companies were bought up and suffered from downgrades when they took on additional debt.

2. *Payment to selling shareholders.*

   The payment to acquire the shares held by the previous shareholders is the biggest expense in a merger. Most public companies have a low level of leverage, and the value of the equity represents the biggest portion of the acquisition value.

3. *Transaction costs.*

Expenses for investment bankers and lawyers as well as smaller items such as Securities and Exchange Commission (SEC) filing fees and shareholder solicitation represent several percent of the total cost. Investment banking fees are by far the largest element of these costs and typically amount to 5 percent of the value of the transaction. Golden parachute payments for managers are also a form of transaction costs.

Investors in debt are mainly concerned with getting paid back. Unlike investors in equity, their upside is limited to the interest received, while their downside risk is the entire loan amount. The interest charged on a loan will depend not only on the riskiness of the underlying venture but also on the order in which the debt is repaid. Every homeowner knows that the interest charged on a mortgage is less than that for a home equity line of credit because the risk of loss is higher for the latter than the former. The same principle is true for debt used in the financing of mergers. We will digress briefly to discuss the hierarchy of repayment for different types of debt if a company goes into default.

Here is a list showing the priority of claims (highest to lowest) in a chapter 11 bankruptcy proceeding. Outstanding payments with the highest priority are paid first, and any funds left over are then available for the payment of the next priority, and so on.

1. Secured debt, to the extent that the value of the asset covers the associated debt
2. Bankruptcy administrative costs
3. Postpetition bankruptcy expenses
4. Wages, subject to limitations
5. Employee benefit plan contributions, subject to limitations
6. Unsecured customer deposits, subject to limitations
7. Federal, state, and local taxes
8. Unfunded pension liabilities, subject to limitations
9. Unsecured claims
10. Preferred stock
11. Common stock

Lenders will try to make secured loans whenever possible. Unsecured loans are much riskier and are not paid until a long laundry list of other claims have been paid. Banks in particular have enough influence on an issuer to negotiate a senior position for themselves in the capital structure. As a result, most bank loans are secured and are held by banks.

The situation changes for bond financing. Bonds are created with the intention of providing an easily tradable instrument to investors. Although investment banks underwrite bond offerings, thereby providing guaranteed initial liquidity for the issuer, it is not their intention to hold on to the bonds for a long period of time. Instead, investment banks sell the loans to investors. The multitude of investors who each acquires a small piece of the pie reduces their leverage relative to the issuer. As a result, most bonds are unsecured.

Another important difference between loans and bonds is the regulatory nature of the two forms of financing. Bonds are publicly traded and are registered with the SEC. This means that the issuer must make periodic filings with the SEC and comply with numerous regulations, in particular Sarbanes-Oxley. In transactions in which the issuer is going private, the issuance of public bonds would negate some of the advantages of no longer being a public company. This problem can be avoided if the bonds are issued as a private placement; however, the transfer of such bonds is restricted, which in turn negates the advantage of having a bond as an easily transferable instrument.

Bank Loans

Although bridge loans are also issued by banks, we are referring here to more permanent loans. For larger buyouts, several loans with different maturity dates are used in order to avoid overwhelming the borrower with a single large repayment. In practice, the debt is rarely paid off; most frequently it simply is refinanced with new loans or bonds. The advantage of loans is that they are held by a small number of banks. More recently, loans have sometimes been resold in the secondary market to institutional holders. This allows banks to free up their balance sheets for new loans and allows other creditors to invest in debt on terms available otherwise only to banks. Collateralized loan obligations (CLOs) were among the most active buyers of acquisition related bank loans in 2005–2006 but have since scaled back their buying. Whether they will return to their peak level of activity depends on investors regaining confidence in these vehicles, which were battered by the credit crisis.

Bank loans often are secured; if unsecured, they are senior to other unsecured debt. Almost anything can be used as collateral. Inventory, receivables, intellectual property, and equipment are the most frequent types of collateral. Banks will lend up to 85 percent of the value of the collateral for accounts receivables, less for equipment. Inventory is often perishable (such as fashion items for a retailer) and may be borrowed against for less than half of its value. For long-term loans, real estate is the principal type of collateral.

The term or maturity is the defining characteristic of bank debt. Most loans pay interest at a variable rate.

Short-term loans are usually promissory notes often issued under lines of credit. They have maturities of less than one year, commonly 90 days. They are payable upon demand by the lender. The borrower has to rely on the strength of its relationship with the lender and also on the willingness and ability of the lender to continue to fund the loan. Short-term loans tend to have simple documentation and are often unsecured. Banks see these loans as low-risk lending because they are paid back quickly, and a borrower's financial condition is unlikely to deteriorate significantly over the short maturity of these loans.

Intermediate and long-term loans have 1- to 15-year horizons and are more complex to close. Due to their longer maturity, they often carry restrictive covenants to protect the interests of the lender. These covenants limit the ability of the borrower to pay dividends, sell assets, or make other noncritical business expenses. Term loans can be amortizing or have a balloon. A "balloon" refers to the entire amount being due at one time. A combination of both is also frequently found: The loan amortizes according to a schedule that stretches beyond its term. The remaining balance is due at maturity. Other sinking fund features are less common but can be negotiated if needed. Larger mergers are structured with several staggered term loans of different maturities.

A new development in the 2000s is the growth of a market in leveraged loans. They are similar to normal bank loans in that they are secured and carry variable interest rates. However, their term is longer and compares to that of junk bonds. More important, the issuers underlying the loan are companies that have a large amount of leverage—hence the name of the loans. Some investors view leveraged as a substitute for junk bonds. It is the demand from such investors, in particular hedge funds and CLOs, that led to an explosive growth in the leveraged loan issuance in recent years. Leveraged loans provide the investor with a more senior position in the capital structure than junk bonds, which are unsecured, yet provide an attractive spread over the London Interbank Offered Rate (LIBOR). For the issuer, the cost of leveraged loans is less than that of junk bonds because the loans are secured and the bonds are unsecured. For banks, the emergence of the market has meant that loans can be made to companies that in past years would not have met underwriting standards. Banks are willing to make the loans and hold them in their inventory briefly because the loans are expected to be sold off quickly to investors, so that the credit risk for the bank is minimal. However, banks can earn generous fee income for arranging these loans.

Bridge Loans

Some debt is expected to be repaid very quickly after the completion of the merger. Only a temporary form of financing is needed, which is called a "bridge loan." Potential sources of funds could be:

- *Proceeds from the issuance of bonds or the remortgaging of assets.* The merger is often completed in a very short time frame, whereas such financing maneuvers can take longer. In addition, potential lenders are not willing to make loans if a merger is pending.
- *Sale of assets or noncore businesses.* Sale-leaseback transactions or the disposition of product lines that the acquirer does not need fall into this category. The factoring or sale of accounts receivable also tends to take longer.
- *Cash on the balance sheet of the target.* The acquirer cannot access cash balances of the target company until the merger is completed but must pay for the shares immediately. A bridge loan is used to overcome the timing difference in the payment. This is particularly relevant for cash-rich target companies.

Sometimes bridge loans are provided as temporary financing until permanent financing in the form of bonds can be secured. Bonds tend to have change of control provisions, so that in many instances they can be issued only after the completion of a merger. For example, in a leveraged buyout, the target company will be the issuer of the bonds. Due to change of control provisions, the acquirer will finance the acquisition with a bridge loan and replace it with bonds issued by the target subsequent to the completion of the buyout. In contrast, in a strategic acquisition, the buyer may be able to arrange for permanent bond financing prior to the closing, because the bonds would be issued by the acquirer. There would be no need for bridge loans.

An atypical form of bridge financing was provided to Countrywide Financial when it was acquired by Bank of America in 2008. Countrywide was experiencing financial distress as a result of credit losses on its subprime mortgage portfolio and needed additional capital. Rather than providing Countrywide with a loan, Bank of America invested in newly issued Series B preferred stock of Countrywide. Had Bank of America provided a loan to Countrywide, its financial leverage ratios would have deteriorated: more debt for the same amount of equity. Preferred stock, however, increased the amount of equity and hence improved generally accepted accounting principles (GAAP) as well as regulatory capital. The Series B preferred stock was canceled when the merger was closed.

Mezzanine Debt

Mezzanine debt derives its name from middle level in theater seating. It represents subordinated debt that structurally is inserted between a firm's senior debt and equity. It is used when banks and other senior lenders have maxed out their credit lines, the buyer is not willing or able to provide more equity contribution, and the resulting borrowing gap must be filled. It is a standard feature in leveraged buyout transactions. It can also used when a strategic buyer has limited cash and is unwilling to incur dilution by issuing stock for an acquisition.

Mezzanine debt is provided by specialized lenders, such as insurance companies or funds, and also CLOs. Mezzanine debt is more expensive than senior debt but cheaper than equity. In some instances, mezzanine debt is structured to receive no interest or principal payments until the senior lenders have been paid off.

Mezzanine debt often comes with a payment in kind (PIK) feature. Instead of paying interest in cash, PIK debt pays interest in the form of additional debt.[1] PIK debt increases the risk of mezzanine debt.

A PIK feature makes debt look more like equity, and this can convince banks to count it as debt. Banks often have leverage limits, above which they will not fund acquisitions. If PIK debt is counted as equity, the leverage of the firm is reduced and banks can lend. Holders of bonds with PIK features suffered significant losses in the high-yield bond meltdown of the late 1980s, and if history is a guidance, a similar outcome might face investors of the current wave of PIK debt.

Finally, mezzanine debt often is coupled with an equity "kicker" in the form of warrants.[2] Warrants reduce the cost of this debt, because mezzanine lenders are willing to charge a lower rate in exchange for the additional upside upon exercise of the warrant.

Bonds

Bonds encompass a wide range of financing arrangements. They differ from loans in that they are structured from the outset as securities that can be transferred easily in small pieces. Most corporate bonds are issued by large corporations to investors who seek a stable stream of income and safety. Bonds issued for acquisitions offer high rates, but at the price of higher risk. Low-grade bonds have been around since the early part of the twentieth century under various monikers. Since the 1970s, bonds issued with high yields have been known under the term "junk bonds," a term allegedly created by Michael Milken. The issuance of junk bonds grew dramatically during the 1970s and 1980s as investors began to be attracted to their risk/return profile. High-yield bonds have become an asset class in its own right.

Today, high-yields bonds play a secondary role in funding mergers to leveraged loans. Loans are easier, cheaper, and faster to arrange than junk bond issuances. Nevertheless, junk bonds continue to be issued to supplement leveraged loans in cases where the additional financing is needed and insufficient collateral is available for leveraged loans. Unlike in the 1980s, most junk bonds issued today are issued by low-rated companies that are not necessarily subject to an acquisition.

As mentioned previously, companies that issue junk bonds to the public must continue to report to the SEC and are subject to all related regulations just as if their equity were still traded publicly, including the burdensome Section 404 certification under Sarbanes-Oxley. For companies that are going private, it makes sense to avoid the issuance of junk bonds if possible.

Sale and Leaseback Financing

Companies rich in real assets are popular targets for financial buyers. During the recent buyout boom, private equity funds often acquired real estate investment trusts (REITs) due to their holdings of real estate. Even less obvious businesses rich in real estate holdings became popular buyout targets, such as self-storage firms or some retailers that had long-term leases for their stores.

In a sale-leaseback transaction, an asset is sold to a third party for cash and then leased back. This generates cash up front that can be used to pay for the acquisition, but in the long run, it reduces flexibility because the company must comply with the terms of the lease. For example, if the asset is no longer needed, it cannot be sold, but the lease must be terminated, most likely with a penalty. In the case of assets that appreciate in the long run (real estate), the company no longer benefits from that appreciation. This concern can be mitigated if the lease contains an option to buy.

There are many ways to structure sale-leaseback transactions. The accounting and tax treatment depends on the details. Title to the sold assets may or may not change hands; if it does not, the lessor is essentially a lender.

Another option to raise cash is an outright sale of assets. One of the largest buyouts of all times, the $39 billion acquisition of Equity Office Properties Trust by private equity group Blackstone, made headlines because within only six months, almost half the properties owned by Equity Office were sold. Blackstone recovered 70 percent of its investment through these sales.[3] This was a traditional sale of assets without a leaseback provision. Blackstone's bet was that it could acquire Equity Office for less than the sum of its parts, similar to the style of 1980s corporate raiders.

Hedge Fund Financing

When the debt markets became impossible to access after the meltdown of the subprime market in 2007, buyers in several mergers sought to access hedge fund financing directly rather than let banks underwrite and subsequently resell the debt. It remains to be seen whether such a disintermediation will become more common.

The largest transaction that used hedge fund financing was the acquisition of Goodman Global by private equity firm Hellman & Friedman LLC. In addition to obtaining financing from banks that had not been very active in the funding of LBOs, the buyers also received funding directly from hedge funds GSO Capital Partners and Farallon Capital Management. Direct financing can lower the cost by eliminating the intermediary, but also may complicate funding. Most private equity funds are small operations that do not have sufficient staff to manage a complete syndication with the same level of professionalism as an investment bank.

Hedge fund financing is no panacea that can substitute for bank financing at any time. Another transaction that sidestepped debt financing from banks was the attempt by producer and financier David Bergstein to acquire the film distribution firm Image Entertainment. Bergstein obtain a $60 million debt commitment directly from hedge fund D.B. Zwirn & Co. Unfortunately, Zwirn was going through some rough times. Its chief financial officer had left, and the SEC had launched an investigation amid allegations of improper booking of expenses. Although the amounts involved were immaterial compared to the $5 billion size of the fund, it was sufficient to rattle investors and trigger a flood of redemption requests reportedly amounting to $4 billion. Zwirn's problems were compounded by its investment strategy: It made loans to firms such as Bergstein's. The value of these loans is difficult to establish, and there is almost no secondary market. Given the problems Zwirn was facing, it was unable to provide the financing, and Bergstein was unable to come up with a replacement lender. The transaction failed to close.

Seller Financing

Financing an acquisition through a loan from the seller is a common practice in the acquisition of small businesses. For public companies, seller financing is rare but does happen in some small- and micro-cap transactions. It can be used to replace bank lending or as a supplemental source of debt. It is probably underused in the acquisition of public companies, even though it would be an attractive replacement for other forms of debt, especially in times when other borrowings are difficult to obtain.

Rather than receiving the purchase price up front, a seller obtains a note from the buyer that will be paid back over time. In effect, the seller doubles as a bank or bondholder. The author believes that in many cases of failed mergers, it would have been more advantageous for the shareholders to receive bonds or notes as payment than hold on to shares of a firm whose acquisition collapsed. Once a merger is dead, it is difficult to find another buyer willing to attempt an acquisition.

An example of seller financing was the installment sale of PDS Gaming, a company that leased and financed gaming equipment for casinos. PDS was taken private by its chief executive officer (CEO), Johan P. Finley, in September 2004. Shareholder received only $1.25 per share of the total $2.75 per-share merger consideration up front; the remaining $1.50 per share were paid in three equal installments of $0.50 over the next three years. Instead of using outside financing, the buyers obtained funding from the public shareholders by paying the merger consideration over time. Not many mergers are structured in this way, even though the author believes that many mergers that fail due to financing could be completed if the sponsors were relying on installment sales to shareholders. The PDS Gaming transaction had a value of only $7.5 million, which is indicative of the type of transaction where funds are held back.

Stapled Financing

Stapled financing is not a form of financing but rather a description of the timing of the commitment by banks. Financing is seen as one of the principal risks in many mergers. Buyers began in the early 2000s to prearrange financing for acquisitions even before the merger agreement was signed. It increases the certainty for the target firm that the buyer will be able to follow through on a transaction. This can be particularly helpful in an auction, where multiple buyers are bidding on a target. A buyer may be able to win the auction even if its price is not the highest if the stapled financing provides enough assurances to the target that its proposal is more likely to succeed than a higher one.

The drawback for a buyer is the additional cost incurred for the stapled financing. The banks arranging the package will do so for an added fee.

FINANCING OF MERGERS VERSUS TENDER OFFERS

There is a subtle difference in the funding of a straight merger compared to that of a tender offer. Tender offers are completed in a two-step process (see Chapter 4), whereas mergers are closed in one single step. In a tender offer, the financing for the first step is subject to Regulation T margin rules of the Federal Reserve. At the time the buyer has acquired shares of the target through the tender offer, there are still shares outstanding and traded. Therefore, the buyer is simply a controlling investor in a public company. Banks and brokers are prohibited from financing more than 50 percent of the market value of an investor's holdings if the stock is used as collateral. Therefore, tender offers are funded through unsecured bridge loans or private placements to the extent necessary to comply with Regulation T.

UNCERTAIN MERGER CONSIDERATION

In most merger transactions, the value to be received by the target's shareholders is predetermined. In a cash merger, a set dollar amount is paid for each share. In a stock-for-stock merger, the exchange ratio is either fixed or fluctuates around a collar. Either way, the value is either fixed or can be computed with reasonable effort through a predetermined formula.

However, there are occasionally transactions, mostly involving smaller companies, where the value that will be received is subject to adjustment in a more complex way than through a simple collar arrangement. These transactions require an extra amount of work by the arbitrageur to evaluate. Sometimes uncertainty can come from adjustments that can be made to the merger consideration based on performance benchmarks. In other mergers, the value of the consideration received can be difficult to determine.

Adjustments to Merger Consideration

Florida-based bank Coast Financial Holdings was experiencing losses when real estate loans in its local market became troubled. At the time, house prices were falling precipitously in Florida, and many borrowers were defaulting on their loans. Developers of real estate were also defaulting on construction loans. Coast struck an agreement with First Banks, Inc. of Missouri to sell itself for $22 million, or $3.40 per share. However, due to the rapid deterioration of Florida's real estate market, First Banks was unwilling to assume the risk of large losses entirely by itself. It created a deal structure whereby the merger consideration paid to shareholders was to be adjusted for losses incurred by Coast prior to the closing. The workings of the adjustment are shown in Exhibit 5.1. The final payment to shareholders came to $1.86 per share.

EXHIBIT 5.1 ADJUSTMENT OF THE MERGER CONSIDERATION IN THE ACQUISITION OF COAST FINANCIAL HOLDINGS

At the effective time of the merger, all issued and outstanding Common Shares will be canceled and converted into the right to receive an aggregate payment of $22,130,793.80 ("Initial Aggregate Purchase Price") less the Adjustment Amount as described below.

On the date that it is determined that all conditions for closing have been satisfied, to the extent that the sum of our allowance for loan and lease losses plus our tangible equity on the effective date of the merger (the "Reserve Plus Equity Amount") is less than the amount (referred to throughout this proxy statement as the Deficiency) that would be required to be added to the Reserve Plus Equity Amount for such amount to equal at least seventy-five percent (75%) of the sum of our non-performing loans and leases plus other real estate owned as of the effective date of the merger (the "NPL Plus OREO Amount") and this Deficiency is greater than One Million Dollars ($1,000,000), then the Initial Aggregate Purchase Price will be adjusted downward.

The actual adjustment will be computed determining the amount that would be required to be added to the Reserve Plus Equity Amount to allow the Reserve Plus Equity Amount to equal exactly seventy-five percent (75%) of the NPL Plus OREO Amount. The amount determined in the immediately preceding sentence will then be rounded, upward or downward, to the nearest $500,000 increment, with the rounded number being the actual adjustment to the Initial Aggregate Purchase Price (this rounded amount being referred to as the "Adjustment Amount"). The Initial Aggregate Purchase Price less the Adjustment Amount is referred to as the "Final Aggregate Purchase Price." For these purposes, the allowance for loan and lease losses, tangible equity, non-performing loans and leases and other real estate owned will be determined in accordance with our past practices, consistently applied.

The amount that will be paid for each Common Share will be determined by dividing the Final Aggregate Purchase Price by the number of Common Shares issued and outstanding immediately prior to the effective time of the merger (the "Per Share Merger Price").

If the Deficiency exceeds $10 million, then Coast Financial and First Banks each will have the right to terminate the Merger Agreement.

Based on the above formula and depending on the amount of the Deficiency, the Per Share Merger Price could be reduced from the initially offered price of $3.40 to as low as $1.86 prior to triggering such termination rights. . . .

For illustration purposes only, set forth is the calculation of the Adjustment Amount and the resulting Per Share Merger Price based on various Deficiency levels.

Deficiency	Initial Aggregate Purchase Price	Adjustment Amount	Final Aggregate Purchase Price	Per Share Merger Price (1)
—	$ 22,130,793.80	—	$ 22,130,793.80	$ 3.40
$ 1,000,000	$ 22,130,793.80	—	$ 22,130,793.80	$ 3.40
$ 1,000,001	$ 22,130,793.80	$ (1,000,000.00)	$ 21,130,793.80	$ 3.25
$ 2,500,000	$ 22,130,793.80	$ (2,500,000.00)	$ 19,630,793.80	$ 3.02
$ 5,000,000	$ 22,130,793.80	$ (5,000,000.00)	$ 17,130,793.80	$ 2.63
$ 7,500,000	$ 22,130,793.80	$ (7,500,000.00)	$ 14,630,793.80	$ 2.25
$ 10,000,000	$ 22,130,793.80	$ (10,000,000.00)	$ 12,130,793.80	$ 1.86
$ 12,500,000 (2)	$ 22,130,793.80	$ (12,500,000.00)	$ 9,630,793.80	$ 1.48

(1) Based on outstanding Common Shares of 6,509,057.

(2) A Deficiency exceeding $10,000,000 provides both of the parties a right to terminate the Merger Agreement.

The preceding is only an illustration of how the Adjustment Amount and the corresponding Per Share Merger Price is impacted by the existence of differing levels of an existing Deficiency. It is not necessarily indicative of the results of operations of Coast Financial now or in future periods or of any level of any future Deficiency.

As of September 30, 2007, the Deficiency was approximately $1,286,000 which would result in a payment of approximately $3.17 per share. In view of our current and anticipated performance, it is likely that the Deficiency will continue to increase in size and the amount that you will receive will be further reduced. There can be no assurance that the Deficiency will not increase substantially between the date of this proxy statement and the date that the Adjustment Amount and the resulting Per Share Merger Price is determined.

Source: DEFM14A filed on October 10, 2007.

Unusual Forms of Payment

Several other forms of payment are similar to seller financing. They are the placement of a portion of the merger proceeds into escrow to cover contingencies and the distribution of contingent value rights. Both forms of payment are used when there is a large element of uncertainty about some aspect of the acquired business. For example, funds are placed in escrow when there is a fundamentally different assessment between the target firm and the buyer about the risk of an aspect of the business. For example, a bank that has a division specializing in underwriting loans to boats may have a higher level of confidence in the loss risk of these loans than a buyer of that bank. Splitting the risk may not be acceptable—the buyer will still fear overpaying, whereas the target firm will feel it is not getting enough. A portion of the merger consideration is placed into escrow for a certain period of time until the actual losses, or lack thereof, become apparent. If there are no losses, the escrow will be distributed in full. If there are losses, the escrow will be reduced, and in some cases, there may be no distribution out of the escrow.

Another form of payment for uncertain future payments is done through contingent value rights (CVRs). A contingent value right pays the former target shareholders additional consideration if the anticipated but uncertain revenue is generated.

When Information Resources, Inc. was acquired by private equity funds Symphony Technology and Tennenbaum & Co. in late 2003 for $114 million, it was in litigation with the Dun & Bradstreet Corp., A.C. Nielsen Co., and IMS International, Inc. over certain anticompetitive practices by A.C. Nielsen that had kept Information Resources out of the European market. Information Resources was seeking damages in the amount of $350 million, to be trebled for punitive damages. The trust was structured so that Information Resources' former shareholders would receive 68 percent of all proceeds up to $200 million and 75 percent above $200 million, with the remainder going to the new owners of Information Resources. Due to the highly uncertain outcome of the litigation, the buyers were unwilling to risk paying the public shareholders a large amount that they may not be able to recover if they were to lose the litigation. Similarly, the public shareholders were not willing to sell Information Resources if they could potentially recover an additional $1 billion through litigation.

The CVR paid $0.7152 per share in May 2006, the shareholders' share of the aggregate settlement of $50 million minus expenses. An interesting twist on the Information Resources' CVRs is that they were traded publicly on the over the counter bulletin board. This additional liquidity benefited shareholders who wanted to sell at the prevailing market price. In contrast, escrow arrangements are not traded publicly. It is not possible to liquidate them. Their holders must wait until they pay out.

CVRs can also be used in large transactions. At the time of writing, Fresenius Medical Care is in the process of acquiring APP Pharmaceuticals Inc. for $3.7 billion ($23 per share) plus a CVR that would pay shareholders an additional $6 per share if APP meets certain earnings before interest, taxes, depreciation, and amortization (EBITDA) thresholds over the three years after the acquisition. Unlike the CVRs of Information Resources, APP's were not structured as a trust but as a debt security of a subsidiary of Fresenius under an indenture.

CVRs are efficient and flexible tools that can help shareholders obtain fair value when a part of the business has considerable upside that is very uncertain. Unfortunately, few boards consider these instruments when they negotiate a sale. Many boards are probably unaware of their existence. Others are swayed into believing that uncertain outcomes must be discounted into small present values. Although that is correct in a statistical approach, it does not make sense to leave a large windfall to the buyer. The boards of APP Pharmaceuticals and Information Resources should be lauded for their strong stance.

CONFLICTED ROLE OF INVESTMENT BANKS

Until recently, the world of finance was separated into two types of institutions: commercial banks that made loans and investment banks that trade and underwrite securities.

This distinction goes back to the instigation of the Glass-Steagall Act in 1933, when commercial banks and investment banks were separated in order to prevent some of the financial disasters that had struck during the Great Depression: Member banks of the Federal Reserve were prohibited from buying securities for their own account and from "issuing, underwriting, selling, or distributing, at wholesale or retail, or through syndicate participation, stock, bonds, debentures, notes or other securities" (Section 16). Similarly, investment banks were prohibited from engaging "at the same time to any extent whatever in the business of receiving deposits" (Section 21). By the 1990s, pressures arising from the evolving nature of the banking business made the separation of commercial and investment banking appear more and more anachronistic. This led to the partial repeal of Glass-Steagall through the Gramm-Leach-Bliley Act of 1999. Interestingly, Sections 16 and 21 were both left unchanged in the repeal. Instead, the two revoked sections, 20 and 32, deal with banks' ownership of investment banking subsidiaries and the interlock of banks' management with that of securities firms. This subtle distinction is often missed by commentators.

Today, the goal of commercial banks is to generate fees from both their commercial and their investment banking operations. A good illustration of their business philosophy is provided by former Citigroup CEO Charles "Chuck" Prince, who said in an unfortunate timing just weeks before the 2007 subprime meltdown began that "as long as the music is playing, you've got to get up and dance." As of mid-2008, Citigroup had written off $69 billion and raised $36 billion in cash.[4] Chuck Prince was no longer its CEO.

Another separation within financial institutions that is relevant for arbitrageurs occurs within investment banks. It concerns the distinction between the advisory and the underwriting activities of the bank. Underwriters earn their fees from the placement of securities with their clients, whereas bankers earn a fee for advising firms on the takeover. Typically, a banker will:

- Advise the target on strategic options well before a merger has been decided upon; this is often part of an ongoing relationship with the firm's executive.
- Assist the firm in selecting merger partners.
- Help with the negotiations.
- Value the firm and the principal terms.
- Issue a fairness opinion.

Investment banks have gone to great lengths in recent years to separate their underwriting businesses from their advisory activities. In street jargon, Chinese walls or firewalls keep personnel in the different divisions from talking to each other about pending deals.

To complicate matters further, investment banks often also take on the role of buyer. Aware of the negative perception that clients will get when a bank acts as buyer, adviser, and underwriter at the same time, some investment banks have spun off their private equity divisions into separate firms.

As a result, today banks play a dual role in mergers: They wear the investment banker hat and also that of the provider of financing. As such, they are slowly drifting toward the European banking industry's model of universal banks.

Merger and acquisition (M&A) advice is a major contributor to investment banks' profits and is particularly popular because, unlike trading and principal investments, providing advice requires little capital and hence boosts not just earnings but also return on capital. Average revenue per investment banking employee in 2007 was $714,572.[5] Global investment banking revenues that year amounted to $84 billion, of which roughly half was made from M&A advisory work. Of that revenue, 44 percent originated in the United States.[6]

In most instances, arbitrageurs have little to worry about banks' activities because mergers get funded and the merger closes. In some instances, however, the conflicts within banks will affect the outcome of a merger. Arbitrageurs must be well aware of the potential problems that can arise from the multiple roles that banks play.

A low point illustrating the drive to get the deal done was reached by investment banking legend Bruce Wasserstein in the 1989 sale of publishing firm Macmillan, Inc. in a leveraged buyout to its managers and private equity firm Kohlberg Kravis Roberts & Co. (KKR). The litigation accompanying this merger gives a rare and interesting insight into the negotiation process. It is not uncommon for the diciest aspects of questionable practice to be revealed only in court. How else would shareholders or the public ever know?

What had started as an attempted management buyout[7] of the undervalued firm Macmillan by its CEO, Edward P. Evans, turned quickly into a full-blown hostile takeover battle when Robert M. Bass, at the time known primarily as a greenmailer[8] and raider, intervened with a $64 per share takeover proposal. The board had formed a special committee that retained Lazard Freres as its financial adviser. Lazard valued Macmillan at $72.57 per share, but the recapitalization proposal at only $64.15 per share. The investment banking firm Wasserstein, Perella was retained by Macmillan's management as a financial adviser. It advised the board that Macmillan should be worth between $63 and $68 per share, and the board announced a recapitalization plan worth $64 per share in lieu of endorsing Bass's takeover. In response, Bass increased his offer to $73 per share. Only 10 days after their $63 to $68 valuation, Wasserstein, Perella issued a new valuation opinion, now claiming that Bass's $73 proposal was inadequate and that Macmillan was worth more. Lazard also issued a new valuation opinion that came to the same conclusion. The Macmillan board rejected the increased Bass offer.

The distinction between Lazard's role as adviser to the special committee and Wasserstein, Perella's advisory function to the full board is critical. The full board included Evans, who had strong conflicts of interest because he favored a transaction that involved himself and KKR. The special committee, however, was supposed to look out for the interest of shareholders.

Management continued pursuing its own buyout plan and brought KKR into the game. KKR was given access to confidential Macmillan information in order to perform due diligence. In the meantime, another bidder entered the scene: Robert Maxwell made several proposals for cash tender offers for Macmillan, bidding up to $86.60 per share. Management first ignored him but eventually decided to put the company through a formal auction process.

Maxwell knew that he was not welcome and that management preferred to buy Macmillan itself with the help of KKR. He even went so far as to call the auction "rigged." It turned out that his opinion was correct.

Wasserstein, Perella set out to manage the next round of bidding. Maxwell proposed a $89 per share all-cash buyout, while KKR offered $89.50 consisting of only $82 cash and the remainder in subordinated debt securities. Moreover, the KKR bid was subject to a number of conditions, including lockup and no-shop clauses, that effectively made it impossible for Macmillan to accept Maxwell's bid. Since KKR's proposal had a debt component with face value of $7.50 but uncertain market value, whereas Maxwell was to pay all cash, albeit marginally less, the financial advisers called both proposals a tie.

Macmillan's CEO then called KKR and tipped them off about Maxwell's bid. In order to create an appearance of a fair bidding process, Bruce Wasserstein scripted a text that he read to both KKR and Maxwell. He informed them that he was unable to recommend either bid to management and gave them a deadline for submitting any new offers. However, he gave KKR valuable additional information: They would have to make additional concessions if they wanted a lockup. Maxwell was not informed of KKR's special tip or that Evans had told KKR about his bid.

In telephone conversations that followed, Wasserstein gave Maxwell the impression that he was already the high bidder. Maxwell decided not to increase his bid to avoid bidding against himself. KKR submitted a revised bid of $90 per share. During the day after the auction deadline, negotiations were held with Maxwell and KKR over other aspects of their bids. Only KKR was encouraged to increase its price, which it did to a marginally higher $90.05. Maxwell was left with the impression that he had submitted the highest bid and was not encouraged to submit a higher proposal.

In the board meeting that followed the end of the auction, Wasserstein recommended KKR's bid, even though Wasserstein was the adviser to the full board, including Evans, rather than to the special committee that ran the auction process. Lazard did nothing to intervene. Unaware of the unequal treatment of KKR and Maxwell during the auction process, the board decided to accept the higher bid by KKR. As part of the acceptance, it awarded KKR a lockup agreement that allowed KKR to acquire subsidiaries of Macmillan at a discount, should Maxwell prevail eventually.

In a subsequent SEC filing, KKR disclosed that it had been tipped off by Evans about Maxwell's higher bid during the auction. In response to this information, Maxwell increased his bid to $90.25 in cash. Nevertheless, the board, by now aware of Wasserstein's and Evans's shenanigans, maintained that the KKR proposal was superior to Maxwell's.

In the ensuing litigation, Maxwell scored two victories: He had Macmillan's poison pill[9] overturned and the lockup agreement with KKR invalidated. KKR had already received two thirds of Macmillan's shares in its tender offer, but following his victory in court, Maxwell was able to complete his tender offer. Shareholders preferred his all-cash bid to KKR's mixed cash/debt payment and withdrew their shares from KKR, tendering them to Maxwell instead.

The Macmillan example illustrate to what lengths some advisers are willing to go to help their clients complete deals that are not in the interests of shareholders. Even though Macmillan is a transaction from 1989, conflicts of interest continue to exist among shareholders, acquirers, and financial advisers. The circumstances today are different than the facts in Macmillan. Few financial advisers will favor their client as openly as Wasserstein did in 1989. But there are other opportunities for advisers to favor one side over another, as will be shown shortly in the discussion about fairness opinions.

A different conflict of interest appeared in the 2007 attempt by shoe retailer Finish Line to acquire its competitor Genesco. Genesco had been the object of a bidding war between Finish Line and Footlocker that saw bids surge from an initial $46 by Footlocker to a winning $54.50 by Finish Line. However, the timing of Finish Line's highly leveraged proposal coincided with increasing difficulties by investment banks to sell merger-related leveraged loans in the secondary market. Finish Line's bankers, UBS, would have suffered a loss if it had sold the loans it had committed to providing Finish Line.

UBS and Finish Line attempted to terminate the merger agreement by declaring that Genesco had suffered a "material adverse effect." However, the merger agreement had a very narrow interpretation of the term, and it was clear that a material adverse effect did not apply in the case. UBS had to find another excuse to avoid having to fund the transaction.

Two arguments were used against Genesco: (1) that Genesco had committed fraud by not providing Finish Line with financial results for May 2007, which showed its deteriorating performance; and (2) that the combined firm would be insolvent due to the large amount of debt used to finance the merger. Therefore, UBS should not be required to fund the deal.

The courts dismissed the fraud claim, but the insolvency argument was never litigated. Instead, UBS and Finish Line settled the litigation. UBS paid $136 million to Genesco, and Finish Line issued preferred stock to Genesco convertible into 10 percent of its outstanding shares. Instead of Finish Line owning Genesco, Genesco ended up owning a big stake in Finish Line.

The irony is that while UBS was arguing that Genesco had suffered a material adverse effect, it fought simultaneously the opposite battle in the acquisition of Sallie Mae by private equity firm J C Flowers. While Flowers argued that Sallie Mae had suffered a material adverse effect, UBS argued that it had not. Had the Sallie Mae acquisition closed successfully, UBS would have made $50 million in fees.

UBS's argument about insolvency is rooted in a real provision of bankruptcy law. There is indeed a section in the bankruptcy code that can be a problem for a secured lender in an LBO. Section 548 is a fraudulent conveyance rule providing that a secured lien can be voided if the company was insolvent at the time the lien was given, or became insolvent as a result of the lien; had "unreasonably small capital"; or incurred debts beyond its ability to pay. To complicate matters further, the definition of "insolvency" in the bankruptcy code differs from that under GAAP. Under GAAP, a company is solvent when its assets are sufficient to pay debts as they occur. Under the bankruptcy code, however, "solvency" means that a company must have sufficient assets at fair value to pay all probable liabilities. In a leveraged buyout, this solvency test is much harder to meet because LBOs are structured on the basis of future cash flows rather than present assets, and liabilities often exceed hard assets, in particular if the acquisition price included payment for goodwill and other intangibles.

The recent innovation of stapled financing can also be problematic. Banks advising the target can have an incentive to push the firm to accept a transaction that is not in its best interests, or that has too low a price, because the bank will earn fees from providing financing for the deal. Even if the provider of the financing and the adviser to the seller are not the same bank, it may be to the advantage of the target's adviser to push the transaction if it expects to be part of the syndicate that will provide financing.

The club of banks that provide financing to mergers is a small world involving the same firms and bankers. Banks are well aware that their advisory revenue depends on getting deals done and that their revenue from financing depends on other banks getting a deal done. If one bank advises a target on a deal, it may not be part of the syndicate that provides financing for the same transaction; however, it will be part of future syndicates involving other targets. Because there is a limited number of banks that syndicate financing, no bank can afford to be too harsh in its advisory role, or it would jeopardize its ability to join future financing syndicates.

FAIRNESS OPINIONS

If Bruce Wasserstein's fairness opinion is an example for the conflicted rule of investment banks, it is also a sign of the sloppy work that sometimes is performed by investment bankers when drafting fairness opinions.

Fairness opinions are issued by an investment bank as an independent party to assure the board of directors of a target that the merger consideration is "fair from a financial point of view." The use of fairness opinions can be traced back to a Delaware Supreme Court ruling in *Van Gorkom*, discussed in more detail in Chapter 6, in which it found that a board of directors had not made a good faith effort to take a well-informed decision. The court suggested that reliance on a fairness opinion could have solved that problem.

Today, fairness opinions have become a standard ingredient in mergers, even though the *Van Gorkom* court stated clearly that they are not a legal requirement. Most boards are unaware of this detail; they are convinced by their advisers that a fairness opinion is needed and believe that it is a checkbox requirement that, if fulfilled, will show that they have acted in the best interests of shareholders. The fairness opinion is provided by the same investment bankers who advise the company on a merger, and they can charge an additional fee for this extra service.

The problem with fairness opinions is, of course, that the same bank that advises the target on whether to merge also provides the opinion on the fairness. If it were to find that the merger is unfair and the merger were not to happen, then the investment bank would be paid less. Therefore, fairness opinions must always be taken with a grain of salt. In many cases, they are irrelevant and constitute no more than bureaucratic paperwork that justifies extra fees.

Fairness opinions will always conclude that a merger is fair to the shareholders of the target. Wasserstein, Perella's opinion about the fairness of the Macmillan buyout, which flip-flopped as the bidding war progressed, is not uncommon. Fairness opinions will go to great lengths to dismiss their own finding that a transaction is actually quite unfair. When Netsmart was acquired by its management team, with the backing of private equity funds Insight Venture Partners and Bessemer Venture Partners, the fairness opinion issued by investment bank William Blair found an implied transaction equity value "by the discounted cash flow analysis ranged from approximately $142 million to $202 million, as compared to the implied transaction price for Netsmart of $115 million." William Blair then dismissed its own analysis by claiming "that the Discounted Cash Flow Analysis was a less reliable barometer of value than other methodologies based on historical results."[10]

This is completely counter to the typical valuation exercises performed in buyouts, where valuation by discounting cash flows is the preferred methodology. Netsmart was going through a rapid growth phase at the time of the transaction. Management forecast annual growth of 14.6 percent for the next few years, with a quadrupling of earnings before interest and taxes (EBIT) and EBITDA growth of 2.7 times. It is clear that a valuation based on historical performance will undervalue a company undergoing such rapid growth and improvement in performance. William Blair's claim that historical methodologies are superior to a forward-looking method such as discounted cash flows can be explained only by its own favoritism of management over shareholders. The litigation about Netsmart's buyout had other important legal implications, which are discussed in Chapter 7.

The fairness opinion usually is rendered by the same financial adviser that has been retained by the target to arrange the sale. The investment bank has two sources of revenue: a percentage of the transaction value, plus a fixed fee for rendering the fairness opinion. Typical fees for fairness opinions range from a few tens of thousands of dollars in small transactions to several hundreds of thousands of dollars in larger mergers. The fee based on a percentage of the transaction size is the larger amount of the two. Therefore, it is not surprising that the fairness opinion will always conclude that a transaction is fair. It would be in the best interest of shareholders if the fairness opinion were rendered by a different firm than the adviser that arranges the transaction. However, under the current disclosure regime, this is not required. Instead, it is sufficient if the fee arrangements are disclosed.

SYSTEMIC RISK

So far, the discussion about availability of financing has focused on the funding of the particular merger under consideration. However, there are times when financing is independent of the characteristics of a transaction but becomes difficult to obtain for any merger. This occurs roughly once every decade and is known as a credit crunch.

Credit crunches generally are triggered by poor oversight of banks, whose lending standards decline and who make increasingly risky loans. Some trigger, such as one large default, leads to a sudden reassessment of all lending risks by all banks at the same time. The result is a drastic reduction of the availability of credit.

The merger boom of the 1980s came to an abrupt end when the junk bond market collapsed. First Boston was unable to place $475 million of 15 percent bonds of the Ohio Mattress Company. The junk bond market had been jittery since the bankruptcy of LTV Corporation in 1986, which was the largest bankruptcy at the time. Spreads widened for several months but returned to normal shortly thereafter. By early 1989, the supply of new junk bond issues had increased to levels that made it difficult for the market to absorb at the current spreads. Some high-yield issuers responded by withdrawing their offerings and launching new ones at much higher yields

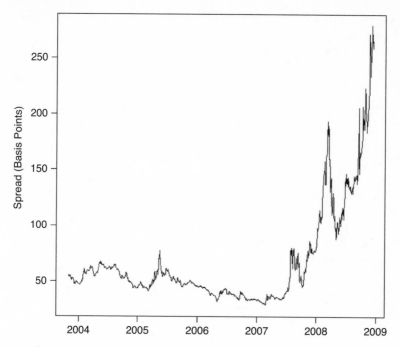

FIGURE 5.2 Leveraged Loans: All in Spreads

of 15 percent and higher. But even at these levels, Ohio Mattress failed to place its bonds.

The going-private boom of the new millennium came to a sudden stop when the effects of the subprime crisis began affecting banks' ability to fund buyout transactions. At the same time, investors became wary of any debt issued for buyouts and were unwilling to acquire such debt from banks. Therefore, the entire debt funding machine came to a halt. A chain reaction was set in motion: Funding vehicles such as CLOs or structured investment vehicles were unable to obtain short-term funding in the money markets and had to end their purchases of leveraged loans. This, in turn, left banks with large inventories of loans that could not be sold and whose market prices were dropping. As a result, banks curtailed their lending to leveraged borrowers, which ended many pending buyouts. Figure 5.2 shows the impact of the credit crunch on spreads in the leveraged loan market. Within a few months, spreads widened from slightly over 200 basis points to over 500.

CHAPTER 6

Legal Aspects

Merger arbitrageurs must combine an investor's mind-set with that of a strategy consultant and a lawyer. This makes merger arbitrage an art rather than a science. It also implies that it is very difficult for quantitative models to replicate a merger arbitrage strategy. Most references on arbitrage focus on the mechanical aspect of merger arbitrage, which we discussed in Part I. Antitrust issues are also popular among writers about the topic. However, the full richness of the arbitrage process becomes apparent only when one considers the legal aspects.

The law of mergers and acquisitions is extremely specialized, and a comprehensive description is beyond the scope of this chapter. Most legal texts covering mergers exceed this book in length. Therefore, this section gives a limited overview of some of the key issues. Readers interested in delving deeper are strongly encouraged to consult the extensive legal literature that exists about this topic.

The legal framework is complicated by a multitude of overlapping laws and regulations that apply to mergers. It would be an exaggeration to suggest that an arbitrageur must be a lawyer. Legal training may be helpful, but a good understanding of the principles is sufficient for most arbitrage investments. Most arbitrageurs will do well using some common sense and a sharp eye for the wording of key provisions in merger agreements.

Aside from antitrust legislation, which is a world of its own, there are at least four levels of legislation that arbitrageurs must be familiar with:

1. Federal regulations promulgated by the Securities and Exchange Commission (SEC) are the rules most investors become aware of when receiving a proxy or information statement about a merger. Like all other SEC rules, the principle of full disclosure underlies these regulations. Almost anything goes as long as it is disclosed to shareholders. The SEC does not judge the fairness of a merger or the adequacy of the consideration received.

2. State corporation codes are relatively static and play no more role than provide a general framework from which court decisions are derived. Corporations are governed by the law of the state in which they are registered, and hence their merger or dissolution is first and foremost controlled by the statues of their state of incorporation. However, state codes tend to remain relatively general in order to provide maximum flexibility to their company citizens. Many states model their codes after Delaware General Corporate Law; even the country of Liberia follows Delaware's example. While this may appear far-fetched, arbitrageurs had to deal with Liberian corporate law in 2004, when Stelmar Shipping, a Liberian container shipping firm founded by British/Greek entrepreneur Stelios Haji-Ioannou, was acquired by Overseas Shipholding Group. Many other U.S.-traded shipping companies are incorporated in Liberia, so other mergers involving Liberian companies are likely to happen in the future.

   Some intricacies of different codes involve not only anti-takeover provisions but also the availability of dissenters' rights for appraisals. This topic is addressed in more detail in Chapter 11. State statutes also define many anti-takeover provisions, discussed later in this chapter.

3. Court decisions are the key to understanding the law of mergers and acquisitions. Although state corporate codes set the framework under which mergers take place, it is the precedent of case law that sets the relevant standards. Judges will look to state statutes, precedent, and SEC rules when making decisions. Readers may be surprised that SEC rules would come into play in a state court, but judges occasionally refer to a company's SEC filings and its compliance with SEC rules in their decisions.

   The most important jurisdiction is, of course, Delaware. Judges in other states will look to Delaware's decisions for guidance but will also try to maintain a certain independence.

   The venue for these decisions is almost always a state court, often the state of incorporation, and otherwise the state in which the corporation has its main place of business. Lawyers for plaintiffs sometimes suggest litigating in western states if a company has its headquarters there, under the theory that courts in those states are more shareholder-friendly than courts on the East Coast. Nevertheless, the law applied will be that of the state of incorporation. Any difference in outcome is due to a different interpretation of facts and circumstances.

4. Company-specific contracts. These are mostly anti-takeover provisions, but restrictions on takeovers can also be found in less obvious places, such as bond or loan covenants or employment agreements. It is common to see so-called change of control clauses in bond covenants. If the issuer is acquired, the bond becomes due immediately.

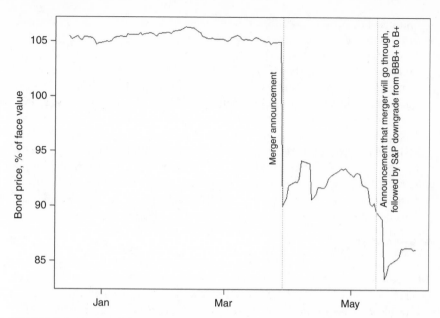

FIGURE 6.1   Price of the ISS Global A/S 4.75% Bond Due 09/10

It should be noted that change of control clauses were, until recently, very uncommon in European bond covenants. As a result, highly rated companies with low debt loads could be taken over and leveraged by the new owners. The bonds continued to pay the low interest rate assigned at issuance, but rating agencies downgraded the bonds to junk level. Effectively, the cost of the buyout was borne by the widows and orphans who suffered a significant capital loss on their high-risk, low-yield bond holdings. A prominent example is the buyout of Danish cleaning firm ISS A/S by entity affiliated with Goldman Sachs and the Wallenberg family. Within hours of the announcement, one bond lost 25 percent of its value (see Figure 6.1). A few weeks later, the rating agencies reacted to the buyout and downgraded ISS's debt from a BBB investment grade rating to a junk level of B. The losses suffered by the bondholders effectively were a wealth transfer from widows and orphans to Goldman Sachs and the Wallenbergs.

It is clear that anyone with advance knowledge of the merger would have profited enormously from a short position in ISS bonds or by buying protection on ISS bonds in the credit derivative markets. Indeed, it was rumored at the time that such insider trading through credit derivatives was rampant in European markets, where regulatory enforcement was completely absent and penalties are much lighter than in the United

States. The earlier warning against insider trading can only be reiterated in this context.

Change of control clauses can also be found in employment agreements of key executives. Typically, they provide for a lump-sum payment (golden parachute) when the firm is taken over. Similarly, stock options and restricted stock vest upon a change in control. These issues are discussed in more detail in Chapter 7.

Merger law evolves discontinuously. It remains static during periods of little activity but changes rapidly in each merger boom. The key decisions emanate from the 1980s and the more recent merger boom of the new millennium.

MERGER PROCESS

Although arbitrageurs take their positions mostly after a merger has been announced, it is helpful to understand the legal requirements that companies have to follow in the adoption of the merger. A poorly conducted process is open to attack in the courts. In this case, there are three possible outcomes:

1. *The deal is delayed or collapses.* An outright collapse rarely happens, but delays can occur and depress the annualized return (see Chapter 2).
2. *The buyout price increases.* This is the dream scenario in every deal.
3. *Another buyer gets involved.* This can also lead to a higher price, but as in all contested transactions (Chapter 2), an arbitrageur may suffer a loss if a short squeeze develops on the short side of the arbitrage.

Maximizing shareholder value has become the holy grail of modern management. Unfortunately, all too often, managers cite shareholder value to justify many strategies that are more likely to destroy rather than create it. "Shareholder value" has become a somewhat meaningless phrase used to justify any corporate activity, from the expansion of new productive capacity to country club memberships for senior executives. Not surprisingly, mergers and acquisitions are also done in the name of shareholder value. As with country club memberships and corporate jets, it is often difficult for outsiders to discern the real motive behind a merger: Will it benefit ultimately shareholders or mainly the company's executives?

In theory, the decision to sell a company lies with shareholders, who vote in a shareholder meeting. In practice, most shareholders vote with the board, so that the de facto power to sell a company rests with its board. The board, in turn, itself relies to a large extent on representations made to it by management executives. Conflicts of interest exist whenever a company is up for sale. Economists refer to this as a principal/agent problem. The shareholders as principals hire an agent (manager) to act on their behalf but cannot be sure that the agent actually will act in their interest. Management and board members may be more interested in keeping their jobs than in maximizing shareholder value. Stock options may help to eliminate this conflict by aligning the interests of managers and shareholders: If managers are paid in stock, then they should act as if they were shareholders. In reality, options and share ownership can introduce new conflicts of interests. For example, options usually vest fully and are cashed out when a company is sold. A manager with sizable unvested option holdings may be more interested in selling the company at a lower price if the options vest immediately than risk waiting for several more years until the options vest. Given such complexities in modern corporations, it can be very difficult, if not impossible, for outside shareholders to understand the true motivations of management.

Courts try to stay out of business decisions and give the benefit of the doubt to management. This principle is known as the "business judgment rule." Judges do not want to second guess every decision taken by boards and only expect boards to act in good faith in their decision-making process and to exercise care and loyalty to shareholders. However, the courts do recognize that mergers and acquisitions present a particular challenge to boards. Through a number of key decisions, the merger process has become a highly structured undertaking. Courts in Delaware have taken the lead; those in other states often use similar approaches when faced with merger-related litigation. Even in states where little established case law exists, legal counsel will advise boards to follow Delaware's lead as a best practice. Therefore, understanding Delaware's requirements helps following the process in other states. We will refer to these requirements as six rules.

At the center of all decisions is the question of fairness in two dimensions: fairness of price and fairness in the procedure of the merger. Courts do not like to rule on the fairness of a price—judges are lawyers, after all, not business executives. They defer to the business judgment of the board for that question by default. This gives a significant amount of protection to board members in the day-to-day management of a firm. Instead of second-guessing price, courts will focus on *how* it was determined. The assumption is that if the procedures were deficient and unfair, then it can be concluded that the price cannot be fair. Some relevant factors are how the merger was negotiated and structured, how information is disclosed to shareholders, and how shareholder votes were conducted. The rest of this section gives an overview of the principles underlying these procedures.

The year 1985 was one of high activity for Delaware's courts, which set the groundwork for modern merger and acquisition (M&A) court decisions. The first decision that year involved the leveraged buyout of rail car leasing firm Trans Union by its chief executive officer, Van Gorkom. The board was confronted with the buyout and was led by Van Gorkom to adopt the merger agreement only minutes after learning that a leveraged buyout was planned. Delaware's Supreme Court ruled that:

> *[...] we must conclude that the Board of Directors did not reach an informed business judgment on September 20, 1980 in voting to "sell" the Company for $55 per share pursuant to the Pritzker cash-out merger proposal. Our reasons, in summary, are as follows:*
>
> *The directors (1) did not adequately inform themselves as to Van Gorkom's role in forcing the "sale" of the Company and in establishing the per share purchase price; (2) were uninformed as to the intrinsic value of the Company; and (3) given these circumstances, at a minimum, were grossly negligent in approving the "sale" of the Company upon two hours consideration, without prior notice, and without the exigency of a crisis or emergency.*
>
> 488 A.2d 858 (Del. 1985)

The Van Gorkom decision is Rule #1: The board must make an informed decision.

Rule #1: The Board Must Make an Informed Decision

Later that year, the Delaware Supreme Court ruled in a landmark decision in *Unocal v. Mesa Petroleum* that a board owes an "enhanced duty" of care to shareholders in its decisions. Mesa, controlled by T. Boone Pickens, had launched a tender offer for the shares of Unocal, and Unocal's board responded by launching a self-tender offer for its own shares, but excluding Mesa from this offer. The ensuing litigation gave birth to the "enhanced" scrutiny of the *Unocal* standard.

> *Because of the omnipresent specter that a board may be acting primarily in its own interests, rather than those of the corporation and its shareholders, there is an enhanced duty which calls for judicial examination at the threshold before the protections of the business judgment rule may be conferred.*

Before a board may reject a takeover bid, it must analyze

*...the nature of the takeover bid and its effect on the corporate en-
terprise. Examples of such concerns may include: adequacy and
timing of the offer, questions of illegality, the impact on 'constituencies' other than shareholders (i.e. creditors, customers, employees, and perhaps even the community generally), the risk of
non-consummation, and the quality of the securities being offered
in the exchange.*

493 A.2d 946 (Del. 1985)

The board's decision to thwart a takeover attempt must pass a two-
pronged test:

1. *Reasonableness test.* The board must have a reasonable belief that a
   threat to the effectiveness of corporate policy exists.
2. *Proportionality test.* The defenses adopted must be reasonable relative
   to the threat.

Rule #2: The Board Has an Enhanced Duty of Scrutiny

If conflicts of interests are present, such as in management buyouts, then
the buyout is considered so tainted that an even higher standard of board
scrutiny is required. In the original case underlying this line of thought,
the Signal Companies were a 50.5 percent majority shareholder of UOP,
Inc. and tried to acquire the remaining 49.5 percent of shares held by public
shareholders through a merger. UOP's management made no serious attempt
to negotiate a price, allowed two of UOP's directors to prepared a valuation
report for Signal using internal UOP data, and failed to disclose a number or
relevant facts about the price and the negotiations (or absence thereof) to the
public shareholders. The Delaware Supreme Court ruled that the damages
award should be "in the form of monetary damages based upon the entire
fairness standard, i.e., fair dealing and fair price" (457 A.2d (Del. 1983)).

Rule #3: "Entire Fairness" Is Required When Directors Are Not Disinterested

The typical procedure to comply with this entire fairness standard is the
establishment of a special committee of independent directors, which leads
the buyout negotiations. It is obvious that legal and financial advisers for
this committee must also be independent.

There is one exception to the entire fairness standard: Delaware law
allows for the squeeze-out of minority shareholders when the buyer holds

at least 90 percent of the shares. This is referred to as a short-form merger, because it requires no shareholder approval and can be done in a very short period of time with only an information statement.

An easy way for companies to get to the 90 percent level at which they can avail themselves of close scrutiny is a voluntary tender offer. This has led to a difficult situation for shareholders in tender offers. If a buyer obtains 90 percent of the shares through a tender offer, it can then launch a freeze-out of the remaining shareholders. Neither the tender offer nor the freeze out will be subject to judicial review if

- The tender offer was noncoercive.
- A majority of the minority shareholders tender their shares.
- The squeeze occurs promptly after the tender offer and at the same price.
- There are not "retributive" threats to the special committee.

The only remedy for shareholders of a squeeze-out is the exercise of appraisal rights. This topic is covered in Chapter 11.

The requirement that a tender offer be of a noncoercive nature goes beyond minority squeeze-outs and applies to all tender offers. It was first established in *Solomon v. Pathe Communications Corp.*, where the court found that "in the absence of coercion or disclosure violations, the adequacy of price in a voluntary tender offer cannot be an issue" (672 A.2d (Del. 1996)).

Rule #4: A Merger Cannot Be Coercive

The most important rule for arbitrageurs came out of the *Revlon v. MacAndrews & Forbes* litigation. Corporate raider Ron Perelman had tried to buy Revlon through his company, Pantry Pride. Revlon rebutted his repeated offers and instead took a number of defensive measures that favored another buyer, private equity firm Forstmann Little & Co.

> [...]When Pantry Pride increased its offer to $50 per share, and then to $53, it became apparent to all that the break-up of the company was inevitable.[...] The duty of the board had thus changed from the preservation of Revlon as a corporate entity to the maximization of the company's value at a sale for the stockholders' benefit. This significantly altered the board's responsibility under the Unocal standards.[...] The directors' role changed from defenders of the corporate bastion to auctioneers charged with getting the best price for stockholders at a sale of the company.
>
> 506 A.2d 173 (Del. 1985)

Rule #5: The Board Must Seek to Maximize the Price Paid to Shareholders

Revlon duties, as this rule is referred to, can be classified easily as the most important of all rules discussed here. It is normal to see a number of shareholder lawsuits filed whenever a merger is announced. Most of these lawsuits will allege that the board breached its fiduciary duty to shareholders by failing to seek the highest possible price.

The board is required to maximize price only if it decides to sell the company. Instead of selling, it is legitimate and legal for the board to determine that the company should remain independent and not be sold, for example, if market conditions are adverse and would lead to a sale below intrinsic value, whatever that may be. In that case, the board can adopt anti-takeover provisions, as discussed in the next section.

Revlon is concerned primarily with the procedural dimension of getting the highest price, and the highest price is the one that can be achieved *reasonably*. If a board were faced with two competing bids, the lower of which is unconditional, whereas the higher highly uncertain, it is justified to go for the bird in the hand rather than the bird in the bush and accept the lower bid.

Note that despite the court's use of the term "auctioneer," it is not necessary for the board to conduct and actual auction. It is possible for a board to sign a merger agreement and then look actively for other buyers at a higher price. This has become fashionable in the current merger boom under the term "go-shop" clause. It allows a company to seek a higher bidder for a limited period of time, usually 30 to 60 days, without having to pay a breakup fee. It is sometimes referred to as a "fiduciary out." Here is how it works in the case of the First Data buyout by KKR:

> *During the period beginning on the date of this Agreement and continuing until 12:01 a.m. (New York City time) on the 51st day following the date of this Agreement (the "No-Shop Period Start Date"), the Company and its Subsidiaries and their respective officers, directors, employees, agents, advisors and other representatives (such Persons, together with the Subsidiaries of the Company, collectively, the "Company Representatives") shall have the right to: (i) initiate, solicit, facilitate and encourage Takeover Proposals, including by way of providing access to non-public information to any other Person or group of Persons pursuant to an Acceptable Confidentiality Agreement; provided that the Company shall promptly make available to Parent and Sub any material non-public information concerning the Company or its Subsidiaries that is made*

available to any Person given such access which was not previously made available to Parent and Sub; and (ii) enter into and maintain or continue discussions or negotiations with respect to Takeover Proposals or otherwise cooperate with or assist or participate in, or facilitate any inquiries, proposals, discussions or negotiations regarding a Takeover Proposal.[1]

Unfortunately, go-shop periods are largely pointless. The bigger and more complex a buyout is, and the shorter the go-shop period, the less likely it is that a potential buyer can be found and conduct sufficient due diligence to make a genuine counterbid. In the case of the $29 billion buyout of First Data, it took KKR four months from expressing an interest until the signing of a merger agreement. Prior to first contacting First Data, KKR must have conducted a thorough valuation study and industry research, because it gave First Data a narrow price range in which it would be interested. It is hard to see how other buyers can replicate this work in less than two months.

Two types of buyers could have topped KKR's bid: a strategic buyer or another financial buyer. Strategic buyers know their industry and competitors well and will not need to do lengthy industry research. However, they tend to move slowly and will find it difficult to react to such a short timeline. Financial buyers can act very quickly; however, they may not have researched the industry before and may not be able to complete thorough research in addition to due diligence during the short go-shop period. Therefore, go-shop clauses should not count as a market check unless they become significantly longer than at present. Three months are probably the minimum, and for large firms like First Data with different business segments, four to six months are more appropriate. In a case where a go-shop period was litigated, Delaware's chancery court considered a five-month period sufficient (in 2004 Mony Group shareholder litigation). It is unclear whether significantly shorter periods would pass legal muster.

Frequently, *Revlon* duties are broken in a more direct manner. It is not uncommon to see companies selling themselves without conducting a proper market test. This happens primarily with small- and micro-cap issuers, where there is less scrutiny by the press and the shareholder base is less aggressive, unaware of its rights or has simply resigned to being taken advantage of.

The *Revlon* decision has continued to evolve over the last 20 years. First, some states have adopted laws that require management to take the interests of constituencies other than shareholders into account. Second, the courts give the parties some leeway in protecting it against interference from third parties, such as competitors with malicious intents.

In 2003, Genesis Healthcare and NCS had signed a merger agreement that did not allow the board to terminate the merger. Omnicare made a higher bid for NCS, and NCS's board concluded that the new bid was better. In the ensuing litigation, *Omnicare, Inc. v. NCS HealthCare*, the Delaware supreme court ruled that the merger agreement was void because the agreement was "coercive."

Hostile takeovers are a special situation where a board decides not to sell a company, or favors one particular buyer over another. The term "hostile" is very appropriate in many instances. One such case was the battle between mining firm Atlas Corporation and financial investor Blasius Industries. Blasius had acquired 9.1 percent of Atlas and wanted Atlas to restructure the firm and sell assets. To that end, Blasius was planning to nominate candidates to its board. However, Atlas preempted that move by expanding the board by two members, whose staggered terms made it much harder for Blasius to obtain control of Atlas. The Delaware chancery court ruled that an action taken by a board without shareholder approval, whose purpose is to disenfranchise shareholders, is not permissible:

> [. . .] in creating two new board positions [. . .] the board was princi-pally motivated to prevent or delay the shareholders from possibly placing a majority of new members on the board. [. . .] A majority of shareholders, who were not dominated in any respect, could view the matter differently than did the board. If they do, or did, they are entitled to employ the mechanisms provided by the corporation law and the Atlas certificate of corporation to advance that view. They are also entitled, in my opinion, to restrain their agents, the board, from acting for the principal purpose of thwarting that action.
>
> 564 A.2d 651 (Del. Ch. 1988)

Rule #6: A Compelling Justification Is Needed If the Board Disenfranchises Shareholders

It is common to include deal protection clauses in merger agreements. The logic is that a deal that has been negotiated in a fair manner should be protected against spoiler bids from rivals who have no real interest in ac-quiring the firm. Also, the buyer, who expends significant amounts of time and money on due diligence, wants certainty with respect to its investment and does not want to be a stalking horse. For shareholders, the risk is that a merger is agreed at a low price with deal protection clauses that make it impossible to obtain fair value. Not surprisingly, this issue is a point of much litigation. In most cases, the methods described next are used in parallel.

Standard language in merger agreements is a no-shop provision. A good example is that of the buyout of Eddie Bauer Holdings (which later was voted down by shareholders):

Section 6.3. No Solicitation. (a) From and after the date of this Agreement until the earlier of the Effective Time or the termination of this Agreement in accordance with Section 8.1, the Company agrees that (i) subject to Section 6.3(b), the Company and the Company Subsidiaries shall not [...] initiate or solicit [...] or encourage any inquiries or the making or reaffirmation of any proposal or offer that constitutes, or is reasonably expected to lead to, an Alternative Proposal [...]

    (b) Notwithstanding anything in this Agreement to the contrary, the Company (directly or through its Representatives) may (i) until receipt of the Company Stockholder Approval, engage in substantive discussions or in negotiations with a Person that makes an unsolicited bona fide written Alternative Proposal [...][2]

Eddie Bauer was not allowed to solicit other bidders. However, the second part of this clause, in section (b), allows it to negotiate with a buyer that approaches it. This is often called a "fiduciary out." If there is no fiduciary out, it is very easy to have a merger agreement voided.

If should be noted that the presence of a fiduciary out does not necessarily mean that shareholders can expect to receive fair value for their shares. First, the signing of the agreement signals to other potential buyers that management favors one particular buyer. Another buyer may have to submit a hostile bid, and not many businesses are willing to do so, if only for reputational reasons. Second, if the buyer is a financial investor, it is unlikely that it will be challenged by another financial buyer. Private equity funds rarely bid against each other. Finally, it has to be remembered that the similar time constraints apply as in the case of go-shop periods.

Breakup fees are another standard feature of merger transactions. They typically vary between 2 and 5 percent of the deal value and tend to be at the high end of that range for smaller transactions. For transactions of $50 million or more, average termination fees amounted to 3.2 percent in 2004, according to a study by investment bank Houlihan Lokey Howard and Zukin.[3]

TAKEOVER DEFENSES

In the 1980s, the stock market witnessed a buyout wave, during which corporate raiders such as Nelson Peltz, Samuel Heyman, Carl Icahn, T. Boone Pickens, Sir James Goldsmith, and Henry Kravis acquired many established and venerable companies. In popular culture, these raiders were immortalized by Gorgon Gekko in the movie *Wall Street*. Raiders purchased of a company with different lines of business or with assets on its balance sheet that were not valued correctly by its market value. After the purchase, which involved usually a long battle with the company's existing management, the raider sold off its components separately. Raiders were an important factor in the unwinding of the conglomerate boom. One effect of this new trend in business was the emergence of the idea that investors best diversify their portfolios themselves, while companies specialize in their core business. Another effect, and an unintended consequence, was the creation of defense mechanisms by management to prevent outsiders taking control of a firm without the consent of the board.

Such takeover defenses are a double-edged sword. The principal justification is that they provide a company's management team with the ability to make long-term decisions. Others argue that if a company receives an unsolicited proposal, takeover defenses give management time and leverage to negotiate a better deal. Relationships with customers and employees are also cited as justification for strong takeover defenses.[4] According to this theory, they have the potential of reassuring customers: During the hostile takeover of Peoplesoft by Oracle, customer orders for Peoplesoft products declined because Oracle had announced it would discontinue Peoplesoft's product line after the merger. Strong takeover defenses might have convinced customers to continue buying Peoplesoft's software. Similarly, it is argued that employees prefer to join a company that is less likely to be taken over. Both arguments appear far-fetched. It is doubtful that takeover defenses actually enter any purchasing or employment decisions, and there is no evidence from surveys or other data.

Some academic studies have questioned the benefits of takeover defenses for shareholders. In a 2003 study, Lucian A. Bebchuk and Alma Cohen of Harvard Law School[5] found that companies with staggered boards (to be described) suffer on average from a 6 percent lower valuation. A recent study,[6] while not addressing the question of company valuation directly, found that analysts do not adjust their earnings forecasts following the adoption of a poison pill (to be described). However, the same study found that poison pills are adopted in response to several downward revisions of earnings, which suggests that they are adopted by boards fearful of losing their jobs.

From any investor's point of view, takeover defenses are a reason for concern. Stocks trade often with a premium if they are takeover candidates, and companies with strong takeover defenses will not be able to get such a premium. Even worse, it will be more difficult for shareholders to organize a change of management in the event the company does poorly. Put simply, takeover defenses entrench management and may even signal to the market that management fears it may become ousted, which means that it is not optimistic for the company's future.

For a merger arbitrageur, takeover defenses generally are not a serious problem. Companies that get acquired will already have waived their defenses in favor of the acquirer. Nevertheless, arbitrageurs can forgo some extra return if the takeover defenses hold other potential acquirers at bay. As discussed in Chapter 2, some of the best opportunities for extra returns come from bidding wars. But in the presence of takeover defenses, another acquirer is not very likely to come forward with a hostile offer. Since inaction does not generate headlines or statistics, it is impossible to quantify how serious this issue is.

Poison Pills

The most popular takeover defense are poison pills, euphemistically called "shareholder rights plans" or "share purchase rights plans." Such a plan gives shareholders the right to acquire additional shares at a steep discount to market value when one shareholder acquires more than a certain threshold of a firm. The trick with the structure is that the acquirer itself cannot participate in the rights plan.

As an example, consider excerpts from the shareholder rights plan of OneSource Information Services:

> *"Acquiring Person" shall mean any Person who or which, together with all Affiliates and Associates of such Person, shall be the Beneficial Owner of 15%, or in the case of a Grandfathered Stockholder, 35%, or more of the Common Shares of the Company then outstanding [. . .]*
>
> *Whereas, the Board of Directors of the Company has authorized and declared a dividend of one preferred share purchase right (a "Right") for each share of Common Stock, par value $0.01 per share, of the Company (a "Common Share") outstanding on the Close of Business on October 6, 2003 (the "Record Date"), [. . .] each Right representing the right to purchase one one-thousandth of a Preferred Share (as hereinafter defined), or such different amount and/or kind of securities as shall be hereinafter provided. . . .*
>
> *[. . .] in the event any Person shall become an Acquiring Person, each holder of a Right shall thereafter have a right to receive, upon exercise thereof at a price equal to the then current Purchase Price multiplied by the number of one one-thousandths of a Preferred Share for which a Right is then exercisable, in accordance with the terms of this Agreement [. . .]*
>
> *From and after the occurrence of such an event, any Rights that are or were acquired or beneficially owned by such Acquiring*

Person (or any Associate or Affiliate of such Acquiring Person) on or after the earlier of (x) the date of such event and (y) the Distribution Date shall be void and any holder of such Rights shall thereafter have no right to exercise such Rights under any provision of this Agreement.[7]

Without going into the details of this plan, it can be seen that whenever someone acquires more than 15 percent of the shares of OneSource, all shareholders receive a preferred share, but the acquirer will not receive any. The result is that the acquirer's stake is diluted and the acquirer would have to purchase the preferred shares from all shareholders. Thus, the purchase of OneSource would become much more expensive.

A remarkable aspect of this particular plan is that one shareholder was exempted. The "Grandfathered Stockholder" referred to in the first paragraph was a private equity fund that was in the process of buying OneSource at the time this poison pill was adopted. Clearly, the motivation of this plan was not to prevent a takeover but to ensure that the private equity fund would be the only possible buyer and that no hostile acquirer could emerge. This private equity fund had bid $8.40 per share.

The board eventually accepted the bid of a strategic buyer, but only after a shareholder, an investment fund managed by this author, had filed a lawsuit. Shareholders received $8.85 per share, 5.4 percent more than under the original deal. We will never know how much more other buyers may have been willing to pay if there had been no poison pill.

It should be noted that boards often adopt shareholder rights' plans when they feel threatened. This is particularly problematic if a buyer has already expressed interest or when an activist investor has called for the sale of the firm. Aggressive investors willing to take on a board may be able to get poison pills adopted under such circumstances overturned in the courts.

Staggered Boards

A buyer faced with a target board that opposes a takeover can bring a proposal to shareholders to replace the board with its own candidates. As a defense against such a scenario, many companies have adopted staggered (a.k.a. classified) boards. Under such an arrangement, a board divides its directors into several classes, and only the directors of one class are elected in a given year. For example, if a board has three classes of three directors each, a buyer needs at least two years to gain a majority on the board, and even that is possible only if it wins all slots in one of the two years. Moreover, because there are fewer positions to be elected in a given year, a larger number of votes is needed to win any board seat. Along with poison pills, staggered boards are the most powerful and frequently used defenses.

Investors who are looking for potential takeover targets should keep an eye on the proposals of activist investors to declassify a board. This is often a prelude to a future merger, but not necessarily so.

Other Defenses

A number of other defenses have been developed over time. Readers interested in details are encouraged to review the extensive specialized literature on the subject. There appears to be no limit to the creativity of corporate lawyers in developing new ones, and it is difficult for most investors to keep track.

Reincorporation in a Less Shareholder-Friendly State   California companies sometimes reincorporate in Delaware, which allows for staggered boards whereas California does not. Reincorporation can be the first step in reinforcing takeover defenses. An arbitrageur will be suspicious when a company is for sale but has recently reincorporated.

Multiple Classes of Stock   Dow Jones had two classes of stock with different voting rights. Outside shareholders held Class A shares with one vote per share, whereas the heirs of the founder, the Bancroft family, held Class B shares with 10 votes per share. When Rupert Murdoch's News Corp. made a takeover bid for Dow Jones, only after lengthy negotiations did the Bancroft family eventually agreed to the transaction. Despite holding less than 25 percent of the company, the family controlled Dow Jones through the bigger voting power.

Cumulative Voting   In regular board elections, shareholders vote for each board candidate with one vote. Cumulative voting, however, allows shareholders to give all their votes to a single candidate. Therefore, small shareholders can control the board more easily.

Pac-Man   One technique that has not been used in the United States since the 1980s is the Pac-Man takeover defense. Like the vociferous character in the video game, a target company turns the tables by offering to purchase the acquirer instead. This strategy was last used in the takeover by Bendix of Martin Marietta, which ended up as a purchase of Bendix by Martin Marietta. This defense is useful primarily for managers who want to maintain and expand an empire, as was common up to the 1980s. With the widespread use of stock options and golden handshakes, the possibility of quick personal enrichment upon the successful completion of a merger makes this defense very unattractive.

Buybacks (Leveraged Recapitalizations) Buybacks can be friendly or unfriendly to shareholders. When management seeks to thwart a takeover threat, increasing leverage can serve to deter potential buyers, while the associated buyback can increase the holdings of management-friendly shareholders.

Freeze-out Many states prevent controlling shareholders from merging with a company for a lengthy period of time, three years in Delaware, unless the board of directors approves the transaction. Note that unlike the other defenses discussed here, a freeze-out is prescribed by state statutes, not company bylaws.

Most states with these provisions give companies the option of opting out of this statute. This is normally stated in a company's bylaws. For example, in October 2007, American Community Properties Trust filed this change of its bylaws with the SEC. At the time, the controlling family was in the early planning stages of taking over the firm.

> *Section 16. Control Share Acquisition Act. Effective October 8, 2007, the Trust elects not to be bound by Subtitle 7 of Title of the Corporations and Associations Article of the Annotated Code of Maryland.*[8]

The provision in Maryland's corporation act goes by the innocuous name of Maryland Control Share Acquisition Act. A shareholder who acquires more than 10 percent loses the voting rights on these shares with respect to a merger or takeover unless the board exempts these shares from the Maryland Control Share Acquisition Act. Of similar state rules, Maryland's is the strictest. When a company opts out of such a provision, it can signal that management may be seeking a sale of the firm.

Another example about the implications of freeze-out provisions was given in Chapter 1 in the discussion about the Pinnacle/Quest Resources merger. At this point, readers should go back to review the letter that Advisory Research sent to Quest's board.

CHAPTER 7

Management
Incentives

Management of a company operates as an agent for the shareholders, the principals of the firm. Conflicts between principals and agents have always existed. Most investors ignore them as a cost of business until a financial crisis erupts, when abuses inevitably come to the forefront. It is only then that investors become aware of the problem.

For arbitrageurs, dealing with corporate management's conflicts of interest is part of the daily investing life. Arbitrageurs usually get involved when a transaction has been announced. It is important to understand the rationale behind a transaction to see whether a higher bid might emerge and whether management has an incentive to support such a higher bid. In management buyouts (MBOs) in particular, it is highly unlikely that a higher bidder will emerge.

Information about management's interest in a merger is supposed to be disclosed in detail. Proxy statements show the different levels of interest that management has in the transaction. The Securities and Exchange Commission (SEC) adopted special regulations under Rule 13E-3 to deal with acquisitions in which management is on both sides of the transaction. Schedule 13E-3 is filed at the same time as Schedule TO or the statements under Regulation 14A, but at least 30 days before any securities are purchased by the acquirer. Much of the material required to be disclosed in Schedule 13E-3 duplicates that of other filings in going-private transactions. As a result, many filings contain little more information that the headings followed by sentences incorporating the other material by reference. Exhibit 7.1 shows an excerpt of such a filing in the going-private transaction of Atari, Inc. There is little substantive information in the filing. The exhibit shows only the information of items 2 and 3. The remainder of the 10-page filing looks similar to the two items shown here. An arbitrageur reviewing this filing learns nothing new.

EXHIBIT 7.1 EXCERPT OF SCHEDULE 13-E3/A FILED BY ATARI, INC.

Item 2. Subject Company Information

Regulation M-A Item 1002

(a) The Company's name and the address and telephone number of its principal executive office are as follows:

Atari, Inc.
417 Fifth Avenue
New York, New York 10016
(212) 726-6500

(b)–(d) The information set forth in the Proxy Statement under the caption "Market Price and Dividend Information" is incorporated herein by reference.

(e)–(f) The information set forth in the Proxy Statement under the caption "Prior Public Offerings and Stock Purchases" is incorporated herein by reference.

Item 3. Identity and Background of Filing Person

Regulation M-A Item 1003

(a)–(c) The information set forth in the Proxy Statement under the following captions is incorporated herein by reference:

"Summary Term Sheet"
"Persons Involved in the Proposed Transaction"
"Directors and Executive Officers of Atari and the Infogrames Parties"

Source: Schedule 13E-3/A filed by Atari, Inc on August 22, 2008

Atari was acquired by its 51 percent owner Infogrames Entertainment SA. Even though there is rarely useful information in a Schedule 13E-3 filing itself, the appendices to the filing can be very useful. In the case of Atari's 13E-3, five presentations were filed as appendices:

- Two presentations given by investment bank Duff & Phelps to the special committee of the board of directors
- Two presentations given by Lazard Freres to the board

- A valuation analysis of Atari's intellectual property by Ocean Tomo that had been prepared for Guggenheim Corporate Funding, which provided funding through a credit facility to Atari

The only benefit of Rule 13e-3 is that additional disclosures are required from buyers about their opinion on the fairness of the transaction. They are required to state whether they believe that the transaction is fair to share-holders. The information is already included in the proxy or tender offer statements and is incorporated by reference into Schedule 13E-3. Needless to say, buyers always believe that the transaction is fair. The disclosures in this section are mostly rephrased repetitions of the determination of fairness made in boilerplate language by the board of directors.

It may be a good idea for the SEC to review its disclosure requirements and simplify 13-E3 filings, which only serve to clutter the EDGAR system. In their current form, they add no information. Appendices such as the opinions could very well be filed with the proxy statements.

MANAGEMENT COMPENSATION

In a corporation organized by Taylorist principles, the value of management is key to the success of the firm. Rank-and-file staff has to be just good enough to complete well-defined tasks that are assigned by management.[1] Retention of key executives is of prime importance in such organizations, and today's levels of compensation reflect management's indispensability.

Modern management compensation consists of a number of different elements:

- Salary.
- Short-term incentives, such as an annual bonus. These incentives are often tied to specific goals, such as financial parameters, improvements in product quality, or market share.
- Long-term incentives, such as restricted stock, options, or stock appreciation rights. These incentives typically are subject to a vesting schedule.
- Benefits, such as pensions, health and life insurance, financial planning assistance, personal use of corporate jets or company cars.
- Indemnification. This benefit is often overlooked. It is highly contingent on extremely rare scenarios where executives are held liable personally for wrongdoing. However, the value of indemnification is very large when such a scenario occurs.

For the executives with the highest overall compensation, variable components constitute the bulk of their income. For executives with lower total compensation, salary makes the largest contribution to their income. An entire cottage industry of compensation consultants has sprung up over the years that advises the board of directors of public companies on the best level and combination of the different types of compensation. What happens if a company is acquired by another is no more than an afterthought in these discussions. However, the payout to top management can be considerable when a firm is acquired.

So-called change of control provisions in the employment agreements of management provide for large immediate payouts when an acquisition is completed. Typical payments under such provisions are listed next.

- Salary and annual bonus is often paid out as a lump sum at a multiple of a single year's total.
- Stock options and stock appreciation rights are cashed out at their intrinsic value. Restricted stock loses its restrictions and is also cashed out or converted into unrestricted stock of the acquirer.
- Benefits usually terminate but sometimes continue to be available. Health insurance in particular is often available for an extended period of time after a merger.
- Indemnification continues to be provided by buyer for executives' actions at the former target.

The large lump-sum payments for salary, bonus, and stock options are referred to as golden parachutes. They were introduced originally to overcome resistance of top managers to mergers that would enhance shareholder value but eliminate their management roles. Rather than work to make their own jobs with their comfortable salaries redundant, managers had an incentive to block mergers so that they could hold on to their highly remunerated positions. An additional incentive for top managers is the difficulty of finding comparable positions elsewhere, especially if their industry is consolidating. Although many top managers like to point out in salary negotiations that their skills are easily transferable to other firms, the reality is that it is difficult for outsiders to obtain highly compensated management positions, as these roles are often filled internally. Management stars in some top companies may find new employment easily, but run-of-the-mill executives from small- or mid-cap firms can have a harder time.

Exhibit 7.2 shows the disclosure of change of control payments for Open Text Corporation. As is typical for firms that have seen a strong appreciation of their stock and are heavy users of options, the bulk of the value of a change of control comes from the immediate vesting of stock options upon the closing.

EXHIBIT 7.2 CHANGE OF CONTROL PROVISIONS OF OPEN TEXT

Quantitative Estimates of Payments upon Termination or Change in Control

Further information regarding payments to our Named Executive Officers in the event of a termination or a change in control may be found in the table below. This table sets forth the estimated amount of payments and other benefits each Named Executive Officer would be entitled to receive upon the occurrence of the indicated event, assuming that the event occurred on June 30, 2008. Amounts potentially payable under plans which are generally available to all salaried employees, such as life and disability insurance, are excluded from the table. The values related to vesting of stock options and awards are based upon the fair market value of our common stock of $32.10 per share as reported on the NASDAQ on June 30, 2008, the last trading day of our fiscal year. The other material assumptions made with respect to the numbers reported in the table below are:

- Payments in Canadian dollars included herein are converted to U.S dollars using an exchange rate of 0.988835
- The salary and incentive payments are calculated based on the amounts of salary and incentive payments which were payable to each Named Executive Officer as of June 30, 2008; and
- Payment under the Long Term Incentive Plan is calculated as though 50% of the target bonus has vested; and
- The number of options available for vesting is equal to:
- The number of options outstanding and exercisable as of June 30, 2008 plus
- The number of options which were scheduled to be outstanding and exercisable by September 30, 2008, plus
- With respect only to a change in control in the ownership of Open Text, the number of options which are subject to the acceleration of their vesting dates as a result of such change in control.

Actual payments made at any future date may vary, including the amount the Named Executive Officer would have accrued under the applicable benefit or compensation plan as well as the price of our Common Shares.

(Continued)

EXHIBIT 7.2 CHANGE OF CONTROL PROVISIONS OF OPEN TEXT (*Continued*)

		Salary ($)	STIP Payment ($)	LTIP Payment ($)	Vesting of Stock Options ($)	Employee Benefits ($)	Total ($)
John Shackle- ton	Termination Without Cause	$625,000	$625,000	$—	$17,382,519	$16,539	$18,649,058
	Change in Control	$625,000	$625,000	$1,000,000	$18,015,894	$16,539	$20,282,433
	Change in Relationship	$625,000	$625,000	$1,000,000	$18,015,894	$16,539	$20,282,433
P. Thomas Jenkins	Termination Without Cause	$618,022	$618,022	$—	$10,996,750	$23,840	$12,256,634
	Change in Control	$618,022	$618,022	$969,058	$11,725,000	$23,840	$13,953,942
	Change in Relationship	$618,022	$618,022	$969,058	$11,725,000	$23,840	$13,953,942
Paul McFeeters	Termination Without Cause	$185,407	$65,475	$—	$1,808,000	$—	$2,058,882
	Change in Control	$185,407	$65,475	$315,438	$4,520,000	$—	$5,086,320
	Change in Relationship	$185,407	$65,475	$315,438	$4,520,000	$—	$5,086,320
Kirk Roberts	Termination Without Cause	$346,092	$312,054	$—	$1,809,275	$—	$2,467,421
	Change in Control	$346,092	$312,054	$286,762	$3,030,725	$—	$3,975,633
	Change in Relationship	$346,092	$312,054	$286,762	$3,030,725	$—	$3,975,633
John Wilk- erson	Termination Without Cause	$200,000	$182,460	$—	$2,263,500	$—	$2,645,960
	Change in Control	$200,000	$182,460	$487,500	$4,527,000	$—	$5,396,960
	Change in Relationship	$200,000	$182,460	$487,500	$4,527,000	$—	$5,396,960

Source: Form 10-K by Open Text Corporation filed on August 26, 2008.

Payments to executives are subject to excise taxes unless they have been approved by shareholders. Section 280G denies a corporation a deduction for a golden parachute payment to the extent that it exceeds three times an executive's annual salary unless shareholders have approved the payment.[2]

A parallel regulation, section 4999, imposes a 20 percent excise tax on the recipient of the excess payment of the golden parachute.

These rules were first introduced in the 1980s after a public outcry over large payments to executives whose companies are acquired. The IRS regulations were well meant but have been diluted quite significantly. When they do apply, they have an adverse effect on shareholders. Companies are allowed to reimburse executives for the 20 percent excise tax. The result is that the cost of the golden parachute has increased for the company, and a sophisticated buyer will take the cost of the nondeductibility and reimbursement of the excise tax into account and reduce the purchase price accordingly. The net effect is a transfer of shareholder wealth to Uncle Sam. In many mergers, golden parachutes are immaterial, but for smaller companies with highly compensated executives, golden parachutes can become significant.

The rationale behind golden parachutes was to provide managers with strong financial security if they give up their jobs to support mergers that are in the interest of shareholders. The reality of change of control provisions is more differentiated than the theory suggests.

The accelerated vesting of restricted stock and options is the largest potential conflict of interest for managers who have to consider the sale of their firm. Mergers provide managers with two types of windfall profits:

1. Most mergers are done at a premium to the trading price of the stock. Options that have been issued at the money or even out of the money suddenly have a large intrinsic value that will be realized when the merger closes.
2. Options vest immediately. Rather than having to wait up to 10 years and going through the associated market risk for such a long period, executive options vest with the closing and can be cashed out immediately.

Therefore, change of control provisions lead to a set of incentives that make mergers potentially more attractive for managers than for shareholders. In a scenario where a firm is expected to generate long-term growth, shareholders may be best off holding on to their shares for the long run. Executives, however, may be better off selling the firm and cashing out immediately.

An example of these conflicts is the $11 billion acquisition of Sungard Data Systems by a consortium of private equity firms in 2005.[3] Sungard's board was considering a spin-off of the firm's Availability Services business when private equity firm Silver Lake Partners made a proposal to acquire Sungard for $33 per share. The board rejected the proposal until it was subsequently increased to $36 per share. The board led lengthy negotiations with the private equity fund, until it decided to discard the idea of the spin-off in favor of the acquisition by the private equity group:

> *On or about March 9, 2005, management advised* [Sungard's Chairman] *Mr. Mann that there were severe resource constraints involved in continuing to work on completing the previously announced spin off of the Company's availability services business by the end of April, while at the same time handling all of the due diligence and other demands of the transaction with Silver Lake Partners and operating the Company's businesses. On or about March 13, 2005, after discussions among the directors, Mr. Mann informed management that, in light of the progress that had been made on the transaction with Silver Lake Partners and the strains imposed on management by continuing to work on the spin off, as well as operating the business of the Company, they should concentrate their efforts on the transaction rather than the spin off.*
>
> Def 14A filing on 5/26/2005

It is hard to see how an $11 billion company can be too small to evaluate two competing strategic alternatives, a buyout and a spin-off. It is even more troubling if the interests of management are taken into account: Chief executive officer (CEO) Cristóbal Conde received over $58 million from his sale of stock and options. At the time of the merger, only $42.6 million worth of stock had vested, so that accelerated vesting alone was worth over $15 million to him. For all 20 senior executives, the payout for their equity holdings was $226 million, and the accelerated vesting was worth $83 million in the aggregate.

The Sungard buyout has a peculiar feature, because management elected to forgo its change of control payments and instead invest in the company after the buyout. Irrespective of the absence of change of control payments, management nevertheless received $11 million in tax gross-up payments for section 4999 excise taxes, of which $3 million went to CEO Conde. The investment by management in the buyout is discussed in the next section.

Changes in executive compensation can signal to shareholders that management is preparing for an acquisition. In the case of Watchguard's acquisition by a management group with the backing of private equity firms Vector Capital and Francisco Partners, CEO Borey requested a change in his employment agreement in April 2005, shortly after receiving an indication of interest from Vector Capital in March to acquire Watchguard. The amended compensation package included change of control provisions on Borey's salary, bonus, and a lump-sum cash payment. More important, the executive stock options were repriced, because Watchguard's stock price had performed poorly recently and the options were underwater. The board adopted the changes to the employment agreement and stock options at its meeting in April 2005, unaware that discussions with a potential buyer had already occurred.

The change in Watchguard's compensation plans was probably a breach of management's fiduciary duties, because it conferred a benefit on management that the board or shareholders would have assessed differently from management. Management knew that there was interest in an acquisition, whereas the board did not. The likelihood of an acquisition, and hence the value of the change, looks differently when one has knowledge of the discussions with the private equity firm.

CONTINUING MANAGEMENT INTEREST IN PRIVATE EQUITY BUYOUTS

The going-private transaction of Sungard Data Systems was not only an example of how management can earn windfall compensation by selling their firms rather than pursuing other strategic initiatives, such as a spin-off. It also shows that management can have significant long-term incentives in selling to private equity funds.

In the case of Sungard, it does not appear that any strategic acquirer was a serious contender for a merger. Had there been one, it is safe to assume that management would have lost its jobs because the acquiring firm already has a management team in place. Replacement of the target management is one of the first areas in which synergies can be achieved. In contrast, private equity funds need a management team in place because they are passive investors that do not get involved in the day-to-day running of the business.

Moreover, had a strategic acquirer purchased Sungard, management would not have had the opportunity to participate in the upside of the company after the merger. Their ability to benefit from Sungard's business would have ended with the merger. In the private equity transaction, however, CEO Conde was given the opportunity to invest $22 million in the post-buyout firm. Other managers whom the private equity buyers wanted to retain were given the same privilege. Total management investment amounted to 3 percent of the post-buyout firm. Management's participation was not limited to the funds that they invested. In addition to the capital they put at risk, management would receive up to 15 percent of Sungard under an executive option plan.

It is hard to see how management could have acted with the benefit of shareholders in mind when they were presented such a win-win opportunity. They received an immediate riskless payout from the change of control provisions and, in addition, continued to participate in the future upside of the firm. Had Sungard not gone private, management would have had only a participation in the upside of a public Sungard without a risk-free payout.

The Sungard buyout is a variation of a management buyout. In a classic MBO, the managers ultimately take control of the firm. Private equity funds are only the providers of temporary capital that is paid back over time until management has taken full control. Management buyouts of this type occur today mainly in the middle market. In the overall buyout market, it is more common to see management as co-investors along with private equity. The problems involving buyouts by private equity are discussed in Chapter 8.

There are many theoretical justifications for MBOs, most of which are valid arguments.

- The increased debt burden of a company that has been taken private instills discipline on managers to run the firm efficiently.
- The regulatory burden on private companies is less than that of public companies. Especially since the advent of Sarbanes-Oxley, the cost of being public has increased. By going private, companies can be run independently of the constraints, burdens, and cost of being public.
- Public companies are judged by their quarterly numbers, and management may have too much of a short-term focus on the next quarter. When a company has been taken private, it is easier for managers to take a long-term view rather than manage to next quarter.
- It is easier to improve efficiency in privately held companies than public ones.

Some of these arguments are disproved easily. If high levels of debt are supposed to make managers work harder and focus more on efficiency, then Microsoft or Berkshire Hathaway must be among the most inefficient firms and must be run by real slackers. Although it is true that the regulatory burden on private companies is lower than for public firms, reporting subject to Sarbanes-Oxley does not necessarily end when a company becomes private. Many firms issue bonds that are traded without restrictions, and therefore they continue to make periodic filings subject to Sarbanes-Oxley. In addition, one of the exit strategies of MBOs is to take firms public again after a few years. When the firm makes its initial public offering (IPO), it needs three years of audited financial statements and, at that point, will have to go through the entire Sarbanes-Oxley process. With many firms going public again after three to five years, the cost savings are minimal to nonexistent.

Even the argument that private companies can make better long-term decisions bears little validity. Public markets are inefficient, but not to the point that they cannot take a long-term view at all. Most biotech firms would not be in business if markets were that shortsighted. If management complains about the market's lack of understanding of its strategic vision, then the fault most likely lies in an inadequate communication of the strategy.

Finally, the argument that improvements in efficiency are easier done in private companies than public ones does not carry much weight. Some of the largest companies have been the object of sometimes dramatic turnarounds. Entire sectors, such as the airlines or electric power, are regularly undergoing restructuring while remaining publicly traded. The question is why public shareholders should not reap benefits of improvements in efficiency.

The fundamental problem with management buyouts lies in the unique position that the management team holds relative to outside shareholders. Not only do the managers as buyers have an information advantage, they are also dealing on both sides of the transaction: As sellers, they provide the special committee of independent directors and its financial advisers with information about the firm's value, and as buyers, they have an interest in acquiring the firm for the lowest price possible. Even though a special committee is established to manage the sales process, management still controls the information that is available to the committee. Assuming that management will act with complete emotional detachment in its role as seller disregards human nature. There are many instances, some of which are discussed in this book, where the true activities of managers were hidden from the special committee. The special committee process is at best a Band-Aid for a seriously conflicted situation.

LONG-TERM PLANNING IN MANAGEMENT BUYOUTS

Management should take the long view. When it comes to preparing for management buyouts, taking the long view can be toxic for shareholders. Unscrupulous managers have many ways to prime a company for an acquisition at a low price. Management controls the company and its operations and can manipulate

- *Choice of accounting principles.* By expensing rather than capitalizing costs or selecting last in, first out inventory management over first in, first out, earnings can be managed. Accounting is a particularly attractive area for manipulation because prudence dictates a conservative approach to accounting. When a company is prepared for a management buyout, some extra prudence can help to decrease the price that management will have to pay.
- *Cost structure.* Managers can avoid making improvements in efficiency and build up an earnings reserve. Earnings will be lower while the firm is public and can be boosted as soon it goes private by making minor changes to costs.
- *Management discussion and analysis.* Overly pessimistic descriptions of the business climate and outlook can depress a stock.
- *Projections.* Withholdings projections or lowballing assumptions to underestimate growth will depress a stock price.
- *Boost investment.* Some categories of investment, such as certain software development costs, are expensed rather than capitalized. It is impossible for outside shareholders to determine the exact nature of a company's expenses. For all they know, profitability is low and the firm is a dud. The benefit of the investment will be reaped by managers after a low-priced buyout.

In an extreme scenario, unscrupulous managers can make long-term plans to take a company private by depressing the stock price through a number of devices. As buyers, managers want to pay as low a price as possible for the company. If they plan an MBO well in advance, they will no longer work in the interests of shareholders but undermine shareholders in their own interest. Unfortunately, it will be almost impossible for shareholders to detect such behavior. Even courts are of little help, because they give management sufficient leeway under the business judgment rule to cover all but the most blatantly abusive actions.

Consider an oil firm that is to be taken private through an MBO. One way to reduce its value is to slow its drilling program. An oil company must drill new wells constantly to maintain its output because yields on existing wells decline after some time. Less output equates to lower profits. There can be many legitimate reasons why drilling slows: difficult geological environment at the drilling location, wear and tear on the equipment, and labor shortages, to name but a few. It will be impossible for shareholders or courts to determine whether a slowing of the drilling program is genuinely due to such factors or whether these are just excuses to drive down the firm's valuation. Once the MBO is complete, managers can then ramp up the drilling program by investing in new equipment or hiring more employees. If sufficient time passes between the slowdown of the drilling program and the MBO and no clear linkage can be established through documentary evidence, a court will give management the benefit of the doubt under the business judgment rule.

Assume that the slowdown was due genuinely to outdated equipment. Even if this fact were disclosed, management could acquire the firm through an MBO and subsequently replace the equipment. Managers doing such an MBO would use their inside knowledge of the firm and the assets of shareholders for their own benefit.

Short of banning MBOs, there is little that can be done to overcome these problems. Disclosures can provide some relief. At this time, management is required only to release its projections performed as management. Projections performed by management as the buyer are not disclosed. Shareholders would get a better understanding of the rationale for MBOs if all projections and business plans were required to be disclosed. Current disclosures are completely inadequate. Consider, for example, the disclosures of the discussion of the board of Netsmart, shown in Exhibit 7.2. The disclosures are mostly boilerplate language and simply rephrase a few simple key points:

- An MBO is better than remaining a public company. No real rationale is given other than the "belief" of the board.
- The price is fair.
- The procedure is fair

The filing from which the excerpt in Exhibit 7.3 is taken did not even disclose management's internal projections. They became public later, only after shareholders had filed litigation. During the litigation, it became known that Netsmart's management had restricted its search for a buyer exclusively to private equity funds. Management did not want the firm to be acquired by a strategic buyer, which probably would have brought in its own management team. From management's perspective, the acquisition by a private equity fund offered not only job security but the ability to participate in any appreciation of the firm's value, since it is common for private equity funds to offer managers significant equity stakes in the firm. It transpired during the litigation that management had actually used the phrase "second bite at the apple" in a presentation that described the advantages of a buyout. That phrase was omitted from the final version of the presentation.

EXHIBIT 7.3 REASONS FOR THE MERGER GIVEN BY NETSMART'S BOARD

In the course of reaching its determination, the Special Committee considered the following substantive factors and potential benefits of the merger, each of which the Special Committee believed supported its decision:

- Its belief that the merger was more favorable to unaffiliated stockholders than the alternative of remaining a stand-alone, independent company, because of the uncertain returns to such stockholders if the Company remained independent in light of the Company's business, operations, financial condition, strategy and prospects; as well as the risks involved in achieving those returns, the nature of the industry in which the Company competes, and general industry, market and regulatory conditions, both on an historical and on a prospective basis;
- Its belief that the merger was more favorable to unaffiliated stockholders than the potential value that might result from other strategic alternatives available to the Company, including, among others, remaining an independent company and pursuing the current strategic plan, pursuing a significant acquisition, seeking strategic partnership arrangements or pursuing a sale to or merger with a company in the same markets, given the potential rewards, risks and uncertainties associated with those alternatives;
- The fact that, prior to entering into the Merger Agreement, the Company had been engaged in a competitive bid process which included the solicitation of indications of interest from seven potential financial buyers, the delivery of corporate and financial information to three potential acquirers that signed a confidentiality agreement with Netsmart, the receipt and response to inquiries from three potential acquirers, and the receipt and evaluation of indications of interest from one potential acquirer, which subsequently determined not to proceed with a transaction at its initial bid price. See "Background of the Merger."
- Its belief that no other alternative reasonably available to the Company and its stockholders would provide greater value to stockholders within a timeframe comparable to that in which the merger

would be completed in light of the fact that the offer from the Sponsors was the highest firm offer received after a competitive bid process;

- The fact that the merger consideration of $16.50 per share is all cash, so that the transaction allows the Company's unaffiliated stockholders to realize in the near term a fair value, in cash, for their investment and provides such stockholders certainty of value for their shares;

- Netsmart's historical and current financial performance and results of operations, its prospects and long-term strategy, its competitive position in its industry, the outlook for the behavioral healthcare market and general stock market conditions;

- The historical market prices of Netsmart common stock, including the market price of the Netsmart common stock relative to those of other industry participants and general market indices, and recent trading activity, including the fact that the $16.50 per share merger consideration represented a 6.7% premium over Netsmart's closing stock price on November 16, 2006 (the last business day prior to the approval of the transaction), and a 24.1% premium over Netsmart's average share price for the 20 trading day period ended November 16, 2006;

- Its belief that Netsmart's stock price was not likely to trade at or above the $16.50 price offered in the merger in the near future. The board based this belief on a number of factors, including: the directors' knowledge and understanding of the Company and its industry; management's projections and the Company's business plan; and the various valuation methodologies and analyses prepared by William Blair and described under "Special Factors—Opinion of Netsmart's Financial Advisor" below;

- The financial analysis reviewed by William Blair at the meetings of the Special Committee on November 16 and 17, 2006 and at the meeting of the board of directors on November 17, 2006, and the opinion of William Blair, described in detail under "Special Factors—Opinion of Netsmart's Financial Advisor" that, as of November 17, 2006 (as confirmed in its written opinion dated November 18, 2006), and based on and subject to the various factors, assumptions and limitations set forth in its opinion, the $16.50 per share merger consideration to be received by holders

(Continued)

EXHIBIT 7.3 REASONS FOR THE MERGER GIVEN BY NETSMART'S BOARD (*Continued*)

of shares of Netsmart common stock (other than the Management Investors, the Sponsors and their respective affiliates) was fair, from a financial point of view, to the holders of such shares;

- The efforts made by the Special Committee and its advisers to negotiate a Merger Agreement favorable to the Company and its unaffiliated stockholders and the financial and other terms and conditions of the Merger Agreement; and

- The fact that, subject to compliance with the terms and conditions of the Merger Agreement, the Company is permitted to terminate the Merger Agreement, prior to the adoption of the Merger Agreement by our stockholders, in order to approve an alternative transaction proposed by a third party that is a "superior proposal" as defined in the Merger Agreement, upon the payment to the Buyer of a termination fee of 3.0% of the total equity value of the transaction and its belief that such termination fee was reasonable in the context of break-up fees that were payable in other transactions and would not impede another party from making a competing proposal. The Special Committee believed that these provisions were important in ensuring that the transaction would be fair and the best available to Netsmart's unaffiliated security holders and providing the Special Committee with adequate flexibility to explore potential transactions with other parties.

The Special Committee also considered a number of factors relating to the procedural safeguards involved in the negotiation of the merger, including, among others, those discussed below, each of which it believed supported its decision and provided assurance of the fairness of the merger to the unaffiliated stockholders of Netsmart:

- The fact that, other than for customary fees payable to members of the Special Committee (that were not contingent on the Special Committee's recommendation of a transaction or the consummation of a transaction), the acceleration of options to acquire an aggregate 15,000 shares of Netsmart common stock and the receipt of payment for stock options that will be cancelled in accordance with the terms of the Merger Agreement, the directors (other than Messrs. Conway and Koop in their capacity as continuing employees) will not receive any consideration in connection with the merger that is different from that received by any other unaffiliated stockholder of the Company;

- The fact that the consideration and negotiation of the transaction was conducted entirely under the oversight of the members of the Special Committee consisting of all members of Netsmart's board of directors other than those directors who are members of management or former members of management, and no limitations were placed on the authority of the Special Committee. Accordingly, the Special Committee was free to explore a transaction with any other bidder it determined was more favorable or likely to be more favorable than Buyer. The purpose for establishing the Special Committee and granting it the authority to review, evaluate and negotiate the terms of the transaction on behalf of the Company was to ensure that the Company's unaffiliated security holders were adequately represented by disinterested persons. None of the members of the Special Committee have any financial interest in the merger that is different from the Company's unaffiliated security holders generally (other than the exchange of options to acquire shares of Netsmart common stock in accordance with the terms of the Merger Agreement);
- The fact that the Special Committee had ultimate authority to decide whether or not to proceed with a transaction or any alternative thereto, subject to our board of directors' approval of the Merger Agreement following its approval by the Special Committee;
- The fact that the financial and other terms and conditions of the Merger Agreement were the product of arm's-length negotiations between the Special Committee and its advisers, on the one hand, and Insight and its advisers, on the other hand;
- The fact that Netsmart is permitted under certain circumstances to respond to inquiries regarding acquisition proposals and, upon payment of a termination fee, to terminate the Merger Agreement in order to complete a transaction with respect to a "superior proposal" as such term is defined in the Merger Agreement;
- The fact that the Special Committee retained and received advice from its own independent legal counsel in negotiating and recommending the terms of the Merger Agreement;

(Continued)

EXHIBIT 7.3 REASONS FOR THE MERGER GIVEN BY NETSMART'S BOARD (*Continued*)

- The fact that the Opinion of William Blair addresses the fairness, from a financial point of view, of the merger consideration to be received by unaffiliated stockholders;
- The fact that the transaction will be subject to the approval of Netsmart stockholders and that members of Netsmart's senior management and of the board of directors do not own a significant enough interest in the voting shares of Netsmart to substantially influence the outcome of the stockholder vote. As of Thursday, February 22, 2007, the record date for the special meeting, these persons collectively owned an aggregate of 492,736 shares, representing approximately 7.5% of Netsmart's outstanding common stock, excluding 549,878 shares issuable currently or issuable within 60 days upon exercise of outstanding options which if exercised would result in ownership of 14.6% of Netsmart's outstanding common stock. These shares consist of 106,348 shares owned by James L. Conway, 104,815 shares owned by Anthony F. Grisanti and an aggregate 281,573 shares owned by the other members and former members of the board of directors. See "Special Factors—Interests of Officers and Directors in the Merger" beginning on page 46; and "Common Stock Ownership of Management, Executive Officers and Certain Beneficial Owners" beginning on page 70;
- The likelihood of the Sponsors obtaining the required debt financing for the transaction, given the solidity of the commitment letter from WFF; and
- The fact that under Delaware law, the stockholders of the Company have the right to demand appraisal of their shares. See "Appraisal Rights" beginning on page 55.
- The Special Committee was aware of and also considered the following adverse factors associated with the merger, among others:
- That the public stockholders of Netsmart will have no ongoing equity participation in the surviving corporation following the merger and will cease to participate in Netsmart's future earnings or growth, or to benefit from any increases in the value of Netsmart stock;
- That if the merger is not completed, Netsmart will be required to pay its fees associated with the transaction as well as, under cer-

tain circumstances, reimburse Buyer for its out-of-pocket expenses associated with the transaction;

- The limitations on Netsmart's ability to solicit or engage in discussions or negotiations with a third party regarding specified transactions involving Netsmart and the requirement that Netsmart pay Buyer a $3,479,527 termination fee (less any amount of reimbursement of the Buyer and Merger Sub's expenses previously paid by Netsmart up to a maximum of $1,159,842) (which amounts assume no exercise of options or warrants since the date of the Merger Agreement) in order for the board of directors to accept a superior proposal;
- That if the merger is not completed, Netsmart may be adversely affected due to potential disruptions in its operations, including the diversion of management and employee attention, potential employee attrition and the potential effect on the Company's business and its business relationships;
- The fact that Netsmart is entering into a merger agreement with a newly formed corporation (Merger Sub) with essentially no assets and, accordingly, that any remedy in connection with a breach of the Merger Agreement by Merger Sub could be limited, although the Sponsors have agreed to fund Merger Sub in the event that it is obligated to pay the Company's expenses upon certain terminations of the Merger Agreement and the Sponsors have provided equity commitment letters;
- The fact that the funding of the financing contemplated by the debt commitment letter issued to Buyer, or alternative financing on terms that are not materially less favorable to Buyer than those contained in the Debt Commitment Letter from WFF, is a condition to Buyer and Merger Sub's obligation to complete the merger; and
- That Netsmart's business operations will be restricted prior to the completion of the merger.

Source: Form DEFM14A filed by Netsmart on March 2, 2007, p. 23.

In a landmark decision, Judge Leo Strine of the Delaware chancery court ruled that Netsmart should not have restricted its search for buyers to financial buyers only but should have considered strategic buyers as well. In particular in light of Netsmart's status as a small-cap company, it is unlikely that all potential acquirers would have known that it was for sale. For larger companies, there are fewer potential strategic acquirers, and a search can be somewhat more restrictive.

> *To test the market for strategic buyers in a reliable fashion, one would expect a material effort at salesmanship to occur. To conclude that sales efforts are always unnecessary or meaningless would be almost un-American, given the sales-oriented nature of our culture.*
>
> Judge Leo Strine, *In re Netsmart Technologies, Inc.* Shareholders Litigation, No. 2563-VCS (March 14, 2007)

MILKING A COMPANY THROUGH RELATED PARTY TRANSACTIONS

The legal term "related party transactions" or "affiliated transactions" describes deals between a company and its managers, board members, or other persons who have influence in the firm and also stand on the other side of the transaction. These affiliates are in a privileged position because they have the power to influence decision making, potentially in their favor. Related party transactions always blur the line between personal assets and those of the firm. The question is only to what extent that separation breaks down. Some of the most infamous related party transactions were partnerships in which Enron's chief financial officer Andrew Fastow bought assets from his employer and subsequently sold them back to Enron for a risk-free profit.

Executives who run businesses in the same industry as the public companies that they manage often have business dealings between their private firms and the publicly traded company. In theory, such transactions are supposed to be conducted at arm's length on terms that are no worse than those an unrelated third party would offer. The more exotic the assets involved, the more difficult it becomes to determine such a fair market value. Transactions with affiliates are a convenient method to milk companies and strip assets from public shareholders.

Whenever a loss-making company with significant related party transactions is acquired by management, shareholders can bet that the company has been milked. The only reason managers would want to acquire such a company is that it is a valuable component of the executive's overall business interests. The losses in the public entity may in fact subsidize gains that the executive makes in the privately held firms. Unfortunately, such suspicions are difficult to prove because the business judgment rule gives management enough room to maintain a seemingly fair process. As we have seen before, as long as the process is robust enough to have sufficient elements of fairness, courts will not interfere even when smoking guns abound.

Related party transactions with a company's affiliates are disclosed in a company's proxy statement. Exhibit 7.4 shows the disclosures of Central Freight's related party transactions.

EXHIBIT 7.4 RELATED PARTY TRANSACTIONS OF CENTRAL FREIGHT

We currently lease 22 active terminals and seven dormant terminals from Southwest Premier Properties, L.L.C. Southwest Premier is owned by some of our directors, executive officers and existing stockholders, including 77% by Jerry Moyes, and 10% by Robert Fasso. In 1998, we sold thirty-four of these properties to Southwest Premier, along with additional terminals that have since been sold, for an aggregate of $27.8 million in a sale-and-leaseback transaction that was accounted for as a financing transaction. We also currently have operating leases for two active terminals owned by Mr. Moyes. We incurred aggregate expense to Southwest Premier of approximately $6.8 million in 2004. We incurred aggregate lease expense to Mr. Moyes of approximately $1.2 million in 2004.

Swift Transportation Co., Inc. and Central Refrigerated Service, Inc. provide us with a variety of transportation services. Mr. Moyes is the Chairman and Chief Executive Officer of Swift and the owner and Chairman of the Board of Central Refrigerated. Together, these companies provided us with approximately 25.7% of all third-party linehaul transportation services in 2004. Under these arrangements, Swift provided us with approximately $12.0 million in services in 2004. At year end, we owed Swift approximately $0.9 million. Central Refrigerated provided us with approximately $2.0 million in services in 2004. At year end, we owed Central Refrigerated approximately $0.1 million. We believe that the amounts paid are equivalent to rates that could have been obtained in an arm's length transaction with an unrelated third party.

We currently lease terminal space from Swift in Memphis, Tennessee at a lease rate of $15,836 per month and in Fontana, California at a lease rate of $60,500 per month. We also sublease portions of our

(Continued)

EXHIBIT 7.4 RELATED PARTY TRANSACTIONS OF CENTRAL FREIGHT (*Continued*)

terminal facilities to Swift at seven different locations. Swift leases property from us in Tyler, Texas, for $3,750 per month, in Houston, Texas, for $15,181 per month, in Little Rock, Arkansas, for $800 per month, in San Antonio, Texas for $7,835 per month, and in Amarillo, Texas for $160 per month. All leases with Swift are, either by their terms or due to expiration of the contract, on a month-to-month basis.

Under these subleases and other subleases we formerly had with Swift, our rental income from Swift was approximately $0.4 million in 2004. We believe that the amounts paid are equivalent to lease terms and rates that could have been obtained in an arms' length transaction with an unrelated third party.

We lease independent contractor drivers and their tractors through Interstate Equipment Leasing, Inc., a company owned by Jerry Moyes. The independent contractors provide linehaul services for us at a rate per mile that we believe is equivalent to rates that could have been obtained in an arm's length transaction with an unrelated third party. We incurred expenses with Interstate of approximately $0.5 million in 2004. At year end, we had no liability to Interstate.

Source: Central Freight DEF 14A filing of April 22, 2005, pp. 17–18.

In many instances, a creeping takeover of a firm by its management team starts with related party transactions such as these. Central Freight was indeed acquired by Jerry Moyes in 2006. The Central Freight story started when Moyes took the firm public through an IPO in 2003. Just before the IPO, the board agreed to a repricing of the leases. Annual lease payments by Central Freight to Moyes increased from $4.4 million to $7.2 million "to reflect fair market value." As a result of this repricing, Moyes earned almost as much from the leases as he paid to outside shareholders when he bought out the 60 percent held by the public in 2006. While public, Central Freight never had a chance to become profitable, partly because of the lease payments to Moyes.

At first sight, it would not make sense for Moyes to acquire a loss-making trucking firm. In the context of this overall business strategy, however, the acquisition of the firm made sense: Had Central Freight remained public, it would eventually have run out of money and gone bankrupt.

Moyes's terminals would probably have been idle. As a stand-alone company, Central Freight was not a viable business, but in connection with ownership of the terminals, the overall complex was likely to generate profits.

Outside shareholders did not fare well while Central Freight was public. Shares in the 2003 IPO were sold at $15 per share, and when the firm went private in 2006, shareholders received only $2.25 per share.

CHAPTER 8

Buyouts by Private Equity

Private equity funds always pay cash when they acquire a publicly traded company from public shareholders. In a few rare cases, public shareholders have been given the opportunity to continue to participate in the upside through continued equity interests or contingent value rights. Even though buyouts by private equity funds are similar to any other cash merger, they deserve extra attention due to the usually high leverage employed as well as the participation of current management in the buyout group.

Many private equity funds are offshoots of the corporate raiders of the 1980s. Private equity had almost disappeared during the 1970s but made a comeback in the 1980s with the buyout boom. Since then, the industry has become institutionalized, and today many of the largest pension funds and insurance companies view private equity as an asset class in its own right.

The rapid ascent of private equity can be explained at least in part by the incentives that its managers receive from their investors. Like hedge funds, typical fee structures consist of a 2 percent management fee, coupled with a 20 percent participation in any gains.[1] Many investment professionals have launched private equity funds to take advantage of this generous fee structure.

It is important to remember that private equity funds, like many other investors, are not a homogeneous group, but can have vastly different strategies and approaches to their business. Not all funds are normally in the business to buy out public companies, but do so only when an opportunity arises. A large number of private equity funds provides capital to privately held firms rather than acquiring public companies. Others purchase unwanted subsidiaries of larger firms or buy out public companies as part of a roll-up strategy. Some specialize in an industry; others are active in many. Nevertheless, the common theme is that they need to sell their investments for more than they bought them at. Buying low is the first step in maximizing profit margins.

In light of the incentives that private equity managers have, it is not surprising that buying low is a key ingredient for maximizing the 20 percent participation in the profits generated by the fund. The incentive to short-change shareholders of a company that is to be taken private is therefore much greater for private equity managers than for the managers of strategic acquirers. A number of factors give private equity an advantage over strategic acquirers. Reputation alone as a driving force is much more critical for a strategic acquirer than a private equity fund in paying public shareholders fair value for their shares. A private equity fund is much less reliant on its reputation than a corporation that must sell goods and services to the public on a daily basis. Several other factors work to the benefit of private equity over strategic buyers.

PRIVATE EQUITY'S ADVANTAGE

Private equity can have a competitive edge over strategic acquirers because selling firms are more willing to let a private equity fund perform due diligence than a rival. In case the transaction does not occur, there is less risk if a private equity fund has proprietary information and a deep insight in the business than a competitor. Even the best nondisclosure agreement is of only limited utility once a deal has collapsed. Even though private equity firms may own other firms in the same business, the perceived risk of divulging information to a financial investor is lower than releasing it to a competitor.

Private equity prides itself in its ability to take the long view and its ability to structure privately negotiated transactions quickly. The decision-making process is indeed simpler in private equity firms, where only a few partners need to agree on the viability of a transaction. The decision makers are all deal professionals who have experience putting transactions together. The situation is different with corporate buyers, where the board of directors must sign off on a transaction after multiple internal committees have given their blessing. Unless a firm is a serial acquirer, many decision makers are not familiar with the procedures for acquisitions.

Public companies often complain about the pressure to manage to quarterly earnings, which impedes management's ability to take long-term decisions. Private equity contrasts its ability to take a long-term approach to investing that looks over short-term fluctuations in earnings, especially when they are caused by investments into the future of the enterprise. Private equity folklore claims that buyouts benefit companies because they can reinvigorate firms, invest in their growth, and reposition them as stronger and more competitive enterprises. This may well happen in some cases, but many buyouts are done simply with the benefit of cheap debt and constitute little operational improvement. They are simply financial maneuvers.

An entire group of private equity funds made private investments in public equity, abbreviated PIPE. Because the Securities and Exchange Commission (SEC) requires that stock acquired in a private transaction be resold only under stringent restrictions, it lacks liquidity and is worth less than regular stock. Therefore, a private equity investor gets to buy the PIPE stock for less than the shares trade at in the market and can make an extra return. Put differently, private equity can buy into public companies at a lower price than the investing public. What is even more significant is that these investments often come with board representation. Private equity firms can familiarize themselves through this channel with the firm and its industry. Then, when the firm is willing to be bought out, the private equity funds have an advantage over other potential buyers because they already know the firm.

Private equity funds do not always invest in common stock. Frequently used instruments are convertible debt or preferred securities that can be converted into common stock. The advantage is that when things work out well, the funds will convert their holdings into common stock, and they will be as well off as if they had invested in common stock from the outset. However, when there are problems, debt and preferred stock get paid first, and private equity funds end up better than the holders of common stock. When venture capital or private equity funds are present with such securities, problems can arise when companies are taken private, as we will see in the example of Aegis Communications.

Aegis Communications was a small operator of call centers and offered its clients related services that fall under the customer relationship management (CRM) label. It had acquired several other firms and was saddled with significant amounts of debt. In 1999, Aegis conducted a strategic review of its activities and issued new preferred shares to a group of investors involving turnaround firm Thayer and private equity fund Questar in order to reduce its bank debt.

Aegis continued to suffer losses, but only half of these losses were due to operations. The other half came from the preferred dividends paid to its majority shareholder, the private equity group, on its preferred shares. To make matters worse for the holders of common shares, the interest on the preferred dividends was paid in additional shares of preferred stock. Thus, the interest-on-interest effect kept diluting shareholders and increasing the burden of preferred dividends. Even though the private equity shareholders owned only 36 percent of the common stock, the convertible preferred shares gave them a 72.8 percent majority.

In March 2001, the same group of investors proposed to acquire the remaining shares from minority investors for $1.00 per share, representing a total of about $33 million. The board formed a special committee of independent directors to evaluate the proposal. The special committee consisted of two independent directors, one of whom had been appointed on the same day the committee had been formed after one director affiliated with the buyout group had resigned. Had he not resigned, not enough independent directors would have been on the board to form a committee. A committee of one would have been too much of a farce.

Three months later, the private equity investors changed their mind and decided not to proceed with the buyout.

Another two years of losses ensued. For practical purposes, Aegis was all but bankrupt. The principal goal of the private equity funds now became the limitation of their losses. As owners of preferred stock, they were in a strong position, which was reinforced further by their control of the board. Outside shareholders were faced with the typical problems that minority shareholders encounter once the going gets tough: They get squeezed by insiders.

In July 2003, Aegis planned a sale to AllServe Systems plc, a British firm in the same sector. The payment of $22.75 million that AllServe was to make was sufficient for the repayment of debt and some of the preferred stock. Common shareholders would have received nothing.

However, instead of the sale, a consortium of Deutsche Bank and Esser injected additional capital into Aegis in return for warrants. Simultaneously, the conversion ratio of the preferred stock held by the private equity funds was adjusted in their favor, diluting common shareholders.

Amid continuing losses and accounting deficiencies, working capital was raised by the sale of receivables and issuance of notes to Essar and Deutsche Bank. The debt was eventually assigned to World Focus and converted to equity. World Focus also acquired the common shares of Questar for $0.0268 per share and committed to paying Questar the difference in case it were to acquire the publicly held shares at a higher price.

In the fall of 2006, World Focus bought out the shareholders for $0.05 per share. The private equity funds were paid additional funds to compensate them for the difference. Series B preferred stockholders were paid $3.60 per share.

This Aegis saga shows how private equity funds can protect their interests even in cases where a company is de facto bankrupt. Public shareholders bore proportionately much worse losses than the private equity funds that controlled the board and were able to invest through privately placed preferred stock.

CEOs DON'T WANT TO SELL TO THE HIGHEST BIDDER

The principal problem with management buyouts is that management deals on both sides of the transaction. As managers of the firm, they coordinate the sales process and have privileged access to confidential corporate information; as buyers, they have an interest in acquiring the company for the lowest possible price. This was discussed in more detail in Chapter 7.

Picture yourself as the CEO of a company whose stock price is depressed even though you are aware that the company will do very well in the near future. For example, you may have invested in new equipment that will lower the cost of production and increase your company's profitability once it is running in production mode. The stock price may not reflect the future benefits of the investment. Efficient market theorists will claim that the market will incorporate this information into the stock price. The reality is, however, that management frequently complains that the market fails to recognize the benefits of long-term investments, and indeed this is one of the arguments used to justify private equity buyouts. As the CEO, if you want to benefit from the upside, you could either get the board to issue more options or get involved even more deeply into the firm by teaming up with a private equity firm and take the company private.

In short, imagine you are CEO Evans of Macmillan, whom we encountered in Chapter 5. His principal motivation was probably to acquire Macmillan for himself. The auction only started because Evans himself initiated the sale of Macmillan with a $64.00 per share recapitalization proposal. It was only after this proposal that Maxwell became interested.

Management buyouts are the flip side of private equity buyouts. Managers must rely on private equity to fund the acquisition, and private equity funds often rely on management's knowledge of the firm, its markets, and its customers for the success of the transaction. A strategic acquirer, however, already has a management team of its own and has no use for duplicate overhead. In fact, eliminating the managers of the target firm is one of the first and easiest steps to achieve the very synergies that justify the transaction.

As a result, managers often have little incentive to sell to strategic acquirers and instead prefer financial buyers who will keep them employed. For example, candy and baseball card maker Topps received two acquisition proposals, one from its rival Upper Deck for $10.75 per share and another from Disney CEO Michael Eisner for $9.75 per share. Eisner acted as a pure financial buyer and indicated from the outset that he intended to keep CEO Arthur T. Shorin and his son-in-law, chief operating officer Scott

Silverstein, to manage Topps. In their desire to sell to Eisner and retain their jobs, Shorin and Silverstein went to great lengths.

Details of attempts to prevent Upper Deck from buying Topps became public during a trial in Delaware's chancery court, where Upper Deck sued Topps. Upper Deck had had signed a confidentiality agreement with Topps when doing its due diligence, as part of which it had agreed not to make a tender offer for Topps shares without Topps' management approval. Given management's conflicted incentives, they had little reason to help Upper Deck make a proposal and worked actively to prevent it. Management refused to approve Upper Deck's tender offer but supported Eisner's, so Upper Deck had no choice but to sue to invalidate this provision of the confidentiality agreement.

In its regulatory filings, Topps misrepresented to its shareholders Upper Deck's acquisition proposal, claiming that there was a financing contingency. In fact, Upper Deck had already arranged financing through CIBC, subject to certain conditions. These conditions, however, all related to information about Topps, and exactly the information that Topps had refused to provide to Upper Deck under the confidentiality excuse.

Similarly, Topps overestimated the antitrust aspect of a combination of the two firms. Upper Deck's own lawyers estimated that there was little antitrust risk in a buyout, and it is difficult to see why Upper Deck would want to buy Topps just to be rebuffed by regulators. Baseball trading cards are not a competitive market, where consolidation would pose a risk to consumers. If regulators were concerned about competition in the trading card market, they would have blocked the 2004 purchase of Fleer Corporation by Upper Deck. The antitrust risk in Upper Deck's tender offer is therefore negligible.

Topps' investment bank, Lehman Brothers, was rendering advice that was clearly partial to Topps' management. Lehman's first fairness opinion used management's five-year projection, exit multiples between 9 and 10, and a cost of capital of 11 to 12 percent (actual: 11.6 percent) and found a range of values for the stock of $9.67 to $12.99 per share. In a subsequent opinion, Lehman eliminated the last two years of management projections, reduced exit multiples to between 8.5 and 10, and increased the cost of capital to 11.5 to 13.5 percent. These changes had the effect of reducing the theoretical value of Topps shares to $8.76 to $12.57. Eisner's then proposal of $9.75 was no longer near the low end of the range and made the price look somewhat less undervalued.

The court enjoined the Eisner transaction, which in itself is unusual, forcing Topps to make additional disclosures and to allow Upper Deck to make a tender offer. Despite its victory in court, Upper Deck eventually withdrew its tender offer, blaming it on Topps' unwillingness to provide it with crucial due diligence information.

PRIVATE EQUITY FUNDS HAVE THEIR OWN AGENDA

In some instances, there can be a large disconnect between the interests of private equity funds and those of public investors. Merisel, Inc., is an example of a transaction that got into trouble when a large investor, private equity fund Stonington Partners, L.P., needed to exit its investment.

Private equity funds are structured as partnerships with a limited duration, typically 10 years. In their early stages, the managers identify investment opportunities and draw on capital commitments from their limited partners. In the middle of their life, managers restructure the business they acquired and seek to maximize value. Toward the end of the life of the fund, managers liquidate their investments by either selling the companies to other firms or funds or by taking them public in an initial public offering (IPO) if market conditions permit. Alternatively, the funds can distribute shares of the investments to the limited partners. The latter option has several disadvantages. First, the value of the shares can be difficult to establish. This can be a problem for the manager, whose incentive fee is based on 20 percent of the profits generated. If cash is distributed to the limited partners, there is no discussion about the profit generated. However, in the case of a distribution of shares, the profit depends on the value assigned to the shares. In the case of illiquid investments, there is likely to be disagreement between the manager and the limited partners about valuation.

Second, the limited partners may have no interest in holding the shares that have been distributed to them, but want to invest the proceeds from the Stonington liquidation elsewhere. This will lead to selling pressure and depress the value of the shares. If market participants anticipate a distribution and an associated selling pressure, the stock price will decline already in advance of the distribution and depress the stock price, which in turn reduces the valuation and the profit share allocated to the manager.

For these reasons, managers of private equity funds prefer to sell rather than distribute shares.

In the case of Merisel, it was exactly this problem that convinced management to sell the firm. Stonington Partners held 60 percent of the company and were in the process of winding down their fund. Merisel's board was concerned that many of Stonington's limited partners would be unwilling to hold shares for Merisel. After all, despite being fully SEC reporting, Merisel was a micro-cap company traded on the pink sheets, and many investors still have an aversion to companies traded on that platform. The proxy statement for the merger states this logic very bluntly:

> *In September 2006, two members of the board of directors of Merisel (which we refer to as the "Board") who represent Stonington Capital Appreciation 1994 Fund, L.P., a privately-held investment fund (which we refer to as the "Fund") and the majority stockholder of Merisel, informed the Board that it believed that Merisel should preliminarily explore the feasibility and advisability of strategic alternatives that would enable the Fund to liquidate all or a significant portion of its holdings of Merisel. According to the representatives of the Fund, termination of the Fund, which was supposed to take place at the end of 2007, would require the Fund to liquidate its security holdings, including its majority common stock interest and preferred stock in Merisel, or distribute such holdings to its limited partners. [...] the Board determined that Merisel should consider the impact on Merisel and its stockholders of the Fund selling or distributing its Merisel shares and begin evaluating strategic alternatives to maximize stockholder value.*
>
> Merisel DEFM14A, May 9, 2008, p. 25

The threat of a liquidation of the private equity fund put significant pressure on the board to sell Merisel, and one wonders whether potential buyers would use knowledge of the situation to depress the price.

The board did eventually find an interested buyer, business development company American Capital Strategies (ACAS), which agreed to acquire Merisel for $5.75 per share in cash. However, when Merisel announced results for the first quarter of 2008 that were below its forecasts, ACAS declared a material adverse effect and sought to renegotiate the price.

> *On May 4 and May 6, 2008, representatives of ACAS informed Merisel's financial and legal advisors that ACAS currently does not intend to proceed with the acquisition of Merisel at $5.75 per share in cash in accordance with the terms of the Merger Agreement. According to the representatives of ACAS, ACAS desires to renegotiate the terms of the transaction (specifically, the per share purchase price) in light of ACAS' view of the performance of Merisel's business during the first quarter of 2008.*
>
> Merisel DEFM14A, May 9, 2008, cover letter

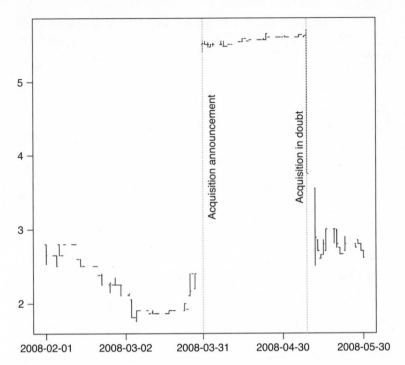

FIGURE 8.1   Stock Price of Merisel at the Time of American Capital Strategies' Acquisition Proposal

Merisel's stock price reacted vigorously (see Figure 8.1) and dropped from $5.50 just before ACAS's announcement to $2.61. Several factors played a role in this drastic drop:

- The deterioration in Merisel's business itself would have justified a lower price absent the pending merger.
- The threat of a collapse led to significant selling.
- The risk that Stonington's limited partners would sell their shares in the market should the merger not happen led to selling.

Nevertheless, the underlying reason for the collapse was the potential overhang of sell orders in Merisel's stock should Stonington distribute shares to its limited partners. ACAS was well aware of this problem, and it can be assumed that the pressure that Merisel was under was factored into the decision to seek a renegotiation of the merger.

The moral of this experience is that private equity funds can have interests that are opposed to those of other shareholders not only when they take firms private but also when they are investors and want to sell. Arbitrageurs must be vigilant about the agenda of these investors.

BUYOUTS AS FINANCIAL ENGINEERING

Private equity returns can be attributed to a large extent to financial maneuvering rather than managerial skill. Increasing leverage of the acquired firm by adding debt and paying out the proceeds from the debt offering to the private equity funds is a popular method for achieving a fast payout. This can be done more quickly and requires less effort than a sale. Nevertheless, a sale of a portfolio company can also be attractive for private equity funds if they can sell it for a valuation that is much higher than that of the original firm when it was first acquired.

For shareholders, the principal problem with these types of transaction is that there is no reason why they should be performed by a private equity fund rather than the management of a public firm. In that sense, financial engineering is tantamount to theft from the former shareholders. The gains from this maneuvering should have accrued to the public shareholders. When the same managers who helped take a firm private then manage it under a dividend recapitalization, the insult to the public shareholders is complete.

Dividend recapitalizations are a form of financial leverage where a company, after it has been acquired by a private equity firm, issues additional debt and then pays out the proceeds from the debt offering to the private equity funds as a dividend. A survey of private equity firms[2] found that most firms are comfortable with a debt/equity ratio of 4:1 following a dividend recap. The sooner a dividend payout is made after the buyout of a public firm, the higher the rate of return of the private equity fund will be. Therefore, private equity funds have an incentive to make a dividend recap as soon as possible after the buyout. Most see a time frame of 12 to 24 months as appropriate. A dividend recap is also an attractive alternative to an IPO: It is faster to accomplish, it can yield comparable returns, and the private equity fund continues to hold the equity for potential future upside.

The downside of dividend recaps is the high debt burden that can crush a portfolio company and drive it into bankruptcy. If this happens too quickly after the dividend recap, the private equity fund faces liability under fraudulent conveyance. As long as the portfolio company survives for an extended period of time after a dividend recap, there is little risk of legal liability for the private equity fund should the firm end up in bankruptcy. In addition, if enough procedural safeguards are in place, such as board review and independent legal and solvency opinions, private equity funds can limit their exposure to liability from recaps.

Multiple arbitrage is another egregious form of financial maneuvering that allows private equity funds to capture gains that normally would belong to shareholders. "Multiple arbitrage" refers to acquiring a firm at a low multiple, for example, a low price/earnings (P/E) ratio, and selling it at a higher P/E ratio. One case of multiple arbitrage was the acquisition of Celanese AG by Blackstone in April 2004. Celanese was listed on the Frankfurt stock exchange, where it traded at a relatively low multiple. When Hoechst and Rhône-Poulenc merged in the 1990s to form life sciences conglomerate Aventis, their chemicals businesses were spun off as a separate firm, Celanese. It became a takeover candidate when Kuwait Petroleum Corporation wanted to sell its 29 percent stake. Blackstone acquired 84 percent of the shares for €32.50 for a multiple of 6.4 times earnings. Although this represented a 10 percent premium to the most recent trading price, the book value of Celanese was €42, or almost one third higher.[3] However, arguably Celanese was partly a U.S. company, because 60 percent of its assets were located in the United States. Blackstone benefited from the disconnect between the location of the assets and the trading market by reincorporating Celanese in Delaware, complete with a classified board and poison pill shortly after the buyout. Only nine months after the buyout, Blackstone sold Celanese Corp. in an IPO to U.S. investors. The buyout required only a cash outlay of $650 million, but Blackstone ended up owning $1.7 billion worth of stock and making $1.4 billion in cash, including $111 million in management fees that Celanese paid to Blackstone as its owners. Why management could not have reincorporated Celanese AG in the United States itself and let the original shareholders reap the benefits of a higher multiple stateside can be explained only by the large payments management made from the buyout. Chairman Claudio Sonder made €7 million in change of control payments, which is uncharacteristically large by European standards. Also, Celanese managers participated with Blackstone in the transaction and benefited directly from a lower buyout price.

It should be noted that a small group of arbitrageurs, including Paulson & Co. and Arnhold & S. Bleichroeder, held out for a higher bid.[4] The arbitrageurs obtained an independent valuation of Celanese AG that initially valued the shares at €42. A third valuation that was done during court proceedings found a value of €65 per share, which was subsequently adjusted upward to €73. Paulson & Co. attributes the low valuation of €32.50 in the original buyout to the "coziness" between Blackstone and the financial adviser that opined on the value, Goldman Sachs. Goldman was an investor in the Blackstone funds that acquired Celanese and therefore had an interest in obtaining a low price. The litigation between Paulson and Celanese was settled in August 2005 for €53 per share. This represents 63 percent more than the original price. Other shareholders who did not tender their shares received €51 per share.

CHAPTER 9

Minority Squeeze-outs

Some of the worst shareholder abuses can be found when a majority owner of a public company seeks to buy out the minority shareholders. The majority owner controls all of the information flow and has an advantage over the outside shareholders that is similar to that enjoyed by management in a management buyout. In fact, the majority shareholder often controls management because it has majority control of the board.

Due to this control, the target company does not operate as an independent business. The larger the proportion of shares held by the majority stockholder, the more the company resembles a subsidiary of the majority shareholder. In many cases, it actually acts economically as a subsidiary, in that most of its business is done with the majority shareholder or it sells products or services that are extensions of the offerings of the majority shareholder. Therefore, minority squeeze-outs are frequently referred to as parent-subsidiary mergers, in which the subsidiary has publicly traded minority interests.

From a minority shareholder's point of view, there are few options to protect itself from an unfair treatment in a squeeze-out transaction. Because the majority shareholder already controls the majority of the company, there is no change in control, and the protection of *Revlon* duties (see Chapter 6) does not apply. The board is not obligated to maximize the price that shareholders will receive.

Nevertheless, minority squeeze-outs are subject to an entire fairness standard. The board only has to ensure only that the buyout price is fair, not that it is maximized. However, it is difficult to demonstrate entire fairness when the buyer controls the board. Boards should take two measures to alleviate the concern over the buyer's control:

1. A special committee of independent directors should negotiate with the majority holder on behalf of the minority shareholders.
2. The closing should be conditioned on the acceptance by a majority of the minority shareholders.

Courts will assume that if these two conditions are met, the squeeze-out of minority shareholders was fair. As we pointed out in Chapter 6, fairness is a procedural concept, not one that sets definitive price levels.[1] The principal drawback of this assumption is that neither of the two conditions deals with fairness of price. The price may not be fair, but large enough to be just acceptable to the majority of minority shareholders. It is perfectly conceivable that an independent committee negotiates too low a price, and a majority of shareholders accepts it for fear of holding an otherwise illiquid position as minority shareholders in a firm of which the majority shareholder takes advantage through related party transactions. Just because a majority of the minority have accepted the offer, one cannot conclude that the squeeze-out was not coercive. The opposite may well be the case: If minority shareholders have participated in the offer to a large degree, then that may be a sign of coercion.

Coercion can come in many forms; for example, if the subsidiary generates losses, then minority shareholders have an interest in selling their shares sooner rather than later, especially if the losses are expected to increase. The subsidiary may eventually end up in bankruptcy and may then be rescued by the majority shareholder, especially if it is of strategic importance to its core business. However, minority shareholders probably would be wiped out in the rescue operation. Another form of coercion is the absence of an alternative to the squeeze-out. Minority shareholders remain at the mercy of the majority shareholder unless they tender their shares. Therefore, any proposal to buy out the minority shareholders will be coercive. The coercion occurs in a more subtle way what than the courts would attach that label to.

Even if one denies the existence of coercion, there is no doubt that many minority shareholders are frustrated if they hold shares in a company that is controlled by a self-interested majority investor. I have seen time and time again that frustrated shareholders will accept any deal, even a bad one, just to be able to get out of the position and move on. Stocks with a large majority shareholder generally have limited liquidity. Shareholders find it difficult to sell without driving down the price. If a majority holder makes a squeeze-out proposal, it constitutes the only liquidity event available to the minority shareholders. Under these circumstances, a bad deal is better than no deal.

BOARDS LACK EFFECTIVENESS DURING SQUEEZE-OUTS

Similarly, the existence of a special committee of independent directors is in itself not necessarily evidence of a fair process. Many supposedly "independent" directors are beholden to management in one way or another. The standards applied to board members to verify their independence are very loose. Even family members are considered independent. In the case of Wilshire Enterprises, the cousin of the chief executive officer (CEO) was deemed to be independent under rules of the American Stock Exchange. Rarely are independent directors completely detached from the majority shareholder. They were often invited to join the board by management, sometimes by that of the majority shareholder. They may work in the same industry that the majority shareholder is in. In any case, independent directors will have relationships of some sort with the majority shareholder and will find it difficult to take a confrontational stance for fear of antagonizing the majority shareholder. The world of board directors is a small one, and board positions are lucrative and prestigious. No independent director will risk jeopardizing future board appointments by being seen as too independent and working against the interest of the majority holder, even if doing so benefits the minority shareholders. The real world is much more complex that the Delaware courts' idealized role of independent directors who are completely detached from social interactions. As long as board members are humans, there will always be a structural bias in committees composed of independent directors.

The mere presence of a special committee also can serve as a charade to mask an entirely unfair process. Committee members must be engaged in the process and actively defend the interests of the minority shareholders. A committee that merely rubber-stamps decisions of the majority shareholder can hardly be regarded as evidence of a fair process. A further complication is the absence of a sufficiently large number of independent directors on the board of the subsidiary.

Directors serving on a special committee created to negotiate a merger are compensated for their extra effort and time. In addition, paying them is supposed to align their interests with those of shareholders. These payments are made in addition to regular directors' fees.

Corporate governance firm the Corporate Library conducted a study[2] of payments to members of special committees in merger and acquisition situations and found that a flat fee is the most common form of compensation. Flat fees at the firms in its study varied between $10,000 and $75,000 with a median of $27,500. Directors who receive fees only for attending meetings of the special committee receive between $500 and $10,500 per meeting, with a median of $750. Other forms of payments are retainers—one time or monthly—combined with per-meeting fees. Monthly retainers range from $5,000 to $12,500. Chairs of the special committee receive higher retainers and per-meeting fees in roughly 40 percent of all cases. Unfortunately, the study did not try to correlate payments to committee members with committee effectiveness in the buyout process.

Once a majority shareholder begins negotiations with a special committee, two implicit assumptions are made:

1. There will eventually be a sale of the minority interests.
2. The majority holder will be the buyer who will be successful in acquiring the shares held by the minority.

In instances where the board of the target takes its responsibilities seriously, its efforts will be frustrated by these two constraints. The target is, after all, a subsidiary of the majority shareholder, and it is hard to fathom another firm acquiring a minority stake in its competitor's subsidiary. Similarly, financial buyers seek control of the target firm and have no interest in a minority position in a subsidiary. Private equity funds often do acquire subsidiaries of larger firms; when they do so, however, they acquire control of the subsidiary.[3]

MINORITY SHAREHOLDERS ARE IN A TOUGH SPOT

Courts assume that in a tender offer, there is no coercion by the majority shareholder if the offer is conditioned on the acceptance by the majority of the minority. In the absence of coercion, the process is deemed fair.

The travesty of the majority of the minority rule in tender offers becomes clear from the 2002 acquisition of Siliconix by its 80.4 percent majority shareholder, Vishay Intertechnology. The independent committee of Siliconix was dragging its feet on Vishay's squeeze-out proposal, attempting to negotiate a better price. Vishay was unwilling to increase its price. The market, meanwhile, voted by bringing Siliconix's trading price above Vishay's proposed price. Unable to negotiate a merger on its terms, Vishay launched a stock-for-stock tender offer. The exchange ratio was based on the prices of Siliconix and Vishay after Vishay's first tender offer. In other words, the buyout premium had all but vanished.

Invariably, a majority of minority shareholders accepted the terms of the deal and tendered. The committee of independent directors did not support the transaction but adopted a neutral stance. In the shareholder litigation that followed, the court maintained that because a majority of the minority shareholders had tendered their shares without coercion and the committee of independent directors had not objected, the transaction was fair from a procedural point of view.[4]

The situation would have been different had there been no special committee of independent directors or no clause requiring the majority of the minority shareholders to tender their shares. The acquisition of ARCO Chemical by Lyondell Petrochemical Company[5] was structured as a merger, and the court ruled that

> [...] *the board cannot abdicate [its] duty by leaving it to the shareholders alone to approve or disprove* [sic] *the merger agreement because the majority shareholder's voting power makes the outcome a preordained conclusion.*

For the Delaware court, the difference between a tender offer and a merger is that in a tender offer, shareholders have the ability not to tender and thereby derail the transaction. In a merger, once the majority holder votes in favor, the transaction will close irrespective of whether the outside shareholders support it.

Since the Siliconix ruling, this standard has been read to apply only to mergers. Under current Delaware law, companies are free to squeeze out minority shareholders through tender offers at unfair prices. The buyer only faces the disclosure requirements of Schedule 13E-3, where the buyer must explain why the transaction is procedurally fair to minority shareholders. As discussed in Chapter 7, the disclosure always states that the buyer believes that the transaction is fair.

Another strategy for a majority shareholder is to acquire shares in the open market until it reaches the threshold at which it can conduct a short form merger. The only risk with that strategy is that it must report its purchases on Schedule 13D or 13G, thus notifying the market of its actions and potentially triggering a rally in the stock price. The higher the percentage owned by the majority owner, the more likely such a strategy is to succeed. Open market purchases take time to effect. If only a small position is to be acquired, the purchase can be completed before the deadline for the filing.

The implications for shareholders of companies that have a controlling shareholder are potentially devastating. Companies that are controlled by a majority shareholder typically trade at a discount to comparable firms that have a well-diversified shareholder base. The market takes the risk of shareholders suffering at the hands of the majority shareholder into account in setting the prices at which shares trade. Shares will trade at a discount to their value absent this risk. Clearly, the market works efficiently in a micro sense, because the risk associated with the control by the majority shareholder is incorporated in the stock price. However, on a macro scale, it is a waste of capital if shareholders do not get the full value of their investment.

The experience of infoUSA (since renamed to infoGroup) shareholders illustrates the difficulties that minority shareholders encounter. InfoUSA's founder and CEO Vinod Gupta owned 37.5 percent of the company in 2005 when he made a proposal to buy out the public shareholders for $11.75 per share for a total transaction value of $390 million. He had been buying shares in the open market prior to his acquisition proposal and had stated that he believed himself that the shares were worth at least $18 per share[6] and that he would acquire more shares in the future. The timing of the proposal was highly suspicious: It came only days after an earnings release had led to a drop in the stock price by more than 20 percent (see Figure 9.1). A special committee of independent directors was formed and rejected the proposal in August 2005. It presented Gupta with two alternatives: Either let the board conduct a market check to find what price other buyers may be willing to pay for infoUSA, or Gupta could negotiate with the special committee under an exclusivity arrangement, but he would have to accept a market check after the signing of a merger agreement. When confronted with these alternatives, Gupta withdrew his acquisition proposal. The special committee of the board was disbanded in a split vote.

The end of the formal buyout negotiations did in no way stop Gupta's attempt to acquire control of the firm. InfoUSA had a poison pill in place that prevented any shareholder from acquiring more than 15 percent of the firm. However, Gupta was exempt from the poison pill and could acquire more shares. He had two methods at his disposal to obtain more shares: open market purchases, which he was doing already, and the exercise of executive options that he received as part of his CEO compensation package. Instead of buying infoUSA in one single transaction, Gupta could take control of the firm in a creeping takeover by increasing his ownership percentage through his option holdings and open market purchases.

Gupta took advantage of his options to increase his holdings when dissent from shareholders emerged prior to the 2006 shareholder meeting. An activist hedge fund, Dolphin Limited Partnership, was dissatisfied with the continued lackluster performance of infoUSA's stock and attempted to have its own nominees elected to the board in a contested election. Just prior to the record date for the shareholder meeting, Gupta exercised some of his options and hence boosted his holdings in the firm by 1.2 million shares to 40 percent. As a result of this increase in share ownership, infoUSA's director nominees were elected in the contest by a narrow margin with 51 percent of the votes. Gupta's share ownership was likely to increase even further: Between 2004 and 2007, he was the recipient of all of the company's stock awards. In 2007, a new stock option plan was put to a vote by shareholders that would have increased his holdings by another 3.5 million shares, equivalent to 6 percent of the shares.

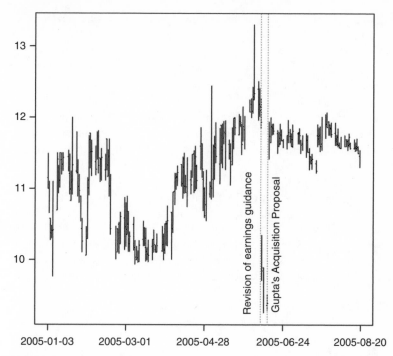

FIGURE 9.1 Stock Price of infoUSA after the 2005 Earnings Release and Gupta's Acquisition Proposal

Shareholders had another reason to be suspicious: Gupta's holdings reported prior to the contested director election to the Securities and Exchange Commission did not include all of his shares, and over 150 transactions were not reported. It was only after Dolphin initiated the proxy contest that Gupta's shares and the missing transactions were reported. To make matters worse, it was discovered later through litigation initiated by Dolphin that Gupta never intended to acquire the company. He stated in a September 2005 letter to that board:

> *After we lowered our revenue guidance due to the Donnelly Market shortfall, our stock got crushed. At that time I had no choice but to support the stock. That was the primary reason for offering $11.75 for the shares. If you recall, the stock had dropped to $9.20 per share. After my offer, even though it has been withdrawn, the stock is hanging in around $10.80 per share. Under the circumstances,*

nobody can sell their shares short because they know I am there to support it.

September 7, 2005, letter by Vinod Gupta to the Board released by Dolphin Limited Partnership on www.iusaccountability.com

Dolphin's litigation also turned up many instances where Gupta's personal expenses appeared to have been paid by infoUSA, such as an 80-foot yacht for which no evidence of corporate usage was found, personal use of company jet, and a skybox.

The overall effect of these revelations was that confidence in infoUSA waned. Shareholders saw a dual threat from a creeping takeover by Gupta. In an attempt to alleviate these concerns, Gupta entered into a one-year standstill agreement in July 2006 under which he agreed not to acquire any additional shares. The agreement was subsequently extended by another year through 2008. But the market had already voted with its feet: infoUSA's stock declined (see Figure 9.2) to a low of $3.78 in 2008. It was

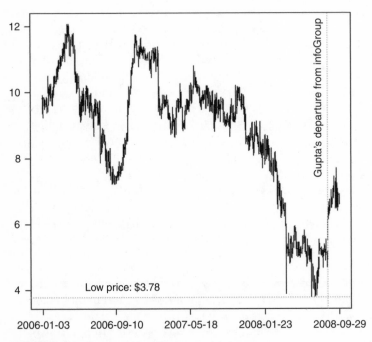

FIGURE 9.2   infoUSA's Stock Price, 2006–2008

only after Gupta's departure as CEO in August 2008 that the trend in the stock's performance reversed. Nevertheless, while Gupta controlled over 40 percent of the shares, the company remained a highly risky investment, and shareholders had to accept a low valuation for their shares to compensate for the risk associated with a majority shareholder.

Gupta was never actually a majority holder of infoUSA in the sense that his ownership never exceeded 50 percent. Nevertheless, his holdings were large enough to make him a de facto majority holder:

- His holdings amounted to 40 percent, giving him the largest single vote.
- As beneficiary of the stock option plan, he was slowly increasing his holdings to the 50 percent level.
- In contested board elections, candidates backed by management won even though the vast majority (roughly 90 percent) of outside share-holders voted for the dissident slate of candidates.
- As CEO, he wielded significant control over the firm.

The problems that shareholders face with quasi-majority shareholders are a hint of what can happen when an actual majority holder controls a firm. Minority squeeze-outs where the majority owner controls more than 50 percent of the firm can be even worse.

Chaparral Resources[7] was a company incorporated in Delaware and traded in the United States that owned oil concessions in Kazakhstan. The government of Kazakhstan wanted to maintain several competing national oil firms to be active rather than having a company from one single nation dominate its oil industry. Because of their geographic location, the oil fields of Kazakhstan were of interest to both Russia and China. China's national oil company, CNPC, and Lukoil had been battling to acquire PetroKazakhstan, a Canadian oil company with fields in Kazakhstan, in 2005. A Canadian court eventually ruled against Lukoil's argument that it had a preemptive right to acquire one of PetroKazakhstan's subsidiaries. CNPC then purchased the company for $4.2 billion.

In the meantime, a sideshow that made fewer headlines was Lukoil's success to acquire Nelson Resources for $2 billion. Nelson was incorporated in Bermuda and traded in Canada. Lukoil's acquisition price amounted to roughly 15 percent less than the trading price of Nelson on the Toronto Stock Exchange prior to the announcement. Luckily for Nelson's insiders, they had exercised their options and sold shares prior to Lukoil's takeunder proposal.

Ironically, CNPC reprocicated by suing Lukoil over a stake in a joint venture that it had with Nelson, claiming to have preemptive rights to purchase Nelson. In the end, Lukoil succeded and acquired Nelson. Kazakhstan's government was happy because Lukoil's win at Nelson restored the balance between Russia and China in its oil fields.

For shareholders of Chaparral Resources, however, the Nelson acquisition was the beginning of a nightmare. Nelson owned 60 percent of Chaparral Resources, and now that it was part of Lukoil through its subsidiary Lukoil Overseas Ltd., that firm's management controlled these shares. The successful takeunder of Nelson emboldened Lukoil's management to attempt the same at Chapparal.

Lukoil began by fudging the 2005 annual report on form 10-K. During its preparations, a Lukoil executive instructed Chaparral's staff to "add something a little negative to the report" and complained that it conveyed a "positive impression" and used "positive words." Production data that would have shown growth was also removed from the report, to make sure that investors saw nothing positive in the firm. Production had already been falling because the lease for the only drilling rig on its Karakuduk oil field had expired. The lease's expiration was in no way an extraneous event. It had been orchestrated carefully by Lukoil. The rig was leased jointly by Lukoil and Chaparral, and Lukoil simply refused to renew its lease. The rig's owner was urging a prompt renewal, fearing a loss of income, but Lukoil prevailed. Moreover, leases for more rigs had already been lined up and an increase in production was forecast by Chaparral internally, but this information was not communicated to shareholders in the annual report. The gloomy tone of the report and absence of good news had the desired effect: Chapparal's stock dropped by 23 percent (see Figure 9.3).

Lukoil's executives regarded the Karakuduk oil field as theirs, even though it was exploited jointly by Lukoil and Chaparral. In an e-mail, the chief financial officer of Chaparral complained about Lukoil's regional director for Kazakhstan, Boris Zilbermints, making "noises" about payments from the oil field's revenue to Chaparral, which "is letting the minority shareholders receive funds." This was an example of what a Chaparral director described in another e-mail as "the Russian way of doing business." So were some of the other scare tactics used by Lukoil. It threatened to shut in the Karakuduk field if no deal were reached, or to cease development or fire the board of directors.

The board of directors did create a committee of independent directors to evaluate Lukoil's buyout proposal. At least one of the two directors on the committee, however, appears to have had more concern for Lukoil's interests than for those of the minority shareholders. He leaked the valuation range that Chaparral's financial adviser had calculated to

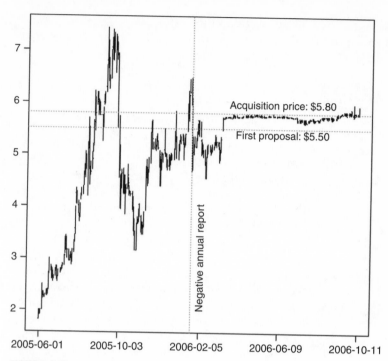

FIGURE 9.3 Chapparal Resources

Lukoil, so that Chaparral was negotiating with a buyer that knew the price range of the seller. The two directors appear to have been well aware of the problematic nature of the buyout, as they negotiated a highly unusual clause in their indemnification agreement: If there were a lawsuit in connection with the merger, they would be paid $300.00 per hour for time spent defending themselves. In other words, the less they represented shareholders, the longer the lawsuits would last, and the more they would be paid.

With the stock price depressed artificially, Lukoil made a lowball offer for the shares of Chaparral's minority shareholders. Lukoil's initial bid of $5.50 per share was soon raised to the final price of $5.80 when it became clear that this was a level at which one institutional holder was willing to sell. While Chaparral and Lukoil were debating whether $5.50 or $5.80 was the right price, Chaparral's financial adviser indicated that the value of the firm was in the $8.00 to $11.00 range.

Lukoil completed the acquisition for $5.80 per share, but this was not the end of the road for the minority shareholders. The rest of the story is discussed in Chapter 11.

FAMILY CONTROL

Governance analysts at the Corporate Library estimate that 170 of the 1,800 firms that it tracks, or almost 10 percent, can be classified as family firms. These are firms where "family ties, most often going back a generation or two to the founder, play a key role in both ownership and board membership." An additional 163 firms are classified as "founder firms," in which the founder owns more than 20 percent of the equity.[8] Overall, almost one publicly traded firms in five is under the influence of a founder or family.

A 20 percent stake in itself is not enough to exercise control. In some cases, a family or founder does own an outright majority of the shares and can exercise control directly. In other instances, companies have a dual share class structure where the founder or family hold A-class shares with more voting rights than those held by public shareholders. Many large firms under family control fall into that category. Prominent examples are many publicly traded newspapers, including News Corp. and the *New York Times*. But even when a 20 percent holder does not have voting control through the ownership of shares with higher voting rights, a 20 percent holding can be the largest single block of shares held. If the remainder of the shares are held widely in small lots, and many of these holders are retail investors who do not exercise their voting rights, then a even a stake as small as 20 percent can yield effective control of a firm.

Family influence is a double-edged sword. Sometimes control by a family can improve performance because interests of shareholders, management, and the majority holders are aligned. Unfortunately, there are also many counterexamples where family control led to a meltdown. Some spectacular failures occurred in companies led by controlling families, most recently at Adelphia and Refco. The differentiating factor between the few family-controlled firms that perform very well, the majority that underperforms, and the isolated cases of meltdowns is governance. The Corporate Library assembled a list of five red flags that help investors distinguish between good and bad family-controlled firms:

1. Multiple share classes
   Some firms with multiple classes of shares have both classes traded publicly, while others have special family-only classes.
2. Special voting rights

Families sometimes have the right to elect a majority of the board of directors, or a number of directors that represents less than the majority but is still larger than the economic ownership of the family in the firm. Special voting rights are usually coupled with multiple share classes.

3. Layered ownership structures

    The Corporate Library warns investors to steer clear from companies owned by multiple nested family trusts.

4. Related party transactions

    Methods managers use to milk public companies through related party transactions were discussed in Chapter 8. In family-controlled firms, the art of related party transactions often is perfected even more. The family earns income from its ownership in the firm, employment by the firm, and transactions with the firm. Leases of corporate headquarters or special loan arrangements are examples of such transactions. The principal problem with related party transactions is that the distinction between personal and corporate assets blurs.

5. Special takeover defenses or change of control provisions

    Change of control provisions are sometimes even more favorable for families that own and manage a company than for employee managers. Stockholder voting agreements can lock owner-managers in even more effectively than other takeover defenses.

Arbitrageurs looking at acquisition proposals involving family firms must take these factors into account when estimating the probability of failure. If a company is to be acquired by its controlling owners, arbitrageurs often will encounter some of the problems described in the first section of this chapter. If outsiders make a proposal to acquire a family-controlled firm, the dynamics can become difficult to judge. The acquisition of Anheuser–Busch Cos. by InBev SA, which was discussed in Chapter 3, led to a split in the founding Anheuser-Busch family. One group of family members around the CEO of the firm, August A. Busch IV, was unwilling to accept InBev's unsolicited initial bid of $60.00 per share. Another part of the family supported InBev's proposal. InBev sought to benefit from the rift in the family by proposing to elect Adolphus A. Busch IV, the CEO's uncle and great-grandson of Anheuser-Busch's founder, to the board to replace August. The strategy worked in that the family eventually consented to an acquisition at a price that was $5.00 higher than the initial bid.

Sometimes controlling families simply are unwilling to sell to outsiders. Consider, for example, the proposal by the Cagle family to take poultry producer Cagle's Inc. private (see Exhibit 9.1). Cagle's is listed on the American Stock Exchange.

EXHIBIT 9.1 LETTER BY THE CAGLE FAMILY TO THE BOARD OF CAGLE'S INC.

Dear Board Members:

This letter is to confirm that James Douglas Cagle together with certain members of his family and Cagle Family Holdings LLC, a Georgia limited liability company (sometimes referred to in this letter as the Cagle Family Group) are pleased to offer $9.00 per share in cash to acquire all of the stock of Cagle's, Inc. (the "Company") not owned by the Cagle Family Group. This offer represents a premium of 19% over the November 8, 2007 closing price. We believe the shareholders will find this proposal, which provides for all cash consideration at a premium value, very attractive.

We propose a transaction in which we will acquire, through a merger, the Company stock we do not own. We are well positioned to negotiate and complete a transaction in an expedited manner with a high degree of closing certainty. To effect this transaction we are close to finalizing the last details on a financing commitment from AgSouth Farm Credit, ACA for $27 million, $17 million of which will be available to fund the transaction.

The members of the Cagle Family Group together hold a controlling stake in the Company's common stock. We are not interested in selling our shares pursuant to an alternative transaction and will only consider a transaction in which we purchase all of the outstanding shares of the Company not now owned by us. Given our controlling stake in the Company and the nature of the proposed transaction, we expect that you will form a special committee of independent directors to consider this offer and respond on behalf of the Company and its other shareholders.

Source: Form SC 13D filed by Cagle's Inc. on November 13, 2007.

The family states unambiguously that it is "not interested in selling our shares pursuant to an alternative transaction and will only consider a transaction in which we purchase all of the outstanding shares." The family eventually withdrew its acquisition proposal. At the time of writing, the stock trades well below the offer price. It is clear that no hostile bidder could ever intervene because the family would simply refuse to sell its shares.

CHAPTER 10

Government Involvement

Despite its institutionalized free market rhetoric, the government takes a strong interest in merger activities. Its different agencies engage in ways that both help and hamper arbitrageurs in their business. The multitude of federal and state agencies that are involved in the regulation of takeovers is confusing and, worst of all, inconsistent. Different actors have conflicting goals and priorities.

In general, the Securities and Exchange Commission (SEC) casts itself as an investor advocate that promotes full disclosure. State legislatures, in contrast, tend to be beholden to the interests of corporate management rather than investors. Other state and federal agencies cater to constituencies with even narrower interests, such as state agencies regulating the power industry, which seek to minimize rates paid by consumers for energy consumption.

Departments arbitrageurs can have problems with various antitrust authorities, most prominently the Federal Trade Commission (FTC) and the Department of Justice (DOJ), as well as industry-specific regulators such as the Federal Communications Commission, the Surface Transportation Board, and the Federal Energy Regulatory Commission.

ANTITRUST ENFORCEMENT

Antitrust concerns are among the most difficult problems for arbitrageurs to make judgments on. The field is highly technical and relies on a thorough understanding of precedent cases where regulators intervened or chose not to intervene. Antitrust regulation is further complicated by the political environment, where enforcement can be weak or strong in different administrations. Moreover, individual transactions can have political overtones, for example, if they risk eliminating jobs in the district of a powerful member of Congress.

Antitrust laws have their origin in the Sherman Act of 1890, which had two principles:

1. All contracts, combinations and conspiracies that restrain trade are prohibited.
2. Conspiracies to monopolize a particular market are prohibited.

Violations of these provisions are punishable. The Sherman Act was ineffective at first because courts interpreted it very broadly and ruled that it was worded so that all contracts would be barred if it were implemented. In 1914, the government responded to this problem through a new law, the Clayton Act. Initially, the Clayton Act addressed only the acquisition of stock in a corporation if the effect was to reduce competition; asset acquisitions were not covered. The act was amended when the loophole began to be exploited. The criteria used to determine whether a merger is anticompetitive were defined in Section 7:

> *No corporation shall acquire the whole or any part of the stock, or the whole or any part of the assets, of another corporation where in any line of commerce in any section of the country the effect of such an acquisition may be to substantially lessen competition or tend to create a monopoly.*
>
> Clayton Act, Section 7

Further improvements in the antitrust treatment of mergers were made by the Hart-Scott-Rodino Antitrust Improvements Act of 1976, commonly abbreviated as HSR. It established the principle that mergers must be reviewed in advance by the FTC and the DOJ. Prior to HSR, the government disapproved mergers after they had been completed already. This led to the logistical nightmare of having to disassemble merged companies, which was difficult and took a long time to litigate. In the meantime, the merged company was benefiting from its anticompetitive behavior. Since HSR, the government no longer *approves* mergers; instead, it gives *clearance* so that the merger can close.

Under HSR, all mergers above a certain threshold value must make a notice filing. The threshold increases every year with inflation; it was $65.2 million for fiscal 2009. The FTC and DOJ then decide among themselves which agency will review the transaction. They must make up their mind whether to challenge the transaction in a set period of time. For all-cash offers, the regulators have 15 days to review the filing; in stock-for-stock offers, 30 days. During this waiting period, the transaction cannot close. If the government does not oppose the transaction, it will either grant early termination of the waiting period or let the period expire unchallenged. Early termination notices are posted on the FTC's Web site.[1] In stock-for-stock transactions, both firms must supply the required information.

If some antitrust concerns are raised in the government's review, the merger will be investigated in more detail. In this process, the agency that reviews the merger asks the company to supply it with more documents voluntarily. The government also conducts interviews with customers and competitors to get a better understanding of the products involved. The typical investigation that leads to no subsequent action lasts 57 days.[2] If this still is not sufficient, the government requests "additional information and documentary material relevant to the proposed acquisition." These are also known as "second requests" and are dreaded by arbitrageurs. A second request leads to a widening of deal spreads because the market perceives the risk of a challenge by the government as having increased significantly. Companies can avoid a second request by withdrawing the initial HSR filing and refiling it with additional information. This will reset the waiting period and avoids the bad publicity of a second request. Second requests often are issued in the last week of the HSR waiting period. The government tries to make full use of the allotted time to avoid unnecessary requests.

Antitrust insiders claim that the government benefits in its investigation often from information that is volunteered by competitors or customers of the merging firms as soon as the merger has been announced publicly.

Most second request proceedings are resolved amicably between the government and the merging companies. In the best-case scenario, the companies will furnish additional information that clarifies the government's concerns. Other second requests can lead to protracted negotiations. The merging firms often come to a settlement with the FTC or DOJ whereby they agree to divest certain divisions of one of the firms prior to closing the transaction. Exhibit 10.1 shows the announcement of Dow Chemical of the intended divestment of some of its subsidiaries in order to facilitate the 2008/2009 merger with Rohm & Haas.

A second request always leads to delays in the closing of the merger and increases costs. The FTC typically requests large amounts of data that can amount to millions of pages of documents. The merger cannot be completed until 20 days after both parties have complied with the second request. In the case of a cash merger, that period is shortened to 10 days. The average time period needed to resolve a second request is 157 days.[3]

Table 10.1 shows the statistics of HSR filings and second requests from 2005 through 2008. Only in roughly 1.5 percent of HSR filings will the government issue a second request. This figure reflects a large number

EXHIBIT 10.1 ANNOUNCEMENT BY DOW CHEMICAL OF INTENT TO DIVEST SUBSIDIARIES TO FACILITATE MERGER WITH ROHM & HAAS

Midland, MI—September 10, 2008

The Dow Chemical Company announced today that it is exploring divestiture options for its Clear Lake Operations acrylic acid and esters, and UCAR Emulsion Systems specialty latex business in North America. Dow has engaged J.P. Morgan to act as financial adviser in support of this effort.

The exploration of strategic options for the business is driven by Dow's interest in proactively mitigating potential anti-trust issues associated with its previously announced acquisition of Rohm and Haas.

The business includes an acrylic acid and esters production plant located in Texas (Clear Lake), and UCAR Emulsion System specialty latex product plants located in Louisiana (St. Charles), Illinois (Alsip), California (Torrance) and a commercial and technical center in North Carolina (Cary). As divestiture options are considered, the business will continue to be sharply focused on effectively managing operations, competing in the market, delivering exceptional value to customers, and the safety of Dow employees.

Source: Press release by Dow Company.

TABLE 10.1 HSR Transactions, Second Requests, and Merger Enforcement Actions from 2005 to 2008

Fiscal Year	HSR Transactions	Second Requests	Merger Enforcement Actions	HSR Premerger Violation
2005	1,610	25	14	1
2006	1,755	28	16	0
2007	2,108	31	22	1
2008*	767	8	5	1

* Represents fiscal year 2008 through February 29, 2008.
Source: Federal Trade Commission, "The FTC in 2008: A Force for Consumers and Competition," March 2008.

of filings of smaller mergers that have no competitive implications at all. However, once a second request has been issued, the risk of regulatory action is very high. In roughly two thirds of all second request cases, the process reaches the point where the government files a lawsuit to block the merger. Once legal action begins, the deal is dead for practical purposes. Resolution of the litigation can take a long time and will be costly. Therefore, the parties to a merger usually terminate the deal once the government challenges it.

Litigation brought by the DOJ is heard in federal court. The DOJ will seek a judgment to enjoin the merger. In contrast, litigation brought by the FTC is initially heard by an administrative law judge. The decision of the administrative law judge is then reviewed by the FTC commissioners and can be appealed in federal court. The FTC's ruling comes in the form of a cease-and-desist order rather than an injunction.

The overriding principle is the question of market power and concentration. The first analysis is whether a merger increases concentration in the relevant market. A market is defined as

> a product or group of products and a geographic area in which it is produced or sold such that a hypothetical profit-maximizing firm, not subject to price regulation, that was the only present and future producer or seller of those products in that area likely would impose at least a "small but significant and nontransitory" increase in price, assuming the terms of sale of all other products are held constant. A relevant market is a group of products and a geographic area that is no bigger than necessary to satisfy this test.
>
> Horizontal Merger Guidelines, U.S. Department
> of Justice and the Federal Trade Commission

This definition of a market is very vague, and regulators have a history of shifting definitions in unpredictable ways. The relevant market has two dimensions: geographic and product reach. "Product reach" is defined by potential substitutes that consumer might use when faced with a price increase. The analysis will try to determine whether there is a group of products for which a monopolist can impose a nontransitory price increase. Consumers' price elasticity is the economic variable that is evaluated here. If consumers' demand is inelastic for a 5 percent increase in the price of the products of both merging firms, then there are potential adverse competitive effects in the product market. The geographic reach is determined analogously: What is the smallest region in which a price increase would not be transitory?

Once a market has been found, the concentration in that market is calculated through the Herfindahl-Hirschman Index (HHI). The

HHI is the sum of the square of the percentage market share of each firm:

$$HHI = \sum_{i=1}^{N} s_i^2 \tag{10.1}$$

where N is the total number of firms in the market.

s_i is the market share of firm i.

The HHI ranges from zero to 10,000, where the maximum of 10,000 is reached when one single firm has a market share of 100 percent. For a hypothetical market with perfect competition of an infinite number of firms each with infinitesimal market share, the HHI will approach zero. The higher the value of the index, the more concentrated the market is. Regulators will consider the anticipated HHI after the closing of the merger. Three threshold levels are relevant for government action:

1. *HHI below 1,000 after the merger.* There is no concentration.
2. *HHI between 1,000 and 1,800 after the merger.* The market is moderately concentrated. If the merger leads to an increase of more than 100 points in the HHI, there is a risk that it may be anticompetitive. An increase of less than 100 points is not considered to have competitive consequences. This allows for the merger of smaller participants.
3. *HHI above 1,800 after the merger.* The market is considered highly concentrated. Nevertheless, if the increase due to the HHI is less than 50, the merger is unlikely to have an anticompetitive impact. Such a small increase occurs when smaller market participants merge.

To put these levels into context, an HHI of 1,000 represents a market of 10 firms each having a 10 percent market share. An HHI of 1,800 corresponds to a market of 5 firms each with 18 percent market share, plus a large number of smaller firms with an aggregate market share of 10 percent.

Table 10.2 shows the government's investigation of mergers as a function of the change in the HHI and the level of the HHI in the industry following the merger. It can be seen that for mergers in highly concentrated industries, there are few closed cases, and the vast majority ends in enforcement. In contrast, for industries with a low HHI after the merger, the ratio of investigations that are closed without action relative to the ones that are enforced is much more balanced.

Since 1984, the index levels are no longer adhered to mechanically but have become flexible guidelines. Qualitative factors are also taken into account now, notably changes in market conditions and the degree of differentiation of products.

TABLE 10.2 FTC Horizontal Merger Investigations: Post-Merger HHI and Change in HHI (Delta), FY 1996–FY 2005 (Enforced/Closed)

Postmerger HHI	Change in HHI (Delta)								
	0–99	100–199	200–299	300–499	500–799	800–1,199	1,200–2,499	2,500 +	TOTAL
0–1,799	0/14	17/28	19/17	17/9	3/2	0/1	0/0	0/0	56/71
1,800–1,999	0/4	5/4	5/5	12/1	12/3	0/0	0/0	0/0	34/17
2,000–2,399	1/2	1/5	7/5	24/12	31/8	1/1	0/0	0/0	65/33
2,400–2,999	1/1	4/1	6/5	16/4	41/12	25/7	0/0	0/0	93/30
3,000–3,999	0/2	2/2	3/2	6/2	16/8	50/16	29/8	0/0	106/40
4,000–4,999	0/0	0/2	1/1	3/1	8/2	9/4	45/2	0/0	66/12
5,000–6,999	0/0	2/0	3/2	3/1	7/0	10/2	90/14	31/3	146/22
7,000 +	0/0	0/0	1/0	1/0	2/0	6/0	16/1	152/2	178/3
TOTAL	2/23	31/42	45/37	82/30	120/35	101/31	180/25	183/5	744/228

Source: Federal Trade Commission, Horizontal Merger Investigation Data, Fiscal Years 1996–2005, issued January 25, 2007.

The Federal Reserve Bank of St. Louis maintains a database of market shares of banks in regional markets named CASSIDI. It is accessible to the public and can be a useful tool in examining bank mergers. The data is based on Federal Deposit Insurance Corporation (FDIC) filings by banks and is usually 12 to 18 months old, so that any conclusions drawn should be taken with a grain of salt. The announcement of the merger between Wells Fargo Bank and Wachovia Bank is a good example of how the HHI works. An arbitrageur can use the CASSIDI system to calculate the HHI in different markets in which the merging banks operate. CASSIDI identifies 46 overlapping banking markets, of which 29 are in California. Each of these markets is analyzed individually. For example, in the market of Davis, California, the total HHI is 1,852 prior to the merger. CASSIDI's calculation is reproduced in Table 10.3.

Following the merger of the two institutions, the HHI in this market increased by 954 to 2,806, as seen in Table 10.4. The Federal Reserve Bank of St. Louis gives the helpful warning that the merger

> *could have an adverse effect on competition in this banking market. Please contact the Buyer's primary federal banking regulator for more information.*

Because most of the overlap is concentrated in California and affects relatively few markets, it is likely that the banks will find a way to divest branches in the affected markets if required to do so by antitrust regulators.

Over time, other factors have been added to the evaluation of anticompetitive effects of mergers. Today, the DOJ will also consider the possibility of entry of new competitors, any efficiency gains from the combination that would offset any anticompetitive effects, and take the potential exit of one of the merger parties into account in the event that the merger were not to occur.

The enforcement of antitrust risk by the government is highly variable and depends on the current political situation as well as the individuals in charge of the DOJ and FTC. The effect of the addition of more and more factors to the analysis of anticompetitive effects of mergers probably has contributed also to the decreasing government antitrust activity this decade.

It is unclear whether regulators are preparing to become more aggressive. In 2007, the FTC failed to obtain a preliminary injunction to block the acquisition of Wild Oats by Whole Foods. Normally, regulators will stop litigating when courts refuse to grant preliminary injunctions, if only because a victory after the merger has concluded makes an unwinding of the combined entity difficult. In the Wild Oats/Whole Foods merger, however, the FTC continued to litigate and won an appeal in the middle of 2008. During the first quarter of 2009, the merged Whole Foods settled the litigation with the government by agreeing to sell 32 stores, mostly in

TABLE 10.3 Banking Market in Davis, California, as Seen by the St. Louis Fed's CASSIDI System

Type	Branch Count	Entity Name	City	State	Unweighted Deposits†	Rank	Market Share	Weighted* Deposits	Rank	Market Share
BHC	1	Wachovia Corporation	Charlotte	NC	301.421	1	26.09	301.421	1	26.09
BANK	1	Wachovia Bank, National Association	Charlotte	NC	301.421					
BHC	2	Bank of America Corporation	Charlotte	NC	280.738	2	24.30	280.738	2	24.30
BANK	2	Bank of America, National Association	Charlotte	NC	280.738					
BHC	3	Wells Fargo & Company	San Francisco	CA	211.273	3	18.28	211.273	3	18.28
BANK	3	Wells Fargo Bank, National Association	Sioux Falls	SD	211.273					
BHC	4	First Northern Community Bancorp	Dixon	CA	122.285	4	10.58	122.285	4	10.58
BANK	4	First Northern Bank of Dixon	Dixon	CA	122.285					
BHC	1	Jpmorgan Chase & Co.	New York	NY	108.451	5	9.39	108.451	5	9.39
BANK	1	Jpmorgan Chase Bank, National Association	Columbus	OH	108.451					
BHC	1	U.S. Bancorp	Minneapolis	MN	56.254	6	4.87	56.254	6	4.87
BANK	1	U.S. Bank National Association	Cincinnati	OH	56.254					
BHC	1	Mitsubishi Ufj Financial Group, Inc.	Tokyo		50.560	7	4.38	50.560	7	4.38
BANK	1	Union Bank of California, National Association	San Francisco	CA	50.560					
BHC	1	Rcb Corporation	Sacramento	CA	24.537	8	2.12	24.537	8	2.12
BANK	1	River City Bank	Sacramento	CA	24.537					

* Deposits of thrift institutions are weighted at 50 percent, unless otherwise noted. Deposits of thrift subsidiaries of commercial banking organizations, however, are weighted at 100 percent.

† Deposit data (in millions of dollars) are as of June 30, 2007, and reflect currently known ownership structure.

Source: Adapted from Federal Reserve Bank of St. Louis, CASSIDI™: Competitive Analysis and Structure Source Instrument for Depository Institutions. Run on October 4, 2008.

TABLE 10.4 Effect of the Wells Fargo/Wachovia Merger in the Davis, California, Market on Competition

| | | | | Postmerger | | | | | |
| | | | | Unweighted | | | Weighted* | | |
Branches	Name	City	State	Deposits**	Rank	%	Deposits**	Rank	%
4	Wells Fargo & Company	San Francisco	CA	512.694	1	44.37	512.694	1	44.37
1	Wachovia Bank, National Association	Charlotte	NC	301.421			301.421		
3	Wells Fargo Bank, National Association	Sioux Falls	SD	211.273			211.273		

	Premerger	Postmerger
Total Organizations:	8	7
Total Banking Organizations:	8	7
Total Thrift Organizations:	0	0

Herfindahl-Hirschman Index	Premerger	Postmerger	Change in HHI
HHI Unweighted Deposits	1852	2806	954
HHI Weighted Deposits	1852	2806	954

* Deposits of thrift institutions are weighted at 50 percent, unless otherwise noted. Deposits of thrift subsidiaries of commercial banking organizations, however, are weighted at 100 percent.

Note: This transaction exceeds established merger guidelines, suggesting that it could have an adverse effect on competition in this banking market. Please contact the Buyer's primary federal banking regulator for more information.

Source: Adapted from Federal Reserve Bank of St. Louis, CASSIDI™: Competitive Analysis and Structure Source Instrument for Depository Institutions. Run on October 4, 2008.

Arizona and Colorado. The significance of this settlement lies in the breakup of a firm that had merged already. Such drastic measures had not been taken in decades and could be the harbinger of a new, more stringent approach to the implementation of antitrust laws.

The analysis of antitrust risk is complicated even more by the increasingly global nature of large corporations. As a result, antitrust concerns arise no longer just from U.S. regulators in U.S. mergers, but more frequently from foreign regulators when two U.S. firms have dominant market share in these foreign markets. One of the largest transactions to stumble over foreign antitrust enforcement was the aborted $115 billion merger of Sprint and MCI WorldCom in 2000. The European Commission (EC), which enforces antitrust laws in the European Union, blocked the transaction. Similarly, in 2001 the $40 billion of GE and Honeywell was blocked by the EC even though it had already been okayed by U.S. regulators.[4]

International antitrust issues can arise in transactions that look solid from a U.S. perspective. As companies become increasingly global, arbitrageurs will run into international antitrust issues more frequently. Antitrust enforcement is a risk not only in the major economies of the world; it also can become a problem if the merging U.S. companies happen to have a dominant position among each other in smaller markets abroad. The author was once invested in a transaction that suddenly was held up in a country in South America where the firm had a dominant position, even though this export market was a small fraction of the firm's overall sales. As globalization progresses, even supposedly domestic deals will increasingly have international implications.

It can be seen from this brief description that the analysis of antitrust risk in mergers is extremely technical and specialized. Some arbitrageurs specialize in transactions that have antitrust risk and profit from their ability to analyze challenges better than the market on average. Other arbitrageurs hire lawyers who specialize in antitrust law to help analyze antitrust risk. If an arbitrageur does not have a good understanding of the risk or access to superior legal advice, it is best to stay away from mergers that have antitrust risk.

SEC'S APPROACH TO REGULATION

The Securities and Exchange Commission takes a relatively passive approach to the regulation of mergers and buyouts. It follows the main tenet of securities laws when companies merge: disclosure. Unlike other regulatory agencies, the SEC does not evaluate the merit or fairness of a merger. Even grossly unfair mergers can pass SEC muster as long as their unfairness is disclosed properly. The review of the quality of disclosure trumps a pro-nouncement as to its merit. This line of regulation is comparable to other SEC mandates, such as the issuance of securities, where the SEC simply reviews the adequacy of disclosures.

The review depends on whether the acquisition is structured as a merger or a tender offer. Tender offer filings apply to both cash tender offers and stock tender offers. The SEC reviews three types of documents:

1. Proxy statements

    These are filings made on Schedule 14A. They are similar to proxy statements sent out with annual meetings. A merger that requires share-holder approval requires a special meeting that is convened for this purpose. Sometimes the timing of the special shareholder meeting over-laps with that of the regular annual meeting, and the two are combined. Target companies sometimes simply skip the regular annual meeting if they are going to be acquired shortly and have a special meeting only for the purpose of approving the merger. If the merger were not to be approved, they would have to reconvene the regular annual meeting later.

2. Tender offer statements

    These are documents that describe the terms of a tender offer. As discussed on Chapter 3, no shareholder approval is needed in a tender offer because shareholders consent indirectly by tendering their shares. These filings are made on Schedule TO.

3. Information statements

    These are statements on Schedule 14C that are similar to 14A filings except that no proxies are solicited. Minority squeeze-outs through short form mergers, for example, do not require shareholder approval, and a Schedule 14C is provided to shareholders.

A number of other, related filings are made in a merger, many of which reproduce information that is filed in the three statements just described. These other filings include:

- Going-private transaction; Schedule 13E-3.
- Schedule 14D-1 and 14D-9.
- Schedule 14E-4.
- Form 15. Once the merger is completed, the company files a Form 15 to announce the termination of the listing of its shares. These filings are made after the completion of the merger and have no relevance to arbitrageurs.

Table 10.5 shows the principal filings made by targets and acquirer as a function of whether the transaction is structured as a merger or tender offer,

TABLE 10.5 SEC Filings Made by Acquirers and Targets in Tender Offers
and Mergers

| | Tender Offer | | Merger | |
	Cash	Stock Exchange Offer	Stock	Cash
Acquirer	Schedule TO, Summary term sheet	Prospectus under Rule 425	Registration statement under Rule 425	Proxy under 14A
Target	Schedule 14D-9	Schedule 14D-9	Proxy under 14A	Proxy under 14A

and whether the consideration is cash or stock. When both cash and stock
are offered, the filings required for stock-for-stock mergers are made.

Documents filed with the SEC are available to the public on its EDGAR
system through the Internet. For arbitrageurs, EDGAR is the first stop in the
collection of information.

As soon as a merger is announced, the press release is filed with the
SEC under Form 8-K along with the merger agreement. An 8-K is required
to be filed within four business days of a material event. When a merger
agreement is signed, the press release and the agreement are filed under item
1.01 of Form 8-K. There is often a duplicate filing of the press release and
the merger agreement because under byzantine securities laws, a merger
agreement is reportable not only as a material event but also, in the event
of a stock-for-stock merger, as an event related to an offer of securities, or
as a tender offer. Therefore, the EDGAR system will also show a Rule 425
filing or a Schedule TO with the exact same information as the 8-K. It is one
of the more annoying aspects of researching mergers that many filings are
duplicative or empty shells. Unfortunately, there appears to be no interest on
the side of securities lawyers to make the system more easily comprehensible
for investors. The more complex the system, the more need for expensive
services of securities attorneys.

Mergers

In general, when stock is issued by the acquirer, the issuance may be subject
to approval by shareholders. This may be required by the laws of the state
of incorporation or by rules of the exchange on which the acquirer is listed.
For example, the stock exchanges require shareholder approval whenever
more than 20 percent of the outstanding shares are issued.

If the acquisition is structured as a merger, a registration statement of
the new shares is filed by the acquirer under Rule 425. For a cash merger,

a proxy statement is filed on Schedule 14A by both the acquirer and the target. The acquirer's shareholders approve the issuance of shares and the merger, whereas the target's shareholders approve the merger only. Duplicate filings are a common annoyance in mergers. Exhibit 7.1 showed an excerpt of such a duplicative Schedule 13-E3 filed by Atari Inc. The information required by Schedule 13-E3 (to be discussed) is already contained in the proxy statement. Nevertheless, because this merger leads the company to go private, it is also required to make a going-private filing on Schedule 13-E3. Documents of this type that are full of references to other documents are common in mergers. The irony is that the SEC requires the information required by the going-private rule to be incorporated into the proxy statement yet also requires the company to make a filing of the going-private schedule.

When a company seeks approvals from shareholders, it seeks proxies to vote the shareholders' shares at the meeting. A proxy statement must be filed at least 20 days prior to the shareholder meeting.

The difference between an all-cash and a stock-for-stock, or mixed cash and stock merger, is the amount of information contained in the proxy statement about the buyer. When cash is paid, target shareholders need to know very little about the acquirer. However, when stock is received in exchange for the target shares, shareholders need very detailed information about the acquirer in order to evaluate the transaction.

The layout of a Schedule 14A in connection with a merger is similar to the next example from the shareholder meeting for Wilshire Enterprises.

14A filings in connection with a merger are initially submitted to EDGAR as preliminary 14A filings labeled as filing type PREM14A. After the SEC has reviewed and approved the materials, the definitive proxy statements distributed to shareholders are filed as definitive filings labeled DEFM14A.

An additional item that is presented to shareholders in many mergers is a proposal to authorize the board to postpone the meeting, if necessary, to solicit additional proxies in case the number of votes present at the meeting is insufficient to adopt the merger agreement. A postponement is rarely necessary, but companies nevertheless include these proposals as an insurance policy.

Tender Offers

Tender offers give rise to multiple and duplicative documents that make life difficult for arbitrageurs who have to review them. For cash tender offers, the acquirer files a Schedule TO and a summary term sheet. For an exchange offer, the acquirer files a registration statement under Rule 425

TABLE OF CONTENTS OF THE DEFM14A FILINGS OF WILSHIRE ENTERPRISES, FILED ON AUGUST 5, 2008

Questions and Answers about the Merger and the Merger Agreement

Summary

Cautionary statement concerning forward-looking information

Market price and dividend information

The special meeting

> Time, place, and purposes of the special meeting
>
> Record date and quorum required votes
>
> Proxies; revocation
>
> Submitting proxies via the Internet or by telephone
>
> Adjournments and postponements
>
> Solicitation of proxies

The parties to the merger

Background to the proposal relating to the merger

Reasons for and benefits of the merger

Risk factors and detriments related to the merger

Proposal 1:

> Adoption of the merger agreement pursuant to which a wholly-owned subsidiary of NWJ will merge with and into Wilshire for a merger consideration to the stockholders of Wilshire of $3.88 per share in cash
>
> The merger
>
> Stock options and restricted shares
>
> Regulatory approvals applicable to the merger
>
> Conditions of closing
>
> Representations and warranties
>
> Interim operations

(Continued)

TABLE OF CONTENTS OF THE DEFM14A FILINGS OF WILSHIRE ENTERPRISES, FILED ON AUGUST 5, 2008
(*Continued*)

as in a stock-for-stock merger. The target files the same documents as in a cash tender offer.

This information is required in a tender offer statement:

1. Summary term sheet
   This is useful as a quick overview of the transaction.
2. The name of the target company, class of securities involved, and indication of any prior purchases of these securities
3. The identity and background of the filing
   The acquirer in a strict sense is often a merger subvehicle that has been established only for the purpose of making the acquisition. This item gives some background as to the ultimate acquirer behind the merger vehicle.
4. Terms of the transaction
   This includes the number of shares being bid for, expiration date, tendering and withdrawal procedures, payment method, and tax consequences.
5. Description of past contacts, negotiations, or transactions with the target
6. The purpose of the transaction
7. Source of the funds used to complete transaction
   This section is particularly relevant for cash mergers. It allows arbitrageurs to estimate the risk associated with the financing.
8. The number of shares bidder already owns
9. Identity of persons and parties employed by bidder for the transaction
10. Bidder's financial statements (two years)
11. Any agreements between the bidder and any of its officers that might be material to target company shareholders
12. Any recommendations that bidder is making to the target shareholders
13. The purposes and reasons for a going-private transaction, and alternatives considered
14. Comments on the fairness of a going-private transaction.
15. Reports, opinions, and appraisals

Shareholders receive an "offer to purchase" and a "letter of transmittal," which are also often published in major newspapers. The offer to purchase describes the principal terms of the transaction.

Rule 14E governs some of the principal requirements for tender offers:

- The tender offer must be open for at least 20 business days. The starting point is the publication of the offer, its advertisement in a newspaper, or the submission of the materials to the target.
- The tender offer can be extended for a period of at least 10 business days. A notice of extension must be sent to shareholders. Extensions are

a frequent occurrence because many companies fail to get the minimum number of shares needed by the time of the expiration of the initial tender period. Good-quality communication can increase the likelihood of a successful tender offer.

- If the tender offer is amended, a notice must be sent to shareholders within 10 days. It must also be delivered to the target and other bidders, if any. The exchange on which the company is quoted must also be notified.
- *Best price rule.* All shareholders must receive the same price. This rule has stopped the practice of greenmailing that was prevalent in the 1980s. If the price is increased during the tender offer period, for example, due to a bidding war, then all shareholders must receive the higher price, including those who tendered prior to the increase.
- Most important, the acquirer must pay for the securities promptly.

Another important rule is the prohibition of the acquirer from purchasing shares of the target from the announcement of the tender offer to its expiration.

In an exchange offer, the acquirer pays for the shares of the target in stock. The stock to be sold must first be registered with the SEC. However, the exchange offer period commences when the registration statement is filed with the SEC. The exchange offer can be consummated once the registration statement has been declared effective by the SEC.

The target must respond to a tender offer within 10 days by filing a Schedule 14D-9 and a summary term sheet, which also contains mainly references the Schedule 14D-9. This filing must state whether the target supports or rejects the tender offer. If the target has no position, it must state the reasons. Schedule 14D-9 is organized in this way:

1. Subject company information
2. Identity and background of filing person
3. Past contacts, transactions, negotiations and agreements
4. Solicitation or recommendation
5. Person/assets retained, employed, compensated, or used
6. Interest in securities of the subject company
7. Purposes of the transaction and plans or proposals
8. Additional information
9. Exhibits

Going-Private Transactions

Rule 13e-3 describes the information that must be furnished to shareholders when a company goes private. Most of this information is already contained in the proxy statement or tender offer document, so Schedule 13E-3 always resembles that of Atari in Exhibit 7.1. Some information that must be furnished to shareholders according to Rule 13e-3 and that is contained in the proxy or tender offer statement includes:

- Whether the company believes that the transaction is fair to shareholders. Needless to say, it always believes it is. The justification usually evolves around trading liquidity of the shares, premia received, prospects for the business, and fairness of the process.
- Whether independent directors have retained independent representation. This is always the case except for the smallest transactions in the nano-cap space.
- Whether independent directors support the transaction.
- Descriptions of all contacts between the target and acquirer for the last two years.
- Appraisals from outside valuation firms, if any. These are often the most interesting materials filed in going-private transactions. Presentations to the board of directors by the investment bankers are required to be filed, and these tend to be a treasure trove of information about the valuation and its assumption.

Going-private transactions with 13E-3 filings are always reviewed by two layers in the SEC: the branch office and the Office of Mergers and Acquisitions. As a result, the SEC makes lengthy comments and requests many changes before a company can go private. This leads to multiple amendments of the filing on the EDGAR system.

STATE GOVERNMENTS

Companies incorporate under state laws and also liquidate or merge according to procedures prescribed by the states. A merger itself is a relatively simple activity in most states: it is sufficient for an authorized company official to file a certificate of merger with the relevant state body. In Delaware, this is the secretary of state's Division of Corporations.

During the merger wave of the 1980s, companies managed to convince their local state governments to implement anti-takeover legislation. States became protectors of entrenched management that sought to fight off hostile takeovers. This put state governments in direct conflict with the SEC, which casts itself as an investor advocate and maintains that state anti-takeover provisions are an infringement to interstate commerce.

The devil lies in the details leading up to the merger. State laws offer companies many takeover defenses to fend of potential suitors and thwart merger attempts. These defenses have been described in detail in Chapter 6.

However, state politicians occasionally do get involved when a local company wants to fend off a hostile acquirer. One of the most notorious cases was the battle for shopping mall owner Taubman Centers, Inc., between a group of Taubman family members and Simon Properties Group, another commercial real estate firm. Australian mall operator Westfield America Trust joined Simon in its attempt to acquire Taubman. In late 2002, Simon Properties and Westfield offered to acquire Taubman for $17.50 per share, a premium to the $14.80 closing price before the announcement. Taubman had an entrenched family that controlled the firm through Series B shares as well as through a voting agreement between the family members and their friends that gave them control over 33.6 percent of the shares. The Series B shares had been issued years earlier when the GM pension fund wanted to swap its interests in some of Taubman's properties into shares of the firm.

Simon first increased its bid to $18.00 and later, in January 2003, to $20.00 per share, a 25 percent premium to its trading price before the offer. Of the outside shareholders, 85 percent accepted Simon Properties' $20.00 bid. When the Taubman family refused to sell, Simon sued in Michigan state court to have the voting agreement voided under that state's control share acquisition act. This in itself is rather unusual: A hostile buyer is normally the victim of a control share act and does not seek to benefit from it. During the litigation, it was discovered that the true reason for the issuance of the Series B shares had been to thwart an attempted takeover by another firm, Rouse Company. This takeover proposal had never been revealed to shareholders.

The court sided with Simon and prevented the Taubman family from voting its shares. However, the battle for Taubman then shifted from the court system to the state legislature of Michigan. Taubman lobbied Michigan's lawmakers to pass a law that would make it legal for groups of shareholders to vote their shares together without triggering the provisions of the Michigan control shares act. After intense lobbying, the Michigan senate passed the law in a vote of 24 to 14 in September 2004.

The day after Michigan's governor signed the law, Simon Properties withdrew its acquisition proposal.

It is very difficult for arbitrageurs to estimate the probability of success of a lobbying campaign on the state level. It is safe to assume that state politicians will bow to the demands of local companies rather than help out-of-state acquirers. However, the intensity of a local defense hardly ever reaches the levels seen in the Taubman case. In the acquisition of Anheuser-Busch by InBev, Missouri governor Matt Blunt opposed the deal publicly and even directed the Missouri Department of Economic Development to see if there was a way to stop it. Despite the high profile of Anheuser-Busch, the transaction was completed because, ultimately, the willingness of the target firm to be acquired trumped the political machinations.

States also have antitrust laws. They are rarely a problem because federal antitrust regulations trump those of states. Other state laws, however, can conflict with federal antitrust regulations. Highly regulated industries, such as utilities or telecommunications, often are mandated by state law to operate in ways that are considered anticompetitive under federal antitrust laws. Fortunately, lawyers have created a state action doctrine, which gives these firms immunity from federal antitrust laws.

Takeovers of utilities often fail because of opposition by state agencies charged with regulating the industry. The bodies often have wide-ranging powers and will block mergers if there is a risk, often more perceived than real, that rates for the state's residents will increase if a merger passes.

Banking and insurance mergers can take a long time to complete because state banking or insurance regulators have to approve the transaction in each state where the banks or insurance companies are active.

One of the more extreme cases of interference of such a state agency with a merger was the acquisition of Unisource Energy by private equity firm Kohlberg Kravis Roberts & Co. (KKR) in 2003. The Arizona Corporation Commission refused to approve the transaction. KKR made a number of proposals to mitigate the concern of the commissioners that rates would have to be raised in order to repay the debt accumulated in the buyout. KKR proposed to "ring fence" customers of the utility by issuing the debt separately through the holding company rather than through the utility. KKR also promised to keep the headquarters and management in Arizona. Nevertheless, the Arizona Corporation Commission refused to approve the transaction. It has been reported anecdotally that the major point of contention was KKR's unwillingness to reveal details of its calculation of the internal rate of return that it expected to make on the transaction. Fortunately for shareholders, the price of Unisource increased after the transaction had collapsed (see Figure 2.1).

It should be noted that the increase in the price only shows that KKR was underpaying for Unisource. The true value of the firm became apparent to the market only due to KKR's proposal.

Some of the most wide-ranging powers to interfere with businesses are available to state gaming regulators. Exhibit 10.1 shows the disclosure in the proxy statement of FX Real Estate & Entertainment Inc. The exhibit describes the power that Nevada Gaming Authorities have over casino companies. These powers include the forced sale of stock if a shareholder is deemed not acceptable.

For arbitrageurs, there is a real risk that a buyer is not acceptable to a gaming commission. For example, New Jersey withdrew the license of the Tropicana Casino shortly after its acquisition of Aztar Inc. had been completed. New Jersey justified its decision with Tropicana's failure to maintain a first-class casino. Fortunately for arbitrageurs, the transaction had closed already. Bond investors, however, took losses when Tropicana had to file for bankruptcy following the loss of its license.

EXHIBIT 10.2 FX REAL ESTATE & ENTERTAINMENT'S DESCRIPTION OF NEVADA GAMING REGULATION REDEMPTION OR MANDATORY SALE OF SECURITIES OWNED BY AN UNSUITABLE PERSON

Our certificate of incorporation provides that, to the extent a gaming authority makes a determination of unsuitability or to the extent deemed necessary or advisable by our board of directors, we may redeem shares of our capital stock that are owned or controlled by an unsuitable person or its affiliates. The redemption price will be the amount, if any, required by the gaming authority or, if the gaming authority does not determine the price, the sum deemed by the board of directors to be the fair value of the securities to be redeemed. If we determine the redemption price, the redemption price will be capped at the closing price of the shares on the principal national securities exchange on which the shares are listed on the trading date on the day before the redemption notice is given. If the shares are not listed on a national securities exchange, the redemption price will be capped at the closing sale price of the shares as quoted on an inter-dealer quotation system, or if the closing price is not reported, the mean between the bid and asked prices, as quoted by any other generally recognized reporting system. The redemption price may be paid in cash, by promissory note, or both, as required, and pursuant to the terms established by, the applicable gaming authority and, if not, as we elect. In the event our board of directors determines that such a redemption would adversely affect us, we shall require such person and/or its affiliates to sell the shares of our capital stock subject to the redemption.

Requirements for Equity Security Holders

Regardless of the number of shares held, any beneficial owner of the voting or non-voting securities of a registered company may be required to file an application, be investigated and have that person's suitability as a beneficial owner of such securities determined if the Nevada Commission has reason to believe that the ownership would otherwise be inconsistent with the declared policies of the State of Nevada. [...]

The Nevada Act requires any person who acquires more than 5% of the voting securities of a registered company to report the acquisition to the Nevada Commission. The Nevada Act requires beneficial owners of more than 10% of a registered company's voting securities to apply to the Nevada Commission for a finding of suitability within 30 days after the Chairman of the Nevada Board mails the written notice requiring such filing. Under certain circumstances, an "institutional investor," as defined in the Nevada Act, which acquires more than 10%, but not more than 15%, of the registered company's voting securities may apply to the Nevada Commission for a waiver of a finding of suitability if the institutional investor holds the voting securities for investment purposes only....

Consequences of Being Found Unsuitable

Any person who fails or refuses to apply for a finding of suitability or a license within 30 days after being ordered to do so by the Nevada Commission or by the Chairman of the Nevada Board, or who refuses or fails to pay the investigative costs incurred by the Nevada Gaming Authorities in connection with the investigation of its application, may be found unsuitable. The same restrictions apply to a record owner if the record owner, after request, fails to identify the beneficial owner. Any person found unsuitable and who holds, directly or indirectly, any beneficial ownership of any equity security or debt security of a registered company beyond the period of time as may be prescribed by the Nevada Commission may be guilty of a criminal offense. We will be subject to disciplinary action if, after we receive notice that a person is unsuitable to hold an equity interest or to have any other relationship with, we:

- Pay that person any dividend or interest upon any voting securities;
- Allow that person to exercise, directly or indirectly, any voting right held by that person relating to our company;
- Pay remuneration in any form to that person for services rendered or otherwise; or

(Continued)

**EXHIBIT 10.2 FX REAL ESTATE &
ENTERTAINMENT'S DESCRIPTION OF NEVADA
GAMING REGULATION REDEMPTION OR
MANDATORY SALE OF SECURITIES OWNED
BY AN UNSUITABLE PERSON** (*Continued*)

- Fail to pursue all lawful efforts to require the unsuitable person to relinquish such person's voting securities including, if necessary, the immediate purchase of the voting securities for cash at fair market value.

Requirements for Debt Security Holders

The Nevada Commission may, in its discretion, require the holder of any debt or similar securities of a registered company to file applications, be investigated and be found suitable to own the debt or other security of the registered company if the Nevada Commission has reason to believe that such ownership would otherwise be inconsistent with the declared policies of the State of Nevada. If the Nevada Commission decides that a person is unsuitable to own the security, then under the Nevada Act, the registered company can be sanctioned, including the loss of its approvals, if without the prior approval of the Nevada Commission, it:

- Pays to the unsuitable person any dividend, interest or any distribution whatsoever;
- Recognizes any voting right by the unsuitable person in connection with the securities;
- Pays the unsuitable person remuneration in any form; or
- Makes any payment to the unsuitable person by way of principal, redemption, conversion, exchange, liquidation or similar transaction.

Source: Form 10-K filed with the SEC on March 24, 2008, by FX Real Estate & Entertainment Inc.

FEDERAL GOVERNMENT

The federal government gets involved in mergers through a plethora of agencies that regulate individual industries or are charged with overseeing the federal antitrust laws. In addition, there are less obvious organization, such as the CFIUS (to be discussed) or good old political pressures and lobbying that can become threats to the completion of a merger.

One such agency that operated in relative obscurity but suddenly came to prominence is the Committee on Foreign Investments in the U.S. (CFIUS), an inter-agency committee that is chaired by the Treasury Department. It was established in 1975 during the Ford administration by an executive order and brought under presidential oversight in 1988 through the Exon-Florio Amendment. Since then, CFIUS has operated in relative obscurity until the sale of British shipping firm P&O to Dubai Ports World, a company controlled by the government of Dubai. P&O operated a number of ports in the United States. Even though CFIUS saw no threat to national security from the transaction, it fell through eventually after another port operator managed to organize congressional opposition to the transaction. The publicity surrounding this merger led to legislative changes that expand the role of CFIUS in approving the acquisition of U.S. assets by foreign acquirers.

Even before the Dubai Ports saga, CFIUS had an impact on occasional transactions that were subject to its review. One such transaction that normally would have flown under the radar screen of regulators was the 2005 acquisition of Cypress Communications by Arcapita, Inc., formerly Crescent Capital Investments. Arcapita is an investment bank in Bahrain that invests according to Islamic principles. "Private equity fund" may be a more accurate description of its business. The value of the acquisition was only $40 million. Cypress submitted the acquisition to a voluntary review by CFIUS on April 4, 2005, and disclosed it in a press release on May 12. It is noteworthy that several other SEC filings between April 4 and May 12 did not mention the submission to CFIUS. Arcapita had already done a number of investments in the United States, including some household names, such as Church's Chicken and TLC Health Care Services.

Cypress filed "voluntarily" with CFIUS. This is a euphemism that the government uses to make the regulation appear less burdensome. In reality, if a company were not to make a "voluntary" filing, it would be contacted by one of the government agencies the comprise CFIUS, such as Homeland Security, Defense, or State, and would be encouraged to make a "voluntary" filing in strong terms.

CFIUS must review mergers in which the acquirer is a foreign government or an entity controlled by a foreign government. However, unlike in antitrust legislation, where clear thresholds are set, the requirements are vague for CFIUS filings. An acquisition must give a foreign entity control over a U.S. firm. CFIUS has 30 days to review whether the transaction affects national security. In order to give CFIUS maximum flexibility, the term "national security" has not been defined. CFIUS takes a number of factors into account when making that determination:

> *(1) domestic production needed for projected national defense requirements,*
>
> *(2) the capability and capacity of domestic industries to meet national defense requirements, including the availability of human resources, products, technology, materials, and other supplies and services,*
>
> *(3) the control of domestic industries and commercial activity by foreign citizens as it affects the capability and capacity of the United States to meet the requirements of national security,*
>
> *(4) the potential effects of the proposed or pending transaction on sales of military goods, equipment, or technology to any country [...]*
>
> *(5) the potential effects of the proposed or pending transaction on United States international technological leadership in areas affecting United States national security;*
>
> *(6) the potential national security-related effects on United States critical infrastructure, including major energy assets;*
>
> *(7) the potential national security-related effects on United States critical technologies;*
>
> *(8) whether the covered transaction is a foreign government-controlled transaction*
>
> *(9) factors involving non-proliferation and government-sponsored terrorism*
>
> *(10) the long-term projection of United States requirements for sources of energy and other critical resources and material*
>
> 50 U.S.C. 2170 (f)

Following the initial 30-day review, there is an extended 45-day investigation period for certain transactions, including:

- A transaction that threatens to impair U.S. national security, and that threat has not been resolved within the 30-day review period
- A transactions involving foreign government control, such as sovereign wealth funds
- A transaction resulting in foreign control over critical infrastructure that CFIUS believes could threaten national securityIf one of the agencies constituting CFIUS requests a full investigation and CFIUS agrees

Legislation was changed in October 2007, and it remains to be seen how CFIUS's new rules will be implemented in practice. It is clear, however, that we have entered an era in which scrutiny of foreign acquirers will expose arbitrageurs to higher regulatory risk. The committee membership has been widened to include the director of National Intelligence, and CFIUS is now answerable to Congress. This increases the political risk substantially. Political oversight rests with majority and minority leaders of the House and Senate, the chair and ranking members of the Senate Banking Committee and the House Financial Services Committee, any House or Senate committee having oversight over the lead agency in the CFIUS review, and implicitly the members of the districts concerned as well as the relevant state governors. As Dubai Ports and 3Com illustrate, the risk is not purely regulatory. The political environment at the time of a merger is the real driver of deal hiccups, and national security concerns can be a pretext for political games. The 2007 legislation only reinforces this threat, because the results of an investigation now have to be provided to Congress. This will open investigations to political scrutiny by politicians, special interest groups, and business competitors. Even arbitrageurs could potentially use the political process to block an acquisition after taking a position that would benefit from a collapse of a deal. It is extremely difficult to estimate deal completion risk under these circumstances, and I expect that deal spreads will reflect this uncertainty in the future. The politicized character of CFIUS became apparent when British hedge fund The Children's Investment Fund (TCI) attempted to obtain board representation on rail carrier CSX in 2008. TCI owned 8.5 percent of CSX and had no plans to acquire CSX itself but rather to force it to sell itself to another firm. Most likely, CSX would remain a U.S.-owned firm. Nevertheless, several lawmakers were pressing CFIUS to investigate TCI for trying to take over critical infrastructure. It appears that CSX had convinced these lawmakers that a harmless proxy contest for board representation had national security implications. Yet political interference sometimes can dissipate when the transaction is friendly: In the acquisition of Anheuser-Busch by InBev, no national security issues existed. The representative in the district of Anheuser-Busch's headquarters acquiesced to the transaction when it turned out to become friendly and did not attempt to create a politically motivated national security problem.

From a public policy perspective, the sudden focus on national security is troublesome because it comes at a time when foreign investment is desperately needed. The United States runs a twin deficit of the current account and budget and relies heavily on capital inflows to finance these deficits in the presence of a negative savings rate. Aggressive enforcement of national security concerns to deflect political pressure can have serious economic repercussions.

TRADE UNIONS

Trade unions are not normally associated with influence in corporate America. It is well known that they play a key role in European companies, but their influence in the United States has been relegated to the history books. Yet there are rare exceptions where trade unions can become a force in mergers. Unlike other stakeholders in mergers, union influence comes into play on both sides of the merger: As employee representatives, unions can have interests that conflict with those of investors. However, unions have also created substantial pension funds for the benefit of theirs members. When these funds are invested in companies that are going through a merger, then union interests are aligned with those of investors. As fewer and fewer workers are unionized and the size of the funds increases through compounding, unions are becoming a forceful defender of investor rights.

In April 2008, India's Essar Steel made a bid to acquire Esmark, a maker and distributor of steel and part owner of Wheeling-Pittsburgh, for $17 per share. Russia's OAO Severstal, controlled by billionaire Alexei Mordashov, matched Essar's price of $17 in May, and a bidding war broke out for the $670 million acquisition of Esmark. Essar raised its bid to $19 per share shortly after the $17 a share bid from Severstal. Despite the higher price, Essar's bid was far from certain to win. In cases discussed in prior chapters, it was management that backed lower-priced bidders. In Esmark's case, management backed the higher bidder, but the support for the lower bid from Severstal came from a trade union.

Esmark had a unionized workforce. The United Steelworkers (USW) had a contract with Esmark that gave the union the right to reject any deal that changes control of the company and find another buyer. When Esmark signed the initial merger agreement with Essar Steel, it failed to notify the union and give it an opportunity to find another buyer, as required by the agreement. The union decided to back Severstal, because it made a "highly credible restructuring plan designed to derive maximum value from Esmark, including a five-year capital improvement plan that carries the full support of the United Steelworkers." USW favored the bid by Severstal and filed for arbitration. Arbitration has been the standard method for dispute resolution between unions and employers in the steel industry since 1976. Each party can seek arbitration without the consent of the other party.

The arbitrator sided with the USW and set aside the merger agreement between Essar and Esmark. USW was given three days to find another buyer, which was not a challenge because Severstal had already expressed a firm interest. In addition, the USW obtained the support of Franklin Mutual Advisers, which managed funds that owned 60.1 percent of Esmark's shares. Franklin Mutual agreed to tender its shares to Severstal. It reasoned that the Essar transaction had no chance of being completed in light of the opposition by the USW and the clear agreement between Esmark and USW.

In June, Severstal raised its bid to $19.25 per share. Essar conceded defeat and pulled out of the bidding. The merger was completed in early August 2008. Arbitrageurs had hoped for a continued bidding war between the two parties. Figure 10.1 shows that Esmark's stock price traded above $20 during the bidding war. Speculating on bidding wars is difficult, and the timing is critical. It does not always lead to profits.

In today's market, it is more common for unions to play a role in corporate governance than to block mergers. When CVS Caremark attempted to acquire Longs Drug Stores for roughly $2.9 billion, or $71.50 a share, a number of shareholders opposed the transaction, and unions took an active role in the fight over the acquisition's price. Pershing Square Capital Management and Advisory Research, two hedge funds that had advocated a sale of Longs, argued that the real estate was valued not sufficiently high in the acquisition—a contention that was somewhat backed by the remark

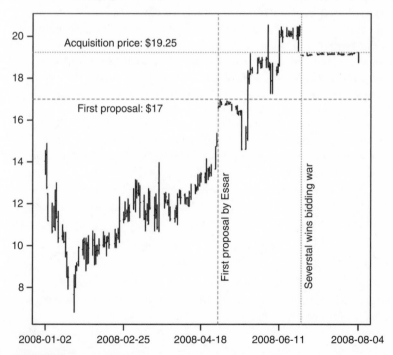

FIGURE 10.1 Stock Price of Esmark

of CVS Caremark's CEO, Tom Ryan, that it had "conservatively valued the store locations alone at more than $1 billion" when the price was negotiated. One investor claimed that Longs' CEO Warren Bryant had even said that there was an agreement between CVS Caremark and Longs not to disclose the real estate valuation publicly.

Trade unions did not enter the fight over Longs directly but indirectly through CtW (Change to Win) Investment Group, an activist organization that provides advisory services to union-backed pension funds. CtW criticized not only the real estate valuation but also a number of other problems: Longs was sold at the lower end of the range that its board had considered adequate, the breakup fee equivalent to $3.00 per share was uncharacteristically large for a transaction of this size, and Longs' assertion that it would not be able to monetize its real estate holdings, even though it had announced earlier that it was considering sale/leaseback transactions.[5]

When the first expiration date of the tender offer approached, only 4.5 percent of the shares had been tendered—shareholders were holding out for a better deal. Walgreens did make indeed a higher offer of $75 per share, which was promptly rejected by Longs, citing antitrust concerns.

Union-affiliated pension funds are likely to continue to play an active role in mergers. Two types of pension fund activism can be distinguished: shareholder activism and social activism.[6]

The term "shareholder activism" refers to activities that improve corporate governance and ultimately increase the value of companies. "Social activism" concerns questions that are often of a political nature, such as health benefits for employees or divestment of investments in certain countries. The value of social activism can be questionable in purely financial terms, but there is no doubt that shareholder activism benefits all investors, including merger arbitrageurs, no matter whether it is done by a union or by any other shareholder.

CHAPTER 11

Four Ways to Fight Abuse
of Shareholders
in Mergers

The last few chapters have painted a gloomy picture of shareholder abuse in mergers. Fortunately, investors have ways to fight back when they feel that a firm is sold on inadequate terms. This chapter discusses the methods shareholders can employ to fight back.

"JUST SELL" IS FOR LOSERS

Some commentators argue that shareholders unhappy with a company's management can just sell their shares. A similar line of argument maintains that investors can always vote with their feet and thereby punish management. Some investors even go so far as to invest only in firms that are liquid enough to allow them to exit easily if they are dissatisfied or disagree with management.

Unfortunately, this simplistic argument actually plays into the hands of unscrupulous management. Many examples in this book deal with conflicts of interest where a buyer tries to acquire a target company at a low valuation. When that buyer of a firm is its management team, it is in a position to make the firm unattractive to investors in order to stage a carefully crafted low-priced buyout. Investors who sell because they are unhappy with management will, in fact, play into the hands of such managers. Chapter 8 describes a plot by majority shareholder Lukoil to squeeze out the minority shareholders of Chapparal Resources. Lukoil caused Chapparal's management to make a number of negative announcements about the company's prospects, thereby driving down the share price. The depressed share price allowed Lukoil to acquire Chapparal for much less than it would have traded at if investors had known the actual drilling schedule that planned an increase in well drilling and hence increased oil production.

It is not even necessary that a company's management engages in such blatantly wrongful conduct in order to depress a stock price. Benign neglect is often sufficient to drive down a share price to a level where a going-private transaction becomes attractive. Unlike open-ended mutual funds, public companies do not trade at net asset value. Instead, the price is set by the law of supply and demand. When there are more sellers than buyers, the stock will drop; conversely, if there are more buyers than sellers, it will rise. Various valuation techniques have been developed to determine an intrinsic value of a company. These techniques are all valid, but there is no guarantee that the market will realize the theoretical price that they come up with. Indeed, value investors have coined the term "value trap": a company that trades at a discount to its theoretical value and remains at a discount forever. The market never recognizes the intrinsic value of a value trap stock.

Value traps get into a vicious circle of poor results and poor stock performance. As the company's financial results deteriorate, selling pressure mounts. The stock price falls, which reduces the company's financial flexibility. Raising new capital becomes expensive, and bank covenants may be broken, which further increases the cost of capital. As a result, financial performance continues to deteriorate and selling pressure increases.

Investors who sell their holdings in a company whose management destroys shareholder value act perfectly rationally from their own narrow perspective. In the aggregate, however, they keep management entrenched when they sell. By selling, investors only aggravate the valuation discount of such a company. After all, not many investors are willing to acquire shares in a firm whose governance is inadequate or whose management is inept.

Activist investors have long recognized this inefficiency and seek out companies where changes in governance can unlock shareholder value. Activists try to obtain control of the firm and hire new management that will improve its performance, or sell the firm outright for a premium. It is an investment style that carries its own risks and will work only in certain circumstances. Not every troubled firm will benefit from the efforts of activist investors.

If shareholders are invested in a company targeted by activists, they stand a good chance that the vicious circle of poor performance and selling pressure will be broken. Shareholders in other companies are out of luck. These companies either will go out of business or, more likely, will be acquired by another firm.

It is the acquisition of the firm that creates problems. If management has a poor record in running the firm, likely it will do as poor a job in selling it. The interests of shareholders and managers are rarely aligned in a merger, as was discussed in Chapter 7. Once the sale of an underperforming firm is negotiated, most shareholders throw in the towel and accept the deal as done. Small investors are relieved to see the end of suffering from poor management; they are forced to give up the hope for a turnaround. Larger holders are happy to see a "liquidity event": Because few investors were willing to buy into an underperforming company, holders of large blocks of shares were unable to sell. The merger provides them with a willing buyer for all of their shares.

It is not unusual to see deals of this type done out of desperation. Shareholders are willing to accept any price as long as they can sell. They are willing to leave money on the table and accept a low valuation. In the case of large-cap companies, disgruntled investors sometimes take their discontent public and oppose a merger, trying to obtain a better price. The record of such actions is variable and often fails. This option is discussed later in this chapter. In the case of small-cap companies, shareholders rarely oppose a transaction. These companies are too small to generate headlines, so that a campaign to oppose a merger is difficult to conduct.

However, it is just in the small- and micro-cap space that most share-holder abuse occurs. Minority squeeze-outs and management buyouts of these smaller companies are particularly at risk. A passive, frustrated, and apathetic shareholder base is an invitation for potential buyers to force a deal on poor terms. Shareholders should question why a buyer is willing to acquire a firm with little prospects. This question is particularly perti-nent in the case of financial buyers. A strategic buyer can always argue that synergies will make the acquisition of an underperforming company a good investment. However, if the very management team that ran a company into the ground partners with a private equity firm to acquire the company, it is not just the buyout itself that is questionable; the entire recent history of the company appears in a different light. Perhaps much of the reason for the company's poor performance was the unwillingness of management to make the necessary operational improvements. The only reason why a financial backer is willing to fund the acquisition is probably management's plan to improve the company; shareholders should wonder why these improvements are not made while the company is held publicly.

Shareholders who just sell under these circumstances effectively are enriching the very group that has caused their losses. Public shareholders lose what management and their financing partners make in excess returns. Selling is the strategy for losers. The winning approach is to try to capture some of the upside for the public shareholders that would otherwise go to the acquirer.

CASE FOR ACTIVIST MERGER ARBITRAGE

Fortunately, shareholders have some tools at their disposal to defend their interests in mergers in which the consideration paid is inadequate or where management was grossly negligent in selling the firm without maximizing shareholder return. The fiduciary duties of a board of directors in the sale of a company have been discussed at length in Chapter 6. Readers may want to revisit that chapter at this point.

Merger arbitrageurs and other investors in companies that are subject to a troubled buyout should not hesitate to adopt aggressive tactics to obtain full value. Although any investor can employ the strategies discussed here, merger arbitrageurs who follow them will be considered to adopt an "activist merger arbitrage" investment style. Activist merger arbitrage is an extension of classic merger arbitrage in combination with tactics otherwise employed primarily by activist investors.

Figure 11.1 illustrates how activist merger arbitrage fits into the life cycle of a corporation and the related investment strategies. While a company

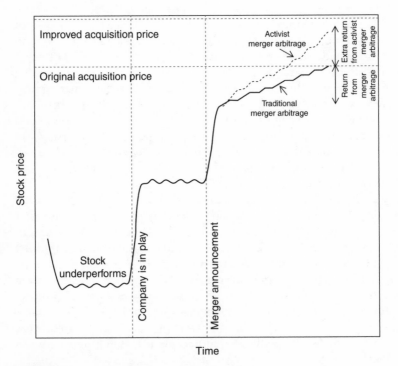

FIGURE 11.1   Late Stages of a Company's Life

underperforms, it is considered a value investment. A value investment may recover through a number of catalysts, when it is considered "value" by a sufficient number of market participants, or when an activist investor gets involved. An activist often will seek to have the company sell itself. In the absence of an activist, the company's management may decide itself that "strategic alternatives," such as a sale, are the best option for the company's future. Either way, once a company is in play, its stock price increases, generating an instant return for its investors. As soon as a merger is announced, the company's stock price will jump to a level just short of the acquisition price. At this point, the firm becomes a merger arbitrage investment. The potential return is the spread between the merger consideration and the price at which the arbitrageur can buy the firm prior to the merger.

Activist merger arbitrage seeks to increase the return available to the arbitrageur by increasing the amount paid in the transaction. Of course, this will work only in cases where the board of the target has not made a serious effort to maximize shareholder value. If the company has been shopped properly and gone through a real auction process with multiple bidders, it will be impossible for even the most determined activist investor to find a buyer that is willing to up the price paid. However, in many of the cases detailed in this book, public shareholders were shortchanged. In such instances, an activist merger arbitrage may be successful.

Various tactics are available to activist merger arbitrageurs. They can be classified broadly into two categories: legal tactics and public pressure.

1. Legal tactics
   - Appraisal rights
   - Class actions
   - Requests for documents
2. Public pressure
   - Proxy campaigns
   - Withholding shares in tender offers

These tactics are detailed in the remainder of this chapter. It should be noted that even though investors may have a good reason to think that they are not getting sufficient consideration in a merger, it is an entirely different matter to make a legal case. For most tactics, the burden of proof is on the plaintiff (i.e., the shareholder). The business judgment rule holds that courts will by default assume that a board took a decision in good faith, even if it turns out to have been a bad decision after the fact. Investors who want to attack a merger must make sure that they can find strong evidence of wrongdoing. In addition, they must show that this wrongdoing had a material impact on the transaction.

LEGAL TACTICS

Appraisal Rights

Many states give shareholders the possibility to get a court to value their shares when a company is acquired for cash. "Appraisal rights," sometimes called "dissenters' rights," are available only in cash deals and not normally in the case of stock-for-stock deals.[1] Shareholders in cash deals who feel that they are not getting a sufficient payment for their shares can apply for a court-supervised valuation of their shares. They will receive the value determined by the court, whether higher or lower than what was paid in the merger.

Appraisal rights are for shareholders what covenants are for bond holders: an implicit contract that protects them from abuses by management or majority shareholders. They are particularly relevant in squeeze-outs of minority shareholders, as will be seen in the Chaparral Resources/Lukoil example later.

Appraisal rights are unappealing because they have to be performed individually and cannot be combined into a class action. That means that each shareholder has to bear its own legal costs.[2] Legal costs can amount to $100,000 or much more, depending on the length and complexity of the litigation. In addition, the cost for valuation studies, court costs, deposition, expert witnesses, and similar expenses also must be borne by the plaintiff. Therefore, perfecting appraisal rights is attractive only for large shareholders. Small shareholders who feel shortchanged can always use traditional class action litigation to get a higher payout. Some prominent large investors who have sought appraisal rights are Mario Gabelli's Gamco Investors Inc. in several instances (8.25 percent holding in a $10.8 billion Cablevision buyout, Carter Wallace, Medpointe Healthcare) and Applebee's director and sixth largest shareholder, Burton "Skip" Sack, who held over $60 million worth of Applebee's stock.

One of the advantages of appraisal rights over litigation for breach of fiduciary duty is that shares are valued based on their intrinsic value. In a breach of fiduciary duty litigation, a shareholder needs to prove first that such a breach occurred. This makes the argument in appraisal litigation a little easier for plaintiffs. However, it can be implied that if an appraisal action is successful, there must have been a breach of fiduciary duty. If there were no breach of fiduciary duty, then the company would have been sold at fair market value, and it would be unnecessary and impossible to sue for appraisal.

The real difference between appraisal rights and litigation for breach of fiduciary duty lies in the compensation of lawyers representing plaintiffs. It is not uncommon to see both types of litigation submitted in parallel to the court. Breach of fiduciary duty litigation often is filed as a class action on a contingency fee basis. This implies that the law firm representing plaintiffs assumes the risk of not getting paid if the class action fails. In return for this risk, the law firm typically is rewarded with one third of the proceeds of the litigation in case of a success. For large holders, one third of their incremental proceeds from the litigation can amount to more than they would pay if they pursued litigation independently from the class action. Therefore, the optimal strategy for large shareholders is to file a demand for appraisal and opt out of the class action.

Because Delaware does not want its courts to be flooded by appraisal cases, it has instituted a complex procedure that makes appraisal actions difficult for investors. The procedure must be adhered to exactly, and any deviation will void an appraisal action. The shareholder will instead receive the default consideration. An investor seeking to perfect appraisal rights needs to meet a number of stringent requirements, which are spelled out in Section 262 of Delaware General Corporation Law (DGCL). This section is included as an appendix in proxy statements in deals for which appraisal rights are available:

1. The shareholder must notify the company of her dissent and plan to seek appraisal prior to the shareholder meeting.
2. The shares must not be voted in favor of the transaction at the shareholder meeting. This means that the shareholder must abstain, vote against, or not vote at all.
3. The company sends a letter to the shareholder who notified it (under point 1) of its intent to seek appraisal, giving the shareholder 30 days to demand fair value for the shares.
4. The shareholder must then notify the company of the number of shares for which she seeks appraisal. The shareholder has 60 days to reverse the election to seek appraisal.
5. The company has 20 days to respond to the shareholder. It must include in its response a list of all the shareholders who are seeking appraisal.
6. The shares must be held through the effective time of the merger.
7. The shareholder must file a petition with the court within 120 days of the effective time of the merger. If no petition is filed, the shareholder will receive the same merger consideration as the other shareholders. This is a last-minute exit strategy for shareholders who seek appraisal rights but then change their mind.

The court will look at the value of the company at the time of the merger in its appraisal decision. This means that all benefits that the company might get from the merger, such as synergies, will be ignored.

Merger agreements frequently limit the percentage of shares for which appraisal rights can be sought. It is typical to terminate a merger agreement if appraisal is sought for more than 5 percent, sometimes 10 percent, of shares. This provision aims to reduce litigation risk for the buyer. In addition, tax-free treatment of some mergers can be lost as a result of appraisal rights under some circumstances.

Beyond the cost of legal fees and uncertainty whether a shareholder will win, there is another important factor that limits the attractiveness of appraisal rights: time value of money. Delaware courts award shareholders who seek appraisal rights interest at a rate of roughly 5 percent over the Federal Reserve discount rate from the time of the merger until the court has a decision or the litigation is settled. This amounted to roughly 10 percent in the last few years and only 8.5 percent at the time of writing. Whether this return is sufficient to compensate a plaintiff for the time value of money is a question that each potential plaintiff must weigh carefully. If the litigation is drawn out over an extended period of time, potentially several years, then the forgone time value of money can more than offset any increase in payouts received. On the other end, the acquirer of a company potentially can benefit from making payment for the shares later if its cost of capital is over 10 percent. The compounding on the ~10 percent rate can be semiannual, monthly, or quarterly at election of the court.

The typical time frame for an appraisal action is one year, and another year should be added in the case of an appeal. An appeal in Delaware must be filed with the Delaware Supreme Court. If the company appeals the appraisal judgment, it is required to post a bond with the court. This bond should be equal to the amount of the judgment that is being appealed. The Supreme Court generally defers to findings of the chancery court, so that most appeals are of little consequence other than increasing legal costs for all parties.

Delaware courts will look at a variety of measures to determine fair value and usually do not put much weight on market value. Instead, the company is valued as a going concern. "Proof of value can be established by any techniques or methods that are generally acceptable in the financial community or otherwise admissible in court."[3] Discounted cash flows (DCFs) are among their favorite tools. Under this approach, cash flow projections are made, a terminal value is estimated, and these are then discounted at a weighted average cost of capital (WACC). Cash flow projections are usually based on management's own forecasts. The terminal value is more difficult to determine; the courts go with multiples or a constant growth rate approach. Finally, the WACC is estimated using the capital asset pricing model. It is clear that these methodologies are highly dependent on the assumptions. As a result, the expert witnesses of the shareholder and the company usually find highly divergent values. The Gordon dividend growth model also is used frequently. It is very sensitive to growth rates and thereby can lead to very high valuations. More recently, comparable company analysis and comparable transactions have become more prominent in appraisal cases. The toolbox used by the courts is evolving. Table 11.1 shows the valuation methods used in some appraisal actions.

One of the key requirements of appraisals is that the fair value determined by the court be "exclusive of any element of value arising from the accomplishment or expectation of the merger or consolidation."[4] This means that any synergies that a buyer expects to realize in the merger cannot be considered in the valuation. Similarly, no minority discount is used in appraisal actions, and costs related to the merger also cannot reduce the appraised value. In a two-step merger, the date on which the company is appraised is that of the second step. This is important in that the new majority holder can already take actions to improve the value of the firm once it gains control after the tender offer. Any such improvements will increase the value of an appraisal action.

In addition to receiving the appraised value of the investment, the shareholder has also the right to interest from the date of the merger until the judgment. Interest rates used vary widely. Table 11.1 lists rates used in some appraisal cases.

Mergers typically will be done at a premium because the buyer expects to achieve savings through synergies and is willing to share these savings with the selling shareholders. Therefore, if the sale had been negotiated in a fair manner, there would be no incentive for shareholders to seek appraisal rights. It becomes an attractive option only in two scenarios:

1. Shareholders feel that the merger consideration is grossly inadequate, and a solid case can be made for a significantly higher payout.
2. The merger agreement stipulates a maximum percentage of shares that can seek appraisal, and a shareholder with a block larger than the maximum seeks appraisal rights. In this case, a buyer sometimes can be encouraged to pay more. A precondition is, of course, that the original merger consideration valued the target at the low end of a reasonable valuation range. Pressing appraisal rights to squeeze additional concessions from a fully priced merger is doomed to fail.

Most shareholders do not hold their shares directly but through a brokerage or trust account. These shares are not held on the books of the corporation in the name of the shareholder but in the name of Cede & Co., which acts as the depository for most brokers in the United States. In legal parlance, the shareholder is a "beneficial" owner, whereas Cede & Co. is

TABLE 11.1 Outcome of Appraisal Actions

Case Name	Date of Decision	Date of Offer	Defendants' Offer per Share	Court's Determination of Fair Value	Premium	Method Used by Court	Annual Percentage Rate
Gboll v. eMachines, Inc., No. Civ. A. 19444-NC	11/24/04	12/31/01	$1.06	$1.64	55%	DCF analysis	6.21%, compounded monthly
Dobler v. Montgomery Cellular Holdings Co., No. Civ. A. 19211	9/30/04	11/14/01	$8,102.23	$19,621.74	142%	Comparable transactions (65%); DCF (30%); comparative companies (5%)	8.25%, compounded quarterly
Cede & Co. v. Medpointe Healthcare, Inc., No. Civ. A. 19354-NC	9/10/04	9/28/01	$20.44	$24.45	20%	DCF analysis	7.50%, compounded quarterly
Lane v. Cancer Treatment Centers of America, No. Civ. A. 12207-NC	7/30/04	3/20/91	$260	$1,345	417.31%	DCF analysis (85%); comparable companies (15%)	9.14% compounded monthly
Cede & Co v. Technicolor, No Civ A. 7129	07/09/04	In 1983	$23	$21.98	(4.44)%		10.32% from 1/24/83 to 8/2/91; 7% from 8/3/91 until date of paid judgment

252

Case	Date				Method	Interest rate
In re Emerging Communications, Inc., Shareholder Litig. No. Civ. A 16415	6/4/04	$10.25	$38.05	271.22%	DCF analysis	6.27% compounded monthly
Doft & Co. v. Travelocity.com, No. Civ. A. 19734	4/1/04	$28	$32.76	17%	DCF analysis; adjusted per share value by adding a 30% control premium	Legal rate,* compounded quarterly
Cede & Co. v. JERC Acquisition Corp., No. Civ. 18648	2/10/04	$13	$13.58	4.46%	DCF analysis	4.73%, compounded monthly
Union Illinois 1995 Investment Limited Partnership v. Union Financial Group Ltd., C.A. No. 19586	1/5/04	$9.40 with possibility of additional $0.80	$8.74	(7.02)%		Legal rate,* compounded monthly
Prescott Group Small Cap v. The Coleman Co., No. Civ. A 17802	9/8/04	$5.83	$32.35	454.89%	Drawn from expert's company-specific transactions	Legal rate,* compounded monthly
Taylor v. American Specialty Retailing Group, No. Civ. A. 19238	5/16/03	$2,200	$9,079.43	312.70%	DCF analysis; comparable transactions	Legal rate,* compounded quarterly

TABLE 11.1 (Continued)

Case Name	Date of Decision	Date of Offer	Defendants' Offer per Share	Court's Determination of Fair Value	Premium	Method Used by Court	Annual Percentage Rate
Gentile v. Singlepoint Financial, No. Civ. A. 186677-NC	3/5/03	10/23/00	$2.46	$5.51	123.98%		11% compounded quarterly
Gonsalves v. Straight Arrow Publishers	3/13/02	1/8/86	$100	$262.96	162.96%		SAP's cost of borrowing based on prime rate of interest less 0.25% and Gonsalves' opportunity cost based on Whitman's prudent investor rate
Paskill Corp. v. Alcoma Corp., No. 321, 1999	1/1/00		$9,480.50	$10,049	6%		Unknown

* 5% over the Federal Reserve discount rate as that rate fluctuates during the period.
Source: Based on Geoffrey Jarvis, "State Appraisal Statutes: An Underutilized Shareholder Remedy," *Corporate Governance Advisor* 13, No. 3 (May/June 2005); Committee on Business and Corporate Litigation, *Annual Review of Developments in Business and Corporate Litigation* (American Bar Association, Chicago, 2006); J. Eisenhofer and M. Barry, *Shareholder Activism Handbook* (Aspen Publishers, New York, 2008 supplement); and author's research.

the owner of record. When a shareholder is required to notify the company of the intent to seek appraisal, the notification actually must come from the record holder of the shares, or Cede & Co. for these investors. The shareholder must contact Cede & Co. and instruct it to demand appraisal for the shares held by the investor. The time required to get the relevant documents from that firm should not be underestimated.

An important aspect is the availability of appraisal rights on shares acquired after the record date under certain limited circumstances. In a recent ruling by Chancellor Chandler of the Delaware chancery court involving an appraisal action brought for shares of Transkaryotic Therapies, which was acquired by Shire Pharmaceuticals, the court ruled that even shares acquired after the record date can be included in an appraisal action. In this case, Cede & Co. had demanded appraisal for shares for which it was the record holder on behalf of a beneficial owner. The beneficial owner subsequently sold these shares, and the new owner sought appraisal. The court ruled that the change in beneficial ownership was irrelevant because the statute requires only that the holder of record make the demand for appraisal. This opens the door for arbitrageurs to obtain full value on shares acquired after the record date. It often can be difficult to buy large positions before the record date, because the proxy statement has been available only for a short time and there may not be enough trading volume in a stock to permit the acquisition of a significant position.

The crucial question is naturally whether litigation for appraisal rights makes empirical sense for shareholders. Geoffrey Jarvis of the law firm Grant and Eisenhofer gives encouraging statistics:[5] Shareholders who exercise their appraisal rights successfully receive a median increase of 80 percent in their merger consideration. Table 11.1 shows a list of appraisal actions and the premia received. Most actions take two to four years to litigate, and a few cases even run for over a decade. The most crucial problem for the investor is that its investment is tied up for the duration of the legal proceedings. If successful, the investor will receive interest in addition to the premium. This interest is intended to compensate for the lost time value. Since 2007, the rate in Delaware is the legal rate, which is 5 percent over the Federal Reserve discount rate, as that rate fluctuates during the period from the closing of the merger to the payment of the award. However, investors still face liquidity constraints for the duration of the case. For example, most investment funds have a need for liquidity to pay redeeming investors. Hedge funds may be able to place illiquid positions in side pockets for the duration of the litigation, but this option is not available for open-ended mutual funds. Therefore, open-ended funds are structurally disadvantaged and may find it optimal not to seek appraisal rights even if they have a very strong case and it would benefit their investors.

A separate problem is the credit risk faced by investors during appraisal proceedings. If the company declares bankruptcy during the appraisal action, the investors become unsecured creditors and may be able to recover only a fraction of their judgment. This problem is particularly acute in leveraged buyouts that use large amounts of leverage to buy out public shareholders.

A better route may be a class action, which we discuss in the next section. The minority squeeze-out of Chaparral Resources' public shareholders by Lukoil saw a group of hedge funds managed by London money manager SISU Capital Ltd., SISU Capital Fund, and SISU Capital Fund II opt out of the class action and instead seek to perfect appraisal rights. The two cases were settled simultaneously after approximately 18 months, with Lukoil paying the same gross per share amount to the public shareholders in the class action and the funds seeking appraisal. However, the net payment to the two groups was not the same due to the different structure of legal fees and the small number of claim forms submitted by the deadline.

One of the most successful appraisal actions of all time is probably that conducted by Bill Fagan in the 2001 going-private transaction of sandwich chain Quiznos. Public shareholders (including this book's author) were cashed out for $8.50 per share, but Fagan managed to get $32.50 per share in the appraisal proceedings. According to data from Jarvis, the record is held by the 1999 action of *Borruso v. Communications Telesystems Intern.*, where the shareholder seeking appraisal received $0.645 instead of the $0.02 per-share merger consideration. This represents an increase of over 3,000 percent. But appraisal actions can also work to the disadvantage of shareholders: In an August 2007 decision, Delaware's Leo Strine set the value of shares of The MONY Group, acquired by AXA in 2004, at only $24.97 per share plus interest for the three years that it took to get to the final decision. For hedge fund Highfields, it was a lot of effort for a disastrous result. AXA had acquired the other shareholders' stock for $31.00 per share.

Class Actions

Class action lawsuits have a bad reputation. Martin Lipton, inventor of the poison pill, labels them "a type of extortion."[6] One of the most prominent law firms that brought the class action format to securities litigation, Milberg Weiss, was indicted, and at least one of its former partners had to serve a prison sentence.

Nevertheless, class actions are an option that can be more viable for shareholders in a merger than seeking appraisal rights. Even though the press reports of an explosion of securities litigation, it is a strategy that is underutilized by investors.

There are two types of securities class actions:

1. Lawsuits under Section 10b-5 of the Securities and Exchange Act; these are federal cases
2. Lawsuits under state law for breaches of state corporation law

Federal class actions under Section 10b-5 are the ones that are most often caricatured by opponents of shareholder litigation. They usually involve claims of false or misleading statements by the company or its officers that have led to a decline in the share price. Various attempts of reform, such as the Class Action Fairness Act of 2005 and the Private Securities Litigation Reform Act of 1995, have limited abuses of class actions filed in relation to 10b-5 claims. Class actions of this type are of no interest to an activist merger arbitrageur.

Class action litigation under state corporation law, however, is a tool that can help activist merger arbitrageurs maximize the consideration paid in a merger. Mergers are always done pursuant to the corporation laws of the state in which the company is incorporated. Therefore, state courts are the proper venue for this litigation. Chapter 6 explained the responsibilities that a board of directors has when selling a company. The most common approach to attack a merger is to find a breach of one of these fiduciary duties and file a class action under state law.

Such a lawsuit can have a number of goals:

- Lawsuits that seek to block a merger
- Lawsuits that seek additional disclosures
- Lawsuits for damages if shareholders believe that their firm has been sold for too little consideration

Legal action to block the sale of a company is hardly ever successful. The courts will weigh whether more damage is done in blocking the sale of a firm than in letting the transaction proceed, and will almost always find that blocking a transaction will cause irreparable harm. Moreover, shareholders who attempt to block a sale do so because they are unhappy with the consideration obtained. Therefore, the court will argue that if there is only disagreement about the price, unhappy shareholders can obtain redress through litigation for damages more easily than through blocking a sale, which would interfere with the ongoing business operations. Motions to enjoin a merger are almost always dismissed. A rare exception was the acquisition of Topps by Michael Eisner. The Delaware court enjoined the transaction, but only to give another buyer, Upper Deck, the opportunity to launch a tender offer for Topps' shares at a premium to

Eisner's proposed price. When this tender offer did not come forth, the Eisner transaction closed.

The second type of litigation is quite common and generally successful. These lawsuits sometimes are driven by plaintiff attorneys. The proxy or tender offer statements filed with the Securities and Exchange Commission (SEC) often are deficient. This is partly due to the haste with which they are assembled, partly due to negligence. In some instances, companies withhold information deliberately in order to make the transaction look fairer than it actually is.

Lawsuits seeking damages are the most difficult and longest of all. They usually end in a settlement. The fact that a settlement has been agreed on is not at all an indication that the original lawsuit had no merit. Instead, it is often optimal for both sides to settle rather than continue to litigate. For the defendant company, the legal costs can be cut when it settles early rather than fight a lawsuit that it knows it will lose anyway. For the plaintiff, time value of money makes an early settlement more attractive, even if it amounts to a slight discount compared to what could have been obtained at trial.

Securities class actions are filed by a plaintiff who represents all shareholders. A subtle difference between 10b-5 cases and merger litigation based on state law is the choice of a representative plaintiff for the class in federal cases, whereas in state merger litigation the first plaintiff to file will be the representative plaintiff. All shareholders who own stock at the time of the merger will be part of the class and are entitled to a payout from the award or settlement. The submission of claim forms is a requirement for obtaining a payout from a securities class action. When a claim form is submitted, the proceeds of the award or settlement have already been deposited and need only to be distributed to shareholders who submit a claim. For most shareholders, the claim form is submitted by their broker or custodian bank. A claim form is equivalent to the coupons that used to be attached to physical bond certificates and allowed the holder to claim interest payments. Contrary to statements made by industry leaders, including Legg Mason's chief operating officer and general counsel Andrew Bowden,[7] after the SEC cited firms for failing to claim the proceeds of class actions for their clients, submitting a claim form is not the same as filing a lawsuit, and it does not require a legal determination. Filing a proof of claim is akin to claiming a dividend payment from a company that has declared a dividend.

For an activist arbitrageur, the principal advantage of filing a class action over filing an individual lawsuit lies in the legal fees charged to the plaintiff. If a shareholder files a lawsuit individually against a company, it must pay its own legal fees. Class actions, however, are based on contingency fees that are charged to the entire class, and only in the case of a success. Therefore, an arbitrageur not only does not face an up-front cost but also will not suffer any expense in case the action is unsuccessful. The corollary is that law firms vet these cases very carefully before taking them on to avoid the substantial up-front costs involved. A law firm that agrees to file a merger-related class action typically will retain a valuation expert at its own expense to determine whether the price is fair. This expert, usually a firm specializing in business valuations, will often cost $100,000. In addition, the law firm incurs costs for depositions and document review, which can add up to another six-figure amount. Due to these high costs, it is unlikely for meritless class actions to be filed against mergers.

Large investors often file individual lawsuits rather than class actions. The contingency fee structure compensating the law firm in a class action is the driver for this decision. Contingency fees are calculated as a percentage of the damages or settlement paid to shareholders. One third is frequently cited, but actual percentages are often lower. For the holder of a large block of stock who expects to receive many millions of dollars of damages, it can be less expensive to retain a law firm on a retainer plus an hourly rate rather than sharing a large fraction of the proceeds. Because such an arrangement eliminates the risk for the law firm of not receiving compensation at all if the case is dismissed, the overall cost of litigation is lower. In order to file individually, the shareholder must opt out of a class action if one has been filed.

Opting out of a class action is what SISU Capital Ltd. did in the litigation against Lukoil. SISU filed a separate legal action. Lukoil settled both the class action and SISU's lawsuit simultaneously. The gross proceeds amounted to a 45 percent increase to the $5.80 offered to shareholders originally by Lukoil. SISU received a settlement of $2.61 per share, out of which it had to pay its legal costs. Public shareholders who participated in the class action received $2.38 per share, partly because not all shareholders filed claim forms. Although SISU received $0.23 per share more than the participants of the class action, it is not clear whether it was worth the effort financially. SISU held 1.3 million shares, so the additional proceeds of $0.23 per share amount to a total of $300,000. SISU's legal costs are likely to have exceeded this amount, so that it would have been better off had it not opted out of the class action.

An important aspect of shareholder litigation is the discovery phase, during which plaintiffs' attorneys review internal documents of the company. Discovery can take two forms: Before a trial, discovery is made to uncover all information needed in the trial. Sometimes, a settlement is negotiated and discovery is made afterward to confirm the representations made in the settlement. If the representations turn out to have been untrue, then the settlement will have to be renegotiated, or the case will proceed to trial.

Because of its favorable cost structure, securities class actions are the best method for small investors to defend their interests in mergers in which they are shortchanged. But even large institutions use class actions to obtain fair value in mergers. Some examples of recent actions are:

- Shareholders of Foodarama Supermarkets were paid initially only $53 per share but stand to receive another $14 per share after a class action lawsuit against the management buyout group.
- When Restoration Hardware was acquired by management and private equity funds for $4.50 per share after it spurred a higher bid from Eddie Lampert's Sears Holdings, shareholders received an extra $0.19 payout through a class action.
- Former shareholders of National Home Health Care Corp., which was acquired by Angelo Gordon in 2007, received an extra payout of $0.10 per share, or just over one extra quarterly dividend payment, thanks to litigation brought by Helaba Invest Kapitalanlagegesellschaft, an investment advisory subsidiary of state-owned Hessische Landesbank.

It should be noted that securities class actions under Delaware law are heard by a professional judge in the court of chancery, which is a court of equity that does not provide for jury trials. Indeed, all cases involving corporate law are decided by the court of chancery, so that decisions tend to be expert and consistent.

Inspection of Books and Records

Activist shareholders have the right to inspect the books and records of a corporation. All states have such statutes. Under Delaware law, any shareholder can inspect the books and records. Other states have more stringent requirements. Texas and Nevada, for example, award this right only to 5 percent shareholders or those investors who have held their shares for at least six months. In Delaware, the right to inspect books and records is also available to beneficial owners, which are those who hold their shares through a brokerage account.

Requests to inspect books and records are often referred to as "220 requests," after Section 220 of Delaware General Corporate Law, which specifies the procedure to be followed:

(b) Any stockholder, in person or by attorney or other agent, shall, upon written demand under oath stating the purpose thereof, have the right during the usual hours for business to inspect for any proper purpose, and to make copies and extracts from:

1. *The corporation's stock ledger, a list of its stockholders, and its other books and records; and*
2. *A subsidiary's books and records [...]*

(c) If the corporation, or an officer or agent thereof, refuses to permit an inspection sought by a stockholder or attorney or other agent acting for the stockholder pursuant to subsection (b) of this section or does not reply to the demand within 5 business days after the demand has been made, the stockholder may apply to the Court of Chancery for an order to compel such inspection. [...] Where the stockholder seeks to inspect the corporation's books and records, other than its stock ledger or list of stockholders, such stockholder shall first establish that:

1. *Such stockholder is a stockholder;*
2. *Such stockholder has complied with this section respecting the form and manner of making demand for inspection of such documents; and*
3. *The inspection such stockholder seeks is for a proper purpose.*

Where the stockholder seeks to inspect the corporation's stock ledger or list of stockholders and establishes that such stockholder is a stockholder and has complied with this section respecting the form and manner of making demand for inspection of such documents, the burden of proof shall be upon the corporation to establish that the inspection such stockholder seeks is for an improper purpose. [...]

(d) Any director (including a member of the governing body of a nonstock corporation) shall have the right to examine the corporation's stock ledger, a list of its stockholders and its other books and records for a purpose reasonably related to the director's position as a director.

8 Del. C. § 220

If a company refuses a request and a shareholder files a lawsuit, as described in Section 220(c), Delaware courts will try the demand expeditiously within a few months. Shareholders almost always win these cases. However, there are a few exceptions where courts routinely deny access to books and records. Most important, shareholders do not have the right to inspection to determine whether to tender shares in a tender offer. The rationale is that the tender offer statement should contain all the information required to take that decision. If the tender offer statement is defective, then shareholders have a basis to sue for additional disclosures.

Typical reasons for demanding books and records include the launch of a proxy fight or preparation for a resolution to be brought to the annual meeting, examination of the independence of directors, communication with other stockholders regarding a stockholder class action against the corporation, and communication with other stockholders to encourage them to dissent from a merger and seek appraisal. Investigation of suspicion of mismanagement is also an acceptable reason as long as the shareholder has a "credible showing, through documents, logic, testimony or otherwise that there are legitimate issues of wrongdoing."[8]

The shareholder can inspect all documents that are essential and sufficient for the request. The court can curtail the scope of documents that must be produced in order to protect the company from excessive costs. A confidentiality agreement usually is required from the shareholder before inspection.

Activist merger arbitrageurs cannot use 220 requests to obtain documents for a tender offer but can use it for related purposes, for example, if the tender offer is canceled or a merger collapses. An investigation of the independence of directors on the special committee should also be a valid reason for a 220 request, and in some mergers, questions about directors' independence do indeed arise.

PUBLIC OPPOSITION

Shareholder activism is associated with shame campaigns held by activists to embarrass management. These campaigns generate headlines and become known to the public. This is, of course, the goal of these campaigns. The headlines will be read by clients, employees, and friends and family of the chief executive officer (CEO). If an activist can generate enough publicity around embarrassing details of management failures, the CEO will be avoided in the local country club. The goal of the activist is that once the shame factor becomes sufficiently large, management eventually will yield to its demand.

Public opposition is an uphill battle that is not often successful. The low success rate is caused partly by the difficulty that shareholders face in rallying opposition and partly by the lack of follow-up of many activists who oppose transactions but run ineffective campaigns or do not even follow through with a campaign.

A campaign to oppose an acquisition takes two forms: In a merger, the activist must wage a proxy campaign to minimize the number of shares voting in favor, whereas in a tender offer, the activist must convince share-holders not to tender their shares.

Proxy Campaigns

In mergers, activists are at a disadvantage to management. The favorite tool used by management to pass a merger proposal is the postponement of the shareholder meeting. This allows management first of all to gather additional votes. These votes are collected by proxy solicitors who call shareholders, sometimes even retail accounts that hold only a few hun-dred shares, and ask the investors to vote over the telephone in favor of the merger. If this is still insufficient, management can reset the record date that allows shareholders to vote. If more arbitrageurs who support the transac-tion have acquired shares after the original record date, then the likelihood of gathering sufficient votes increases.

Activists that seek proxies to oppose a transaction face a number of obstacles. First, the cost of running a proxy contest can be significant. Many observers give numbers well into the six figures. This is definitely the case when a proxy solicitation firm is retained. In the absence of a proxy solici-tation firm, campaigns can be run at a much lower cost, but the activist has to design a campaign carefully to ensure its effectiveness. The principal cost is the printing and distribution of the proxy materials to shareholders. Most investors hold their shares through Cede & Co., and these shareholders are serviced by Broadridge (formerly ADP). The processing fee is approximately $1 per account in addition to materials, printing, and postage. Due to new SEC regulations allowing electronic delivery of proxy materials, it should be possible to run campaigns at very low cost. As mentioned before, the critical factor for a successful campaign will be its planning, and not the retention of a proxy solicitor.[9] One of the reasons that Stilwell's campaign against the acquisition of SCPIE by The Doctors' Company (see Chapter 1) failed is that Stilwell's proxy materials were designed poorly and did not convey his message in a clear and concise way. Investors who did not take the time to read the entire long letter had no idea what the issues were and why it would have made sense to vote against the company's proposal. A concise bullet point format with highlighting may have changed the outcome of the contest.

Unfortunately, Broadridge designs its proxy ballot forms in a way that makes them confusing to investors. In uncontested elections, the control number, a reference number needed to vote, is displayed prominently in a box with a red border. In contested elections, however, the dissidents' proxy forms tend to be cluttered with text, and the control number is not displayed prominently. This places the activists at a slight disadvantage.[10] In close contests, this disadvantage can make the difference between winning and losing.

Withholding Shares in Tender Offers

Withholding shares in tender offers usually is more difficult to do than a campaign in a merger, where the activist asks shareholders to vote against the transaction. A shareholder who does not tender will be at a disadvantage if the minimum tender condition is satisfied: The shares will become illiquid and it may take several weeks until the second step of the transaction is completed and the investor is cashed out. In the meantime, the shareholder not only has an illiquid investment, possibly relegated to the pink sheets, but also loses the time value of money. In contrast, in a merger, the company will continue to exist and the shareholder is not forcefully cashed out in a disadvantageous way.

A rare instance where opposition to a tender offer gained traction is the attempted acquisition of Longs Drug Stores by CVS Caremark in 2008. A key factor in the success of the opposition was the number of unhappy shareholders: Hedge funds Advisory Research and Pershing Square owned a combined 18 percent of Longs, and CtW Investment Group representing several unions also opposed the transaction. This gave the opposition a large enough block of shares to make a credible case against tendering. In addition, the opposition generated significant publicity, which caused other investors to follow them into not tendering. Their credibility was enhanced further when they convinced Walgreens to partner with two commercial real estate investment trusts and submit an acquisition proposal. As a result, at the first expiration of the tender offer, less than 4.5 percent of all outstanding shares had been tendered.

Investing in Merger Arbitrage

CHAPTER 12

The Role of Merger Arbitrage in a Diversified Portfolio

Portfolio theory reduces investments to two dimensions: risk and return. Both variables are forward looking and hence difficult to capture without perfect foresight. Therefore, analysis relies on historical relationships that are extrapolated to the future. It is assumed, or rather hoped, that the historical relationships will also hold in the future. This may or may not be the case.

Risk is a variable that is particularly difficult to define. The most common substitute for risk is price volatility. An asset's historical price fluctuations are observed, and it is assumed that these historical fluctuations incorporate all the risks that stockholders faced in the past. This historical volatility is then used in forward-looking analysis, and it is assumed that any risks that this stock faces have already occurred in the past and hence are incorporated in the historical volatility. The length of time over which historical volatility is calculated is the most important determinant of whether there is any validity to this approach. It clearly makes no sense to produce 10-year forecasts based on historical volatilities observed over only 1 or 2 years.

More fundamentally, it is a strong assumption that all risks inherent in a stock have already manifested themselves in the past. The economy evolves constantly and markets are in flux; assuming that future fluctuations will somehow resemble those of the past is not obvious. However, it is the only practical approach that can be taken when forecasts are made.

An improvement over a static forecast can be achieved through the use of GARCH models. In these models, volatility is autocorrelated. These models are better at replicating some of the basic observations about volatility, notably that volatility occurs in clusters and is mean reverting. Volatility clusters are periods in which markets are highly volatily for longer periods of time or exhibit low volatility for long periods of time.[1] In the words of

B. Mandelbrot, "Large changes tend to be followed by large changes, of either sign, and small changes tend to be followed by small changes."[2]

In the long run, however, volatility tends to revert to a mean value.

Other than volatility, another statistical term that plays an important role in the construction of portfolios is correlation. It is just as important as return and risk. Even though the risk/return trade-off has become a household term, correlation somehow has been left out. The popular business press does not refer to risk/return/correlation trade-offs.

Correlation describes the comovement of two different assets and can range from −1 to +1. A perfect correlation of +1 means that prices of the assets move exactly in parallel, whereas −1 means that they move exactly in the opposite direction. When building financial portfolios, it is best to have assets that have no correlation at all.

VOLATILITY OF STOCKS GOING THROUGH A MERGER

Once a merger is announced, the volatility of a stock declines markedly. Figure 1.6 shows the stock prices of Trustreet Properties before and after the announcement of the merger. It can be seen that price fluctuations following the announcement of the merger are much smaller than before. Figure 12.1 shows daily price changes of Trustreet Properties. It is clear from the picture that daily price variations are much smaller following the announcement of the merger than before.

Daily total returns differ from daily stock price returns in that they incorporate dividends. For dividend-paying stocks, price return will be negative on the ex-date of a dividend, even though the investor receives a separate cash flow from the dividend payment. Therefore, total returns are the appropriate measure that will be used for the remainder of this book.

To demonstrate that this is not just an effect in isolated cases, the data set from Chapter 2 was used to estimate the pre- and postannouncement volatilities of 311 mergers. To recapitulate, the data set consists of 311 cash mergers for the period of 1/1/2002 until 12/31/2004 retrieved from the Bloomberg database.[3] The original data set of 797 transactions announced in that period, of which 648 had closed, was reduced to 311 stocks for which sufficient data was available to perform this analysis. Total returns for these stocks were retrieved from the CRSP database. This is a database of historical return information from the Center for Research in Security Prices, part of the University of Chicago's Booth School of Business. This database is used widely in the analysis of historical stock and bond returns. Logarithmic returns were calculated for the daily returns in order to descale the data,[4] and a volatility was calculated for each stock before and after

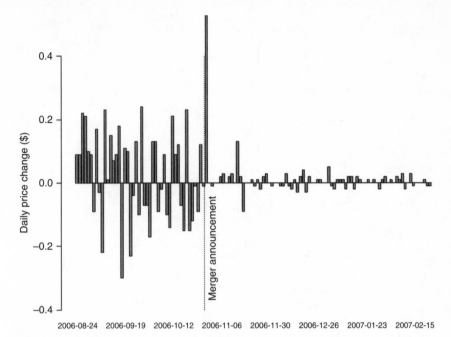

FIGURE 12.1 Daily Price Changes of Trustreet Properties before and after the Merger Announcement

the date of the announcement of a merger. The calculation for premerger volatilities starts 250 trading days before the announcement, and postmerger volatilities are calculated from the day following the announcement until completion. Figure 12.2(a) and Figure 12.2(b) show the resulting cross-sectional distribution of returns. The height of the bars in these histograms shows the number of stocks that have a given return.

It can be seen that both distributions are spread out before the announcement but collapse to a much narrower shape once a merger has been announced. Preannouncement stock returns span a wide range, whereas postannouncement stock returns fall into a very narrow range. A similar phenomenon can be observed for volatilities. This means that daily fluctuations in the prices of stocks going through a merger are much lower once a merger has been announced than the fluctuations of stocks that are not subject to a merger. This effect is even more visible when the variance of returns is plotted, as in Figures 12.3(a) and (b).

There are several implications of these observations.

Evaluating stocks going through a merger on the basis of their historical volatility and return characteristics will lead to incorrect conclusions.

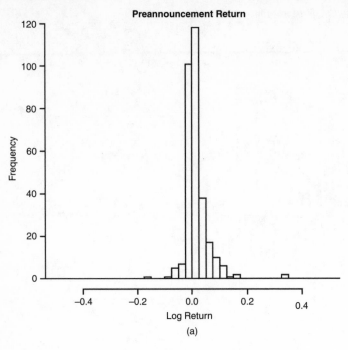

(a)

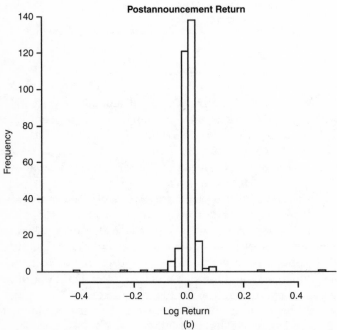

(b)

FIGURE 12.2 (a) Cross-sectional Distribution of Daily Returns before the Announcement of a Merger, (b) Cross-sectional Distribution of Daily Returns after the Announcement of a Merger

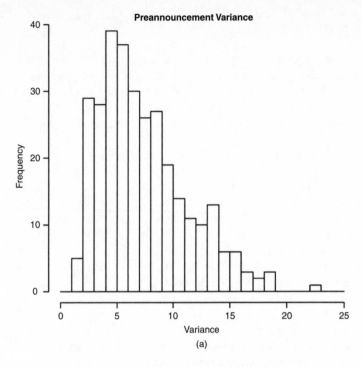

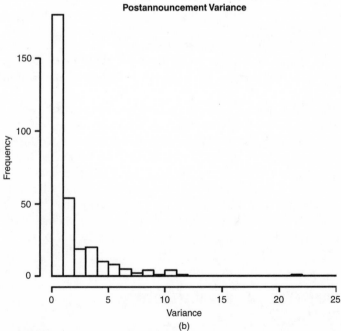

FIGURE 12.3 (a) Variance of Daily Returns before the Announcement of a Merger, (b) Variance of Daily Returns after the Announcement of a Merger

Many asset managers use value-at-risk (VAR) methodologies in their risk assessments. These methodologies will yield incorrect results for stocks going through a merger. After the announcement of a merger, a VAR system will look back at the recent much higher volatility and extrapolate this into the immediate future. However, actual price fluctuations are much smaller for merger stocks than before the announcement, so that the VAR is overestimated. As the merger seasons, a more dangerous error enters into VAR: The algorithm will look back at recent volatility and project a low volatility into the near future. As Table 3.3 showed, the average time until a merger collapses is about 130 days, or more than four months. Therefore, a VAR methodology will underestimate the price risk of a merger stock. This is even more so if the VAR algorithm is based on the RiskMetrics methodology, which uses exponentially declining moving averages. The VAR will decline soon after the merger announcement and will remain low even as the deal approaches the time of the average deal collapse.

Another implication is that combining stocks that are going through a merger into a portfolio should produce an overall volatility that is significantly lower compared to that of a portfolio of nonmerger stocks for which no merger has been announced. A portfolio of stocks going through a merger is no longer a portfolio of stocks but a portfolio of merger spreads. The characteristics of that portfolio are hence those of merger spreads. Although the analysis for Figure 12.2(a) and (b) was based on cash mergers, the same qualitative observation is also true for stock-for-stock mergers or mixed stock/cash mergers. The difference between these two types of mergers is primarily the degree to which any residual market volatility is contained in the spread.

It was shown in Chapter 1 that spreads in stock-for-stock mergers exhibit negative correlation to the market, all else being equal; refer to Table 1.3 in particular. Cash mergers should exhibit a positive, albeit small, correlation with the overall market. By combining cash and stock-for-stock mergers in a portfolio, arbitrageurs can create a net correlation that is almost zero. Unfortunately, all this theoretical elimination of all correlation is not achievable in practice, and most merger funds do have a small positive correlation with the overall stock market. However, the beta coefficient of merger arbitrage funds tends to be small and is of the magnitude of 0.5 to 0.6 for many funds.

RETURN AND CORRELATION CHARACTERISTICS OF MERGER ARBITRAGE

Merger arbitrage has been practiced by securities dealers for a long time. Investments have become available to investors since the 1980s, when private partnerships and mutual funds began to be rolled out more widely. With the growth of hedge funds in the 1990s, various data vendors began to track the performance of merger arbitrage hedge funds, and with the growth in interest in the strategy, academic literature began to investigate the potential of merger arbitrage.

Researchers approach merger arbitrage from two different angles. The first approach is to examine the returns of hedge funds that specialize in merger arbitrage. The second approach is more detailed. It examines each announced deal and constructs a hypothetical portfolio of stocks going through a merger. A number of rules for purchase and sale of stocks is assumed, and the return of this portfolio is then measured over time. The second approach mimics an arbitrageur's activities in the construction of a portfolio rather than analyzing descriptive fund data, as the first approach does.

Each approach has its strengths and weaknesses. Using merger arbitrage hedge fund returns compares apples and oranges because funds can have different fee and cost structures. Although most hedge funds have a 2 percent management fee and 20 percent performance fee, some funds deviate from this 2/20 fee structure. In addition, hedge fund databases are known to suffer from inaccuracies, most notably an incomplete sample of the universe of merger arbitrage funds, and survivorship bias. The construction of a hypothetical portfolio is also problematic. It assumes an index-like investment strategy, whereas actual arbitrageurs select their targets carefully. It also does not incorporate inefficiencies that can make some mergers less investable than others, for example, when an acquirer's stock cannot be borrowed to engage in a short sale. Finally, placing orders carefully around the bid/offer spread is an important ingredient in any arbitrage strategy that deals with tight arbitrage spreads. It is difficult to capture bid/offer spreads accurately.

The second approach has been practices for a longer time than the analysis of merger arbitrage fund data. This is probably caused by the paucity of data on funds for earlier years, because most merger arbitrage occurred in the broker/dealer community and merger arbitrage vehicles open to outside investors are a more recent development.

An early study[5] of merger arbitrage investigated 761 cash tender offers that were announced from 1971 to 1985. It concluded that a merger arbitrageur earns a daily abnormal return of 0.47 percent. On an annualized basis, this corresponds to an abnormal return of 171 percent, a return that any merger arbitrageur is dreaming of. The flaw in this study that led to this outsized return is the way in which the return was calculated: For each merger, the return was annualized. These returns were then averaged across all mergers in the sample. The implicit assumption of this cross-sectional approach is that all mergers happen at the same time. In reality, the mergers were spread out over a 14-year period, with only limited overlap, and the average daily return could not have been achieved on a time-weighted basis. A study by Jindra and Walkling[6] suffers from the same error. It examines 361 cash tender offers between 1981 and 1995 and finds annual excess returns of up to 115 percent for purchases of target stock on the day after the announcement and a sale one week later.

Bhagat et al.'s[7] analysis of cash tender offers describes the nonlinear nature of merger arbitrage. The capital asset pricing model (CAPM) is inadequate because it does not capture all risks, most notably the deal-specific risk of noncompletion.

Mitchell and Pulvino[8] find excess returns of almost 4 percent per year using a contingent claims analysis. Their study remains one of the most thorough and detailed studies of merger arbitrage performed to date and will be discussed at greater length. They examine 4,750 cash and stock mergers and tender offers between 1963 and 1998. Rather than examining merger arbitrage transactions at a deal level and then averaging over transactions, they create a hypothetical portfolio that is managed on a daily basis. This creates what is effectively a passively managed risk arbitrage index, which is subject to a number of rules that are adhered to mechanically. For example, no single position can amount to more than 10 percent of the portfolio. An important finding of their study is the correlation characteristics of merger arbitrage. Under most market conditions, merger arbitrage is uncorrelated with the returns of the overall stock market. However, in severely declining markets, the correlation becomes positive. Mitchell and Pulvino estimate a piecewise linear regression of a CAPM model that separates returns in upmarket and downmarket series:

$$R_{RiskArb} - R_f = (1 - \delta) \left[\alpha_{Mkt\ Low} + \beta_{Mkt\ Low} (R_{Mkt} - R_f) \right]$$
$$+ \delta [\alpha_{Mkt\ High} + \beta_{Mkt\ High} (R_{Mkt} - R_f)] \qquad (12.1)$$

where R_{MKT} is the market return.

           R_f is the risk-free rate of return.

           δ is a dummy variable that is 1 when the market return is above a threshold level (upmarket) and 0 when the market return is below that threshold (downmarket).

           α_{MktLow}, $\alpha_{MktHigh}$, β_{MktLow}, and $\beta_{MktHigh}$ are the alpha and beta coefficients of a CAPM model for up- and downmarkets.

The advantage of running a piecewise linear regression of this type over a normal CAPM model is that the piecewise model take nonlinear return characteristics into account, albeit limited to those returns that have been observed historically. The model is estimated through trial and error so that the threshold level that is found is the one that yields the highest R^2 for the model.

The most important conclusion of this study is that linear mean-variance analysis is inappropriate for evaluating merger arbitrage returns. The authors find a monthly excess return (alpha) of 0.53 percent over the risk-free rate with zero beta in upward-trending markets, but a beta of 0.49 percent in downward-trending markets. The threshold level was a monthly return of −4 percent, which minimizes the residuals of the model. Therefore, all markets with performance worse than −4 percent are considered downmarkets, those with performance better than −4 percent are upmarkets. This result is depicted graphically in Figure 12.4. It can be seen that the slope of the graph has a kink at the −4 percent (monthly) threshold level. The three panels in Figure 12.4 show different periods of time, and the effect can be seen clearly for all three periods. For downmarkets with a worse performance, the beta of the merger arbitrage portfolio increases. This effect is more pronounced for cash transactions than stock-for-stock mergers. For stock-for-stock transactions, the beta remains a modest 0.12 in downmarkets, whereas it increases to 0.72 for cash transactions. Even though this is a large discrepancy, it should be stressed that 0.72 is still a low beta coefficient when compared to other asset classes. It should be noted that the authors also estimate a standard CAPM model that does not incorporate a kink but is one single straight line. This model generates an alpha of 0.29 percent and beta of 0.12 percent. To what extent the finding in the bear market is relevant is another question: There are only few occurrences of monthly returns of less than −4 percent, whereas the bulk of the months has a return better than −4 percent.

Mitchell and Pulvino take an additional step in their analysis. Rather than just describing the nonlinear nature of merger arbitrage, they use Black-Scholes analysis to value the optionality. Whenever an investment strategy has nonlinear returns, an option is embedded and hence option theory should be used in its evaluation. Black-Scholes is a good enough approximation for the purposes of this academic study. The authors build a portfolio of written index put options and Treasury bills. The put options are written at a strike price 4 percent below the market at a given time. They find that merger arbitrage generates excess returns of 0.33 percent per month even when options analysis is used based on theoretical Black-Scholes option prices. When actual put option prices are used, the excess return is still a healthy 0.29 percent. Therefore, even if merger arbitrage has characteristics that resemble those of a strategy of writing put options, it still outperforms that strategy.

Mitchell and Pulvino do not limit their analysis of merger arbitrage to a hypothetical portfolio but also apply their analysis to returns of actual

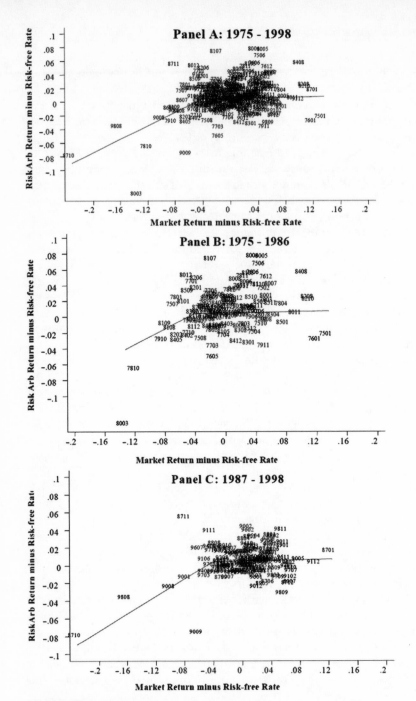

FIGURE 12.4   Piecewise Linear Regression of Excess Merger Arbitrage Returns versus Market Returns
Source: Mark Mitchell and Todd Pulvino, "Characteristics of Risk and Return in Risk Arbitrage," *Journal of Finance* 56, No. 6 (December 2001).

merger arbitrage hedge funds. Hedge funds from HFR's database over the period from 1990 to 1998 exhibit the same nonlinear characteristic as the artificial index created in the first part of the study: In upmarkets, the merger arbitrage hedge fund beta is a low 0.10, which rises to 0.60 in downmarkets.

Another conclusion reached by Mitchell and Pulvino is the importance of transaction costs. They find that much of the excessive outperformance of merger arbitrage found by other studies can be explained by the neglect of transaction costs.

Eliezer Fich and Irina Stefanesco[9] take a different approach: They construct an equally weighted portfolio of 1,928 cash and stock mergers that occurred between 1985 and 2000 where the bidder is a Standard & Poor's (S&P) 500 firm. They find that such a portfolio yields a monthly excess return of 1.2 percent, which is 85 percent higher than that of a portfolio of non-S&P 500 bidders. Despite the higher return, the likelihood of deal completion is higher when a bidder is in the S&P 500 than when not. These results hold for cash and stock-for-stock transactions.

Malcolm Baker and Serkan Savasoglu[10] examine 1,901 mergers between 1981 and 1996 and find excess returns of 0.3 percent per month. Table 12.1 shows their findings in detail. An earlier study by these authors in 2000 had found excess returns of approximately 1 percent per month, or annual excess returns of 12.5 percent. Their main concern is the question why the excess

TABLE 12.1 Merger Arbitrage Returns for Different Portfolios

Portfolio	Value-Weighted			Equal-Weighted		
	Mean (%)	SD (%)	Sharpe Ratio	Mean (%)	SD (%)	Sharpe Ratio
Panel A: Arbitrage portfolios, all offers						
All deals	1.54	4.25	0.23	1.55	2.54	0.39
Cash deals	1.62	4.84	0.22	1.48	3.13	0.29
Stock deals	1.67	4.42	0.25	1.97	4.81	0.29
Panel B: Arbitrage portfolios, first offers						
All deals	1.63	3.49	0.3	1.51	2.72	0.35
Cash deals	1.76	4.32	0.28	1.4	3.3	0.25
Stock deals	1.4	4.62	0.18	1.95	5.03	0.27
Panel C: Market returns						
Market	1.21	4.16	0.15	1.41	5.08	0.17
T bills	0.57	0.24		0.57	0.24	

Source: M. Baker and S. Savasoglu, "Limited Arbitrage in Mergers and Acquisitions," *Journal of Financial Economics* (April 2002), 64 Issue 1, 91–115.

returns achieved by merger arbitrage do not disappear. Economic theory suggests that excess returns should disappear as a result of arbitrage activity. Baker and Savasoglu contend that arbitrageurs are limited in number and constrained in capital, and that this limited arbitrage explains excess returns.

Ben Branch and Jia Wang[11] are the first academic researchers to examine stock-for-stock mergers with a collar. Their sample consists of 187 collar deals between 1994 and 2003. Their findings replicate the nonlinear return characteristics of merger arbitrage: In severely declining markets, returns from merger arbitrage are highly correlated with the market, but they remain largely uncorrelated under normal market conditions. They quantify the mischaracterization of excess returns if mean-variance analysis is applied to merger arbitrage. Under CAPM, excess returns are 11.88 percent, but they amount to only 6.3 percent when contingent claims analysis is used. The threshold level for severely declining markets found by Branch and Wang is −3.7 percent, which is close to the −4 percent level found by Mitchell and Pulvino.

Branch and Wang construct two merger arbitrage portfolios. The first, Strategy I, consists of the target common stock, which is held until the closing for fixed value collars, or delta hedged for fixed share collars. The second portfolio, Strategy II, is always delta hedged irrespective of the type of collar. Figure 12.5 shows the result of these two strategies. It can be seen that merger arbitrage returns are most often negative when the market also has negative returns. These events are the dots in the lower left quadrants of the charts.

In a 2006 update of the study, Ben Branch and Taewom Yang[12] find that fixed value collars yield better merger arbitrage performance than fixed share collars.

MERGER ARBITRAGE OUTSIDE THE UNITED STATES

This book deals with merger arbitrage in the United States. The general idea and some of the principles described here are also applicable to merger arbitrage in other countries. However, the devil is in the details. Arbitrageurs must understand the legal framework for mergers very well before venturing into another jurisdiction. For cross-border mergers, two or more jurisdictions are implicated, and special cross-border rules apply that complicate the analysis even further.

U.S. regulators have a long history of extraterritorial application of their rules, and the SEC is no exception with its merger rules. Much to the chagrin of non-U.S. companies, they can find themselves subject to U.S. merger regulation under certain circumstances. For example, when a

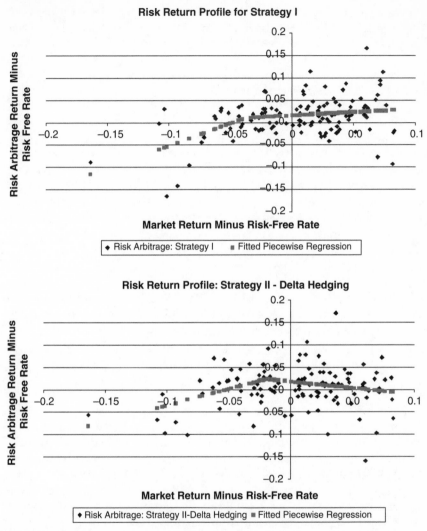

FIGURE 12.5   Piecewise Linear Regression of Excess Merger Arbitrage Returns

non-U.S. company wants to acquire another non-U.S. firm whose shares are traded as American Depository Receipts (ADRs) in the United States, the acquirer may suddenly find itself subject to U.S. laws.

Shares of many foreign companies can be purchased in the United States. over the counter. Regulators are concerned, quite rightly so, that when such a company is acquired, the absence of comparable disclosure requirements that can leave U.S. shareholders less well informed than if their investment had been acquired by a U.S. buyer. A number of exemptions make life easier for non-U.S. companies.

Tier I exemptions apply when U.S. holders own fewer than 10 percent of the shares of the target. In that case, a tender offer is exempt from the disclosure requirements of Schedule TO. U.S. holders must be treated as least as favorably as any other investors, for the consideration offered as well as for the other terms of the offer. In addition, in a stock-for-stock merger, the securities issued by the acquirer do not have to be registered if fewer than 10 percent of the target's shares are held by U.S. investors. The 10 percent threshold also allows acquirers to purchase shares outside of a tender offer.

Tier II exemptions are available to companies fewer than 40 percent of whose shares are owned by U.S. investors. Companies are subject to the same filing requirements as U.S. firms but get some relief in the form of timing of the payment of shares and of extensions of a tender offer, or the payment of interest when allowed under foreign law. The goal of tier II is to prevent conflicts between U.S. regulations and certain foreign merger rules.

Tier III exemptions are available if more than 40 percent of the shares of a foreign company are held by U.S. investors. In this case, the company is subject to the same requirements as U.S. firms.

In both cases, the bidder must provide U.S. holders with information in English that is comparable to that received by other holders. These documents are also furnished to the SEC. However, they are not considered "filed" with the SEC. This is an important distinction because only "filed" documents are subject to the antifraud provisions of the securities laws. Therefore, these regulations allow foreign corporations to offer securities to U.S. investors without the customary regulatory protections.

It should also be noted that for going-private transactions, the disclosure requirements of 13E-1 do not apply.

Many companies still find compliance with the exemptions too burdensome and decide to structure their acquisitions so that they exclude U.S. shareholders. The result of this avoidance strategy is extremely disadvantageous for U.S. investors: They can find themselves holding extremely illiquid shares. U.S.-based arbitrageurs must understand well whether they will be excluded. It may make sense for U.S.-based arbitrageurs to establish a non-U.S. vehicle to engage in merger arbitrage of foreign companies.

Several studies show that merger arbitrage can be successful in non-U.S. markets. However, arbitrageurs must be careful because the legal framework differs drastically from that in the United States. Most European countries, for example, have takeover regimes that are based on the U.K. City Code. The advantage of these regimes is that the timeline for the closing of a merger is very well defined. The drawback is that shareholders have fewer rights to influence management. On the positive side, this is offset by easier access to courts and generally lower cost of litigation, although shareholders do not have the benefit of pooling resources through class actions.

Andrew Karolyi and John Shannon[13] (1999) examined 37 Canadian acquisitions during the year 1997 with a deal value of at least $50 million. They conclude that a portfolio invested in these merger arbitrage transactions has a beta of 0.39 and an annualized excess return of 33.9 percent over the Toronto Stock Exchange index TSE 300.

Christoph Maxheim[14] studies merger arbitrage between August 1999 and October 2006 in three countries: Austria, Germany, and Switzerland. The results for Austria look unfavorable due to the uncharacteristically strong performance of the Austrian Traded Index ATX benchmark over the period of the study. He finds that merger arbitrage in Austria outperforms the ATX index by 2.41 percent; in Germany, it outperforms the Deutscher Aktienindex DAX by 3.97 percent; and in Switzerland, it outperforms the Swiss Performance Index SPI by 2.73 percent annually. Maxheim considers stock-for-stock deals, cash deals, and mixed stock and cash deals. His results are difficult to compare with those of other studies because he does not include transaction costs and calculates raw returns rather than risk-adjusted returns.

A study of 193 mergers in Australia between 1991 and 2000 by Krishnan Maheswaran and Soon Chin Yeoh[15] finds excess returns of 0.84 to 1.20 percent before transaction costs. Once transaction costs of 0.15 percent stamp duty, commissions of 0.30 percent, and 0.50 percent market impact are taken into account, excess returns are no longer significant. They structure a time-weighted portfolio following Mitchell and Pulvino's methodology. Interestingly, they do not find that the market-neutral behavior of merger arbitrage disappears in down markets. The threshold level that minimizes squared residuals in their piecewise linear regression is located at −2 percent rather than the −4 percent found by Mitchell and Pulvino for the U.S. market. However, they do not find that there is a statistically significant difference between the two segments of the piecewise linear regression. In other words, merger arbitrage in Australia does not behave differently in severely declining markets than under normal market conditions.

In China, there are very few investable mergers and acquisitions to date in which arbitrageurs could have invested. The first public tender offer was only made in June 2003 after securities regulators issued Administrative Measures on the Acquisition of Listed Companies. A particularity of the Chinese market is the existence of mandatory tender offers that holders of more than 30 percent of the shares are required to make to the holders of the freely circulating (i.e., not held by the state) shares. Because many 30 percent holders do not actually intend to acquire the firm they are invested in, these tender offers are made at a discount (sometimes at more than a 50 percent discount) to the market price in order to discourage shareholders from tendering their shares. As a result, the only merger arbitrage study[16] in the Chinese market has to work with a limited data set of only 22 tender offer bids between 2002 and 2006 in which a real acquisition attempt was made. The results of merger arbitrage in the Chinese market are discouraging for any hopeful arbitrageur: Annualized abnormal returns are −4.14 percent. Therefore, it is better to invest in the Chinese market directly than to conduct merger arbitrage in China.

RISK AND RETURN OF MERGER ARBITRAGE FUNDS

The previous sections discussed academic studies of merger arbitrage and analyzed hypothetical passive portfolios. These portfolios were constructed on the basis of some assumption about the allocation of capital in a passive manner to mergers active at any one time. Merger arbitrageurs, however, take an active approach to managing their portfolios. Two types of arbitrageurs are active:

1. *Concentrated arbitrageurs* invest in a small number of mergers only and take big bets on each of these transactions closing. Most arbitrageurs in investment banks and broker/dealers fall into this category. Each transaction they invest in has a high probability of closing and hence provides only a small expected return. In order to get to a double-digit level of return expected by investors, the arbitrageurs leverage their portfolios. In investment banks, the funding can be achieved near the London Interbank Offered Rate (LIBOR), whereas merger arbitrage hedge funds finance their leverage at a higher cost of capital. Therefore, the latter need a higher level of leverage in order to achieve the desired level of return. A drawback of this approach is that any unforeseeable event that leads to a widening of spreads, or even a collapse of a deal, will have a large impact on the portfolio and lead to a substantial drawdown. However, many arbitrageurs and investors find the prospect of extended periods of stable returns appealing, even if they are achieved at the price of short bouts of significant losses.

2. *Diversified arbitrageurs* invest in a larger number of transactions. Therefore, they are more likely to be affected by the collapse of a merger. Through a careful analysis of the severity of each transaction, combined with position limits and diversification, the impact of any losses after a deal's collapse on the overall portfolio can be managed.

The returns of hedge funds are tracked by a number of databases. Each of these databases calculates a number of subindices, including indices of hedge funds that specialize in merger arbitrage.

Barclay Hedge. Formerly The Barclay Group, this database began collecting hedge fund data in 1985 and has over 6,000 hedge funds.

Cogent Hedge. This database consists of over 2,000 hedge funds. The merger arbitrage index of Cogent Hedge consists of 33 hedge funds at the time of writing.

Crédit Agricole Structured Asset Management Center for International Securities and Derivatives Markets (CASAM CISDM). Formerly known as Managed Accounts Research (MAR), this database was created in 2005 when Crédit Agricole partnered with the University of Massachusetts Amherst and took over the MAR data. MAR started collecting data on hedge funds in 1992, and has data back to 1990.[17] The merger arbitrage index is a category of its own, unlike in the other databases.

FTSE Hedge. FTSE Hedge Fund Indices consist of only 40 hedge funds in total, and each strategy index can have as few as three hedge funds. Therefore, they are not representative for the performance of each strategy. Participating funds are selected on the basis of investability, such as minimum assets under management, regular reporting and openness to new investments as well as regular redemptions. Merger arbitrage is a subset of event-driven strategies. These indices were launched only in January 2004.

Greenwich Alternative Investments. Formerly known as Van Hedge Fund Advisors, this database covers 7,000 hedge funds. Merger arbitrage is classified as a substrategy of event-driven funds within the market-neutral equity strategy.

Hedge Fund Research (HFR). The HFR database contains over 7,000 funds. The Merger Arbitrage Index is considered a subcategory of the event-driven index.

Hennessee Group. This database has collected hedge fund data since 1987. Merger arbitrage is classified as a substrategy of the broader Arbitrage/Event-Driven category.

Lipper TASS. Formerly Tremont TASS, it was acquired by Lipper/Reuters in 2005. This database contains over 7,000 hedge funds.

Morningstar/InvestorForce. Morningstar acquired this database in 2006 with the intention of applying its mutual fund analytics to the hedge fund universe.

MSCI Hedge Invest. This index is designed to consist only of investable hedge funds (i.e., those that are open to accept new investors). As of September 2008, the merger arbitrage subindex consisted of 33 hedge funds. Merger arbitrage is classified as an element of relative value strategies.

Merger arbitrage hedge funds have grown in size since the 1990s, when they were first offered on a larger scale to the investing public. The growth of total assets managed by merger arbitrage funds is shown in Figure 12.6. This reflects only the post-Internet bubble years, where growth was particularly strong. Some funds will use leverage to increase their exposure, so that the

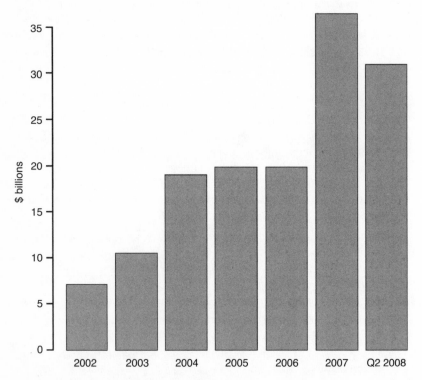

FIGURE 12.6 Assets Managed in Merger Arbitrage Funds
Source: Barclay Hedge, LTD.

total dollar amount of merger arbitrage investments controlled by hedge funds is higher than the net shown in the figure. Since merger arbitrage is a low-volatility strategy, a higher level of leverage can be justified than for other hedge fund strategies.

One of the problems of constructing merger arbitrage fund indices is that many merger arbitrage managers do not restrict themselves to a pure merger arbitrage strategy but also invest in related strategies, notably liquidations, spin-offs, activist situations, or restructurings (bankruptcies). These styles are not necessarily constant but can drift over time. Other problems are related to more fundamental weaknesses of the databases that make their numbers biased. Some databases drop funds that close down from the calculation of the returns, not only after the date of the closing of the fund but even for historical returns when the fund was operating. As funds that close typically do so after poor performance, the averages include only well-performing funds and are biased to the upside. Some data providers are said to have fixed this problem and now provide indices without this type of survivorship bias. Nevertheless, other problems remain. For example, the data providers rely on voluntary reporting by managers, and not all managers choose to report. Managers do not necessarily report from the time their fund was started but often run their funds for a year or two before reporting their historical performance since inception. In cases where the fund had poor performance, the manager will simply shut down the fund without ever reporting.

CASAM reports an annualized 9.77 percent return for merger arbitrage, which compares to 10.30 percent for the S&P index over the same period. However, due to the lower risk of merger arbitrage, as measured through its standard deviation, the risk-adjusted return of merger arbitrage is more than three times as high as that of the S&P 500: The Sharpe ratio of merger arbitrage is 0.3 compared to 0.09 of the S&P 500.

For the remainder of this section, the properties of six of the hedge fund indices will be compared to the S&P 500 and the Lehman Aggregate Bond Index. The S&P 50 and Lehman indices represent the performance of the stock and bond markets overall, respectively. The six merger arbitrage hedge fund indices selected were those of Hedge Fund Research, CASAM CISDM, Hennessee, Barclay Hedge, Greenwich, and FTSE. Data for all of these indices is available through the end of October 2008. However, the indices have different start dates. Hedge Fund Research covers the longest period of time, starting in January 1990. CASAM and Hennessee both start in January 1993. Greenwich starts in January 1997, and FTSE one year later, January 1998. The Barclay Hedge is by far the shortest index, starting only in January 2001.

Monthly returns for the five indices are shown in Figure 12.7. The S&P 500 index is by far the most volatile. Bonds move often in the opposite

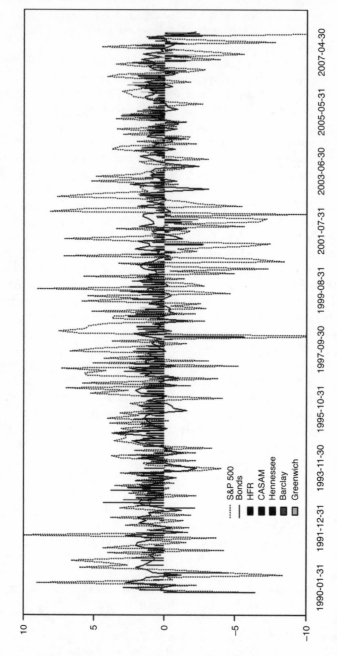

FIGURE 12.7 Monthly Performance of Merger Arbitrage Hedge Funds, the S&P 500 and Bonds

TABLE 12.2 Statistics of Monthly Return for Merger Arbitrage Hedge Fund Indices Compared to Stocks and Bonds

	HFR	CASAM	Hennessee	Barclay	Greenwich	FTSE	SP500	Bonds
Observations	226	190	190	94	142	130	226	226
Minimum	-6.46%	-5.61%	-4.71%	-3.59%	-4.90%	-5.61%	-16.79%	-3.36%
Quartile 1	0.32%	0.29%	0.27%	0.07%	0.18%	-0.14%	-1.71%	-0.09%
Median	0.96%	0.83%	0.90%	0.59%	0.68%	0.39%	1.24%	0.66%
Arithmetic Mean	0.75%	0.77%	0.79%	0.47%	0.63%	0.21%	0.71%	0.55%
Geometric Mean	0.75%	0.76%	0.79%	0.46%	0.62%	0.21%	0.62%	0.55%
Quartile 3	1.50%	1.39%	1.43%	1.07%	1.33%	1.02%	3.40%	1.31%
Maximum	3.12%	4.34%	3.31%	3.00%	2.76%	2.62%	11.44%	3.87%
SE Mean	0.08%	0.08%	0.08%	0.11%	0.09%	0.11%	0.28%	0.07%
LCL Mean (0.95)	0.59%	0.61%	0.64%	0.25%	0.45%	-0.01%	0.16%	0.41%
UCL Mean (0.95)	0.92%	0.93%	0.95%	0.69%	0.81%	0.44%	1.26%	0.69%
Variance	0.02%	0.01%	0.01%	0.01%	0.01%	0.02%	0.18%	0.01%
Stdev	1.26%	1.12%	1.09%	1.07%	1.08%	1.29%	4.19%	1.10%
Skewness	-2.18	-1.09	-1.08	-0.84	-1.61	-1.72	-0.68	-0.4
Kurtosis	8.21	5.54	3.59	1.98	5.43	4.43	1.49	0.54

direction when the S&P 500 falls, except in some instances where a severe drop in the S&P 500 drags down bonds as well as the hedge fund indices. For the remainder of this chapter, monthly returns are used to analyze performance, unless noted otherwise. Monthly data have the disadvantage of masking the true volatility, because extreme moves are so rare that they are not captured by monthly data that cover at most 18 years. However, since hedge funds report their performance only monthly, daily data cannot be used. Summary statistics for these data are shown in Table 12.2. The comparison of the series is difficult due to their different length. For example, the worst drawdown of the shortest index, Barclay, appears to be only roughly half as bad as the drawdown of the longest index, HFR. However, the −6.46 percent drop in the HFR merger arbitrage index occurred in January 1990, the first month that this index was constituted. The other indices did not even exist at that time. It is impossible to extrapolate what their performance would have been in that month. Similarly, the indices that have been in existence for longer appear to have higher returns than the ones that started reporting later. This finding reflects mostly the high returns generated by merger arbitrage during the 1990s, whereas the new millennium saw returns that were generally lower. Therefore, the indices that started later appear to perform more poorly than the older indices.

Figure 12.8 shows the cumulative performance of the six merger arbitrage hedge fund indices, the S&P 500 index, and bonds. It can be seen in the upper chart that the three merger arbitrage indices have a performance that lies close to each other. The S&P 500 overall exhibits a similar cumulative performance, albeit with much larger fluctuations. Bonds have a much lower overall performance but fluctuate in similar ways as the merger arbtirage hedge funds. For this reason, merger arbitrage is often labeled as a strategy with equity-like returns at bondlike volatility.

The lower chart in Figure 12.8 shows the drawdown from the most recent peak of each index. Drawdowns for the three merger arbitrage fund indices as well as for bonds are so small that they are difficult to discern visually on the chart. In contrast, the S&P 500 index experiences frequent losses. Its most dramatic drawdown occurred between early 2000 and late 2002, where it lost over 40 percent of its value.[18] The S&P 500 was going through another severe drawdown at the time of writing.

The risk/return trade-off for merger arbitrage compared to the S&P 500 and bonds is shown in Figure 12.9. All indices are shown from their respective inception. All merger arbitrage hedge fund indices exhibit a volatility that is comparable to that of the Lehman Aggregate Bond Index. However, returns are mostly higher. The FTSE and Barclay Hedge merger arbitrage fund indices underperform bonds. This can be attributed in part to the shorter length of these indices. However, both indices do

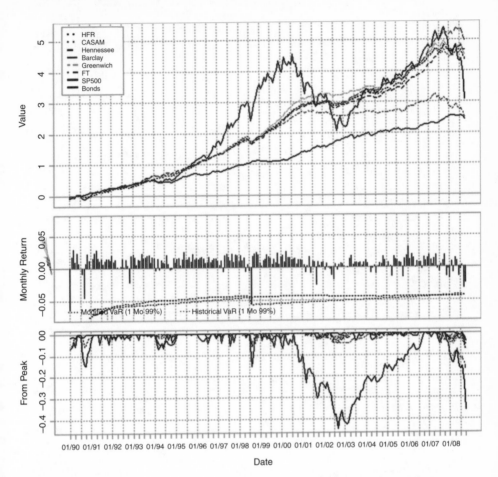

FIGURE 12.8 Performance of Three Merger Arbitrage Hedge Fund Indices Relative to Stocks and Bonds

actually underperform the other hedge fund indices, as can be seen in Figure 12.9.

Figure 12.10 shows the discrepancy between the merger arbitrage hedge fund indices. The HFR index is used as a baseline, and the performance of HFR is calculated relative to each other index. Overall, the indices are quite close to one another, with a divergence emerging most notably during the market turmoil of 2008. It is striking how the HFR index outperforms that of the FTSE; this is consistent with the observation in Figure 12.9. The consistently poorer performance of the FTSE index can be attributed only

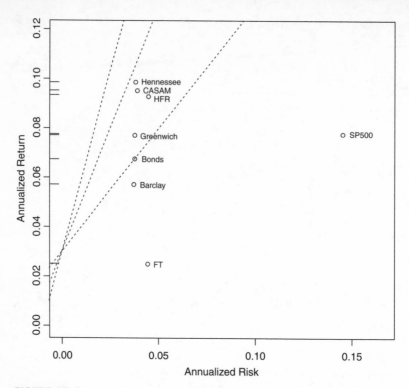

FIGURE 12.9 Risk/Return Trade-off for Merger Arbitrage

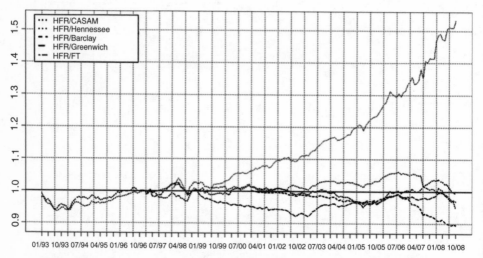

FIGURE 12.10 Performance of Various Merger Arbitrage Hedge Fund Indices Relative to the HFR Hedge Fund

TABLE 12.3 CAPM[*] Statistics of the Merger Arbitrage Hedge Fund Indices, Relative to the S&P 500

	HFR	CASAM	Hennessee	Barclay	Greenwich	FTSE
Alpha	0.0032	0.0022	0.0051	0.0052	0.0030	−0.0023
Beta	0.2346	0.2211	0.1644	0.2057	0.2477	0.3083
R-squared	0.3923	0.3695	0.2097	0.3174	0.3994	0.3932
Annualized Alpha	0.0388	0.0267	0.0632	0.0647	0.0370	−0.0270
Correlation	0.6264	0.6078	0.4580	0.5634	0.6320	0.6271
Correlation p-value	0.0000	0.0001	0.0050	0.0003	0.0000	0.0000
Tracking Error	0.1713	0.1525	0.2218	0.2186	0.1665	0.0463
Active Premium	0.1031	0.0923	0.1328	0.1309	0.1002	0.0320
Information Ratio	0.6017	0.6053	0.5988	0.5987	0.6015	0.6915
Treynor Ratio	0.0798	0.0358	0.2947	0.2261	0.0638	−0.1699
Sharpe Ratio[†]	2.1411	2.4015	2.4645	2.5066	2.4836	2.0931
Sortino Ratio (MAR = 0)	0.3954	0.4955	0.5807	0.3552	0.3629	0.1160

[*]The Lehman Aggregate Bond Index is used as a proxy for the risk-free rate.
[†]The risk-free rate is set to zero for the calculation of the Sharpe Ratio.

to the method by which its constituent funds are selected. As few as three funds are used to calculate the FTSE merger arbitrage index, whereas the other index providers typically use well over 100 merger arbitrage funds. It appears that FTSE was unlucky in selecting funds that underperformed for its index.

Similar effects can be seen when the indices are compared to the S&P 500. Table 12.3 shows some risk statistics in a CAPM framework. The statistics shown are frequently used to evaluate performance and risk. Some of the less common statistics are:

Tracking error. The standard deviation of the difference between the portfolio and index returns. It measures how closely an investment follows the benchmark.

Active premium. The annualized return minus the benchmark's annualized return.

Information ratio. Measures the active return of an investment manager divided by the amount of risk the manager takes relative to a benchmark. It is defined as active return divided by tracking error.

Treynor ratio. The excess performance of the portfolio per unit of market risk (beta) assumed.

Sharpe ratio. The risk-adjusted return. For comparison, the Sharpe ratio for the S&P 500 since 1990 is 0.64.

Sortino ratio. A variation of the Sharpe ratio that incorporates only volatility to the downside. By excluding volatility to the upside, only the harmful aspect of fluctuations is considered. After all, upside volatility is beneficial to the investor. For comparison, the Sortino ratio for the S&P 500 since 1990 is 0.15.

It was discussed earlier that CAPM risk measurements are of limited use when nonlinear strategies such as merger arbitrage are evaluated. A number of other measures have been developed that evaluate the risk of loss. Table 12.4 shows these risk metrics for merger arbitrage funds, bonds, and stocks. It can be seen that most of the merger arbitrage measures are of comparable magnitude as those of bonds, confirming the earlier observation.

Semi deviation. Calculates the standard deviation only for observations that are below the mean.

Gain deviation. The standard deviation only of observations that generate a gain.

Loss deviation. The standard deviation in months in which there is a loss. It is a subset of the semi deviation.

Downside deviation. The standard deviation for months in which the index had a worse performance than the Minimum Acceptable Return (MAR) of 10, 3, and 0 percent.

BENEFITS OF MERGER ARBITRAGE IN A DIVERSIFIED PORTFOLIO

One of the most important insights of modern portfolio management is that investments should not be judged on a stand-alone basis but in the context of a portfolio. This does not mean that an investment does not need to be evaluated carefully. Investors in merger arbitrage funds regularly go to great lengths to conduct due diligence on each of their funds and its portfolio managers. Rather, what the portfolio context refers to is that the characteristics of a risky investment can change when it is used in connection with other investments. For example, selling short a stock is a risky undertaking, because losses are potentially unlimited if its price rises. However, as we have seen, when short selling is used as part of a merger arbitrage strategy, it is a prudent investment strategy that captures the arbitrage spread in a stock-for-stock deal.

Similar arguments can be made for merger arbitrage as an investment strategy. Although it can be argued that merger arbitrage has a large down-

TABLE 12.4 Various Downside Risk Measures

	HFR	CASAM	Hennessee	Barclay	Greenwich	FT	SP500	Bonds
Semi Deviation	0.0165	0.0123	0.0125	0.0120	0.0124	0.0171	0.0485	0.0121
Gain Deviation	0.0062	0.0075	0.0071	0.0065	0.0063	0.0059	0.0236	0.0068
Loss Deviation	0.0148	0.0113	0.0103	0.0094	0.0122	0.0141	0.0314	0.0070
Downside Deviation (MAR=10%)	0.0165	0.0126	0.0127	0.0128	0.0127	0.0163	0.0489	0.0129
Downside Deviation (rf=3%)	0.0184	0.0138	0.0129	0.0122	0.0134	0.0172	0.0479	0.0113
Downside Deviation (0%)	0.0190	0.0155	0.0137	0.0132	0.0170	0.0184	0.0471	0.0102
Maximum Drawdown	−0.0824	−0.0571	−0.0513	−0.0607	−0.0731	−0.1763	−0.4473	−0.0515
VaR (99%)	0.0217	0.0184	0.0175	0.0203	0.0189	0.0278	0.0904	0.0200
Beyond VaR	0.0219	0.0185	0.0176	0.0204	0.0191	0.0278	0.0910	0.0201
Modified VaR (99%)	0.0434	0.0369	0.0305	0.0290	0.0349	0.0430	0.1187	0.0239

side potential, this effect can be mitigated if merger arbitrage is used as one element of a well-diversified portfolio. Diversification is the key: If one investment zigs, the other might zag. This will keep the overall value of the portfolio more stable. The key is to select investments that have a low correlation with one another.

The effect of adding merger arbitrage to an investment portfolio can best be shown graphically. Charts that denote the risk/return trade-off of merger arbitrage have already been presented several times. In modern portfolio construction, these charts usually contain an upward-sloping line referred to as the efficient frontier. The efficient frontier denotes the optimal portfolio for a given level of risk. For example, Figure 12.11 shows the efficient frontier for a portfolio consisting of the S&P 500 and the Lehman Aggregate Bond Index. As previously, the Lehman index is used as a proxy for bonds. This portfolio will be referred to as a traditional portfolio because it contains only standard assets. The efficient frontier denotes the best return that can

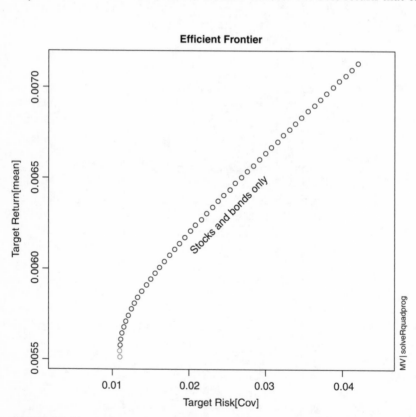

FIGURE 12.11 Efficient Frontier for Combinations of Stocks and Bonds

be achieved for a given level of risk. For example, if an investor is willing to accept a risk level of 3 percent (i.e., 0.03), then the best return that can be achieved by combining the S&P 500 and bonds is roughly 0.66 percent per month. The different points along the efficient frontier represent different combinations of stocks and bonds in steps of 2 percent. The leftmost point on the frontier is a portfolio that consists entirely of bonds; it has the lowest risk and the lowest expected return. The rightmost point of the efficient frontier is a portfolio that consists entirely of the S&P 500. It has the highest return of all feasible portfolios but also the highest risk. The middle point represents a portfolio consisting half of stock, half of bonds. The gray part of the efficient frontier represents linear combinations of the S&P 500 and the Lehman Aggregate Bond Index that are suboptimal. They are included because they are possible. There are two such portfolios: 0 percent stocks with 100 percent bonds, and 2 percent stocks with 98 percent bonds. In both cases, an investor can get the same level of risk but a higher return by selecting a slightly higher level of stocks—these are the black points just above the gray points. The efficient frontier shown here is based on monthly data ranging from January 1990 to October 2008.[19]

When merger arbitrage is added to a traditional portfolio consisting of stocks and bonds, the returns that can be achieved for the same level of risks increase. Figure 12.12 shows two efficient frontiers: The lower line is the same efficient frontier that was depicted in Figure 12.11 for the S&P 500 and bonds; the upper efficient frontier represents a portfolio that contains a third asset, the HFR merger arbitrage index. It can be seen that for a given level of risk, the portfolio with merger arbitrage will generate a higher expected return than that consisting only of stocks and bonds.

The same observation can be made when a combination of several risk arbitrage indices is added to the traditional portfolio of stocks and bonds. Figure 12.13 shows the efficient frontier of the traditional portfolio and the higher frontier that a portfolio consisting of the HFR, CASAM, and Hennessee indices in addition to the traditional assets, the S&P 500 and bonds. The improvement in returns is approximately 0.08 percent per month for the same level of risk. In terms of compounded returns, the portfolio will yield roughly 1 percent more per year. Each index was constrained to a weight of no more than 10 percent of the portfolio. If this restriction were relaxed and each index could represent more than 10 percent of the portfolio, then an even higher improvement in returns can be achieved.

The weakest aspect of this analysis is that it is impossible to invest in an index. An index is a theoretical construct that assumes frictionless investments without transaction costs and infinite instantaneous liquidity for all of its constituents. This assumption is not even valid for standard stock indices like the S&P 500 index, and index funds inevitably underperform their own

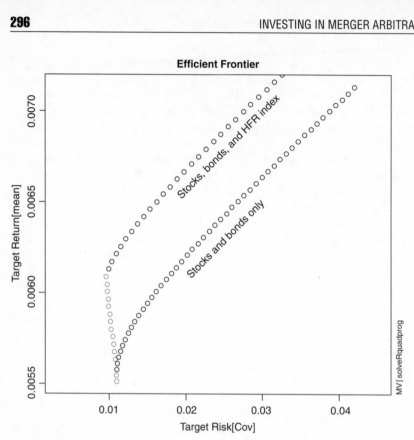

FIGURE 12.12 Efficient Frontier for a Portfolio of Stocks, Bonds, and the HFR Index

indices. For hedge funds, the assumptions implicit in indices are even less valid, because investors can access them only through private placements. Therefore, it is debatable whether hedge fund indices can even be called investable. To make their indices investable, some index providers attempt to include in their indices only funds that are open to new investors. Others seek to build indices that correspond to the entire universe of hedge funds representing the merger arbitrage strategy, including funds that no longer accept new investors. The indices used in the preceding analysis all fall into the latter category. Their advantage is that they represent the performance that can be achieved by the merger arbitrage strategy overall.

Moreover, comparing an actively managed portfolio with an unmanaged index is a conceptually questionable approach. Doing so overstates the performance that can be achieved with an index. An investor could at best invest in an index fund, which will underperform the index. It is

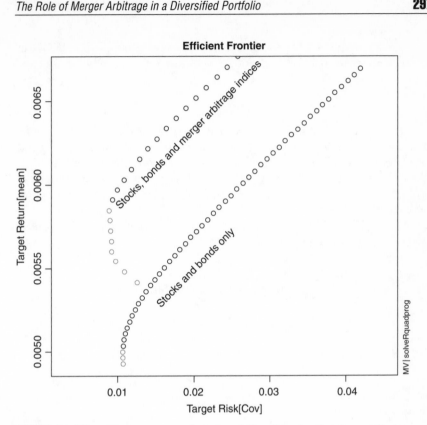

FIGURE 12.13 Efficient Frontier for a Portfolio of Stocks, Bonds, and Various Merger Arbitrage Indices

not only management fees and expenses that make the fund underperform but also other frictions, such as commission costs and timing differences when constituents are added and removed from an index. A more realistic comparison of any managed vehicle should compare its returns to those of an index fund rather than the index itself, because the index is a purely theoretical construct.

Instead of using merger arbitrage hedge fund indices, the next analysis uses several mutual funds that employ merger arbitrage.

The Merger Fund (symbol: MERFX) is the oldest mutual fund that invests exclusively in merger arbitrage. It was launched in 1989.

The Arbitrage Fund (symbol: ARBFX) was launched in 2000 and also invests exclusively in merger arbitrage.

The Pennsylvania Avenue Event-Driven Fund (symbol: PAEDX) was launched in 2003 and utilizes several strategies, including merger arbitrage.[20]

Several other mutual funds invest in merger arbitrage but are not included in this analysis in order to prevent the model from overfitting due to too much data: These funds include The Enterprise M&A Fund (symbol: EMAXX) and the Gabelli ABC Fund (symbol: GABCX). Several funds of Mutual Series also invest in merger arbitrage, among other strategies, going back to the days of Max Heine.

The S&P 500 index and Lehman Aggregate Bond index are replaced, respectively, by these index funds:

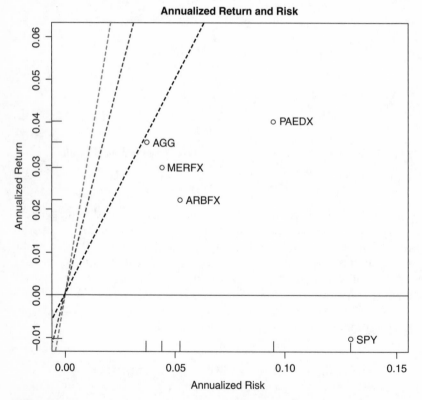

FIGURE 12.14   Risk/Return Trade-off for Mutual Funds that Use Merger Arbitrage

S&P Depositary Receipts, commonly abbreviated SPDR (symbol SPY), an index exchange-traded fund (ETF) on the American Stock Exchange (now NYSE Alternext)

iShares Lehman Aggregate Bond (symbol AGG), an exchange-traded fund by Barclays that replicates the Lehman Aggregate Bond index

The analysis covers the five years from November 2003 through November 2008. The scatter diagram of returns of the five funds can be seen in Figure 12.14. As before, the risk of the merger arbitrage funds is bond-like. PAEDX has higher volatility, which is due to the other non–merger arbitrage strategies used by this fund. Due to the poor performance of the S&P index in late 2008, performance of all funds is superior to that of the S&P index fund, which actually shows a loss over the five-year period.

The efficient frontier is shown in Figure 12.15. The lower frontier shows a portfolio that consists only of the index funds SPY and AGG. The upper

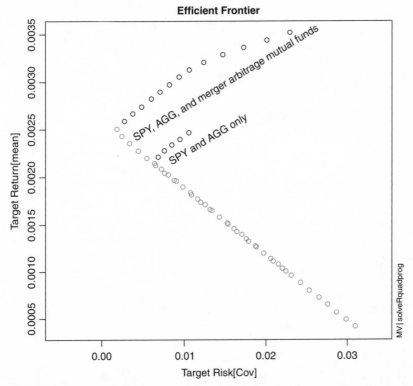

FIGURE 12.15 Efficient Frontier for Mutual Funds that Use Merger Arbitrage

frontier shows portfolios that consist of all five funds, the index funds as well as ARBFX, MERFX, and PAEDX. The same effect that was seen in Figure 12.11 can be observed here: When adding the merger arbitrage funds to a portfolio of stocks and bonds, a higher return can be achieved at the same level of risk.

It should be noted that the efficient frontiers look slightly deformed in Figure 12.15. This is caused by the negative performance of the S&P index fund over the five years covered by the analysis. The optimizer that calculates the frontier had to be fed with constraints on the portfolio composition in order to accept the S&P index as a valid asset class, which leads to the sharp kinks in the frontiers.

CHAPTER 13

Investing in Arbitrage

This chapter looks at number of practical aspects of investing in merger arbitrage strategies. Some topics have been touched on earlier, such as short selling and leverage. Risk management is an area that has not yet been discussed. Despite its exponential growth in finance in general, the tools used in merger arbitrage are still rudimentary. Finally, different vehicles that investors can utilize to participate in merger arbitrage strategies are discussed.

TRADING VERSUS INVESTING

Merger arbitrage investments are held for a short period of time. As we saw in Chapter 3, the average time for the closing of a merger is 136 days. This short holding period qualifies merger arbitrage as a short-term trading strategy by the standards of most investors. For ultra-short-term traders who hold positions for a few days only or even as little as a few minutes or seconds, the time horizon of merger arbitrage is long. Most investors, however, have longer horizons and will consider merger arbitrage a short-term or trading strategy.

The short-term nature of merger arbitrage investing has implications on taxes, which have been discussed in Chapter 3. Merger arbitrage will generate primarily short-term gains and hence will be tax-inefficient. Many institutional investors are pension funds or endowments that are exempt from taxes and do not put much weight on the tax characteristics of merger arbitrage. Taxable individuals, however, often prefer to invest in the strategy through tax-deferred vehicles such as individual retirement accounts (IRAs), variable annuities, or private placement life insurance. The flip side of benefiting from the tax deferral of these vehicles is that the investment must be held long enough for the compounding on the deferral to work as intended. Therefore, an investment in the strategy requires a commitment in the context of an asset allocation strategy. It is not suitable for investors who are chasing after the latest hot strategy. Unfortunately, the nature of financial market is such that asset classes go through cycles and perform well sometimes while underperforming at other times. Merger arbitrage is no different. The market correction in late 2008 is a good example of how short-term cycles can affect merger arbitrage as a strategy. Unfortunately, at the time of writing there were anecdotal reports that many investors reduced their merger arbitrage allocations. Similar sharp drawdowns were experienced in 1998, when investors also dropped merger arbitrage, only to pile back into the strategy shortly thereafter. Investors who make such tactical withdrawals should have a clear idea of when to reenter the strategy. This is, of course, true not just for merger arbitrage but for any investment. If investors exit simply out of panic and enter for the same reason (more commonly called "chasing returns"), then they are effectively pursuing a strategy of selling low and buying high.

The asymmetric payoff of merger arbitrage makes the evaluation of a manager more complex. As discussed on several occasions in this book, merger arbitrage has a high probability of producing a small payoff and a small probability of generating a large loss. An aggressive investor therefore can be tempted to take large risks, because the probability of loss is low. For an outside investor, it is difficult if not impossible to estimate why these risks have been taken: Is the manager an aggressive risk taker or a compulsive gambler? In the author's experience, both personality types gravitate toward the financial markets, and in particular to short-term trading strategies. It is possible to distinguish between the two types only if one makes a deliberate effort to understand the thought process behind each investment decision. Even then, one must be well familiar with each investment to distinguish between empty financial phraseology and actual thoughtful decisions.

Many institutional investors have developed due diligence questionnaires (DDQs) that are supposed to standardize the selection of investment managers to whom they allocate assets. As with all formulaic processes, a clever compulsive gambler will not find it difficult to game the selection process. Check-box investing is necessary if decisions are taken by committee. Unfortunately, it has become widespread, and many institutions will pay the price for this overly simplistic decision making.

LEVERAGE AND OPTIONS

Merger arbitrage is a low-volatility strategy. As such, it lends itself to the use of leverage. Because leverage is a double-edged sword, amplifying both returns and losses, it is risky to use on investment strategies that produce widely fluctuating returns.

Arbitrageurs have two main sources of leverage: the use of derivatives and borrowing. Borrowing can be done either through margin loans from a broker, which is the most common form of borrowing for hedge funds, or through loans. These forms of leverage were discussed in Chapter 3. Derivatives provide more flexibility to managers seeking leverage than margin loans. Not only can the implied interest rate be more favorable, because derivatives are priced using the risk-free rate rather than the (presumably much higher) actual funding rate that is available to the arbitrageur, but also the leverage that can be achieved is much higher. Margin loans are constrained by Regulation T, as described in Chapter 3. Derivatives can provide much higher levels of leverage. Leverage is constrained only by any collateral required by the counterparty, if any.

Single stock futures have been offered by OneChicago, a joint venture of the Chicago Board Options Exchange and the Chicago Mercantile Exchange, since 2002. Single stock futures are similar to other financial futures in that they are cash settled. They require an initial and maintenance margin of only 20 percent of the underlying and thus offer higher leverage than what can be achieved through a margin loan. In addition, certain positions can be used to offset each other, for example calendar spreads. Each contract is offered on an underlying of 100 shares. However, these futures contracts are offered only on a limited number of stocks. At the time of writing, single stock futures were available on approximately 1,200 underlying stocks. Liquidity is also a problem: Toward the end of 2008, the aggregate daily volume on all of these contracts rarely exceeded 10,000. This is equivalent to trading of not even 1 million shares. In comparison, the daily volume on each of the New York Stock Exchange and the Nasdaq was about 10 billion shares over the same period.

Options are another source of leverage. Options have already been discussed in Chapter 3 in the context of call writing to enhance returns. Arbitrageurs can also purchase calls to obtain additional leverage. Implied volatilities fall significantly after the announcement of a merger, so that option premia become affordable despite the tight spreads. An arbitrageur probably will acquire in-the-money options to mimic long positions and in-the-money puts for short positions, because they have the highest deltas.

The pricing of options of stocks in a merger is more difficult than that of options on other stocks. The standard model to calculate prices of financial options on stocks it the Black-Scholes model. One of its crucial underlying assumptions is the continuous movement of prices. For stocks that are going through a merger, prices will go through sudden and instantaneous jumps when a merger is called off. The stock will suffer a sharp correction (or a short squeeze in the short leg of a stock-for-stock merger) that is discountinuous. The risk of such a sudden jump in prices is not captured correctly by the Black-Scholes model. A model that captures this effect was developed by Ajay Subramanian.[1] It uses a jump diffusion process rather than the continuous diffusion, also called Brownian motion, of the Black-Scholes framework. Subramanian examines options on stocks undergoing stock-for-stock mergers and starts with jump diffusion processes of the form

$$dS_1(t)1_{N(t)=0} = 1_{N(t)=0}[(\mu_1(t-) - d_1)S_1(t-)dt + \sigma_1'S_1(t-)dW_1(t)]$$
$$dS_2(t)1_{N(t)=0} = 1_{N(t)=0}[(\mu_2(t-) - d_2)S_2(t-)dt + \sigma_2'S_2(t-)dW_2(t)]$$

$$(13.1)$$

where S_1, S_2 are the prices of the stocks.
        μ_1, μ_2 are the drifts of the diffusion processes.
        σ_1, σ_2 are the respective volatilities.
        $1_{N(t)=0}$ is 1 before the jump. $1_{N(t)=1}$ is 1 after a jump, if any.
        $t-$ is a notation for the time just prior to t.
        d_1, d_2 are the respective dividend yields.
        dW_1, dW_2 are random draws as in a Brownian motion.

If the merger is called off, the stocks will revert to a standard Black-Scholes process:

$$dS_1(t)1_{N(t)=1} = 1_{N(t)=1}[(\mu_1(t-) - d_1)S_1(t-)dt + \sigma_1 S_1(t-)dW_3(t)]$$
$$dS_2(t)1_{N(t)=1} = 1_{N(t)=1}[(\mu_2(t-) - d_2)S_2(t-)dt + \sigma_2 S_2(t-)dW_4(t)]$$

$$(13.2)$$

where σ_1, σ_2 are the respective volatilities after the jump.
        dW_3, dW_4 are random draws as in a Brownian motion.

Subramanian derives a closed-form solution for the price of a European call option, which is significantly more involved than the classic Black-Scholes equation:

$$P_1(0, T_0, K) = e^{-\lambda T_0} \left\{ S_1(0)e^{-d_1 T_0} \frac{e^{\lambda T_0} + A_1}{1 + A_1} N(\alpha_1') - Ke^{-r T_0} N(\alpha_2') \right\}$$

$$+ \frac{\lambda S_1(0)e^{-d_1 T_0}e^{(\lambda \sigma^2 T_0/\sigma'^2 - \sigma^2)}A_1}{(1 + A_1)(\sigma'^2 - \sigma^2)} \int\limits_{\sigma^2 T_0}^{\sigma'^2 T_0} dt e^{-\frac{\lambda t}{\sigma'^2 - \sigma^2}} N\left(\frac{x + 0.5t}{\sqrt{t}}\right)$$

$$-\lambda K e^{-rT_0} \frac{e^{(\lambda\sigma^2 T_0)/\sigma'^2 -\sigma^2}}{(\sigma'^2 - \sigma^2)} \int\limits_{\sigma^2 T_0}^{\sigma'^2 T_0} dt e^{-\frac{\lambda t}{\sigma'^2-\sigma^2}} N\left(\frac{x-0.5t}{\sqrt{t}}\right)$$

(13.3)

where $x = \log[\frac{S_1(0)(A_1)}{K(1+A_1)}] + (r - d_1)T_0$.

A_1, A_2 are chosen so that the stock jumps by a factor. $\beta_i(t) = A_i \exp t(-\lambda t)/(1 + A_i \exp(-\lambda t))$ if the deal is called off.

λ is the risk-neutral probability that the deal is called off in the period $[t, t + dt]$ is $\lambda \, dt$.

The integrals can be replaced by

$$\int\limits_0^\tau dt e^{-\omega t} N\left(\frac{x-\rho t}{\sqrt{t}}\right) = \frac{1}{\omega}\left\{\frac{1+\text{sgn}(x)}{2} - e^{-\omega t} N\left(\frac{x-\rho t}{\sqrt{\tau}}\right)\right\}$$

$$+ \frac{e^{(\rho-\xi)x}}{2\omega} N\left(\frac{x-\xi t}{\sqrt{\tau}}\right) + \frac{e^{(\rho+\xi)x}}{2\omega} N\left(\frac{x+\xi t}{\sqrt{\tau}}\right) - \frac{e^{(\rho-\xi)x}+e^{(\rho+\xi)x}}{4\omega}(1 + \text{sgn}(x)) \quad (13.4)$$

$$+ \frac{\rho e^{(\rho-\xi)x}}{2\xi\omega} N\left(\frac{x-\xi t}{\sqrt{\tau}}\right) - \frac{\rho e^{(\rho+\xi)x}}{2\xi\omega} N\left(\frac{x+\xi t}{\sqrt{\tau}}\right) + \frac{\rho(e^{(\rho+\xi)x}-e^{(\rho-\xi)x})}{4\xi\omega}(1 + \text{sgn}(x))$$

where $\xi = \sqrt{2\omega + \rho^2}$

Subramanian uses these formulas to invert the problem: rather than calculating option prices, he uses option prices as the input to derive the implied probability that a merger closes. His results, shown in Table 13.1, show that the options market sets probabilities of the closing of mergers that are good predictors of the actual outcome. The time between announcement and anticipated closing is split into three periods. In each of these periods, the implied probabilities of the options are averaged. The average for the final month before closing or cancellation of the deal is also shown. For successful deals, the average probability implied by the options is twice as high as that for deals that ultimately are unsuccessful.

This result is consistent with other studies that have found that mergers that close have narrower spreads than those that eventually collapse.

Some of the highest leverage can be achieved by swaps. A total return swap allows an arbitrageur to obtain exposure to an asset without taking

TABLE 13.1 Implied Probabilities of the Closing of Mergers Derived from Option Prices

Successful Deals

Target	Acquirer	Average Success Probability (First Third)	Average Success Probability (Middle Third)	Average Success Probability (Final Third)	Average Success Probability (Final Month)	Overall Average
DS	MXIM	0.48	0.64	0.79	0.74	0.61
TOS	P	0.56	0.79	0.95	0.91	0.81
CATP	NOVL	0.79	0.8	0.95	0.93	0.86
CIT	TYC	0.4	0.63	0.74	0.74	0.58
BBC	AAS	0.38	0.44	0.57	0.6	0.43
KNT	AVNT	0.6	0.65	0.76	0.74	0.68
AZA	JNJ	0.81	0.85	0.95	0.94	0.87
SEM	VSH	0.49	0.58	0.79	0.77	0.59
WB	FTU	0.43	0.68	0.86	0.91	0.68
NIS	USB	0.69	0.93	0.98	0.97	0.87
SAW'S	TQNT	0.44	0.6	0.69	0.64	0.57
MRL	PDE	0.38	0.61	0.76	0.77	0.55
HM	ABX	0.4	0.57	0.71	0.82	0.58
DRMD	BRL	0.25	0.42	0.59	0.58	0.38
GEN	TER	0.44	0.49	0.63	0.62	0.52
W	MEA	0.47	0.6	0.79	0.79	0.61
CPQ	HWP	0.16	0.23	0.58	0.77	0.33
GLM	SDC	0.33	0.47	0.65	0.64	0.51
COC	P	0.29	0.35	0.58	0.82	0.41
AVIR	MEDI	0.68	0.79	0.94	0.85	0.83
CORR	MLNM	0.5	0.56	0.72	0.67	0.58
AVNT	SNPS	0.25	0.46	0.62	0.74	0.44
SRM	TYC	0.85	0.85	0.93	0.91	0.87
SCI	SNM	0.29	0.45	0.67	0.73	0.45
Mean		0.47	0.6	0.75	0.76	0.6
Median		0.44	0.6	0.75	0.77	0.58
q Max		0.83	0.91	0.96	0.98	

Unsuccessful Deals

Target	Acquirer	Average Success Probability (First Third)	Average Success Probability (Middle Third)	Average Success Probability (Final Third)	Average Success Probability (Final Month)	Overall Average
NTPA	PROX	0.33	0.29	0.26	0.29	0.3
PRXL	CVD	0.25	0.19	0.3	0.26	0.25
AZA	ABT	0.29	0.43	0.41	0.44	0.38
NR	TBI	0.27	0.3	0.49	0.46	0.35
CYM	AR	0.3	0.25	0.49	0.49	0.36
WLA	AHP	0.01	0.05	0.07	0.08	0.04
GLIA	GLFD	0.15	0.47	0.52	0.51	0.37
REL	LUK	0.49	0.47	0.6	0.53	0.52
FSCO	ZION	0.18	0.22	0.09	0.11	0.17
Mean		0.25	0.3	0.36	0.35	0.3
Median		0.27	0.29	0.41	0.44	0.35

Source: Ajay Subramanian, "Option Pricing on Stocks in Mergers and Acquisitions," *Journal of Finance* 59, No. 2 (April 2004).

possession. As discussed previously, margin borrowing can be expensive, in particular for smaller arbitrageurs or entities that are highly leveraged. A total return swap allows an arbitrageur to borrow the funding capability of a large investment bank or dealer and pay a much smaller spread on the reference rate than if it had taken out a margin loan. The structure of a total return swap resembles that of other swap contracts, such as interest rate swaps. It has two legs: a funding leg and a return leg. In the terminology of total return swaps, the party that receives the return leg, which is the return on the underlying asset, is the buyer. The seller pays the return on the asset. In exchange, the buyer pays the seller a funding cost, which is a spread over the London Interbank Offered Rate (LIBOR). In addition, the buyer pays the seller any depreciation of the underlying assets. The net effect of these cash flows is that the buyer pays the cost of funding and receives any appreciation and dividends on the underlying. If the underlying loses value, the buyer pays the seller.

Sellers of total return swaps are broker/dealers that hedge themselves by acquiring the underlying assets. Therefore, an arbitrageur who acquires a total return swap gets the benefit of paying LIBOR plus a modest spread rather than a higher margin rate.

Similar levels of leverage can be achieved through contracts for difference (CFDs). However, for regulatory reasons, these instruments are not available in the United States at this time.

It is well known to financial practitioners as well as academics that the use of leverage is a double-edged sword. Not only does it amplify positive returns, but it also increases losses. An aspect of leverage that is less well known in academic circles is that the combination of leverage and short selling introduces costs that are a drag on returns. This problem is especially acute for 130/30 strategies. These are investment strategies where 100 percent of the assets are invested in an index, 30 percent are sold short, and an additional 30 percent invested in long positions. The combination of 30 percent short/30 percent long is supposed to add returns that are independent of the direction of the market and add to the return achieved from the index component.

The academic literature regarding these strategies assumes that the proceeds from the short sales are used to acquire the long position. This is not possible because most brokers do not allow an investor to access all of the proceeds from a short sale. Figure 13.1 illustrates this problem. At least some fraction of the proceeds of the short sale have to remain at the broker in cash and cannot be invested. The broker will, of course, pay interest in the form of a short rebate (to be discussed; see also Chapter 3) on the cash balance of short proceeds. Nevertheless, the investor cannot access these funds to purchase additional securities. Therefore, sufficient funds must be borrowed

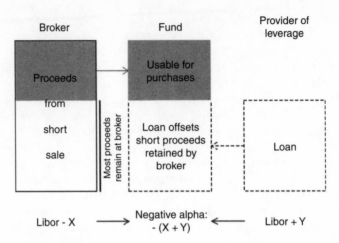

FIGURE 13.1   Leverage Coupled with Short Selling Leads to
Negative Alpha

to compensate for the unavailability of the funds retained by the broker.
The investor needs to pay a higher rate of interest on the amounts borrowed
than received through the short rebate. This is a net cost of the long/short
component that must be offset through investment gains. Therefore, even
before any gains are made, the long/short component will impose a cost on
the fund. This cost also can be viewed as a negative alpha built into the long
component of the strategy.

Some simple calculations can illustrate the extent of a negative alpha. It
is determined by three factors:

1. The amount of leverage used
2. The fraction of the short sale proceeds that the short broker allows the
   arbitrageur to access for purchases
3. The interest rate differential between the short rebate and the borrowing
   cost.

Table 13.2 shows various levels of negative alpha for different levels of
these three variables.

Merger arbitrageurs face the same challenge when using leverage to
finance a portion of the long/short component of their arbitrage portfolio.
In a stock-for-stock merger, they cannot utilize all of the proceeds from the
short sale for purchasing the long leg of the arbitrage. If they leverage, they
must borrow these funds. Their arbitrage position will experience the same
type of negative alpha just described.

TABLE 13.2 Negative Alpha for Different Levels of Leverage, Interest Rate Spreads, and Withdrawal Levels from the Brokerage

20% leverage		Short Proceeds Retained by Broker		
		30%	50%	100%
	1.00%	0.06%	0.10%	0.20%
Spread	2.00%	0.12%	0.20%	0.40%
	5.00%	0.30%	0.50%	1.00%
30% leverage		Short Proceeds Retained by Broker		
		30%	50%	100%
	1.00%	0.09%	0.15%	0.30%
Spread	2.00%	0.18%	0.30%	0.60%
	5.00%	0.45%	0.75%	1.50%
50% leverage		Short Proceeds Retained by Broker		
		30%	50%	100%
	1.00%	0.15%	0.25%	0.50%
Spread	2.00%	0.30%	0.50%	1.00%
	5.00%	0.75%	1.25%	2.50%

SHORTING STOCKS

The shorting of stock is generally regarded as a high-risk activity and sometimes is associated with illegal activities. There is no doubt that short selling exposes the seller to potentially unlimited losses on the short. The short seller takes the opposite position of a buyer; while the buyer has the potential for unlimited gains on their holding, the short seller faces the opposite risk. Short selling as a stand-alone investment strategy is indeed a risky undertaking that is best left to investors who master this discipline well.

Since the stock market goes up most of the time, a simple short position is more likely to generate losses than gains. Returns on funds that specialize in short selling only confirm the difficulty of making a profit on this strategy. Table 13.3 shows the returns of the Hennessee Short Biased Index of short-selling hedge funds. On average, these funds had a negative performance, with a Sharpe ratio of −0.34 compared to a Sharpe ratio of 0.31 for the Standard & Poor's (S&P) 500 index. Some observers unfamiliar with arbitrage strategies may argue based on these numbers that using short selling is a losing strategy. However, when short selling is used as an element of a more complex strategy, such as merger arbitrage, comparisons to pure short selling are not relevant. The short position changes its character from a bet on the drop of a stock price to an attempt to capture a price differential.

TABLE 13.3 Performance of Short Biased Hedge Funds According to Hennessee Group

Year	Return (%)
2006	(4.32)
2005	10.11
2004	(2.37)
2003	(22.65)
2002	15.87
2001	12.81
2000	29.94
1999	(9.91)
1998	(23.29)
1997	4.95
1996	(16.37)
1995	(28.47)
1994	10.78
1993	(4.81)
Average	(3.38)
S&P 500	8.80

Source: Based on data from Hennessee Group.

A short seller is required to deliver the shares that have been sold to the buyer. The buyer is not concerned with whether the purchased shares have been sold by someone who held the stock or who sold it short. The buyer simply expects to obtain the acquired shares. Many institutional investors, including public pension funds and endowments, lend their shares to short sellers and charge a fee for that service. In most cases, the actual lending is done not by the institution itself but by the custodian. A securities lending agreement stipulates whether the custodian must obtain permission from the institution before lending the shares, or whether the shares can be lent on a discretionary basis without prior approval.

Lenders receive a fee from the borrower. Table 13.4 shows the fees charged and returns achieved by lenders of securities in the year 2007. In the table, bp stands for basis points, which represent 0.01 percent.

Most arbitrageurs that sell short do not borrow shares directly from a lender but instead rely on their broker to borrow the shares either out of their clients' inventory or from other sources. Brokers usually borrow from other sources only if the size of the trade is large enough to make doing so economical. An arbitrageur who borrows shares from the broker does not normally pay a lending fee. Instead, the cost of lending is incorporated into the short rebate in the form of a lower rebate. Only hard-to-borrow shares command extra fees.

TABLE 13.4 Fees and Returns Earned by Lenders of Securities

Asset Class	Lendable Assets (US $m)	Total Balance (US $m)	Utilization (%)	Securities Lending Fee (bp)	Securities Lending Return to Lendable (bp)	Total Return to Lendable (bp)
USA Equity	4,529,328.7	636,653.6	10.41	41.84	3.76	5.2
USA Equity (S&P500)	3,388,388.2	302,196.3	6.33	20.77	0.98	1.82
USA Equity (Russell 2000)	424,958.9	173,988.1	31.65	60.9	17.51	5.2
USA Equity (Others)	715,981.7	160,469.2	16.8	61.7	8.54	10.95

Source: Securities Lending Yearbook 2007 (London: Spitalfields Advisors Limited, 2008).

Short rebates vary widely and are subject to negotiation. Most retail brokerage firms pay their customers no short rebate at all. One such firm, Interactive Brokers, pays a rate between based on the Fed Funds rate, and charges between Fed Funds minus 0.25 percent and Fed Funds minus 1.25 percent, depending on the dollar balance of short proceeds. The section about leverage in this chapter has a more detailed discussion of the impact of the short rebate on the use of leverage. Consulting firm Spitalfields Advisors Ltd. has estimated the annual cost incurred in borrowing securities at $50 billion.

Merger arbitrageurs who want to generate extra income also can take the opposite side and lend out shares that they hold as part of the arbitrage. The income generated thereby can offset some of the borrowing costs. Many arbitrageurs will forgo this additional revenue in order to maintain voting control over the shares that are subject to a merger. When shares are lent out, the ultimate holder of the shares will exercise the voting rights, not the original owner who has lent them. For an arbitrageur who wants a merger to happen, it is more critical to vote in favor than to generate additional revenue. The larger the position, the more relevant this consideration becomes.

The borrowing of shares also can be used to acquire votes beyond the actual number of shares owned. An investor can borrow shares with the sole intent of voting them. The cost of borrowing is minimal in most instances; however, the upside of influencing the outcome of such a vote can be considerable. One of the most prominent examples of such "empty voting" occurred during the failed merger of King Pharmaceuticals and Mylan Laboratories in 2005. Hedge fund Perry Corp. owned shares of King, which had risen following the news of the merger. Perry acquired 9.9

percent of Mylan and hedged all its exposure to the stock price. Therefore, Perry[2] had voting rights to Mylan's stock but no economic interest. Perry could have pushed Mylan to pay a higher price for King. The transaction unraveled following the revelation of accounting problems at King, so that Perry's strategy was never tested in practice. However, it has led to calls by Securities and Exchange Commission (SEC) official for action on "empty voting." Because the SEC does not want to disrupt the securities lending markets, no action had been proposed by the time of writing, but it is likely that this area will be regulated in the future.[3]

The SEC has issued a rule that governs all short sales, Regulation SHO. It became mandatory in January 2005. This rule forbids brokers from entering into short sales on behalf of a client unless the stock to be shorted has been borrowed previously. Many brokers will handle both the borrowing and the execution of the short sale. Execution-only brokers now require confirmation from arbitrageurs that the stock has been borrowed (or located for borrowing) prior to placing a short sell.

Short sellers will cover their position only if they cannot borrow the shares from another lender. Under normal market conditions, there are many willing lenders of stock. However, in some instances, an individual stock can be shorted heavily, and only few shares are available to be borrowed. Such stocks are at risk of going through a short squeeze. An arbitrageur who shorts a stock that goes through a short squeeze will suffer a loss, albeit temporarily. The problem with such a loss is that at some point, the arbitrageur will feel compelled to cover the short position to avoid further losses. Unless the arbitrageur is lucky or unusually skilled in timing the market, it is unlikely that it will be possible to reenter the short position at a more favorable level. Market movements in short squeezes are very rapid. The most prominent example of a short squeeze was the increase of Volkswagen (VW) ordinary shares following the revelation that Porsche SE had acquired control over 75 percent of the shares. With 20 percent held by the state of Lower Saxony, the free float amounted to only 5 percent, while short positions were estimated to amount to 15 percent. Within two days, VW's stock price increased from €210 to as much as €1,000. Cumulative losses to short sellers were estimated to amount to €15 billion. It should be noted that the short sellers were for the most part arbitrageurs who had attempted to arbitrage the wide spread between VW's ordinary and preferred shares.

Retail investors usually do not have to worry about borrowing stock themselves. Their clearing broker gives them access to their clients' inventory and will reject orders to sell short if there is insufficient inventory. The direct access to substantial inventory sometimes can give retail investors an edge over institutions when dealing in hard-to-borrow stocks. Retail brokers may have a small number of shares available that are too few to be shown to the street but are still available to their lucky clients.

A short sale in which the arbitrageur is not able to deliver the stock is referred to as a naked short and is illegal. Nevertheless, occasionally naked short sales can happed as trade errors, but this should be an exception and should not occur with any regularity. It has been alleged by anti–short-selling activists and some politicians that some market participants use foreign exchanges to skirt Regulation SHO. Arbitrageurs should refrain from such activities, which are bound to unwind at the time of the closing of the merger. In July 2008, the SEC reiterated Regulation SHO through an emergency order that prohibited naked shorting for equity securities of 19 financial firms.

By issuing this list, the SEC intended to prop up shares of financial companies that had dropped precipitously in the previous weeks. Although this emergency ruling was hailed widely as a tough measure, it merely reiterated the existing prohibition against naked short sales under Regulation SHO. Its impact was more psychological than logical, sending a message that short sellers might face regulatory scrutiny. It worked as intended and led to a rally in financial stocks as short sellers covered their positions in a squeeze. Nevertheless, the effectiveness of the list is at best dubious. Many of the companies listed are not even based in the United States and their principal trading exchange is located in Asia or Europe and does not fall under the purview of the SEC. A short seller who is not subject to SEC oversight, such as a London-based hedge fund, would be able to engage in unlimited naked short selling without violating the SEC's order.

A study[4] conducted shortly after the ban of short selling showed that the effect of the ban was a deterioration of the market quality in the affected stocks. This led to a sharper decline in their stock prices than short selling would have. The study analyzed a number of different metrics to determine the effect of the emergency order.

The study started by noting that short selling the 19 stocks on the list had been comparable to that of other financial companies between 2006 and 2008. When controlling for firm and market characteristics, the author, Arturo Bris, found that there had been less short selling for most stocks on the list than for other financial companies. An important difference between the 19 stocks and other financial companies is the propensity of the firms on the list to issue convertible bonds. Many convertible bonds are acquired by arbitrageurs who hedge the conversion feature by selling short stock. As a result, on an absolute level, there is more short selling in these stocks. This higher absolute level is not evidence of bearish activity but of convertible arbitrage that takes no view about the direction of a company's stock.

More important, the SEC's action led to a deterioration of the market quality in the stocks that the it was hoping to protect. Measures of daily price volatility as well as quoted spreads deteriorated after the emergency order took effect. Also, the comovement of the individual stocks with the overall market increased. In more efficient markets, individual stocks should be less dependent on the overall direction of the market and more dependent on company-specific information.

Despite the mixed results of the first short selling ban, a more comprehensive prohibition against shorting in 800 financial companies was enacted from September 19 to October 8 that same year. Even the nonfinancial company General Motors was included in the prohibition. At the same time, the SEC required the disclosure of short sales that exceed 0.25 percent of an issuer's outstanding shares or $1 million of market value. Only money managers who were already required to file 13F reports are subject to these reporting requirements. These are managers with at least $100 million assets under management.

Regulators outside of the United States were even more drastic in their measures to restrict short selling. The United Kingdom banned short selling of 30 financial stocks for four months. Australia banned all short sales for two months and, like the SEC, instituted reporting requirements. The Netherlands banned naked short sales of financial stocks for three months. Taiwan banned short selling in stocks amounting to 80 percent of the country's market capitalization for three weeks. Ireland and Germany also imposed restrictions on short sales.

A study on the efficiency of short sales[5] that was conducted prior to the worldwide short selling bans found that restrictions on short selling have lower price efficiency. Restrictions on short selling were measured through the availability of shares available for shorting, and the level of borrowing fees. Price efficiency was defined as the lag with which an individual stock responds to market shocks. At the same time, the skewness of returns increased. This was associated with an increase of the number of large positive returns on stocks that suffer from short sale restrictions rather than a decrease in the number of large negative drops. Therefore, like Bris's study, this study confirms that short sale restrictions fail to meet their goals of reducing sharp declines in the affected stocks.

Dividend payments complicate the shorting of stocks. When a stock is sold short, there are two holders of the stock: the original buyer who has lent the stock out, and the buyer who is the counterparty to the short sale. The buyer of a stock is ignorant as to the nature of the stock acquired. The buyer does not know whether the stock was purchased out of a seller's inventory or whether the stock had been borrowed and was sold short. Each buyer of a stock expects to receive a dividend and obtains the right to receive it through the purchase.

Short selling activity increases over dividend dates, as shown in Figure 13.2. Both the percentage of shares available for shorting, labeled "Utiliza-

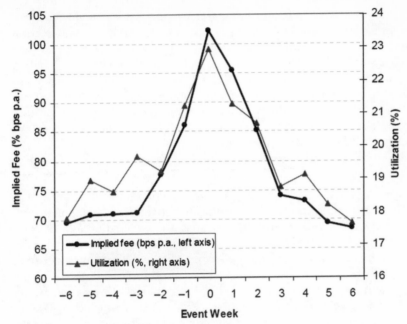

FIGURE 13.2 Fees and Short Sale Activity (Utilization of Shares Available) around Dividend Payments
Source: P. Saffi, K. Sigurdsson, Price Efficiency and Short Selling. Working Paper, London Business School, January 2007, p. 48.

tion," and the level of lending fees increase over dividend dates. Arbitrageurs must be careful if they maintain short positions over dividend dates or attempt to short around that time. The data underlying Figure 13.2 are based on a global data set and may not translate identically to each country. Shorting activity around dividend dates probably increases more in countries that give shareholders tax credits along with dividend payments.[6]

TRANSACTION COSTS

Merger arbitrage spreads are very tight, and arbitrageurs must keep transaction costs under control. Transaction costs come in three forms: brokerage commissions, bid/offer spreads, and market impact.

Brokerage Commissions

As discussed in Chapter 3, commissions have fallen significantly over the last few years. Many mergers would be uneconomical at commission levels of just a few years ago. However, this is somewhat of a chicken-and-egg argument. One of the reasons why spreads have become tighter is the reduction in the overall level of trading commissions. If commissions were larger, then trading costs of arbitrageurs would be higher, and this would be reflected in wider arbitrage spreads. In this way, the fall in the cost of brokerage commissions has benefited not the arbitrage community but rather the investors who sell their shares after the announcement of a merger in order to capture the premium. They obtain a higher price from the liquidity providers, the arbitrageurs, because commissions are lower.

Brokerage commissions bundle a number of services into a single fee:

Execution. This is the basic activity of routing and order to an exchange or electronic communication network (ECN) and matching it with a counterparty. Most trades are executed today electronically. Computer algorithms have been developed to split large orders into smaller ones to reduce market impact (to be discussed). Many brokers offer specialized execution services for arbitrageurs and long/short investors whereby orders are not executed at set price levels; instead, a spread level is entered at which both sides of the trade will be executed. The computer will show one side of the trade in the market in a way that if that side is filled, the other side can be executed instantaneously. For large trades, markets may not be liquid enough to execute the order in a reasonable time frame. Brokers often match buyers and sellers based on knowledge of their clients' investment preferences. Despite increased automatization of trading, the human element will remain an important factor for transactions of this type for some time to come. The cost of pure execution without any added value is currently below $0.01 per share.

Idea generation and market surveillance. Many brokers add value to arbitrageurs by monitoring the market and pointing arbitrageurs to trading activity in stocks going through mergers. Such market intelligence can be very valuable because arbitrageurs generally do not have the time or resources to monitor all trading activity themselves. Commissions charged by brokers who offer such extra services can be as low as $0.02 per share.

Clearing. Clearing is the act of settlement and paying for the shares bought or sold during the execution of the order. It is a highly automated process that benefits from scale effects. The cost of clearing is below $0.005 per share.

Soft dollars. In addition to monitoring the market and making suggestions to their customers, many brokers offer added services that they pay for through commissions. This practice is legal and used widely by money managers that seek to reduce costs at the expense of their clients. The idea of soft dollars is that the broker charges a higher commission than necessary and uses the extra payments to purchase services that the investment advisor can use to help with its research. Services typically paid for with soft-dollar commissions are third-party research, data services, and certain investment-related software. The use of soft dollars is particularly pervasive by hedge fund managers, who trade frequently and thereby accrue significant soft-dollar credits. Instead of paying for research out of the management fee, it is paid for by soft dollars, so that the manager's overall profitability increases. For most arbitrageurs, soft dollars are not attractive because they reduce the spread that is already very tight.

Brokerage commissions are highly variable between different firms and even within a single firm for different clients and types of orders or securities. A common fee structure is based on the number of shares that are executed, often coupled with a minimum ticket charge or base fee per ticket.

Bid/Offer Spreads

Bid/offer spreads were discussed in Chapter 3 in the context of liquidity as a determinant of the profitability of merger arbitrage. Arbitrageurs have to place orders carefully in less liquid stocks with wide bid/offer spreads. For wide bid/offer spreads, it is not economic for an arbitrageur to pay the entire spread unless the arbitrage spread is unusually wide. The arbitrageur will try to work with limit orders that are placed within the bid/offer spread. The disadvantage of this strategy is that there is no guarantee that the order will be filled. Other investors may jump ahead of the order. The advantage is that the arbitrageur becomes a genuine provider of liquidity and contributes to the tightening of the bid/offer spread. A tighter spread, in turn, may encourage some sellers to come forward and either hit the arbitrageur's bid or place an offer in the market that is below the previous best offer and thereby again reduce the bid/offer spread.

Mark-to-market valuation adds an impediment to paying the entire bid/offer spread: Many arbitrageurs are required to value their long positions at the bid and short positions on the offer. Some can use midmarket pricing. Under these circumstances, if an arbitrageur pays the entire bid/offer spread, an immediate loss has to be booked. The loss will, of course, be recovered once the spread tightens. Nevertheless, it complicates the setup of an arbitrage position further.

For the short side of stock-for-stock offer, the previous arguments are also true, albeit in reverse.

Market Impact

Whenever an arbitrageur places an order to acquire shares of a target, the order influences the supply and demand balance. The increase in demand will have an impact on the price. This may not necessarily translate into an immediate jump of the target stock price. It could simply prevent the price from making a correction that would have occurred in the absence of the arbitrageur's order. This effect is known as market impact. Although several consulting firms specialize in measuring market impact as part of an evaluation of execution and trading quality, the measurement of market impact is very difficult and is associated with a certain degree of speculation.

Nevertheless, there is no doubt that arbitrage activity does have a market impact. In the aggregate, market impact by all arbitrageurs helps sellers of a target's stock to obtain a better price than they would in the absence of arbitrage activity. This is a corollary of the argument made in Chapter 3 in the discussion of liquidity.

This discussion of market impact applies also to the short sale in a stock-for-stock merger.

MANAGING THE CASH POSITION

Portfolio managers view cash holdings as a strategic or operational tool. Strategically, cash holdings are treated as an asset class, and operationally, they are needed to meet redemption requests.

Cash can provide a cushion to the downside and represents liquidity that can be put to use when attractive investment opportunities become available. In addition, cash is held in case redemption requests are received from investors. This is a problem that is more acute for mutual fund managers than for arbitrageurs who work in hedge funds or broker/dealers. The latter do not have to worry about cash holdings because cash is part of the firm's overall asset/liability management. Hedge fund managers are in an intermediate position: Typical investment conditions include a 90-day notice period for redemptions, so that the fund manager has sufficient time to liquidate positions and raise cash. Mutual funds have daily redemptions and therefore must keep a portion of their portfolio in cash to meet redemption requests.

The downside of cash holdings is that they do not generate returns. Because the market increases over time, cash holdings act as a drag on performance. This effect is true not only for traditional portfolios but also applies to merger arbitrage portfolios. Merger arbitrage generates positive returns most of the time, which are higher than the return on cash that is invested in short-term products. Holding cash instead of being fully invested diminishes the overall return on a merger arbitrage portfolio.

For traditional investors, the decision to hold cash beyond the amount required to meet redemption requests is a voluntary choice of the manager. The portfolio can be invested in cash or other assets as the manager sees fit. Increases in cash occur when the manager takes an active decision to sell assets and substitute these investments with cash holdings.

For a merger arbitrageur, cash holdings are based less on choice and more on deal flow. Whenever a merger closes, the arbitrageur will receive cash that must be reinvested. In the case of a cash merger, the position is liquidated when the merger closes. In a stock-for-stock merger, the arbitrageur receives cash indirectly when the proceeds of the short sale become available once the short position is closed out. In both scenarios, the arbitrageur will hold cash rather than an investment. The important difference to a traditional money manager is that this cash holding is not based on the arbitrageur's decision to reallocate assets but is out of the arbitrageur's control. It depends on the timing of the closing of the mergers that the arbitrageur is invested in. Mergers close more or less randomly. Even though the arbitrageur can make a rough guess about the closing, the date cannot be pinpointed precisely. For mergers, the closing date is often within a few days of the shareholder meeting. However, when regulatory approvals are required for a merger, then the shareholder meeting is often well before the actual closing date. Even when the arbitrageur has a high level of confidence in a closing date, there can still be delays in the settlement of the cash or stock proceeds.

Due to this uncertainty, the arbitrageur receives cash as a result of the closing of a merger and now faces the decision to

- Invest in other mergers, currently held in the portfolio or not
- Hold on to the cash in case another merger is announced shortly

Like the liquidation of investments, the decision of how to invest cash is different from that faced by a traditional money manager. The traditional manager has a well-defined choice of investment. The arbitrageur also has a defined choice of mergers to invest in. However, mergers are announced at random intervals. In addition to the already announced mergers that the arbitrageur can invest in, there is a probability that another attractive investment opportunity will be announced shortly after the arbitrageur receives a payout from a closing merger.

Assume the arbitrageur spreads the cash across the mergers currently held in the portfolio. The risk characteristics of the portfolio change as the concentration of individual position increases. If another merger is announced shortly thereafter that the arbitrageur deems attractive, all positions must be reduced to free up sufficient funds to invest. In light of the tight absolute spreads, cost of commissions, and bid/offer spreads, this is not a good proposition. Arbitrageurs are more likely to hold the cash until a new merger is announced that is attractive to invest in.

A direct and visible result of this problem is that average cash balances are higher in merger arbitrage funds than in traditional investment vehicles. Cash holdings are considered a cash drag on performance in most portfolios. They are also a drag on performance in merger arbitrage portfolios, but the drag is less of a problem than the alternative. If the cash was invested and subsequently redeployed in a newly announced merger, transaction costs would be much higher than the opportunity cost of holding cash. A back-of-the-envelope calculation illustrates this. Assume the average stock has a price of $20 and the bid/offer spread is 4 cents, while commissions are 2 cents per share. This implies trading costs of 12 cents per share for a round trip, or 0.6 percent. For a long/short merger, the total cost would be twice as high, or 1.2 percent. If cash is held, it can be invested in short-term instruments (money market funds) to yield a return, which reduces the opportunity cost. This compares to a typical monthly return of 1 percent on a merger arbitrage strategy. It is clear that it is best to hold cash rather than incur transaction costs if the arbitrageur thinks that another attractive merger is likely to be announced within no more than a few weeks.

The timing of the closing of mergers is subject to a small seasonality effect. Companies often try to close a merger prior to the end of their fiscal year, which ends on December 31 for most firms. Firms with fiscal years not ending with the calendar year typically have fiscal years that end on another calendar quarter-end. Companies strive to close the transaction in the current fiscal year, or before the completion of a fiscal quarter, in order to simplify the accounting by being able to show financials for the merged entity for an entire fiscal year or quarter.

This effect is apparent from the data. Figure 13.3 shows the number of mergers closing in each calendar month between the years 1990 and 2006. Only cash mergers were considered, of which there were 2,659 over this period. It can be seen that most mergers closed in the calendar month of December. March and September quarter-ends also show slightly more mergers closing than the months just before and after. July is an exception; there may be more merger closings in this month because companies try to close deals before the summer break when many employees take vacation.

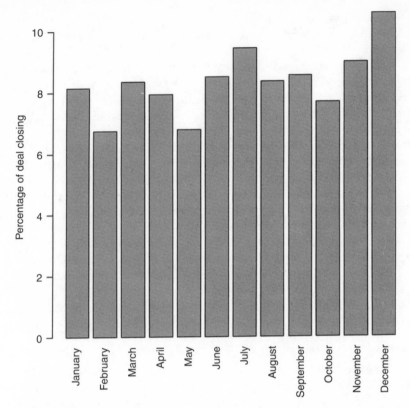

FIGURE 13.3 Frequency of Merger Closings by Calendar Month, 1990–2006

Publicly available mutual funds that employ merger arbitrage are required to report their portfolio holdings quarterly. The annual and semi-annual holdings are included in reports sent to shareholders, whereas the holdings at the end of the first and third quarters are reported to the SEC. Most funds have a fiscal year that ends either in October 31 or December 31. Hedge funds do not report their holdings publicly but, depending on their jurisdiction of incorporation and prospectus, may be required to send audited financial statements to their investors. Investors who are unaware of the cash management problem will assume mistakenly that the fund manager has taken the decision to hold a large amount of cash, even though that holding is of a transitory nature only.

A different type of cash management problem faced by a fund manager is the holding of a certain amount of cash to meet redemption requests.

This problem arises in all open-ended funds that have a high frequency of redemptions. Hedge funds have normally negotiated a notice period of 90 days prior to the calendar quarter-end, sometimes 45 days. This gives the manager sufficient time to liquidate positions after redemption requests are filed by investors. The cash drag created by a structure of quarterly redemptions will affect all investors and can be worse than in the case of open-ended funds if redemptions represent a large percentage of the hedge fund. In that scenario, the manager will sell positions throughout the quarter to raise cash to the level necessary to pay for the redemption. The period of time for which the cash is held can be up to three months, and all investors will suffer a cash drag in that quarter. For small redemptions, this effect will be negligible, but it can become material for sizable redemptions. In an open-ended fund, in contrast, redemptions occur much more rapidly, and managers have tools (to be described) to minimize the impact of cash holdings on performance. Hedge funds justify the lengthy notice periods for redemptions with illiquidity of investments; this is not a valid reason for merger arbitrage funds, which invest mostly in equity securities that are highly liquid or in derivatives positions that also can be closed easily. It is difficult to understand why merger arbitrage investors are willing to accept 90-day notice periods for merger arbitrage hedge funds despite the high liquidity of the underlying instruments.

A commercial solution has been developed to help open-ended mutual funds minimize cash holdings to meet redemption requests. ReFlow Management Co. of San Francisco will acquire the shares redeemed by investors for up to 30 days and thereby smooth the fluctuation in cash requirements. For the duration of its holding period, ReFlow assumes the full market risk of owning the fund's shares. A fund participating in ReFlow's program benefits in several ways: Overall cash balances can be lower than if the fund were to hold a large cushion against redemptions, and the costs related to selling and buying shares in the fund's investments are eliminated. In addition, the adverse tax effects of realizing gains merely to satisfy redemption requests are avoided. The fund can redeem ReFlow's shares later when cash becomes available through investments, or liquidate investments in a more orderly manner. The key requirement is that under an SEC no-action letter, ReFlow's investment must be redeemed within 30 days. Because ReFlow owns shares in the fund that are not senior to other investors, it is not considered to own senior securities, which would be prohibited under the Investment Company Act. Redemption in kind for ReFlow's shares is also available for funds that seek to avoid triggering tax events.

ReFlow's service does not come for free. Its capital is allocated through an auction mechanism. Funds looking to access ReFlow's funds submit a bid of at least 0.25 percent of the amount requested. ReFlow will fill all requests for fund above the minimum winning bid in a Dutch auction. ReFlow's service has also become available to European funds registered in Luxembourg.

To date, the most sophisticated approach to handle the cash management problem analytically has been developed by Juliana Nascimento and Warren Powell of the Department of Operations Research and Financial Engineering at Princeton University[7] in response to an inquiry by this author whether the newsvendor inventory solution can be applied to the mutual fund cash problem. The newsvendor formula is used widely for optimizing inventory when demand is stochastic and there are costs of holding excess inventory.

For a mutual fund, the cash level R_t at time t after new investments, D_t^i, must be sufficient to cover redemptions $D_t^l + D_t^s$, which are large and small redemptions. The incidence of large redemptions will have a more dramatic impact on costs than smaller redemptions, so that they should be modeled independently. When the cash holdings after new investments are insufficient to meet redemptions, $R_t < D_t^l + D_t^s$, the fund incurs a cost of shortfall, ρ^{sh} in liquidating its holdings. A financing cost P_t^f will accrue for large amounts of redemptions where positions cannot be liquidated immediately. Whenever the fund holds too much cash, it incurs an opportunity cost in the form of the rate of return on the portfolio, P_t^r.

The cash management decision x_t that must be taken by the fund manager in each period t is the move x_{t1} from the portfolio into cash and x_{t2} from cash back into investments: $x_t = (x_{t1}, x_{t2})$. The transaction cost is ρ^{tr} $(x_{t1} + x_{t2})$. After the decision x_t has been taken, the cash level is R_t^x.

$$R_t^x = \max(0, \ R_t - D_t^l - D_t^s) + x_{t1} - x_{t2} \text{ and } R_{t+1} = R_t^x + D_{t+1}^i \quad (13.5)$$

The cost for one period is given by

$$C_t = \rho^{sh} \times (D_r^l + D_t^s - R_t) \times 1_{\{D_t^l + D_t^s \geq R_t\}} + P_t^f \times (D_t^l - R_t) \times 1_{\{D_t^l \geq R_t\}}$$
$$+ P_t^r \times (R_t - D_t^l + D_t^s) \times 1_{\{D_t^l + D_t^s < R_t\}} + \rho^{tr} \times (x_{t1} + x_{t2}). \quad (13.6)$$

The problem is to minimize this cost.

The variable are combined into a state of the system before and after the decision x_t taken at time t:

$$S_t = (W_t, \ R_t) \text{ and } S_t^x = (W_t, \ R_t^x), \text{ respectively,} \quad (13.7)$$

where $W_t \ (P_t^r, \ P_t^f, \ D_t^i, \ D_t^l, \ D_t^s)$ represents the exogenous inputs known at time t.

The key to dynamic programming is the definition of a Bellman equation. It represents the problem that is to be optimized, coupled with one or several constraints. In the mutual fund cash problem, the Bellman equation is a recursive value function V such that

$$V_{t-1}^{*,x}(W_{t-1}, R_{t-1}^x) = \mathrm{E}[\max_{x \in \chi(W_t, R_t)} -C_t(W_t, R_t, x)$$

$$+ \gamma V_t^{*,x}(W_t, R_t^x) | (W_{t-1}, R_{t-1}^x)] \tag{13.8}$$

The problem can be solved through a piecewise-linear optimization using Approximate Dynamic Programming (ADP). Nascimento and Powell use an algorithm SPAR-Mutual, shown in the box, and prove that this algorithm converges. The algorithm breaks the value function into piecewise linear functions $\bar{v}_t^n(W_t, R_{t1}^x)$, ..., $\bar{v}_t^n(W_t, R_{tN}^x)$ that approximate the concave shape of the actual value function. The algorithm determines the slopes of those pieces that are close to optimal cash levels, thereby reducing computational effort.

At the beginning of time period t, the algorithm creates a Monte Carlo sample of all the variables in W_t, projecting these values forward over n periods until time N. Temporary approximations of the slopes are calculated in the vector $z_{t-1}^n \times \bar{\alpha}_{t-1}^n \times (S_{t-1}^x)$ is a stepsize rule that is state dependent.

Nascimento and Powell use data to examine the performance of the algorithm based on data from the Center for Research in Security Prices (CRSP) at the University of Chicago Booth School of Business and redemption information from Investment Company Institute for the period from July 2005 until June 2006 for 4,623 stock funds. Further implementation of the algorithm with more granular investment and redemption data is expected to be conducted in the future.

SPAR-MUTUAL ALGORITHM

STEP 0: Algorithm Initialization:
STEP 0a: Initialize $\bar{v}_t^0$ (W_t, R_t^x) for all t and (W_t, R_t^x) monotone decreasing in R_t^x.
STEP 0b: Pick N, the total number of iterations.
STEP 0c: Set $n=1$.
STEP 1: Planning Horizon Initialization: Observe the initial cash level $R_{-1}^{x,n}$.
Do for $t=0$; ... ;T:

STEP 2: Sample/Observe $P_t^{f,n}$, $P_t^{r,n}$, $D_t^{i,n}$, $D_t^{l,n}$ and $D_t^{s,n}$.

STEP 3: Compute the pre-decision cash level:

$R_t^n = R_{t-1}^{x,n} + D_t^{in}$.

STEP 4: Slope Update Procedure:

If $t > 0$ then

STEP 4a: Observe $\hat{v}_t^n (R_{t-1}^{x,n})$ and $\hat{v}_t^n (R_{t-1}^{x,n}) + 1$.

STEP 4b: For all possible states S_{t-1}^x: $Z_{t-1}^n (S_{t-1}^x) =$

$(1-\bar{\alpha}_{t-1}^n (S_{t-1}^x)) \bar{v}_{t-1}^{n-1} (S_{t-1}^x) + \bar{\alpha}_{t-1}^n (S_{t-1}^x) \hat{v}_t^n (R_{t-1}^x)$.

STEP 4c: Perform the projection operation $\bar{v}_{t-1}^n =$

$\prod_{C, W_{t-1}^n, R_{t-1}^{x,n}} (Z_{t-1}^n)$.

STEP 5: Find the optimal solution R_t^n of

$$\max_{x \in \chi (W_t^n, R_t^n)} -C_t (S_t^n, x) + \gamma \bar{V}_t^{n-1} (W_t^n, R_t^x)$$

STEP 6: Compute the post-decision cash level:

$R_t^{x,n} = \max(0, R_t^n - D_t^{ln} - D_t^{sn}) + X_{t1}^n - X_{t2}^n$.

STEP 7: If $n < N$ increase n by one and go to step 1. Else, return $\bar{v}^N$.

Source: Juliana Nascimento and Warren Powell, "Dynamic Programming Models and Algorithms for the Mutual Fund Cash Balance Problem," *Management Science*, in press.

RISK MANAGEMENT

A centerpiece of modern finance is the concept that risk can be calculated and analyzed. The principal parameters that drive the theory of financial risk are standard deviation (volatility) and correlation. In Chapter 12, some of the shortcomings of these measures were discussed when dealing with merger arbitrage and other event-driven strategies. For the measurement and management of the risk of a merger arbitrage portfolio, the metrics used by traditional risk managers are not very useful.

The reason for the inadequacy of financial risk measures based on modern portfolio theory lies in the noncorrelated nature of the risks inherent in merger arbitrage. Most investment strategies rely in one way or another on the dynamics of stocks relative to the overall market. For example, a long/short equity portfolio might hold long positions in stock with high valuations and short positions in stocks with lower valuations. In the short run, it can be expected that these stocks will exhibit similar dynamics relative to the overall market as they have historically. In this case, financial risk management can rely on the plethora of statistical risk measures that have been developed.

For merger arbitrage, the situation is different in that it is known that the dynamics of a stock's behavior have changed at the time of the announcement of a merger. It is not reasonable to assume that it will behave in the near future similarly as it has historically. It was illustrated earlier with Figure 12.2(a) and (b) how the dynamics of stocks change after a merger. Therefore, value at risk, shortfall, and similar risk management techniques do not provide meaningful results for merger arbitrage portfolios.

Merger arbitrageurs are well aware of these restrictions and rely on other methodologies that will appear antiquated to risk managers used to sophisticated statistical techniques. Most arbitrageurs use variations of classic position limits to manage their risk.

In its simplest incarnation, a position limit is a simple cap on the size of any single merger in a portfolio. For example, an arbitrageur may decide not to hold more than 5 percent of the portfolio in a single arbitrage position. Limits can be hard or soft. A hard limit is not exceeded under any circumstance. A soft limit can be exceeded if the arbitrageur has a particularly strong opinion about the likelihood of success of a merger.

A corollary of limiting the percentage of a portfolio that can invested in a single arbitrage deal is to target the number of transactions in which the arbitrageur invests. There are two types of arbitrageurs, as discussed in Chapter 12: concentrated and diversified. Concentrated arbitrageurs seek to limit the number of transactions in which they invest and seek to minimize the incidence of collapsing deals that generate a loss through extremely deep and thorough analysis. Diversified arbitrageurs try to limit the impact of the inevitable deal failure by spreading the risk over a larger number of transactions. A survey of the risk management practices of risk arbitrageurs[8] reveals that the average number of positions held by the 21 arbitrageurs who responded to the questionnaire was 36, with a minimum of 25 and a maximum of 40.

A slightly more sophisticated version of position limits considers the downside risk of a position and limits that to a percentage of the portfolio. The arbitrageur will estimate the severity of each position, as described in Chapter 3, and define a percentage of the portfolio that the aggregate severity (long and short) of any position cannot exceed.

Additional methods for limiting exposure can be set for the types of transactions that an arbitrageur can invest in. For example, arbitrageurs may want to limit their exposure to any individual industry or sector. This is easier said than done, because mergers often occur in waves in certain industries. As a result, deal flow is biased toward the industries undergoing consolidation.

An arbitrageur with strong industry limits may have to forgo arbitrages with high risk-adjusted returns. Therefore, sector limits in arbitrage strategies are not comparable to the use of these limits in stock picking or asset allocation strategies, and their effectiveness is less apparent in controlling risk.

Another type of position limit looks at the structure of the transaction. Arbitrageurs may want to restrict the proportion of leveraged buyouts (LBOs) in their portfolio because these transactions have a higher risk due to the purely financial interest of the buyer. In a strategic transaction, a buyer still may proceed with an acquisition even if the financial circumstances change, because the primary reason for the transaction is a strategic fit of the two firms. In contrast, an LBO relies exclusively on financial considerations to be successful.

Similarly, some hedge funds are constrained by implicit position limits on the payment type in a merger. Some hedge funds promise their investors in their offering materials to sell short at least a certain percentage of their portfolio. Many investors believe erroneously that the short positions will protect the arbitrage portfolio from market movements. As a result, they must invest at least that percentage in stock-for-stock transactions. Such a restriction can become as problematic as limits on industries or sectors. At a time when corporations have large amounts of cash available, more cash transactions are likely to be done than stock-for-stock mergers. Arbitrageurs who are subject to a minimum short sale requirement then will all chase after the limited number of stock-for-stock mergers, thereby driving down spreads and annual returns of these transactions.

Besides, as discussed earlier, the belief that the short position in a stock-for-stock merger protects against market movements is misguided. More precisely, the short position is irrelevant to protecting against market risk. This belief has its origin in standard long/short equity strategies, where it is applicable. The idea is that if the market falls and the transaction is canceled, then both the long and the short leg of the arbitrage will trade at lower levels, so the gain on the short side will offset the loss of the long leg. However, this is not necessarily the case for merger arbitrage investments, because market risk is at best a second-order effect. The principal risk remains event risk—the collapse of the merger. In a long/short position, the cancellation of a merger can lead to significantly higher losses than the termination of an otherwise identical cash deal. First, the long side loses value, and, second, the arbitrageur experiences a short squeeze on the short leg. Therefore, the assumption that losses on the long leg will be offset by gains on the short leg is incorrect.

A more quantitative approach to risk management for event-driven investment strategies was introduced recently by Philippe Jorion.[9] He relies on correlations between events to compute a value at risk. The approach is modeled after credit default analysis pioneered by Moody's Investor Services in the analysis of collateralized debt obligations. It allows for the use of structural models to determine probabilities of deal failure. It also helps to determine the number of transactions (diversification) needed in an arbitrage portfolio to achieve a certain risk level. Another way of looking at dollar risk is to consider it economic capital needed for survival, which conversely determines the leverage that can be employed by the arbitrageur.

The author believes that the use of correlations is an inadequate approach to determine economic capital, whether for collateralized debt obligations or merger arbitrage portfolios. Economic capital should be set so that the portfolio can withstand a stress scenario. This is the traditional approach used by insurance companies. As recent events have shown, the traditional approach has been more successful than the more modern methodologies used in the evaluation of credit risk. Financial risk managers should familiarize themselves with actuarial techniques. Historical correlations are average values that are of no use in the estimation of stress cases. A better approach in the determination of economic capital is the computation of a distribution of outcomes for the portfolio, either through trees or through Monte Carlo projections. Economic capital should be set so that the portfolio can withstand one of the worst outcomes of this simulation. As in credit, seasoning effects do play some role in the risk assessment of merger arbitrage. This timing dimension is missing from Jorion's approach but can easily be implemented in such a simulation.

Mitchell and Pulvino (see Chapter 12) pointed to the poor performance of merger arbitrage in sharply declining markets. One strategy to mitigate losses that can arise in a sharply declining market is to buy out of the money index put options. Most of the time they will expire worthless, and the arbitrageur will lose the option premium. When there is a decline in the market, these options will be in the money and can at least partially offset the losses suffered from collapsing deals. A portfolio following this strategy will have a slightly lower return in most market conditions due to the cost of acquiring options that expire worthless. However, the benefit is a sharply improved risk profile.

Managing downside risk with equity put options may be insufficient, because this method overhedges most of the time but underhedges when the hedge is most needed. An approach to hedging based on finite mixture models has been developed by Adam Tashman.[10] Finite mixture models combine two return distributions from two different states: when the market is in a regular state or in a sell-off state. These two distributions are combined to calculate a hedge ratio that is more accurate than one based solely on linear regression of returns. This approach is similar to hedging through regime switching models.

STANDARD & POOR'S MERGER ARBITRAGE INDEX

Standard & Poor's is best known for its S&P 500 stock index but provides a range of other indices. As part of its efforts to introduce specialty indices, S&P developed a series of arbitrage indices, including a long-only merger arbitrage index that began to be calculated in 2008. Data were backfilled to December 31, 2003, where the index value is set to 1,000.

The index contains up to 40 stocks from any developed market[11] that are in the process of being acquired. Each company has an index weighting of 2.5 percent at the time it is included, or less if the index contains insufficient cash (more on the indexes cash component later). Only companies with an equity of more than $500 million are included if the premium at the time of the announcement is at least 5 percent. Both cash and mixed cash/stock deals are included, but pure stock-for-stock deals are not. For mixed cash/stock deals, the cash component must represent at least 25 percent of the value.

A company is included in the index for one year at the most. If the deal has not closed after one year, the company is removed. A company is also removed once a merger is completed. Similarly, it is removed from the index if the merger is canceled.

No more than 40 companies are in the index at any time. If there are more than 40 eligible merger candidates available, then the company that has the lowest return since entering the index will be replaced by another target. The 2.5 percent weighting of each constituent firm will fluctuate over time with the change in its market value. Therefore, a company can exit the index with a weighting of less than 2.5 percent if its price dropped during the time it was in the index. Its replacement then will be added at that lower weighting. This mimics the management of an actual portfolio. An arbitrageur can put to work only that capital that has been received from the sale of an existing position.

If there are fewer than 40 eligible companies, the index will contain a cash component, because the weighting of each firm is limited to 2.5 percent at the time of inclusion. Interest on that cash balance accrues daily based on U.S. dollar LIBOR. Dividends are added to the cash position on the ex-date. However, the tax treatment of these dividends is assumed to be punitive: It reflects the rates paid by a nonresident institutional investor based in Luxembourg who does not benefit from a double-taxation treaty.

Figure 13.4 shows the performance of the S&P merger arbitrage index from inception in January 2004 through November 2008 compared to the S&P 500 index and bonds. Table 13.5 shows a number of key statistics for the index over the same period. It can be seen that the index exhibits similar properties as the merger arbitrage hedge fund indices discussed in Chapter

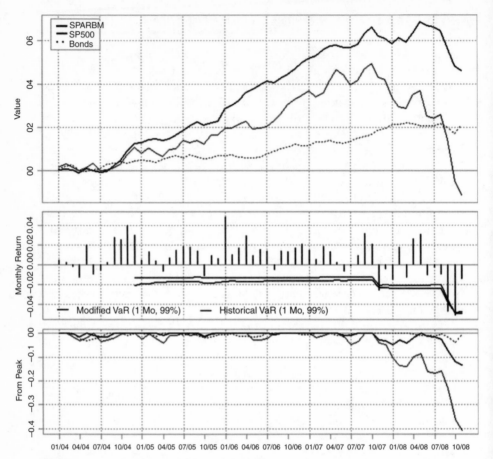

FIGURE 13.4   Performance of the S&P Merger Arbitrage Index Relative to Other Asset Classes

12: The median return is comparable to that of the S&P 500 index, whereas volatility is more akin to that of bonds. The period from 2004 through late 2008 includes the severe market decline in the summer of 2008, so that the S&P 500 index underperforms the merger arbitrage index significantly; the short period of time for which the index has existed exaggerates its outperformance due to the severe decline of the market. In the long run, the S&P 500 index should perform more like the S&P Merger Arbitrage Index, although the volatility of the latter will be closer to that of bonds. This is consistent with the experience of merger arbitrage funds discussed in Chapter 12.

TABLE 13.5 Statistics of Monthly Returns of the S&P Merger Arbitrage Index

	Standard & Poors Merger Arbitrage Index	Standard & Poors S&P 500 Index	Lehman Aggregate Bond Index
Observations	59	59	59
NAs	0	0	0
Minimum	− 0.0521	− 0.1679	− 0.0260
Quartile 1	− 0.0050	− 0.0166	− 0.0025
Median	0.0090	0.0108	0.0044
Arithmetic Mean	0.0066	− 0.0013	0.0033
Geometric Mean	0.0065	− 0.0021	0.0032
Quartile 3	0.0178	0.0192	0.0095
Maximum	0.0486	0.0487	0.0326
SE Mean	0.0024	0.0049	0.0013
LCL Mean (0.95)	0.0018	− 0.0111	0.0006
UCL Mean (0.95)	0.0114	0.0084	0.0060
Variance	0.0003	0.0014	0.0001
Stdev	0.0184	0.0374	0.0102
Skewness	− 0.7134	− 1.8991	− 0.3082
Kurtosis	1.3385	5.2210	0.8658

Figure 13.5 shows the risk/return relationship among the S&P Merger Arbitrage Index, stocks, and bonds. Table 13.6 shows the downside risk. Readers should refer to the explanation of this graph and table in Chapter 12.

SEPARATE ACCOUNTS

Some merger arbitrage managers offer their clients the management of separate accounts in the strategy. There are a number of advantages to separate accounts over pooled investment vehicles such as hedge funds or mutual funds. The account is held in the name of the client, and all securities are in the name of the client. The manager simply has investment authority with respect to the account. Holders of separate accounts receive statements that show all the holdings in their account. For some institutional investors, notably insurance companies, there are restrictions on their ability to invest in pooled vehicles. It is easier for them to ask an arbitrageur to manage a separate account than to allocate assets to a pooled fund. Taxes are also simplified, because the investor will receive a tax Form 1099 rather than a Schedule K-1. Hedge funds in particular are notorious for sending out their tax information late, requiring their investors to file extensions and

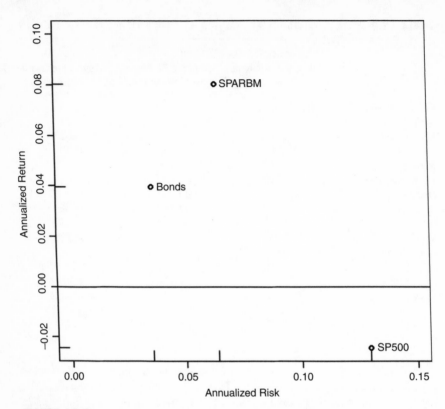

FIGURE 13.5   Risk/Return Trade-off for the S&P Merger Arbitrage Index since Its Inception

potentially incur penalties for underpayment. In fact, individualized tax management is one of the biggest advantages of separate accounts. Whether an arbitrage manager should get involved with optimizing taxes for clients is a different question.

For a manager, it is more complicated to manage separate accounts than a pooled vehicle. Managing a plethora of separate accounts requires additional effort compared to a pooled vehicle that is managed in a single account. Most providers of separate account platforms are now offering tools to streamline order placement. Nevertheless, when a new account is opened or an existing account is closed, there is a significant effort in establishing the initial position or liquidating the holdings. In a pooled vehicle, additions or withdrawals of capital are simply one element of the overall cash management.

TABLE 13.6 Various Downside Risk Measures

	Standard & Poors Merger Arbitrage Index	Standard & Poors S&P 500 Index	Lehman Aggregate Bond Index
Semi Deviation	0.0207	0.0516	0.0111
Gain Deviation	0.0106	0.0130	0.0062
Loss Deviation	0.0140	0.0381	0.0069
Downside Deviation (MAR=10%)	0.0216	0.0512	0.0131
Downside Deviation (*RF*=3%)	0.0198	0.0509	0.0109
Downside Deviation (0%)	0.0194	0.0525	0.0099
Maximum Drawdown	− 0.1321	− 0.4068	− 0.0383
VaR (99%)	0.0362	0.0884	0.0205
Beyond VaR	0.0365	0.0882	0.0206
Modified VaR (99%)	0.0481	0.1355	0.0245

More important, the investment ideas of arbitrageurs are proprietary information that they do not want to share with others. If clients access their account and see the deals in which the arbitrageur has invested, information about the positions can leak into the market and potentially can lead to problems such as front running or a squeeze in the lending market for short positions. For this reason, many arbitrage managers prefer to offer their clients only pooled vehicles.

HEDGE FUNDS AND MUTUAL FUNDS

The arbitrage community was a close-knit community of investment houses until the emergence of hedge funds and mutual funds that invest in merger arbitrage. Suddenly what had been an exclusive niche became available to a much wider group of investors.

Hedge funds and mutual funds are both structured to pool the assets of their investors. Their difference is more one of aura than substance. In fact, hedge funds are modeled after mutual funds: In the United States, a fund is a stand-alone entity that enters into a management agreement with an investment adviser.[12] The principal difference between the structures is one of regulation. Hedge funds are unregulated partnerships that can be sold only to clients who meet qualification requirement in terms income and wealth. At the time of writing, an annual income of $200,000 (or $300,000 if filing jointly) or a net worth of $1 million are required. These amounts are not indexed to inflation. Therefore, the percentage of households that can invest in hedge funds increases steadily.[13] Hedge funds are not required to make regulatory filings or report to their investors. However, the initial offering document must contain information that is equivalent to what would be contained in a mutual fund prospectus.[14] This lack of transparency can be an advantage for a fund manager because the fund's investments can be kept confidential. However, if the manager has more than $100 million under management, it is required to file a 13-F holdings report quarterly. The public can get an idea from these holdings reports which securities are held by hedge funds, despite the aura of secrecy. Even offshore funds that are managed by U.S. managers will have their holdings revealed through this mechanism. The absence of transparency is also a problem for investors, because it complicates their oversight of the manager to whom they have entrusted their assets.

Mutual funds do not have the transparency problem. They report their holdings on a quarterly basis and offer several other advantages over hedge funds:

> *Lower fees.* Typical mutual fund expense ratios are between 1.5 and 2 percent, whereas hedge funds charge 2 percent plus a part of the profits as a "performance fee."[15] A performance fee also can be levied by mutual funds, but it must be symmetric. For example, if the manager of a mutual fund were to receive 20 percent of the gains, then the fund would have to be reimbursed for 20 percent of the losses. For hedge funds, however, the performance fee is asymmetric and applies only to gains. Losses are entirely paid out of the investors' assets. Both symmetric and asymmetric performance fees have their advantages and problems. Proponents of performance fees argue that they align the interest of the investor and the manager and are a strong incentive to attract the best managers. An asymmetric performance fee is always more attractive for the manager but creates problems for the investor: Many managers simply close their funds after losses and start new ones so that they can charge performance fees on any rebound. A symmetric performance fee risks bankrupting the manager under extreme market conditions. Therefore, mutual funds that have performance fees limit them in order to avoid reimbursement of potentially devastating amounts. If the incentive argument is true, then a limited symmetric perfor-

mance fee is inferior to an asymmetric one. The principal problem with asymmetric performance fees in vehicles that have little to no transparency is that investors cannot control whether the manager takes unreasonable risks in order to maximize earnings.

Performance reporting. Mutual funds report daily net asset values, whereas hedge funds report their performance only monthly.[16] This is another aspect of insufficient transparency of hedge funds.

Liquidity. Mutual funds allow their investors to redeem on a daily basis. Hedge funds have created complicated withdrawal schedules, under which investors can redeem their shares only quarterly with at least 90 days' notice. If more than a certain percentage of investors seek to redeem in the same quarter, some funds will prevent all others from redeeming in the same quarter. These provisions were introduced originally because many hedge funds use illiquid instruments that can be difficult to unwind. It is hard to see why these provisions should apply to merger arbitrage funds, however, since these funds are invested in liquid publicly traded securities.

Lower minimum investments. Mutual funds can be invested in with small amounts, generally a few thousand dollars. Hedge funds have higher minimum investments that are sometimes in the millions of dollars.

Tax reporting. Mutual funds furnish their investors with a Form 1099, whereas hedge funds are partnerships that report on a Schedule K-1, which complicates tax reporting for their investors. Both entities are pass-through vehicles, whose gains are taxable only on the level of the investor, not on the level of the fund.

Custody. Mutual funds are required to place their assets with a bank custodian whereas hedge funds typically hold their assets with a prime broker. The prime broker uses the fund's securities as collateral for margin borrowing. The drawback of this method is that the fund is fully exposed to the well-being of the prime broker. If the prime broker fails, the funds become a credit and may not get their assets back for a long time, and then only at a rate of cents for the dollar. Some hedge funds discovered this problem painfully in the bankruptcy of Lehman Brothers, which acted as prime broker for many funds.

One of the biggest misconceptions about mutual funds is their alleged inability to invest in strategies that are the bread-and-butter business of hedge funds. Many commentators claim falsely that mutual funds cannot use leverage or derivatives and sell short. Today a number of mutual funds are available that use hedge fund strategies, including merger arbitrage, and engage regularly in short selling, leverage, and the use of derivatives.

The use of short selling was banned for mutual funds for a long time. To this day, the Investment Company Act of 1940 (commonly called the 1940 Act) states that

> *It shall be unlawful for any registered investment company, in contravention of such rules and regulations or orders as the Commission may prescribe as necessary or appropriate in the public interest or for the protection of investors:*
>
> *[...]*
>
> *3. to effect a short sale of any security, except in connection with an underwriting in which such registered company is a participant.*
> Section 12(a) of the Investment Company Act of 1940

The SEC clarified this provision in 1972 in an interpretive release[17] and stated that despite the wording of the statute, it was the intention of Congress not to limit shorting per se but to prevent the use of short proceeds as equity for further leveraged transactions. Under the current interpretation of the law, short sales are allowed as long as the shares that have been shorted are delivered to the buyer and the mutual fund has segregated sufficient funds to cover the purchase the shorted assets. The requirement to deliver shares forces a fund to short only shares that can be borrowed and prevents naked short selling. The intent of this rule is to limit the ability of funds to leverage through the proceeds of short sales. Similar rules apply for written options and futures contracts. Nevertheless, the urban myth that mutual funds cannot short continues to make rounds.

Similarly, mutual funds can use leverage, albeit not in the form typically used by hedge funds. Margin borrowing is a common method for hedge funds to increase their buying and shorting capacity, and it is limited only by the prime brokers' willingness to extend credit. Mutual funds are precluded from using margin borrowing. Instead, they have to use bank lending within strict limitations: The fund must maintain an asset coverage of 300 percent after borrowing. This means that the fund can borrow up to 50 percent of its preborrowing assets from banks. These strict limits on borrowing were imposed because funds also have the ability to leverage through the use of derivatives. The restrictions prevent the excessive use of leverage on top of leverage.

Overall, there are few restrictions on mutual funds to implement strategies such as merger arbitrage that are typically found in hedge funds. Relatively few mutual funds have chosen to implement these strategies. This has more to do with the eagerness of financial intermediaries to sell hedge funds, whose richer management fees allow for higher compensation of the intermediary, than with actual restrictions on the ability of funds to engage in arbitrage strategies.

Notes

CHAPTER 2: Incorporating Risk into the Arbitrage Decision

1. J. R. Hoffmeister and E. A. Dyl, "Predicting Outcomes of Cash Tender Offers," *Financial Management* 9 (1980): 50–58.
2. Mark Mitchell and Todd Pulvino, "Characteristics of Risk and Return in Risk Arbitrage," *Journal of Finance* 6, No. 6 (2001): 2135–2175.
3. Ibid.
4. Eliezer M. Fich and Irina Stefanescu, "Expanding the Limits of Merger Arbitrage," University of North Carolina Working Paper, May 18, 2003.
5. Ben Branch and Taewon Yang, "Predicting Successful Takeovers and Risk Arbitrage," *Quarterly Journal of Business and Economics* 42 (Winter 2003): 3–18.
6. Fich and Stefanescu, "Expanding the Limits of Merger Arbitrage."
7. The author thanks Mr. Ashish Tripathy for his significant contribution to this study.
8. *In re IBP, Inc. Shareholders Litigation*, 789 A.2d. 14, Del. Ch. 2001.
9. Ben A. Plotkin, "Attacks on Sovereign Unfair, Short-Sighted," *American Banker* (December 2005): 7.

CHAPTER 3: Sources of Risk and Return

1. Roger G. Ibbotson and Peng Chen, "Stock Market Returns in the Long Run: Participating in the Real Economy." *Financial Analysts Journal* 59, No. 1 (January/February 2003): 88–98.
2. Executive stock options are designed to pay off only based on the price appreciation of the stock, not its total return. Managers who receive a significant part of their compensation in stock options will cut their own option payouts if they recommend large dividend payouts. The smaller the dividend, the larger the value of the options. Compensation committees would be well advised to include a total return factor in option awards, for example, through automatic adjustment of the exercise price by dividend payments on the ex-date.
3. There is an undercurrent of companies that pay dividends out of capital, fooling investors into believing that they are highly profitable and helping to prop up the stock price. Such a strategy is bound to fail eventually, at the latest when the stock of capital is depleted.

CHAPTER 4: Deal Structures: Mergers and Tender Offers

1. In *Epstein v. MCA, Inc,* 516 U.S. 367 (1996).

CHAPTER 5: Financing

1. This feature is similar to negative amortization or option mortgages.
2. There is some confusion with the terminology "warrant." I refer here to warrants issued by a corporation to allow the holder of the warrant to acquire newly issued shares from the corporation. The term "warrant" is also used by European investment banks for over-the-counter options sold mainly to retail investors.
3. Jennifer S. Forsyth, "Blackstone's Slick Flip," July 26, 2007, http://online.wsj.com/article/SB118541177778978399.html?mod=googlenews_wsj.
4. Justin Owings and Aaron Krowne, "Citigroup," http://bankimplode.com, accessed on July 15, 2008.
5. "Deal Makers: Ripe for Layoff?" *Wall Street Journal,* February 21, 2008.
6. Marko Maslakovic, "Banking 2008," International Financial Services, London (February 2008).
7. Strictly speaking, Evans was proposing a recapitalization rather than an MBO. The result would have been similar in that he would have owned a majority of the shares.
8. Greenmailers acquired a company's shares and threatened a takeover until the company acquired their shares at a premium.
9. Poison pills will be discussed in Chapter 6.
10. Schedule 14A filed by Netsmart on February 2, 2007, p. 25, http://sec.gov/Archives/edgar/data/1011028/000110465907006593/a06-25740_3prer14a.htm#OpinionOfNetsmartsFinancialAdviso_134828.

CHAPTER 6: Legal Aspects

1. Agreement and Plan of Merger Among New Omaha Holdings, Omaha Acquisition Corporation and First Data Corporation dated April 1, 2007, www.sec.gov/Archives/edgar/data/883980/000119312507072154/dex21.htm.
2. Preliminary Proxy of Eddie Bauer Holdings filed on November 24, 2006, http://sec.gov/Archives/edgar/data/1345968/000089102006000362/v25397prprem14a.htm.
3. Richard De Rose, Marc Asbra, and Josh Langdon: Houlihan Lokey 2005 Transaction Termination Fee Study. Houlihan Lokey Howard & Zukin (2006), 3.
4. Martijn Cremers, Vinay B. Nair, and Urs C. Peyer, "Weak Shareholder Rights: A Product Market Rationale," Yale ICF Working Paper (October 2006).
5. Lucian A. Bebchuk and Alma Cohen, "The Costs of Entrenched Boards," *Journal of Financial Economics* 78, No. 2 (November 2005): 409–433.

6. Thomas A. Turk, Jeremy Goh, and Candace E. Ybarra, "The Effect of Takeover Defenses on Long Term and Short Term Analysts' Earnings Forecasts: The Case of Poison Pills," *Corporate Ownership & Control* 4, No. 4 (Summer 2007): 127–131.
7. Rights Agreement, October 7, 2003, http://sec.gov/Archives/edgar/data/1079880/000095013503005101/b48030okexv4w1.txt.
8. American Community Properties Trust, Amended and Restated Bylaws, October 10, 2007, http://sec.gov/Archives/edgar/data/1065645/000106564507000044/amended_bylaws.htm.

CHAPTER 7: Management Incentives

1. Consumers are frustrated every day by the disadvantages of hiring just good-enough staff. Retail businesses have cashiers who cannot even give change without the help of an electronic cash register.
2. There are numerous other exemptions, such as payments by qualified retirement plans.
3. The consortium consisted of an unusually large number of private equity firms: Silver Lake Partners, Bain Capital, The Blackstone Group, Goldman, Sachs & Co., Kohlberg Kravis Roberts, Providence Equity Partners, and Texas Pacific Group. While it is not unusual to see two private equity funds team up to make acquisitions of firms worth many billions of dollars in order to spread the risk, the large number of firms joining in one single buyout is unprecedented. To the author's knowledge, by the time of writing, it had not been repeated.

CHAPTER 8: Buyouts by Private Equity

1. The term "performance fee" is used for hedge funds, whereas private equity funds refer to this as "carry."
2. Pepper Hamilton and PricewaterhouseCoopers in association with mergermarket.com, "Private Equity Insight: Dividend Recapitalizations" (March 2007).
3. The shareholder meeting to approve the transaction was tumultuous. Police had to be called to remove one irate shareholder from the meeting.
4. Under German takeover rules, holdouts can receive higher payouts than shareholders who tender their shares. This is different from the situation in Delaware and elsewhere in the United States. In this case, the outside shareholder held their shares until after the U.S. IPO.

CHAPTER 9: Minority Squeeze-outs

1. This is a philosophical difference from European regulatory regimes on minority squeeze-outs, where fairness of price is codified. Regulations require a lookback at minimum or average historical trading ranges to set a minimum price for a squeeze-out.

2. Annalisa Barrett and Beth Young, "M&A Special Committees: Structure and Compensation," The Corporate Library (December 2006).

3. In some cases, the formed parent then becomes a minority shareholder itself. The most prominent example is the acquisition of General Motors's subsidiary General Motors Acceptance Company (GMAC) by private equity fund Cerberus Capital in 2007. Cerberus acquired 51 percent of GMAC, and GM retained a 49 percent minority interest.

4. *In re Siliconix*, CA No. 18700, Del. Ch., June 19, 2001.

5. *McMullin v. Beran*, 765 A.2d. 910, Del. 2000.

6. Based on the financial performance of infoUSA at the time, this valuation appears overly optimistic.

7. Not to be confused with a number of other firms that carry Chaparral in their name, most prominently Chaparral Steel.

8. Beth Young, "'It's a Family Affair': Succession Planning, Family Control and the Public Corporation," The Corporate Library (August 2005).

9. Ric Marshall, "Corporate Governance at Family Firms," The Corporate Library (July 2004).

CHAPTER 10: Government Involvement

1. "Early Termination Notices under the Hart-Scott-Rodino Act," Federal Trade Commission Web site: www.ftc.gov/bc/earlyterm/index.shtml.

2. Statement of Thomas O. Barnett, Assistant Attorney General, Before the Subcommittee on Antitrust, Competition Policy and Consumer Rights Committee on the Judiciary, March 7, 2007.

3. Ibid.

4. Arguably, part of the problem was the unwise attempt of GE's CEO, Jack Welch, to obtain support from the U.S. government in lobbying European governments. This angered the EC's antitrust regulators and made a compromise difficult to achieve.

5. Sale and leaseback transactions are a way to monetize real estate.

6. Brad Barber, "Pension Fund Activism: The Double-Edged Sword," University of California Working Paper, 2008.

CHAPTER 11: Four Ways to Fight Abuse of Shareholders in Mergers

1. California gives appraisal rights also in stock-for-stock mergers. In some states, appraisal rights are also available for amendments of the certificate of information. For example, New Jersey gives appraisal rights to shareholders of an acquirer if more than 40 percent of shares are issued in an acquisition; Ohio awards appraisal rights also in stock-for-stock mergers.

2. Although the court has some latitude to allocate legal fees, anyone thinking of perfecting appraisal rights should work on the assumption of hefty legal bills. The court generally will spread the cost incurred for experts and similar

across all shareholders who seek appraisal. However, this is not a statutory requirement and is at the discretion of the court.

One clever strategy was proposed by Kevin Cameron and Greg Taxin of proxy advisory firm Glass Lewis during the acquisition of Providian Financial by Washington Mutual: An investor can seek appraisal rights and find out how many other investors do so. If there is a sufficient number of other investors, it can be worthwhile for a relatively smaller holder to remain in the process. Otherwise, smaller holders can drop out within the 120-day period and obtain the same consideration as the other shareholders who did not seek appraisal rights. This option can make appraisal rights attractive for holders for whom the cost/benefit calculation is marginal at the outset.

3. *M.G. Bancorp, Inc. v. Le Beau*, 737 A.2d 513, Del. 1999.
4. DGCL 262 (h).
5. Geoffrey Jarvis, "State Appraisal Statutes: An Underutilized Shareholder Remedy," *Corporate Governance Advisor* 13, No. 3 (May/June 2005): 2.
6. Marty Lipton, "Shareholder Activism and the 'Eclipse of the Public Corporation,'" keynote address at the 25th annual Institute on Federal Securities, Miami, Florida, February 2007.
7. Sara Hansard, "Legg Mason Resisting Class Action Pressure," *Investment News*, March 6, 2006.
8. *Security First Corp. v. U.S. Die Casting and Development Co.*, 687 A.2d 563 (Del. 1997).
9. In many ways, a proxy campaign resembles a political election campaign. There is a long history of candidates building grassroots support with minimal financial investment.
10. Again, an analogy to political elections is applicable. It has been argued that the poor design of ballot papers confused voters in Florida during the 2000 election.

CHAPTER 12: The Role of Merger Arbitrage in a Diversified Portfolio

1. As an aside, periods of high volatility tend to be accompanied by high trading volumes, at least in developed markets.
2. B. B. Mandelbrot, "The Variation of Certain Speculative Prices," *Journal of Business* 36 (1963): 392–417.
3. As in the estimation of default probabilities, this analysis was performed in cooperation with Ashish Tripathy.
4. This is a standard statistical technique, the justification for which is beyond the scope of this book. Interested readers can find it in most introductory statistics texts.
5. William Dukes, Cheryl Frohlich, and Christoppher Ma, "Risk Arbitrage in Tender Offers: Handsome Rewards—and Not for Insiders Only," *Journal of Portfolio Management* (Summer 1992): 47–55.

6. Jan Jindra and Ralph A. Walkling, "Speculation Spreads and the Market Pricing of Proposed Acquisitions," Dice Working Paper No. 2000–18 (2001).

7. Sanjai Bhagat, James Brickley, and Uri Loewenstein, "The Pricing Effects of Interfirm Cash Tender Offers," *Journal of Finance* 42 (1987), 965–986.

8. M. Mitchell and T. Pulvino, "Characteristics of Risk and Return in Risk Arbitrage," *Journal of Finance* 56, No. 6 (2001): 2135–2175.

9. Eliezer M. Fich and Irina Stefanescu, "Expanding the Limits of Merger Arbitrage," University of North Carolina Working Paper, May 18, 2003.

10. Malcolm Baker and Serkan Savasoglu, "Limited Arbitrage in Mergers and Acquisitions," *Journal of Financial Economics* 64, No. 1 (2002), 91–115.

11. Ben Branch and Jia Wang, "Risk Arbitrage Performance for Stock Swap Offers with Collars," University of Massachusetts, Amherst Working Paper, 2006.

12. Ben Branch and Taewon Yang, "Merger Deal Structure and Investment Strategy: Collar Merger." University of Massachusetts, Amherst Working Paper, September 2006.

13. A. Karolyi and J. Shannon, "Where's the Risk in Risk Arbitrage?" *Canadian Investment Review*, 12, No. 1 (Spring 1999): 11–18.

14. Christoph Maxheim, "Merger Arbitrage in Austria, Germany and Switzerland," University of Basel Working Paper, January 2007.

15. Krishnan Maheswaran and Soon Chin Yeoh, "The Profitability of Merger Arbitrage: Some Australian Evidence," *Australian Journal of Management* 30, No. 1 (June 2005).

16. Jason Tuan, JinXin Zhang, Jason Hsu, Zhang Qiusheng, "Merger Arbitrage Profitability in China," International Conference on Management Science and Engineering, Press of Harbin Institute of Technology Working Paper, 2007.

17. The database also contains returns of Commodity Trading Advisers, with some data starting in the 1970s.

18. On a daily basis, the drawdown is even more severe. Monthly data mask the true extent of volatility of extreme events.

19. It is assumed implicitly that the portfolio is rebalanced monthly.

20. Disclosure: The author of this book also manages this fund.

CHAPTER 13: Investing in Arbitrage

1. Ajay Subramanian, "Option Pricing on Stocks in Mergers and Acquisitions," *Journal of Finance* 59, No. 2 (April 2004), 795–831.

2. Hedge fund Citadel was rumored to have taken similar positions.

3. It is questionable whether the SEC has jurisdiction, because voting is a matter of state corporate law.

4. Arturo Bris, "Short Selling Activity in Financial Stocks and the SEC July 15th Emergency Order," IMD, Lausanne, Switzerland, August 2008.

5. K. Sigurdsson and P. Saffi, "Price Efficiency and Short Selling," London Business School Working Paper, December 2007.

6. A related tax strategy known as dividend stripping is illegal in many jurisdictions.

7. Juliana Nascimento and Warren Powell, "Dynamic Programming Models and Algorithms for the Mutual Fund Cash Balance Problem," *Management Science*, in press.

8. Keith Moore, Gene Lai, and Henry Oppenheimer, "The Behavior of Risk Arbitrageurs in Mergers and Acquisitions," *Journal of Alternative Investments* (Summer 2006): 19–29.

9. Philippe Jorion, "Risk Management for Event-Driven Funds," *Financial Analysts Journal* 6, No. 1 (January/February 2008): 61–73.

10. Adam Tashman, "Modeling Risk in Arbitrage Strategies Using Finite Mixtures," Columbia Practitioner's Conference, April 2007.

11. Currently Australia, Austria, Belgium, Canada, Denmark, Finland, France, Germany, Greece, Hong Kong, Ireland, Italy, Japan, the Netherlands, New Zealand, Norway, Portugal, Singapore, South Korea, Spain, Sweden, Switzerland, the United Kingdom, and the United States.

12. Bank funds and certain insurance products have a similar structure. Non-U.S. funds often are set up as products under the control of a sponsor.

13. It is likely that regulators will increase these requirements at some point.

14. This requirement is often overlooked by hedge fund proponents. See Rule 502(b)(2)(i)(A) under the 1940 Act.

15. For private equity funds, the performance fee is termed "carry."

16. There are exceptions. Some hedge funds have an even lower frequency and report only quarterly, whereas a small subset of funds reports daily.

17. Release IC-7221 of June 9, 1972, and also IC-10666 of April 18, 1979.

Thomas Kirchner, CFA, is president of the Pennsylvania Avenue Funds and manages the Pennsylvania Avenue Event-Driven Fund, a mutual fund that uses merger arbitrage as one of its investment strategies. Prior to launching this fund, he worked in fixed income trading at Banque Nationale de Paris S.A. and as a financial engineer for Fannie Mae. He holds a B.Sc. from King's College, University of London; a Diplôme from the Institut d'Etudes Politiques de Paris; and an MBA from the University of Chicago Booth School of Business.

Index